More Brief Therapy Client Handouts

More Brief Therapy Client Handouts

Kate Cohen-Posey

Published by John Wiley & Sons, Inc., Hoboken, New Jersey.

Published simultaneously in Canada.

For general information on our other products and services please contact our Customer Care Department within the U.S. at (800) 762-2974, outside the United States at (317) 572-3993 or fax (317) 572-4002.

Wiley also publishes its books in a variety of electronic formats. Some content that appears in print may not be available in electronic books. For more information about Wiley products, visit our website at www.wiley.com.

Library of Congress Cataloging-in-Publication Data:
Cohen-Posey, Kate.
  More brief therapy client handouts / Kate Cohen-Posey.
     p. cm.
    ISBN 978-0-470-49985-6 (pbk.)
  1. Brief psychotherapy—Problems, exercises, etc.   2. Mental health education—Forms. I. Title.
RC480.55.C642 2010
616.89'14—dc22
                                      2010023268

10 9 8 7 6 5 4 3 2 1

To my darlin' Harry
who stayed steadfast
while I took a leave of absence
from our marriage to finish this book.
I could have never made it without all your support!

CONTENTS

Section II   Thinking Mind   87

PREFACE

I think you're the author we've been looking for. Those were the astonishing words I heard approximately 12 years ago when Kelly Franklin called me from John Wiley & Sons, Inc. proposing that I write a book of handouts for clients. I was virtually unpublished at the time. Franklin had a keen intuition for what counselors need. *Brief Therapy Client Handouts* became a great seller in the therapy world, and clinicians wanted more material.

Thankfully, Wiley was patient with me while I finished two writing projects. Then the exciting task of amassing and distilling another library of self-help literature began. Each work was refined to its essential pearls of wisdom in a two-page handout format. The book began to organize itself into three important areas that dominate current mental health trends: (1) the mindfulness movement and self-calming techniques; (2) cognitive therapy, which emphasizes efficacy; and (3) enhancing relationships between people. This new collection of handouts preserves the integrity of the original book and adds new features.

Continuity From the Original Book

- **A Therapist's Guide** starts each chapter with (a) learning objectives, (b) an index of topics covered, (c) suggestions for using material, and (d) acknowledgment of any resources not cited in the handouts.

- **Contents of the handouts** describe problems and list strategies and tasks for clients to do on their own or in the office with therapist.

- **An easy-to-read format** is used, with bullets, numbers, boldface, and tables that help information stand out at a glance.

- **Handouts that are adapted from self-help books** have citations so clients who want more information can read the original source. Clients who have already read the original source may still want the handout to review important points—again and again.

- **Assessment questionnaires** are included that target specific issues: Personality Traits, Automatic Thoughts, Core Beliefs, Directing and Distracting Voices, Symptoms of Panic, Repetitious Thoughts and Behavior, Types of Temper, Upsetting Memories, Criteria for Anorexia and Bulimia, Self-Esteem Rating Scale, Distinguishing ADHD From Moodiness, Sensory Integration Dysfunction, Relationship Disaster Detectors, Codependent Checklist, and more.

- **Exercises and worksheets** are provided to address problems: *Power Thinking Worksheet, Thought Record and Evaluation Form, Thought Changer Forms, Self-Talk Worksheet, Self-Talk Record, Selves and Parts Record, Daily Food Log, Anger Log, OCD Exposure Practice, AAAH Response Worksheet, Verbal Interaction Worksheet, Strategies for Dealing With Teens, Couples trivia questions, and A fable and questions for families.*

- **Supplemental information** is accessible for issues that are not the main focus of therapy. Even experienced counselors can use a quick reference and strategies to approach unexpected situations that surface during the course of treatment.

- **Procedures are described** that therapists may want to review to reacquaint themselves with a particular method. This can serve as a guide or script during sessions, rather than as a client handout.

New Features

- **Chapters from *Brief Therapy Client Handouts* were condensed into single handouts** on panic disorder, obsessive-compulsive disorder, managing anger, and dysfunctional families. This was done to give people an even faster understanding of their difficulty and strategies to handle them.

- ***Informed Consent* Handouts** are offered to give clients information and research data about treatment approaches. Because in psychotherapy a client is not a passive recipient of a formal procedure, the limits of the approach and other treatment options are not emphasized. Rather, the underlying principles of the method are explained so the client can work collaboratively with the therapist; these handouts are listed in the *Therapist's Guide* section of each chapter. See *Information About Trances, Information About Meditation, Therapy for Self-Empowerment, Therapy for Faulty Thinking, Creative Cognitive Therapy,* and *Transcending Trauma.*

- **Handouts for and about children** are included: *Entrancing Kids: Wetting, Soiling, Pain; Bedtime Trances for Tots; Mini Meditations for Minors; Be the Boss of Your Brain; How to Talk to All Your Parts; Distinguishing ADHD from Moodiness; Sensory Integration Dysfunction; Hard-Core Bully Busting; Surviving Picky Parents.*

- **Workshop scripts** are offered to help therapist offer programs that promote their practice, give talks to employees in the workplace (for EAPs), or present at conferences: *The Drama of the Subdivided Mind, Beyond Assertive Language,* and *The Tale of the Tiger's Eye Treasure.* The last two handouts can be used in the commercial sector to promote workplace unity. *Entering Trance* and *Maintaining and Deepening Trance* can be used as scripts for a group induction and follow-up discussion.

- **Workshop handouts** are supplied to support the scripted programs: *The Self and Its Counterparts, Connecting With Your Self, Turning Thoughts Into Parts, Self-Talk Case Study, Self-Talk Worksheet, Learned Responses,* and *Verbal Arts Terms.*

- **Guided fantasy exercises** are included: *Trance Guidance and Advisors, Spiritual Guidance, Aspirations and Abilities, Pictures of Personality,* and *Fantasy Self-Talk.* These are excellent to do in small groups.

I experienced many transformations and incarnations as I wrote these handouts. My practice of meditation improved during Mindfulness Matters, and I conquered my old foe—irksome insomnia. I adopted Judith Beck as a near goddess while working on *Thinking Thin* and almost vanquished urges to snack. *Relationship Fundamentals* explained how my husband and I have managed to remain tethered, in spite of the fact that we are both ruggedly independent.

One day I had a young female client who would not allow herself near anything with the faintest odor. I searched my office high and low for information on sensory integration dysfunction, only to find I had notes on my hard drive from reading *The Out-of-Sync Child.* They immediately turned into a rating scale for *More Client Handouts.* That information will now be at my fingertips.

I originally conceived of handouts as a way of providing clients didactic information so I could focus on the mysterious process of therapy. Now I find that they are an integral part of the clinical hour. The printed word lends authority to therapeutic concepts. I may go over a particular strategy with a client and ask, *Are there any thoughts that would keep you from executing this task?* I am assured that the way these info tracts will be used by other professionals will be endless as each person imbues them with his or her own spirit.

ACKNOWLEDGMENTS

Many thanks to:

- The folks at John Wiley and Sons, Inc., and Lisa Gebo for their willingness to publish the empowering dialogue books so I could purge them from my system and return to writing more handouts.

- Marquita Flemming, my current editor at Wiley, who wooed me back to handout world and was an ever-present beacon of light—guiding me with her thoughtful comments.

- My clients, who are always my best teachers. When they told me about a great self-help book they read, I added it to my list, and you can find it nestled in the references. Or they might say, *Do you have a handout on self-esteem?* I'd reply, *Not yet, but I will shortly.*

- The myriad authors of self-help books—some classics and some less well known. You will find old-timers like Melody Beattie and a more recent arrival—Judith Beck. Several of my clients suffering from affairs found their way to the mother-daughter team of Marie and Marlene Browne. Although their title did not rank as high as some others on that topic, I took my client's advice and had to have two handouts on infidelity because their book had so much wisdom. Although I have made digests of many works, extracting 2 pages from a 250-page book does not allow for direct quotes—just a mingling of minds that, hopefully, does not dilute the message.

- The many theorists and other authors in the field whose ideas and research can be found in footnotes throughout this text. You are the collective conscious out of which all literary works are birthed.

- Pamela Colman Smith, who illustrated Arthur Waite's tarot deck and was my first inspiration to combine visual imagery with distressing thoughts in a cognitive therapy that utilizes both hemispheres of the brain. Thank goodness for the other cyber artists who are willing to lend their images to demonstrate this technique, and to my young friend Devon Collins, who may have helped me more than I helped him.

- Karen Calle, Nina Rehberg, and Karen Vanderford, who make my professional life livable by taking care of all the details of managing managed care. Without you, my labors of love might have been buried under an avalanche of paperwork.

SECTION I
QUIET MIND

CHAPTER 1
TREAT YOURSELF TO A TRANCE

MINI INDEX TO CHAPTER 1

Help clients:

1. Collaborate with treatment by providing information about trance (informed consent).
2. Discover the ability to enter, deepen, and maintain trance.
3. Use imagery and inner guides to work through issues.
4. Report relief from unwanted habits, pain, or insomnia.
5. Report improved concentration in daily tasks or involvement in sexual activity.
6. Identify ways to help children with pain, wetting, soiling, anxiety, or going to sleep.

Using the
Handouts

- **Informed consent.** *Information About Trances* meets the ethical obligation to provide information about self-hypnosis.
- **General literature.** *Entering Trance, Maintaining and Deepening Trance, The Language of Trance, Trance Imagery, Trance Guidance and Advisors.*
- **Literature that addresses specific problems.** *Entrancing Unwanted Habits, Trance-Forming Pain, To Dream . . . and Then to Sleep, Erotic Trances.*
- **Literature for parents.** *Trances for Hyperactivity; Entrancing Kids: Wetting, Soiling, and Pain; Bedtime Trances for Tots.*
- **Preparation for and closure after intensely processing traumatic experiences.** *Maintaining and Deepening Trance* (see especially Safe Place Exercise p. 10).
- **Workshops and presentations.** A group induction can be done using many of the techniques from *Entering Trance, Maintaining and Deepening Trance,* and *Trance Dialogue.* Having participants share their experiences of relaxation cues, eye-closure cues, mantras, safe places, or inner advisors can reinforce ideas in the handouts. Because group inductions are so relaxing, participants will often have many spontaneous questions for presenters about the safety and uses of trances. Copies of handouts can be offered for self-practice.

Cautions and
Comments

- **First, introduce relaxation and trance techniques in the office** and use literature to reinforce their use at home. This is especially true when teaching parents protocols to use with their children.
- **State regulations can affect the use of handouts.** Many state licensing bureaus have requirements that clinicians complete a specified number of training hours before using hypnosis or guided imagery with clients. However, most states do not regulate the use of literature on self-hypnosis or meditation. Become familiar with any state regulations that could affect your use of handouts on trance.
- **Handouts offer clinicians a quick review** of hypnotic techniques in general and protocols to address specific problems. Experienced practitioners will notice that the words *conscious, unconscious,* and *trance* have been replaced in hypnotic scripts with more descriptive terms: *intentional mind, automatic mind, calm, still, focused,* and so on.
- **Handouts focus on the *process*** of going into trance. That process is broken down into three steps (predicting, observing, and directing) rather than giving a plethora of hypnotic suggestions. The goal is to teach clients to adapt this process to unique situations that they face.
- **Trances for hyperactivity** can be supplemented by walking meditation found in *Mindfulness: Step by Step.*

Sources Not Referenced in the Handouts

Advanced Techniques of Hypnosis and Therapy, edited by Jay Haley (Harcourt Brace Jovanovich, 1967) describes Ericksonian utilization techniques found in *Trances for Hyperactivity*.

Handbook of Hypnotic Suggestions and Metaphors, edited by D. Corydon Hammond (W. W. Norton, 1990) inspired scripts used in several handouts: "Truisms for Developing Anesthesias," by Milton H. Erickson, p. 54; "Gradual Diminution of Pain," by Milton H. Erickson, p. 56; "Procedure With Difficulty Swallowing Pills," by Irving I. Secter, p. 266; "Eating as an Art," by Sheryl C. Wilson and Theodore X. Barber, p. 381; "Suggestions About Craving," by D. Corydon Hammond, p. 385; "Concentration Suggestions," by William T. Reardon, p. 440; "Hypnosis With Children," by Daniel P. Kohen, pp. 480–481, 490–491.

Handout 1.1—Information about Trances

Trance is a state of focused attention that suppresses unnecessary thoughts, activity, or sensations, allowing a fuller involvement with an outer or inner experience. Everyone has experienced trance at some time in his or her life:

- The beauty of a sunset can be *entrancing*.
- An archer cannot make his mark unless she is *transfixed* on the bull's-eye.
- Dancing to the beat with perfect rhythm *transforms* a person into poetry in motion.
- A sexual climax occurs when a person is in an *erotic trance*.
- A blank stare can momentarily *transport* someone into another realm.

During trance, the chatter, chatter, chatter of the mind is brought to a stop. It is as though when all your brain *busy-ness* slows down there is something else that observes and knows. This *observant self* can transcend your worst fears, recall memories too painful for a waking state, or, in some cultures, walk on hot coals without being burned. Although the inner peace of trance is everyone's natural birthright, it has mystified people for ages.

Certain mental states commonly thought of as trances are not that at all. Missing your turn on the freeway or forgetting what you came in a room to get are signs of preoccupation. In trance your mind is unoccupied, quiet, and open. The African bushman finding his way through unfamiliar territory is in a trance state in which he is totally aware of his environment. Westerners are more likely to navigate the inner realm via three routes:

Types of Trances

1. **Meditation** is the act of consciously putting yourself in trance. The word *meditate* is Latin for being moved to the center. During a trance, brain activity moves from the outer cortex to the hypothalamus in the center of the brain. In all forms of meditation, thoughts are stilled by (1) focusing attention on an object, mental image, or breathing; (2) adopting a passive attitude of observing random thoughts; or (3) constantly repeating a word or phrase. Meditation has no other goal than to quiet the mind.

2. **Hypnosis** comes from the Greek word *hypnos*, which means to sleep. However, in hypnosis a person is fully alert without interference from distracting thoughts. Hypnosis has been defined as a heightened state of internal concentration in which nonordinary responses can be evoked or suggested. These handouts use a three-step process of: predicting (P) approaching signs of trance, observing (O) what *is* happening, and subtly directing (D) a person toward a desired outcome:

   > Don't start to stare at your spot (D) until you are comfortably settled.... And while you examine the tiniest details about it (D), it may be difficult to just notice when your breathing will start to slow down (P).... And discover how good that deep breath just felt (O).... You may be surprised that you can watch your thoughts without placing any special importance on them (D).... And even remember a forgotten phrase (D) that replaces thoughts with poetic repetition—peace be still ... and you can discover stillness at the most surprising times (P)....

3. **Self-hypnosis** uses exactly the same process of inducing trance, but instead of listening to a hypnotist, you talk to yourself. The advantage of self-hypnosis is that you are the keenest observer of yourself. The trick is to continue to talk to yourself. If you just sit and stare at a spot and wait for trance to come, nothing is likely to happen. But by predicting (P), observing (O), and directing (D) yourself into trance, you shut off random mind chatter, and this is trance-inducing in itself:

   > I know that as I stare at my spot, many changes will happen (P) ... like how my jaw just dropped (O) even though my mouth is still closed ... and the muscles in my face are starting to become smooth and ironed out (O).... And now my field of vision seems to be narrowing down, getting blurry around the edges (O).... And

I can let my eyelids drop, too, (D) and wonder how still my mind will become (P) while I notice how long it takes before I need another breath (D) . . . . And I can put my attention on my intention . . . (D) to be still . . . now and even if my boss yells at me sometime in the future . . . .

Why Trance Is Important for You

During a trance you switch from being a thinker to being an observer. At its best, thinking is energizing and fun. But it is also the source of *all* tension. A parade of *what ifs*, *if onlys*, *have tos*, *shoulds*, *awfuls*, and *nevers* can march through your mind, literally trapping you inside yourself. Even constructive mental activity, when overdone, can make it hard to unwind. After a mentally exhausting day, you can toss and turn at night. The brain waves that occur during trance are slower and more synchronized than those that happen during alert or dream states. Thus, trance offers a kind of rest that cannot be obtained from sleep.

As mental chatter decreases, it is possible to gain access to the *automatic mind* that controls breathing, heart rate, perception of pain, habit patterns, and so on. In this way, a person's conscious intentions can realign repetitive, unconscious routines. Two brief periods of meditation a day can significantly lower high blood pressure.[1] Because meditation and trance are so beneficial, the following facts are important to remember:

- Hypnosis and meditation are natural states similar to the time just before awakening and falling asleep, or becoming completely absorbed in a movie or a book.

- People will come out of a trance when they are ready. There has never been a case in which a person did not return to a waking state.

- In many instances one or two sessions of hypnosis may enable a person to break a habit, but usually it requires a number of sessions before change is made.

- The best subjects for hypnosis are motivated, imaginative, and intelligent. People need some ability to reason and use their mind to go into a trance.

- As mental chatter reduces, *people become more aware* and less vulnerable to others imposing their will or complying with unacceptable suggestions.

- Hypnosis is not a truth serum or lie detector. You cannot be compelled to say things in a trance state.

- If people fall asleep during hypnosis, it is because they needed sleep; they will awake refreshed. People do not respond to or remember suggestions when they are asleep.

- People need not be in a deep state of hypnosis for behavior change to occur.

- People do not instantly go into a trance, but with practice, trances come more easily.

- Trance should not be practiced when people are engaged in activities that require their eyes to be open (like driving a car). Eye closure can signal that the automatic mind is being activated, so the intentional mind can take a break from its usual waking-state duties.

---

1. *The Relaxation Response* (p. 144), by H. Benson, 1975, New York: Avon Books.

Handout 1.2—Entering Trance

One of the most natural methods to enter the quiet stillness of trance is by staring. There are many times when you have stared into space and been in a light trance without realizing it. When you add intention and awareness to staring, trance deepens and you can learn to calm yourself at will. Three methods are suggested below for achieving automatic eye closure that often occurs with staring. This is your signal that you have opened the door to trance. After preparing for trance, practice all of them and discover which one works best for you.

Preparing for Trance

- **Plan a distraction-free block of time**. Interruptions can be mentally arousing.
- **Find a comfortable position** with your head aligned over a straight spine. Lying down or reclining may be too restful and promote sleep rather than concentration. Do not cross your legs in a way that would cut off circulation.
- **Choose a focal point** for staring at or above eye level. You can hold up your hand and study a spot where two lines cross. A glow-in-the-dark star or candle flame is good to use when the lights are out.

Method 1—Opening and Closing Eyes. When you are awake, the part of your brain that directs purposeful action is in charge. During a trance the automatic part of your mind that controls your breathing and blood flow comes forward. One of the easiest ways to become aware of your *automatic mind* is to notice the difference between closing your eyes intentionally and allowing them to do what they "want" to do. After achieving a good fixed stare, close your eyes on purpose. They may stay closed or they may open. If they open, simply close them again to find out what they do the next time.

The following *self-talk* gives you steps to predict (P), observe (O), and direct (D) this process. Read it over and practice it from memory. Trust your mind to remember what it needs to do. After doing it once, read it again and find out if there is any difference in the way you follow the steps this time.

1. **Focal point**. *I wonder what changes can happen (P) as I concentrate on my spot. I notice I'm becoming more still (O), as though a ship dropped its anchor.*

2. **Eye fixation**. *I can tell my stare is fixed (O) . . . my eyes are locked on that spot (O).*

3. **Trance cues**. *In fact, my whole self seems to be calmer and quieter (O).*

4. **Automatic response**. *Now I can start to close my eyes on purpose (D) and find out what they want to do . . . . If they want to stay closed, they can stay closed; if they want to open, they can open . . . . It's not important what they do, only that I pay attention to the truth that my body is telling me (O).*

5. **Eye closure cues**. *This time my eyes seemed to stay closed longer . . . . For a moment it felt like they were glued shut and then they opened (O). . . . Now I notice that when they closed, my lids fluttered (O). . . . This time it doesn't seem worth the effort to even open them (O).*

6. **Confirming trance**. *I wonder if by the count of three my eyes can become so lazy that it won't be worth the effort to open them (P). . . . **1** . . . , closed and comfortable; . . . **2** . . . , glued shut; . . . **3** . . . , so heavy, so peaceful . . . the more I try to open them, the more they want to stay closed . . . and now I stop trying and feel myself becoming limper, looser- all over, and at peace (O).*

Method 2—Staring[1]. Once you've experienced automatic eye closure, it can happen rapidly. Often, it is not necessary to open and close your eyes. Simply take more time in steps 3

---

1. *The Self-Hypnosis Kit: Discover the Power of Hypnotherapy to Improve Your Life*, by C. Powell and G. Forde, 1995, New York: Viking Studio, also uses an eye closure induction and clearly explains the process of going into trance.

and 5 above to observe relaxation and eye closure cues. You may notice one or two or several of the following:

Relaxation Cues		Eye Closure Cues
Fixed stare	Jaw drops with mouth closed	Eyes blink slowly
Shoulders drop	Breathing slows down	Light seems dimmer or streaks
Tummy muscles sag	Breaths become fuller and deeper	Eyes tear due to burning sensation
Face muscles "iron out"	Body feels heavy or detached	Field of vision narrows or blurs at the edges
Sinuses clear	Light, floating sensation	Lids close and flutter
Urge to smile	Body rocks inwardly	

Recognizing these natural, calming reactions is important. People who are overly sensitized to their bodies often worry about any change that is different from their usual state of tension. Relaxation can even feel like a loss of control. During trance you may detach from your surroundings, but you become increasingly aware, present, and connected to your *Self*. You can come out of trance any time you wish. The preceding signs of relaxation and eye closure are completely natural and good for you. Use the phrase, *Now I'm aware* ... as you do your self-talk to predict (P) and observe (O). Generally, it is not necessary to give yourself any direction in this trance induction method. It would be perfectly fine if your eyes remained in a good fixed stare.

Self-Talk . . .

Now my eyes seem to be locked on their spot (O), and I wonder what signs of calm stillness I will start to notice (P).... I'm aware of my jaw dropping, although my mouth is closed (O) ... and I took a nice, deep breath (O).... My tummy muscles are letting go and my face feels ironed out (O).... Now I'm getting that clearing sensation in my nose (O) and I wonder when my eyes will want to close (P).... I'm blinking slowly (O) and my lids are starting to feel so heavy (O).... Things are looking blurry (O) ... and now they close (O). They've opened again, but only to narrow slits and now they close (O) ... There is a fluttering and then the fluttering goes away (O).... My eyes rest peacefully shut.

Method 3—Floor-to-Ceiling Eyeroll. The last method of eye closure produces rapid relaxation and may be the fastest way to enter trance. It does not require a focal point and uses more directed self-talk than the previous approaches:

- Look forward at eye level and hold your head still (D).

- Gaze downward, moving only your eyes (not your head) until your lids are almost closed (D).

- Slowly roll your eyes up as if you were trying to see your own eyebrows, and then look all the way toward the top of your head (D).

- Take a deep breath and hold it, while noticing if your eyes can continue to look upward (O).

- When it is too tiring to look up anymore (O), allow your lids to flutter closed, and let your breath all the way out (D).

- Discover all the signs of relaxation (P) as you continue to exhale any tension right out of your body (D)—jaw dropping, shoulders drooping, tummy sagging, muscles ironing out, profound stillness (O).

Handout 1.3—Maintaining and Deepening Trance

Even master hypnotists will not keep people "under" unless they continue to give suggestions that predict, observe, and direct the experience of trance. One of the most *trance*-forming things to observe is your breathing. Practice the following scripts for *directed self-talk* during a waking state and use the breathing exercise that is most relaxing for you once you've entered trance:

- **Complete breath.** *First, I breathe in through my nose and bring air all the way down until my tummy starts to push out.... After my chest fully expands ... I hold my breath for three counts ... 1 ... 2 ... 3.... Now I release air slowly out my mouth as I let go all the way ... noticing when I'm ready for my next breath.*

- **Cleansing breath.** *I breathe in through my nose for three counts ... 1 ... 2 ... 3.... I hold for three counts ... 1 ... 2 ... 3.... I breathe out of my mouth for six counts ... 1 ... 2 ... 3 ... 4 ... 5 ... 6 ..., and wait ... asking myself, "Am I ready for my next breath yet?"*

- **Breathing imagery.** *I imagine myself in a lovely sparkling pond.... I am submerged up to my lips.... I can hear birds and insects and teeming life and feel mud squishing through my toes.... A leaf falls in front of me.... As I breathe in, the leaf floats to me.... When I breathe out, it floats away.... I watch this leaf come back and forth until it seems that the leaf is a part of me and that I am a part of it.*[1]

Mantra Making

Many forms of meditation use a *mantra* to induce and maintain trance. A mantra is a *sacred* formula in the form of a word, phrase, or chant repeated over and over to invoke inner quiet. Some people even pay hundreds of dollars for a "master" to give them a mantra. The following scripts for directed self-talk can help you discover your mantra, free of charge, from your own inner master:

Finding Your Mantra. As I notice myself becoming more peaceful, I can wonder what word or phrase best describes my experience ... now.... It may be the purring of a cat ... the word *quiet, clear,* or *noodle,* ... a phrase—"Peace be still...," words from another language.... *Que sera sera....* I can wait in the quiet of my mind until I am surprised by whatever comes and be thankful for this gift from my inner Self.

Using Your Mantra. (After the previous exercise)... Now that I know my own calming words, I listen to the quiet of my mind ... and any time a thought dares to enter, I can repeat my mantra until everyday mental chatter becomes a chant of peace.

Grounding, Floating, Detachment

Much of the language of trance suggests downward movement—going *deeper* and *deeper,* counting *down* from 5, or walking *down* steps. Some cultures explain this as the need to *ground* energy and establish a connection with the earth. When energy is not grounded, it (supposedly) degenerates into nervous tension and irritability. After a person is fully connected with the earth, energy can flow upward, making a person feel light and buoyant. Then energy can flow endlessly inward, creating feelings of utter detachment. Such ideas offer useful images to deepen trance and explain sensations of sinking, floating, or release. Pick one or two of the following to deepen your trance experience:

Grounding. Now that I've entered trance, I'm ready to start sinking *downward* as I count backwards from **5** and imagine a lovely, gentle pressure pushing on my shoulders.... **4** ... I go a few steps *deeper* and feel my shoulders dropping.... **3** ... *descending* further into myself.... **2** ... drifting *down* with that gentle pressure helping me.... **1** ... I go all the way *down* where it is peaceful and still....

---

1. Imagery from *The Reluctant Shaman* (p. 62), by K. Whitaker, 1991, New York: HarperCollins.

Going Into and Out of Trance. (After the previous exercise): Just as it takes several bobs down and up to reach the bottom of a deep pool, I can float up and back *down* to reach great *depths* of peace.... Now that I'm all the way *down*, I can begin floating right back up again.... **2**... to a more alert ... **3** ... aware ... **4** ... outward state.... And now my eyes open ... **5** ... and I am present but relaxed as I let myself sink right back *down*, my eyes close ...**4**. ... I go *down* those steps ... **3** ... those lovely hands pushing me lower ... *deeper* ... **2** ... further *down* until ... **1**... I'm even *deeper* inside myself..., experiencing such a pleasant, heavy, *sinking* sensation....

Grounding Imagery. As I feel the weight of my head resting on the top of my spine, I notice how that weight is carried *down* one vertebra at a time.... I can feel that weight pressing down on the floor (chair) I'm sitting on.... Through the force of gravity, the earth is pulling my weight toward it ... all the way through the substructure of my house (or high-rise) to the very center of the earth.... So I imagine the column my weight makes as it bores into the earth ... allowing excess energy from my outer brain to move through my body and descend to the very core of the earth.

Scaling. On a scale of **10−1**, I can allow a number to come to mind of how deep down I feel, **1** being all the way down.... Now I can notice if that number can decrease by **1** or **2** points, just enough to go further *down*. ... And find out if I sink *deeper*. ... So I might notice the number **4**. ... And I can just wonder if it will deepen to a **3** ... and watch or feel when it changes.... Will it *sink* to a **2**? ... Can I watch the change? And if it goes to a **2**, will that **2** turn into a swan and float off? ... And on another scale of **10−1**, I can allow a number to come to mind of how *still* (focused, limp) I feel, and begin to notice if that number can decrease by 1 or 2 points....

Centering

Finally, the experience of trance is inward. As you detach from your surroundings, you become more connected to your *Self*. The following scripts for directed self-talk can move you infinitely inward to a place of peace and power:

Centering Imagery. My mind reaches into itself.... Within itself it has no limits. I travel through the "black hole" of my mind ... and experience being transported, as I become less aware of my body and more aware of joining something else.... I travel ever *inward* through a quiet melting in.

Safe Place. As I travel *inward* toward the center of my center, I know I am moving toward a place of comfort.... I don't need to know what this place looks like until I get there.... It may be a place I've been before, or never been ... an indoor place or outdoors ... or totally imaginary.... And when I arrive, I can explore it effortlessly with every sense that I have ... noticing colors, shapes, sounds, fragrances, textures, temperatures.... And, I can find a spot to rest and savor everything around me ... absorbing what I need as I just *observe* and keep my thoughts from thinking me.

Core. So many things have a core.... An apple has a core.... The earth has a core.... A galaxy has a center where spiraling arms meet.... Even your brain has a core: the almond-shaped lobes of the thalamus.... On imaging scans it becomes energized during *deep* meditative states and the rest of the mind slows *down*. ... So I might wonder what is at the center of my being ... and be surprised by any symbol that comes to me ... and stay pleasantly focused on it.

Handout 1.4—The Language of Trance

You may wonder, *When I put myself in a trance, exactly who or what am I talking to?* Your intentional, logical mind is speaking to deeper brain structures that oversee automatic functions that control heart rate, muscle tone, transmission of nerve impulses (experience of pain), and *aha* moments. Traditionally, such trance talk has been thought of as self-suggestions. But it is actually a way of evoking responses that are present within. A person whose throat tightens at the sight of a pill needs to remind his or her muscles that they know how to let loose, using a special type of communication:

SELF-TALK

Before I completely relax the throat muscle that allows me to swallow, I can slowly ask myself some questions: Did I ever have trouble from swallowing or from something being in my mouth? . . . When I was young, was I given the wrong information about children being able to . . . swallow pills that stuck in my mind? (See below.*) . . . . Was so much of my life managed that I decided to control the way I took medicine? . . . I don't have to have answers to these questions for my mind to stop gagging on erroneous thoughts and my body to . . . start to swallow what it needs . . . .

My body works automatically. There have been many times when I've yawned because someone else yawned . . . . My eyelids blink to redistribute tears, and *my throat swallows* to remove saliva . . . . I don't have to tell myself to salivate when there is food in my mouth or to . . . swallow after chewing . . . . My body knows what it's doing . . . . In fact, even thinking the word "swallow" *can make me swallow,* now . . . . I could try not to swallow . . . and find it impossible . . . .

But there are many ways to forget the gag reflex . . . . Sword swallowers do this by brushing the rear of their tongues further and further back every day . . . and, eventually, that throat muscle remains . . . wide open. They have taught the back of their tongues to . . . lose sensation . . . and that muscle in their throats does not do anything anymore . . . . The back of their mouths become comfortably lazy, limp, loose, or numb . . . . I would never have to do such an extraordinary feat . . . because my body knows when my throat needs to close and when . . . it is fine to be comfortably open . . . .

*We give small children liquid medicine because we think they cannot . . . *swallow a pill* . . . and yet we don't allow these same children to play with small objects because we know they will . . . swallow them . . . . It is astonishing how well . . . they can swallow . . . .

And now the mystery begins to be solved because I've seen people . . . *swallow pills effortlessly* . . . . Now I can imagine seeing a person . . . . noticing the pill resting comfortably on the front of the tongue . . . a drink of water filling up the mouth . . . telling the throat muscle to open wide and the pill washing over the back of the tongue . . . . And as the pill and the water flow down the food tube with a wavelike motion, I notice how satisfied the person looks . . . . I see myself swallowing a pill with pleasure and satisfaction . . . knowing that the touch of the pill to my tongue can trigger an amazing sense of letting go . . . .

Evocative Language Forms[1]

Does the preceding self-talk sound slightly odd—full of interesting word usage, curious grammar, and unusual punctuation (. . .) signaling pauses? Your purposeful mind can use sophisticated language rules to defeat its control patterns and reach the automatic, spontaneous brain. It is not necessary to use long soliloquies like the one here. One or two phrases embedded in trance talk will deepen your experience.

1. **Truisms** are statements of truth that disarm resistance. They may refer to people and situations in general or use the word can: I *can* imagine seeing a person swallowing . . . . *They* have taught their throats to lose sensations . . . . *Everyone* has habits that are helpful and others that defeat them. There have been *times* when I have achieved a goal that I once thought of as impossible . . . .

---

1. The use of evocative language is fully explored in the book *Making Hostile Words Harmless: A Guide to the Power of Positive Speaking*, by K. Cohen-Posey, 2008, Hoboken, NJ: John Wiley & Sons.

2. **Predicting all possible responses** focuses attention and anticipates success: The back of their mouths become comfortably lazy, limp, loose, or numb . . . . My eyes may start to blink slowly, narrow down to slits, begin to tear up, or remain fastened to my spot with a good fixed stare . . . .

3. **Not doing, not knowing** reinforces the idea that responses will happen automatically because they are natural: I would never have to do such an extraordinary (sword swallowing) feat . . . . It really isn't important what my eyes do . . . . I don't need to know the exact moment when . . . this craving will pass . . . .

4. **Questions** focus attention, stimulate associations, or assume that something is happening. The word *wonder* offers a way of asking a hidden question: Did I ever have trouble from swallowing? . . . Can I feel the first sensations of how tired my body is, even if part of my mind thinks it wants to think? . . . I wonder, if I lose 20% of my pain, what I will start to notice? . . .

5. **Timely words** indicate that something will happen later or sooner: Even thinking the word *swallow* may cause me to swallow; *now* . . . I wonder *when* my eyes will want to close . . . . I can *begin* to notice if I am *becoming* more still, *yet* . . . *After a while* the feeling can fade . . . .

6. **Shocking words** focus the mind on the next prediction to promote it: It is *astonishing* how well they can swallow . . . . Be *surprised* by any symbol that comes . . . . Could I *dare* to focus on my breath instead of the next thought that tries to come . . . .

7. A **blocking word** inhibits the prediction that follows it. It encourages resistance and yielding simultaneously, which helps a person let go: I could *try* not to swallow . . . . The more I *try* to lift my hand, the more peacefully it lies on my leg . . . . I can *try* to keep my eyes opened . . . .

8. **Positive, repetitive words** create images of what you want to happen: *That throat muscle remains wide open,* was used in the soliloquy instead of mentioning the gag reflex or *the throat closing.* The word *swallow* was used 16 times with different images or contexts.

9. **Opposing opposites** create confusion that inhibits the logical mind: My mind can *stop* gagging on thoughts, and my body can *start* to swallow . . . . There will be many times when I will *remember* to *forget* the urge to eat . . . . Sometimes what I think I *know* about the way I look, I really *don't know* . . . . The opinions formed about myself may be *true* or *false* . . . . They can *appear* and *dissolve* . . . .

10. **Utilizing unwanted behaviors and thoughts** removes the reason to resist them. Distressing ideas and actions can be accepted, encouraged, or slightly modified to promote their opposite: If I catch a pill on the back of my tongue enough times, the tissue can become used to being touched and my throat muscle can learn to . . . stay loose . . . . As I jiggle my leg, I wonder if it will move faster, slower, or swing to the rhythm of "Amazing Grace" . . .

It is not necessary to memorize these evocative language forms. You only need to thoroughly understand each one to discover that they will come to you at opportune times during your trance talk. You can learn to speak to yourself in a slow, rhythmic way: full of embedded suggestions and underlying assumptions that build up expectations. A pregnant pause (. . .) preceding a hidden hint makes it that much more powerful—*I don't have to have answers to these questions for my body to . . . start to swallow what it needs.* This sentence also implies that the desired change *is* going to happen. Just knowing that you can use words on purpose to evoke automatic, spontaneous responses will inspire a different way of talking when you become calm and still.

Handout 1.5—Trance Imagery

Sometimes, in order to get past your usual ways of thinking, it helps to use preverbal language—pictures, symbols, images, and sounds. Physical ailments, diseases, aches, and pains are particularly important to address in this way because raw sensory data is the language of the body. However, common everyday worries, beliefs, fears, and even relationships can be represented through images:

- Daily worries may look like a pile of ants crawling all over each other.

- A woman thinking of her dying father might see herself in a rowboat about to be overwhelmed by an approaching storm.

- A hay fever attack could appear as a dripping faucet.

- A husband may see himself as a jewelry case, enclosing and protecting a valuable diamond—his wife.

It is good to observe (O), predict (P), and direct (D) signs of relaxation before working with images: *As I stare at my focal point* (D), *I notice my body becomes more still* (O).... *If I bothered to ... pay attention ... I might notice that my breathing has slowed down* (O), *and even my thoughts can find a pause* (P) *and, at some point, it will be too much effort for my eyes to stay open ...* (P). However, attending to a symbolic representation of a problem is, in itself, a focal point that quiets the mind and induces trance. The following steps can be used to play with imagery in a way that transforms problems on a whole different level:

Imagery Transformation

1. **Focus your attention on the symptom or problem** that has been bothering you. You may want to project the problem on a movie screen so you can stay detached from it and maintain a level of relaxation.

2. **Ask yourself for an image or symbol that would represent the problem**. Accept whatever comes, no matter how strange or trite it seems.

3. **Fine-tune the image**. Make sure you can see it clearly. Examine it from different angles. Explore its texture, size, and shape. You can even let the image get worse. If you can increase difficult symptoms (like pain), you can also decrease them.

4. **Notice what is wrong with the image**. How is it dysfunctional, or what problem is it creating?

5. **Represent a healed image.** Allow another form to appear. Ask yourself what the problem image will look like when it is no longer an issue.

6. **Compare the two images.** Which is stronger, larger, or more vivid? Adjust the size and detail of the two images so you can discover what would enable the problem image to change into its healed form.

7. **Watch the transformation take place**. Use whatever resources or tools you need to transform the problem image, no matter how fanciful or illogical. Will the change be slow and gradual, or rapid?

8. **Repeat the transformation from the problem image to the corrected image** a few times. Notice how the change happens. Is it sudden or regular? Become adept at healing the problem image in your mind.

9. **Focus on the corrected image.** Tell yourself that this change is happening now and that it is ongoing whether you are awake, asleep, or going about your daily business. When you are ready, take time to count slowly to 5 to come back to the outer world.

The person overwhelmed with worries (above) became a soaring eagle, looking at the pile of ants from a great height. Daily problems seemed puny and insignificant. The woman who felt totally alone without her father allowed her fear of the storm to build (step 3 above).

She suddenly realized that she had her own oar and that she could row herself to safety. Images do not need to be medically accurate to have healing effects. It is more important that they are personally meaningful. A dripping faucet image was corrected with various sizes of washers until the allergy attack it represented subsided.

Using imagery for physical symptoms can produce immediate effects or may have to be practiced regularly. Along with traditional medications, it has proven to increase survival rates for people fighting cancer but should be practiced for 15 minutes, three times a day. Dr. Martin L. Rossman (2000) recommends 10-minute sessions, twice daily, for other serious medical problems.[1]

Imagery for Relationship Problems

Couples can argue over trivial details, zigzagging from one loosely related topic to the next. Often, it is hard to understand the unifying themes underlying their conflicts and how to intervene without dealing with minutia. The following imagery exercise provides an opening:[2]

1. After taking a few moments to become focused and still, visualize how your partner might appear to you in a dream, fairytale, or cartoon. What object, character, or symbol could represent him or her?

2. Visualize a form that you would take in relation to your partner's. Pick an object, character, or symbol that is connected to the one you chose for your partner.

3. Allow the two forms to interact in some fantasy way. Does each character or element seem stuck in the role it is playing? What would the danger be if one of the forms began to change or if the interaction became different?

Differences that originally attracted people to each other can become sources of conflict: rigid/chaotic, emotional/reserved, distancing/pursuing, helpless/competent, dominant/yielding, and so on. Do the images you and your partner created say anything about patterns that are contributing to your ongoing arguments? What image would you like for you and your partner? Would you pick completely different figures or would you change the interaction in your current scenario? The husband who saw himself as a case protecting a valuable jewel (his wife) gradually realized that they could both be diamonds on a crystal-studded crown, able to observe and interact with the world around them.

---

1. Using imagery to dialogue with and transform problems is discussed in greater depth in *Guided Imagery for Self Healing*, by M. L. Rossman, 2000, Tiburon, CA: New World Library.
2. The idea for couple imagery is fully explained in *The Process of Change*, by P. Papp, 1983, New York: Guilford Press.

Handout 1.6—Trance Advisors and Guidance

Imagery is an excellent way to deepen and maintain trance. It provides an internal focus of concentration in which people can *observe* shapes, colors, sounds, textures, and perhaps even notice tastes and smells. Normal waking thoughts are replaced by vivid dreamlike scenes that warrant exploring.

Sometimes images are actively chosen—*as I walk along my favorite beach, I can notice the time of day . . . the color of the ocean . . . the calmness or roughness of the water . . . the sounds of the seagull . . . the feeling of the sand squishing through my toes . . . .* Or images can be received— *I can see a frightened child approaching a curtain in an empty theater. As she (he) peeks behind the heavy drapes, all anxiety is banished by the scene and characters that bring understanding . . . and I, too, discover what is on the stage, fascinated by the drama . . . showing when to believe and when all is make-believe.*

Guidance From Within

Creating or evoking inner advisors adds another dimension to imagery. They give form and voice to wisdom that you may not know that you have. Your automatic mind not only controls your heart rate and respiration, it is the storehouse of all your memories, instincts, intuitions, and inspirations. Its language is pictorial, spatial, and symbolic. It is effortless for your automatic mind to conjure images of wise and loving beings who can be approached in dialogue. Asking them questions creates opportunities for a focused inner search to deepen trance. Begin by making contact[1]:

1. **Enter trance** using whatever method is best for you—staring at a focal point, closing your eyes and finding out if they want to open, observing how your body can become more still and how your breathing and your thoughts can slow down until it is too much effort for your eyes to stay open.

2. **Imagine your safe place**. Allow the image to come to you—a place where you would be completely comfortable and secure all by yourself. It can be real or imaginary, indoors or outdoors, a beach, woods, garden, field, mountain, or your very own bedroom. Notice the time of day, the temperature, colors, sounds, any fragrances, and look for a place where you would like to stand or sit to wait.

3. **Imagine your guide** by wondering, *How would a loving, wise guide appear?* It may take form as an animal, a human, someone you know or have known, an author of or character from a book, or an effect of light. Or your advisor may have no form and be a disembodied voice. You may discover that you have your own personal cabinet made up of historical figures and scientists. Notice where your guide(s) appears in your safe place. Is it waiting for you to approach, or do you take the first step?

4. **Make contact** by asking a question like *Do you have a name? Are you here to help me? Do you believe in me and care about me?* Until now, your advisor has only been able to talk to you periodically through intuition. It is a symbol of what is within you that knows. It has spoken to you before with quiet calmness when you have been troubled, but you may have dismissed its words. Trance imagery creates opportunities for more formal meetings and enduring relationships.

Using Inner Guidance

Describe a problem that is causing you difficulty (even physical ailments) and ask, *What do I need to know, understand, or do?* Take time, using the four steps above to have an encounter with your advisor(s). Before leaving your guide, make physical contact (if any is desired) and plans for future meetings. Some sample questions follow. Remember that asking one question slowly is more important than receiving an answer. Questions can be repeated like a mantra to block

---

1. Many methods for using imagery and inner advisors can be found in *Guided Imagery for Self Healing*, by M. L. Rossman, 2000, Tiburon, CA: New World Library.

distracting thoughts and keep your attention focused on issues. Answers can come at surprising moments during your waking life.

- **Anxiety and worry.** What is making me feel upset? What do I need to understand to let go of this worry? What can I remember when signs of panic start?

- **Self-confidence**. What false belief keeps me from feeling good about myself? Do I gain something from holding on to that false belief? What is the truth about my goodness, desirability, and belonging? What would I like to believe? Who is placing so much importance on appearance?

- **Relationship conflicts**. Why am I upset with my partner (child) right now? Why is my partner (child) upset with me? What do I need to understand to move past this? Are my expectations of this person unrealistic?

- **Criticism**. Who is my real judge? Can I consider others' opinions without making them my judge? What is the underlying reason why this person is difficult? What do I need to remember about myself to be less hurt?

- **Abuse**. Why do I blame myself for what happened? What would it mean if I stopped blaming myself? Why do others say I could *not* stop my abuse? Am I less of a person because of what happened? What do I need to do or understand to release this consuming anger (or sadness)?

Recognizing Your Inner Advisor

How can you discern if inner advisors are figments of your imagination *or* reservoirs of knowledge? People who have used this approach on a regular basis describe the guidance they receive as astonishing, uncanny, or practical. You may be reluctant to ask some of the above questions because you are concerned your advisor will have answers you do not want to hear—to forgive, not to forgive, or to confront someone. Surprisingly, guidance always leads to peace and relief. There are four ways to recognize authentic inner wisdom:

1. **Answers will be more personal or creative than common clichés**. You may be told to simply acknowledge consuming anger, to express it in a game of darts, or to wink at an offender each time you realize he or she no longer has power over you.

2. **Answers focus on understanding.** Even if you committed some terrible act, inner guides will help you realize you are a good person who did something wrong and *why* you went astray. Any berating or disapproval comes from an *inner critic*. The quiet authority of your advisor can dispel past misinformation.

3. **Answers promote perception rather than quick-fix solutions** and illuminate what makes a problem a problem. They come in a slow, focused way that leads *toward* the direction you need to go. Ask for clarification of ideas that are confusing.

4. **Answers can be nonverbal.** You may gain what you need by feeling an overwhelming sense of compassion or simply being hugged by your inner advisor.

Handout 1.7—Entrancing Unwanted Habits

Over a lifetime, people acquire habits—some good, some bad. They brush their teeth, stop at red lights, and say *please* before asking someone to pass the peas. But there are those other habits that have unpleasant consequences: eating sugary, high-fat foods; indulging cravings to eat between meals; keeping snacks handy; smoking; and so on. Some habits are labeled *addictions*, which gives them even more power. All habits are governed by the automatic mind, where they gain a life of their own. When a person's intentional mind is able to give direction to this storehouse of behavior and thought patterns, habits can change with a minimum of effort.

Heavy-Hand Trance. The following induction is especially designed to help conscious intentions take root in your other mind. Read over the steps and then trust yourself to execute what you need to remember. Read the script again and repeat it often, adding your own flourishes. Practice the Heavy-Hand Trace once a week while you are losing weight:

1. Stretch one of your hands out above eye level, focusing on a finger of choice. Tell yourself: *The more I concentrate on that finger, the heavier my hand will become . . . so heavy that it will begin to slowly move down toward my leg. . . .* Take time to feel the heaviness, to allow it to build, before your hand and arm start to descend.

2. Notice where your arm and hand feel the heaviness as they move slowly downward and begin to wonder which fingers will touch your leg first and how your hand and arm will eventually rest . . . knowing that your eyes don't need to close until your hand and arm are all the way down.

3. And when you discover your arm and hand lying comfortably on your leg and your eyelids fluttering, drooping, resting shut; your head can float up . . . perfectly balanced on your spine.

4. Say to yourself, *Now I can begin to wonder how my hand could become so heavy that I would not want to lift it if I tried. . . . On the count of 3, I could make that effort, only to . . . 1 . . . savor the sensations of heaviness, laziness, limpness to . . . 2 . . . notice how it touches or sinks into my leg and . . . 3 . . . the more I try to lift my hand, the more peacefully it lies on my leg and as I stop trying, I sink deeper into calm stillness.*

5. Now with your arm lying there, inert, picture in your mind's eye what you just did . . . your arm outstretched, finger pointed . . . arm descending slowly onto your leg . . . taking your time . . . until it rests profoundly still on your leg. . . .

6. Say to yourself, *Now I begin to notice other parts of my body that are heavy . . . especially my jaw . . . so that my mouth can be closed but my jaw hangs slack, motionless . . . and maybe even my tummy feels heavy, full, or distended. . . .*

7. Finally, picture yourself sitting wherever you might be eating (or about to reach for a cigarette). . . . Your body will know when it has had enough nourishment. . . . Your arm comes to rest on your leg or table top . . . impossible to move. . . . Your jaw drops with your mouth closed and you see yourself feeling this pleasant heaviness . . . all desires banished . . . and you get up and move on to the next task . . . or something else of interest. . . .

Trance Enhancers[1] The following exercises can be used with the Heavy-Hand Trance. Read one of your choosing and think about it after doing the first three steps of the Heavy-Hand Trance (physically or mentally). Practice the ones that address the habits that are hurting you most on a regular basis.

---

1. Using trance for weight control can be explored further in *The Self-Hypnosis Diet: Use the Power of Your Mind to Reach Your Perfect Weight*, by S. Guigenvich and J. Guigenvich, 2007, Boulder, CO: Sounds True, Inc.

Attention on Intentions. Formulate your intention by adding five or fewer words to the statement—*What I want to achieve most is*.... State it in positive terms: ... *to weigh 125 pounds, ... to walk with ease, ... to stick to my (food) plan, ... to be free of smoking,* and so on.

Once your hand and arm are resting on your leg, repeat your intention to yourself slowly, pausing between every word—*I ... want ... to....* Visualize the number on *your* scale at your desired weight. Imagine that each time you repeat your intention, it is a laser beam, breaking up unwanted habits that have accumulated in your automatic mind.

> This is a good exercise to do every morning, while driving, and at bedtime.

The Art of Eating. Picture yourself before a delicious meal. Before eating, you notice colors, textures, and aromas. You can observe both your food and your breath at the same time. After knowing your attention is on your breath, you see yourself lift your fork and take small bites of food.... Each taste bud on your tongue is absorbing flavor as you chew many times, moving food around in your mouth slowly and finally swallowing it. There are no thoughts in your mind.... You see yourself doing the dance of tasting, chewing, swallowing, and at the same time you are aware of your breathing.... But now you notice something peculiar. Time seems to be slowing down.... As you eat, there is so much time between each bite ... and you chew your food more and more slowly. Each second is a minute, until you see yourself reaching the point of feeling satisfied. Finish with step 7 of the Heavy-Hand Trance.

> This is a good exercise to do shortly before eating or going out to dinner.

Food Rules. Everyone has acquired practices that they do not do—not running red lights, not leaving periods off of sentences, not telling store clerks their private business. People do not feel deprived because they follow the rules of the road, punctuation, or social behavior. Ask yourself, *What food rules do I want to follow today? ... knowing that I can stick to them without feeling deprived*—no desserts, no snacks, three servings of bread, and so on. Remember *stressed* spelled backwards is *desserts*. Hold this image in your mind: *d-e-s-s-e-r-t-s = s-t-r-e-s-s-e-d.*

> This is a good exercise to do every morning.

Cravings. Imagine a food that stirs desire, and let the picture go as soon as you can sense a craving. If necessary, go to the kitchen, look at something tasty, and remove yourself to the place where you practice trance. Pay exquisite attention to all the areas in your body where you feel the craving. Is it in the roof or the back of your mouth? Do you feel tingling or salivation? Are there any sensations in your stomach or in your head? Keep noticing ... and watch how the craving eventually passes. Focus on observing rather than controlling cravings. Take a breath and let your hand become heavy. Think of each urge as an opportunity to practice letting go. Sip water if it is too hard to allow cravings to pass.

> Do this exercise intentionally, before situations where you might act out on a craving or while preparing meals.

Helium Delight. Picture helium balloons being filled for every year you have lived. Notice how the gas goes into the first balloon ... filling it until the rubber stretches taut. Watch it float away, carrying an unwanted habit with it. What color is the second balloon? Watch it become stretched, filled, and float off with another unwanted habit. Really notice the next balloon ... how it reaches a point where it cannot take any more helium and how the opening must be tied off before the balloon pops. Keep examining the balloons being filled, but allow something strange to happen with the next balloon. Imagine that it is your stomach being filled with light gas from an unknown source. Notice the feeling of fullness. Your balloon stomach can float away to be replaced by another one, until a balloon for every year you have lived has been filled.

> Do this exercise when you are famished to distinguish real hunger from cravings. When you do not have access to food, imagine your stomach filling and your body burning excess fat.

Handout 1.8—Trances for Hyperactivity

While the quiet stillness of a trance is usually a deeply pleasurable experience, people who need to be moving all the time can find it excruciating. Some research suggests that people with hyperactivity have slower brain waves, and constant activity may be a means of speeding up frontal lobe activity. Rhythmic activities take focus and concentration. Natural methods for people who require movement to soothe themselves are coloring, rocking, shooting baskets, knitting, or the martial art of *tai chi*.

Meditation on Movement

One of the hallmarks of hyperactive people is to drum their fingers or jiggle a leg. These very movements can become the vehicle for entering a trance. You can use a special self-talk that supplies three steps to predict (P), observe (O), and direct (D) this process. The following script is an example of what can happen when you take advantage of restless moments. Each person's experience will be unique:

1. **Focus on a current (habitual) movement**. As I drum my fingers (move my leg), I wonder if I'll tap faster, slower, keep a steady beat, or change the order of tapping (P).

2. **Focus on rhythm**. I can count (to myself) the rhythm I'm using—one, two, three, four; one, two three, four (D).... I can speed up the rate of my tapping and make it more rhythmic by moving to the tune of *Jingle Bells* (D) ... and I can slow down by moving to the rhythm of *Amazing Grace* (D), ... or I can alternate phrases from each tune to speed up or slow down, ... just noticing what my fingers (leg) want to do (O).

3. **Spontaneous (automatic) changes**. Now I can notice if any tune comes to mind to give my fingers direction (O) ... and find out how long will they follow that tune ... that rhythm (P).... It's not important what happens.... I can be surprised and pleased by any changes that do or do not happen ... just watching ... just sensing (O).

4. **Imagination exercise.** If I discover that my fingers (leg) want to stop moving, I can begin to imagine a box ... noticing its color... its size ... what it's made of (D).... And I can wonder what is inside ... and how to open the box (D).... And as I move the box around in my mind, I know that inside I'll find a message or an object that has a meaning to help me focus and concentrate (P).... And I enjoy the process of finding out how to unlock the truth of the box, taking all the time I need....

5. **Concentration imagery**. I can take a couple of minutes to notice my breath (O) and allow an image to come to my mind to help me concentrate in the most amazing ways ... I can picture a large sponge soaking up water (D), and without exactly understanding how, I know that my mind can absorb information (P) so I can get twice as much work done in half the time.... I notice how nothing stops the sponge from absorbing water (O) and nothing can distract me from my purpose (P).

The goal of this trance activity is *not* to change the perpetual motion of hyperactivity into calm stillness, but to utilize restlessness to develop focus and awareness any time it occurs. If movement does stop, an imagination exercise supplies a continued avenue for concentration. Because people with attention deficits are good multitaskers, step 4 can be started while there is still finger drumming or leg swinging. With practice, you can train yourself to use old habits that energize your brain to add new powers of calm focus.

Moving Meditations

Trance has been defined as a state of focused attention, which suppresses *unnecessary* thoughts, activity, or sensations, allowing a fuller involvement with inner or outer experience. This inclusive definition invites methods to activate sluggish brainwaves while preparing people to focus and concentrate. Because these activities are so energizing, they can be followed by traditional trances or concentration imagery (see meditation activity number 5, above).

- **Cross-crawl brain balancing.** While marching in place, touch your right knee with your left hand or elbow and then your left knee with your right hand or elbow.

For variety, touch each heel behind your body alternately. Perform 25 times, slowly, with awareness. Slow cross-lateral movement stimulates the manufacture of dopamine in the frontal lobe, limbic area, and basal ganglion of the brain. This neurotransmitter is enhanced by medications prescribed for people diagnosed with hyperactivity.[1]

- **Alternate cross lateral and bilateral marching.** When you get good at the cross-crawl, switch to a one-sided march. Raise and lower the same side (hand/leg) together. Imagine a string from each hand pulling each leg. This fires one side of the brain at a time. Now do eight cross-crawls, eight one-sided marches, and finish with eight cross-crawls. This increases concentration and the ability to shift brain hemisphere activity.

- **Hand-clapping games** involve two people and make use of crossing the midline, which stimulates the brain. Claps commonly include patterns of clapping one's own hands, clapping both hands of a partner, and each player alternately clapping right hands and then left hands. Clapping patterns are trancelike because they move quickly to a tune or a rhyme and take great concentration. It is easy to Google the words for *Miss Mary Mack* or others and make up your own clap patterns for a *brain break*.

- **Walking on a balance beam** also requires a person to cross his or her midline, to move slowly, and to concentrate. Balance beams can be made by having a lumberyard cut a 4-by-4 to the desired length and nailing it to a piece of wood on each end for stability. Extra challenges can be added by propping one end on a chair and walking on an incline. For a brain break, have a person walk the beam 10 times.

- **Juggling**. Use smallish balls or beanbags that easily fit in the palm of your hand. Simply throw the ball from one hand to the other at waist level. Next, toss the ball in an arc with a maximum height at eye level. With continued practice, a second and third ball can be added for excellent cross-lateral stimulation.

- **Gotcha**. Two people face each other with their palms up and the index finger of the opposite hand pointed just over each other's palm. On the word *Go*, they each try to capture the other's index finger. For more of a challenge and cross-lateral stimulation, they step closer and do the same activity with hands crossed.[2]

- **Line dancing**. Practice or make up steps to the Electric Slide, the Macarena, or the Chicken Dance. A circle dance like the Hora uses the grapevine step that makes use of cross-lateral brain stimulation.

---

1.   This is a well known strategy in Educational Kinesiology and described in the book *Making the Brain Body Connection*, by Sharon Promislow (Enhanced Learning & Integration Inc., 1997).
2.   Another excellent resource for active trances is *Pick and Plan: 101 Brain Compatible Strategies for Lesson Design*, by Brenda Utter, 2007, Thousand Oaks, CA: Corwin Press.

Handout 1.9—Trance-Forming Pain

Pain has a purpose. When it is acute, it signals current or imminent harm to body tissue. Unpleasant sensations send nerve impulses up the spinal cord to the brain, where they are interpreted and then sent back down the spinal cord to direct muscles to react. Neurotransmitters that boost activity of nerve fiber are adrenaline and cortisol. Serotonin and noradrenaline dampen upward transmission of pain impulses.

Chronic pain reminds diseased or injured people of their limits. However, a neurological circuit can be imprinted in the central nervous system (CNS), and that continues to fire in the absence of real sensory input. Repeated thoughts and emotions also cause impulses to travel along well-worn pathways. The memory of pain is experienced as real and present.[1] How can these neurological facts help make the shift from disturbing to tolerable body sensations?

- Regular trances teach the CNS to be less sensitive to pain signals, to calm down, and to build new nerve pathways, making pain conduits less active.

- Neurons that do not transmit pain can interfere with signals from pain-transmitting neurons and inhibit or reduce the experience of pain. This is the *Gate Control Theory* of *Pain*.

- Muscles react to pain with tension and spasm that intensifies it. Trance can relax muscles.

- Trance states increase the output of neurotransmitters that oppose adrenaline and cortisol. Dopamine, the pleasure neurotransmitter, can increase by 65% during some trance states.[2]

Emotional Component of Pain

In addition to *sensations* from tissue damage or interference with body functions, pain includes unpleasant *emotions* related to body sensations. A soldier who breaks his leg in battle may experience his pain differently than a person who is the victim of a drunk driver. Although you may not have any control over the cause of your pain, its distressing sensations, and the limitation it creates, only you can decide what role it will play in your life.

Review the questions below and notice which ones stick in your mind. Take time to enter trance by staring at a focal point, observing how your body can become more still, and how your breathing and your thoughts can slow down . . . until it is too much effort for your eyes to stay open. After becoming focused and still, ask yourself any of the questions that you remember and listen to the silence or wait for answers to come:

- *How does telling myself that my pain or limitations are awful help me?*

- *How much time do I want to spend being sad for what I can no longer do? How much time do I want to spend strategizing ways to do things I can still do?*

- *What can I learn from my pain—to be more compassionate, to take better care of myself, to work within my limits, to slow down, to appreciate what I can do?*

- *Do I need to be more or less angry at the person who caused my injury? Do I need to take action or move past my anger?*

Distraction, Distortion, and Detachment

The following story shows how the intentional part of your brain can use distraction to detach from pain while your mind works on automatic pilot:[3]

A famous psychiatrist named Victor Frankl was interred in a concentration camp. He fully believed he would survive his nightmare and give lectures on his ideas in Vienna following the war. But

---

1. ''Drug-Free Remedies for Chronic Pain,'' by L. Khazzoom, 2009, *AARP*, January & February, pp. 30–33.
2. *Why We Believe What We Believe*, by A. Newberg, 2006, New York: Simon & Schuster.
3. See *Hypnotize Yourself Out of Pain Now*, by B. Eimer, 2008, Bethel, CT: Crown House Publishing, for more exercises to reduce pain.

Frankl's health was waning. On a work detail one day he could barely walk due to pain from his frozen, festering feet. He was about to falter, but that would mean certain death from the SS guard's bayonet. He wondered, *Don't I have a greater purpose than to die here?* Suddenly, his intentional mind conjured an image of being in a warm, beautiful lecture hall where he was giving a talk on his experiences at the camps. That night he found himself back in his bunk with no recall of how he went through the motions of doing the work detail.

Like Frankl, you can relegate your pain to your automatic mind while you purposely focus on tasks that detach you from your discomfort. Take time to become focused and still with your favorite trance induction. Read the scripts below (or have them read to you) to create your own recipes for healing. Repetition will build new nerve pathways.

1. **Remember to forget; forget to remember.** Many people forget to remember the feeling of their shoes on their feet, their glasses on their nose, or their shirt on their shoulders. You can intentionally notice some part of your body, but after a while the feeling can fade and all sensation can be placed under the control of your automatic mind while your intentional mind recalls something more interesting … like the times you've watched great movies and forgotten the hardness of your chair…. How can you forget the feeling of shoes on your feet or the hardness of the chair? Because of lifelong learning, you have the ability to … turn off sensations and discover something interesting … a memory … a fantasy that brings … comfort and more

2. **Pain change**. You can focus intently on your pain, describing it in all its dimensions—what is its shape, color, texture (smooth/rough, hard/soft). Are its boundaries firm or fuzzy? How far does it go below the surface of your skin? What qualities can you change—its depth, area, color, or size? Do the dimensions of your discomfort remind you of something—electricity, a nail, a knife, crab claws? … What would you need to do to change this imaginary source of discomfort? See the change happening. After removing the imaginary source, what would the injured area need—lotion; warm, wet towels; stretching? Apply whatever is needed.

3. **Physical change.** Visualize the physical cause of your discomfort. What is happening in your body that is sending signals of pain up your spinal cord to your brain? Now picture an actual medical treatment or the drugs you are taking working. Watch medicine flow along neurons to receptor cites for opiates—bringing a wonderful feeling of relief. See vertebrae being pulled apart to take pressure off of bulging disks. Imagine the cartilage between arthritic joints becoming thicker and the fluid between those joints gradually beginning to flow….

4. **Count down.** Look up in the corner of your mind, and notice a number from 1 to 10 that represents your pain. Watch that the number begins to change. I don't know what it will be like … maybe it slowly fades and a smaller number begins to emerge from the background. The lines of an 8 can become a 7… and so on… slowly on and on…. A 2 can remind you of a swan, and you begin to feel you are gliding gently: a beautiful swan on the coolness of a clear, glassy lake….

5. **Flow and discard**. Breathe in; breathe out. As you breathe in, clench your fists tighter and tighter. As you breathe out, relax your hands. Imagine your pain in the form of a substance that could flow like syrup, hot lava, or goo. Take a third slow breath, clench your fists, imagine you are drawing the substance into your arms and legs, hold your breath, then let your breath all the way out, and relax your hands. See the substance flowing down your arms and legs, out fingertips and toes. On the next breath in and out, let oily droplets of pain leave your fingers and toes.

Handout 1.10—To Dream . . . and Then to Sleep

There are many reasons why sleep evades people. Chronic conditions like sleep apnea, decrease in estrogen due to menopause, hyperthyroidism, and so on require the help of professionals. However, the common problems of worry, not being able to wind down from a day's work, and body tension will respond to many trance techniques. The first step is to recognize the transition from waking thoughts to the illogical ideas and images of predream states. It may seem like a giant leap from trance to sleep, but it is one small step from self-hypnosis to a hypnagogic state.

The Mysterious Hypnagogic State

The technical term for the brief transition between wakefulness and sleep is *hypnagogia*. In this predream state, images can be fleeting and change rapidly. There is no story line connecting one picture to the next, but they can gradually change from formless patterns to objects to dreamlet scenes. Thoughts are disjointed and lack the purpose and emotional content found in dreams.

A psychologist named Andreas Mavromatis[1] suggested that during hypnagogia the brain cortex is inhibited and the midbrain and brain stem start to take over. The cortex is associated with clear, logical thought. The subcortex is attuned to imagery and symbols. During hypnagogia there is just enough cortical arousal to observe the strange antics of the old brain. Even if you have never heard of a hypnagogic state, you have probably had one or two of the following experiences while falling asleep, waking up, or starting to nod off during the day:

- **Mental:** Strange, nonsensical, irrelevant thoughts; made-up words; flashes of inspiration; meaningful answers to puzzling questions.

- **Visual:** Formless images, speckles, lines, flares, sparks, or cloudlike splashes of color; geometric designs, diamond shapes, or jewels; objects, faces, or animals; landscapes, seascapes, or gardens; scenes with people, writing, or print.

- **Auditory:** Hearing music, humming, a doorbell ringing, crashing, hissing, buzzing, banging, roaring, explosions, warnings, one's name being called, or quotations.

- **Olfactory:** Cigar smells, roses, and others.

- **Sensations:** Sudden muscle contractions; heat or coldness; energy flowing through the body; feelings of floating, weightlessness, heaviness, falling, rocking, spinning, or disorientation; body expansion or elongation; body paralysis, numbness, or tingling; sexual arousal; or a sense of a presence.

- **Repetitive activity:** Recurrence of activities that happened continuously before sleep or throughout the day— playing a computer game, the rocking of waves, or a baby crying.

Mavromatis also pointed out that the relay center between the three brains is the thalamus. Located just behind it is the pineal gland, which is photosensitive. In response to darkness, the pineal gland is signaled to convert stored serotonin (that balances moods) into melatonin. Its release into the brain and blood induces sleepiness throughout the night. Trances for sleep need only mimic the mechanics of hypnagogia. These predreams are the prologue to nighttime dramas that set the stage for deep sleep cycles.

Predream Trances

Spinal Twist. Thoughts produce tension. Likewise, tension causes the mind to think and be wakeful. A day full of mental activity makes muscles tight without physical activity to discharge tension. One of the easiest ways to release stress is with a yoga position called a *Spinal Twist*. Lying in bed on your back (without your pillow), pull your knees to your chest, open your arms

---

1.   Mavromatis' book, *Hypnagogia: The Unique State of Consciousness Between Wakefulness and Sleep*, 1987, London: Routledge & Kegan Paul Books Ltd, is considered one of the most definitive works on hypnagogia.

to the sides, let your knees flop to one side, look in the opposite direction, and exhale. Observe your breathing, and notice what parts of your body are stretching. Imagine which internal organs are being toned and how this helps digestion. Now let your knees fall to the other side and turn your head away from your knees. Do not do this if you have severe lower back problems, if you're pregnant, or have just had surgery.

Rag Doll. Continue lying on your back with your arms bent at the elbows. Cradle your head in your hands and gently rock it from side to. Let all the turning action come from your arms, not your neck. Use one of your middle fingers to press and rub the center hollow in the base of the skull in the back of your head. Gently put your head down. Lift one of your arms a few inches above your bed, count to three, and let it flop. Pay exquisite attention to the sensations in your arm after it falls and let it sink deeper and deeper into the bed. Count to three and imagine that your arm will become too heavy, lazy, or limp to lift. Use the same procedure to flop your other arm and both of your legs (one at a time). Feel the stillness, numbness, and even paralysis that are part of half-sleep.

Tongue and Eyes. (1) Continue lying on your back with no pillow. With your eyes closed, roll your eyes upward as though you were looking at your forehead. Let your jaw drop with your mouth closed. (2) Imagine that you are stimulating your pineal gland (that lies behind your eyes) to release more melatonin. Choose a color for it, and picture melatonin oozing from that tiny, pinecone-shaped organ throughout all your veins, lulling you into a lovely, dreamy sleep. Just before your eyes drop, ask, *What . . . do . . . I . . . need . . . to . . . understand, . . . know, . . . or . . . do . . . to . . . sleep . . . through . . . the . . . night?* You may receive an answer . . . or not, but continue to ask the question slowly until you lose consciousness. Ask the question again upon awakening in the morning: *What do I need to understand, know, or do to fall peacefully asleep tonight?*

Word Association. Word associations mimic the random thought flow of hypnagogic states. Do the first part of the Tongue & Eye Trance and think of a word that describes your experience—perhaps, *quiet*. What is the next word that comes to you? . . . For example, *still*. Continue on, joining two words together: *quiet-still, still-calm, calm-lake, lake-water, water-wet . . . .* Again, pick a word that best describes your experience and repeat it every time you exhale, until you notice hypnagogic signs or loss of consciousness.

Favorite Things. Begin with the first part of the Tongue & Eye Trance or move your eyes back and forth as far as you can go in each direction slowly. These slow eye movements (SEMs) have been observed during hypnagogic states, while rapid eye movements (REMs) occur during dreams. Make up a story about your favorite things—*I'm in my favorite place, at my favorite time of year, wearing my favorite clothes. My favorite person from history* (a book or movie) *shows up and we start to . . . .* You might be joined by your favorite animal or hear your favorite tune. Continue until your mind wanders off and you notice hypnagogic signs or lose consciousness.

Impossible Things. Begin with the first part of the Tongue & Eye Trance or SEMs. Practice hypnagogic thinking by making up strange, impossible things as fast as you can, nonstop. Imagine a purple fried egg rolling off a plate, slithering up the wall, sprouting wings, and flying away. The words to *Lucy in the Sky With Diamonds* (Lennon and McCartney, 1967) describe the hypnagogic state perfectly.

Handout 1.11—Erotic Trances

Sexual enjoyment does not come from using the right technique, position, or the best places to touch. It is about suspending mental chatter, attending to bodily sensations, and following an inner direction about what movements or sounds to express. Just as focusing on a spot will naturally lead to eye closure and trance, focusing on the sight of your partner's body, the sounds of lovemaking, and the sensations of touch create the choreography of the dance of love. Simply repeating the phrase, *Now I am aware of,* ... will block mind chatter and put you under the spell of an erotic trance:

SELF-TALK

I'm aware of the lovely furry texture of my partner's skin and how warm his body feels.... I like the way that touch felt and *I'm noticing* a tingling, sensation. *I'm aware of* my breathing becoming slower and deeper, and it almost feels like I'm moving in slow motion.... Now my body seems to want to move and push harder against his ... and I can feel him pushing back.... *I'm aware of* the rise and fall of his chest as he breathes ... and I want to move with that rhythm.

Meditation Foreplay

People who are sensuous are tuned into the sights, sounds, and textures of their environment. They do the above naturally and can stay focused on sensations without using self-talk. People who are thinkers need to notice sensations. Partners can help each other do this with a script that creates a progression from relaxation to arousal. It is best to start in comfortable (night) clothes, sitting cross-legged on the bed or floor, facing each other with your head balanced over your spine. The person reading the script should speak slowly and rhythmically, pausing each time he or she inhales and speaking on the exhale. Ellipses (. . .) also suggest pauses:

1. **Focal point and trance cues** (partner speaking). *Focus your attention on a spot and notice the signs of relaxation that begin to occur. Although I can see how still you are becoming, you can notice so many more changes, until you are aware of at least two ways your body and mind have become quieter ... more loose ... more still....*

2. **Imagery focus.** *Now with your eyes opened or closed you can picture a staircase leading down.... I don't know how long it is, but at the bottom you can notice a door.... As you go downward, I'll help by lightly touching your shoulders and counting backwards from **5** ... so nod your head slightly when you are ready....*

3. **Deepening trance**. *With each count ... **5** ...* (touch shoulders) *you may take one or several steps down toward the door ... because ... **4** ...* (touch) *I don't know how many steps you need to go down to be in the place where you need to be.... And ... **3** ...* (touch) *as you get closer to the door, its size, color, and design can become clearer.... You know that I will be waiting on the other side ... maybe my current age or younger ... maybe this year or far back in history ... **2** ...* (touch). *For now, just concentrate on the door, what it is made of, how to open it.... Remember that when you join me we may be ... someplace comfortable and expected or someplace surprising ... but keep noticing the door now as you descend to the bottom ... **1** ...* (touch) *and when you open the door, you can describe the scene ... if we are alone or with others ... anything you would like to share....*

4. **Imagery transition.** *Now you can open the door and find me waiting for you.... And you can tell me what you're seeing in your mind.* (Partner responds.) *What is the lighting like?* (Partner responds.) *Are there any sounds or music or fragrances?* (Partner responds.) *Where do you see me in the scene?* (Partner responds.) *How old are we? ... How am I dressed? ... How are you dressed?* (Partner responds.) *Who approaches whom?* (Partner responds.)

5. **Initiating contact.** *What do I say or do that you've always wanted ... maybe something I've said or done before or something you didn't even know that you wanted me to say or do....* (Partner responds.) *What are we doing now?* (Partner responds.) *What is it like when I do that?* (Partner responds.) *What happens next?* (Partner responds.) *Do you want to show me how I'm touching you or just tell me? ...*

The partner leading the exercise can guide the fantasy through to its completion, or it can easily drift into actual lovemaking. Sexual fantasies are a well-known way to block distracting mental chatter. Using guided imagery has the advantage of involving partners together. It may not be necessary for each person to initiate a fantasy on the same night.

Erotic Facts

You may wonder if the meditation foreplay exercise is only for sexual adventurers or if it can rouse a lazy libido in a partner with a puny sexual appetite. A few important facts supply surprising answers and remove roadblocks to a satisfying love life.[1]

- **Desire vs. arousal**. A woman may have to be stimulated (mentally and physically) for 10 or 15 minutes to experience even 2 or 3 minutes of sexual desire or arousal. The older a woman is, the more stimulation she may need. Eight out of 10 women need clitoral stimulation and cannot have an orgasm during intercourse. Men can be stimulated visually or by random thoughts and feel desire *before* arousal.

- **Other circumstances add to low desire.** Early sexual abuse (only for some), poor self-esteem, poor body image, preoccupation due to grief or loss, motherhood, stress, anger, resentment, fatigue, menopause, and too much initiation by your partner.

- **The question of closeness.** Women want to feel close to have sex. Men feel close *by* having sex with their partners. It helps them feel loved, tender, accepted, appreciated, virile, and confident. It is a fallacy that sex is simply a physical release for a man.

- **Love and sex.** There are many reasons to be together—to raise children, pool financial resources, enjoy companionship, share memories, combat loneliness, and face the unknown. The endorphin high of romance always wears off and is not required for lovemaking.

A simple solution for many people who have no sexual desire is to just do it. The want-to and arousal can come after stimulation starts! Sexual activity releases the feel-good hormone (endorphin) and the feel-close hormone (oxytocin). Sex can be used to fall asleep, reconcile, prevent prostate cancer and heart attacks, and increase levels of testosterone. Women who resent unhelpful husbands can have a pleasant surprise when they make specific requests *and* start being sexual before wishes are fulfilled. Because erotic activity may be one of the only forms of meditation that Westerners regularly practice, the following ideas can help remove obstacles to this sensuous observance.

- If you and your partner have different levels of desire, agree on a minimum number of sexual encounters (not less than once a week) and stick to it! You partner needs to show that he will *not* go over your minimum so you do not have to worry about being nagged.

- If you have to say no, say when—"I have to finish this right now, how about in a half an hour."

- If you think your libido is gone, it's just changed to a more subtle form. It is normal for sexual thoughts to become more fleeting with age and when life is hectic. Look for exceptions—sexual turn-ons change over time. If hormone levels are low, do not hesitate to ask your doctor if you are a candidate for testosterone injections or vaginal estrogen creams.

---

1. *The Sex-Starved Marriage*, by M. W. Davis, 2003, New York: Simon & Schuster, offers many solutions for couples with intimacy problems.

Handout 1.12—Entrancing Kids: Wetting, Soiling, and Pain

Once parents understand trance, they can use everyday challenges to help children. Traumas are great opportunities to focus attention by observing what is happening (O); predicting positive outcomes (P); and offering suggestion and direction (D). This initiates a calming process:

- **State the truth**. *That's an awful boo-boo. It must hurt terribly* (O) . . . . *It will keep right on hurting. . . . And you really want it to stop* (P).

- **Predict change**. *Maybe it will stop hurting in a little while or a couple of minutes* (P).

- **Reframe trauma as a trifle**. *Do you think there's enough blood coming out of that cut? It looks like the good, red strong kind, not the bluish weak kind* (O). *I wonder if it will leave the right pink color on the tissue when we dab it with the cut cleaner* (P). *Is it swelling just right?* (O/P) *It's too bad that cut won't take very many stitches . . . so you can be proud* (D).

Preparing for Trance Through Drawing

Drawing pictures is a natural way to begin the first step of starting trances with imagery. The problem of bedwetting in children over 5 offers an excellent example of how to make the transition from drawing to trance imagery. *Step 4 makes use of a type of Kegel exercise in which people stop and start the flow of urine. Children should be encouraged to drink lots of fluid during the day and rewarded for delaying urination in order to stretch their bladders. Use the following scripts with young people:

1. **Drawing to enhance body understanding.** First, we need to draw the part that pumps blood all over the body—*the heart*. Then, we draw the washers (filters) that clean out the blood—*the kidneys*. Next, we draw the bag where the water (pee, urine) that was cleaned out of the blood gets stored—*the bladder*. Now, that bladder needs a gate to let out the urine into the tube that goes outside the body. Finally, we need to draw the part of the body that is the boss of the whole operation—*the brain* and the nerves that connect the brain to the bladder.

2. **Using the drawing to further understanding.** I wonder how you know when you have to pee. The bladder says to the brain, *I'm full*. And what do you think the brain says back? *I'm busy now, so remember to stretch and keep the gate closed*. Or it says, *That's fine, I'll send a message to the legs to get to the potty . . . and when you get there, I'll tell the gate it can open up and let the pee in the toilet where it belongs*.

3. **Suggestions for scripts that reduce bedwetting**. Do the brain and bladder keep talking to each other when you're sleeping? When the bladder remembers that the brain is always paying attention, what will it say? *I'm full*. Then, what will the brain say? —*I'll wake up the rest of you so you can get to that toilet, open up the water gate, let the pee out, and walk back to a nice, warm, comfortable bed*. Or, *You've got plenty of room left in that bladder after all the stretching it's been doing, so just keep the gate closed for the rest of the night*.

4. **Imagery or trance practice during the day.** Now, you can use your daydreaming, imagination, or pretending to see and hear how your brain and bladder talk to each other. Your brain might be telling your bladder, *Just hold that pee a little longer so you'll keep stretching out*. Can you see/feel the bladder stretching? Or your brain might say, **Close and open that gate while you're peeing so the gate will get strong enough to hold the pee all night*. Watch in your mind how the gate can close to stop pee and then open to finish peeing.

5. **Trance practice before bed.** As you sink down comfortably in your bed, you can hear your brain saying to your bladder, *Be sure to let me know when you're feeling full. . . . I'll either wake up your legs so they can get you to the bathroom or I'll remind you to keep the gate closed and stretch just enough to get through the night. . . .* Don't fall asleep until your brain and bladder have made all their plans.

Two
Additional
Problems

There is no limit to the number of childhood problems that can be addressed through drawings for trance imagery. Children should make their own drawings even if these are physiologically inaccurate. The following examples can stimulate parents' imagination to help their children with the soiling, pain, or other unique problems:

Soiling [1]

- **Draw pictures of the "food tube"** with the esophagus, stomach, small intestine, large intestine, bowel, and "bowel gate" (anal sphincter). Draw the brain with nerves connecting it to the bowel.

- **Draw pictures of the problem**. (A) a bowel gate that gets tight when a person feels angry or tense; (B) a bowel stretched by too much poop (feces) that can't send messages to the brain when it is full; (C) poop becoming hard (impacted) when the gate doesn't open often enough; (D) some of the poop seeping around the impaction and out the gate when the bowel is too full.

- **Draw pictures of how the problem gets fixed.** (A) stool softeners making the poop mushy enough to get out the gate; (B) a bowel gate that can open and close easily, even when a person is tense; (C) a bowel that is big enough to hold poop but not so stretchy that it forgets to send messages to the brain. Cut an extra hole in a balloon. Push mud or peanut butter in it. Notice what amount can easily be squeezed out.

- **Suggest a dialogue between the brain and bowel.** The bowel says, *I'm full*. The brain responds, *I'll relax the bowel gate so the poop can come out*.

- **Imagery or trance practice.** See the full bowel sending alerts to the brain. Watch the brain sending messages that make the gate relax and open wide.

Pain Control for Shots

- **Draw pictures** of nerves bringing messages to the brain from all parts of the body. Draw pictures of *nerve-numbers* or switches (endorphins) that cut off the ouches before they reach the part in the brain that makes people feel.

- **Suggest a dialogue between the nerves and the brain.** The nerves say, *There's a big needle headed straight for my arm*. The brain replies, *I'll send in some nerve numbers to your arm so you don't feel any ouches*.

- **Imagery or trance practice.** Draw a circle several times around the part of your child's arm where he or she will be given a shot. Say: *Look at your brows until your eyes close and imagine the nerve-numbers coming to switch off the ouches. . . . The circle gets number and number each time I draw*. Then pinch the numb part so children can feel how well their off switches work before they face the real situation. Remind children to look up and watch their nerve-numbers during an actual situation.

---

1. *Sammy the Elephant*, by J. C. Mills, 2005, and *Clocks and Clouds*, by M. Galvin, 2007, Washington, DC: Magination Press, are stories that aid imagery and help children overcome bedwetting and soiling.

Handout 1.13—Bedtime Trances for Tots

Children who can imagine and daydream are old enough to experience trance. Because trance is such a natural phenomenon, even parents who have not had special training can safely help their children relax by using hypnotic techniques of focusing on imagery, intensifying observation, and identifying trance cues. It is only necessary to use language that confuses the child's intentional mind while being age appropriate:

1. **Suggest an image**. *You know how during daydreams you can pretend to be whereever you want and still be where you are . . . . If you started to imagine something right now, only you would know what it was. Even if you were petting a kitten, going down an escalator, talking to a horse, floating, flying, or something else, no one would know what you see in your mind . . . . And while you are daydreaming, pretending, or imagining, make sure it's fun because you are the boss of your imagination.*

2. **Become observant**. *Just notice what you see in your imagination—Who is with you? Are you alone, with friends, family, or animals? Notice where you are—whether you're inside or outside . . . . Is the weather hot, or warm, in-between, or snowy? Hear the sounds in your fun place—people talking, music, snow falling, or even how something smells or tastes so good.*

3. **Identify trance cues**. *You can close your eyes or keep them open until they want to close while you just look at something carefully . . . . And even though I don't know what you are discovering, I can see what a good job you're doing of concentrating . . . . You've probably already noticed how smooth the muscles in your face can be, how your jaw wants to drop, how your breathing is slower, and that's because you're doing this exactly right.*

4. **Deepen trance**. *Since you and your brain are the boss of your body, you can make yourself even more comfortable . . . . Your body already knows so well how to let go . . . . It even does it a little more each time you breathe out . . . . Just notice how your shoulders drop . . . . I can see that . . . . And I bet your imagination doesn't stop you from saying, 'Calm' or, 'limp' or, some other quiet word with your inside thinking every time you breathe out . . . . So you can just notice how good it feels to be still inside.*

Relaxation Activities

If the preceding script seems too formal, it can be broken down into simple activities until you build confidence in yourself to help your child relax.

- **Massage and rocking** are methods of relaxation that even soothe babies.

- **Rag doll game**. Pick up a child's arm or leg and drop it. Children must let their limbs flop rather than putting them down themselves. If they have difficulty with this, shake their arm or leg a little or have them practice on you.

- **Tense and relax**. Have children tighten themselves into a little ball. Tell them to squeeze tighter and tighter. When they cannot squeeze anymore, tell them to let go all at once. Then play the rag doll game while they lie limply on the floor.

- **Staring game**. Tell children to stare at a shiny object as hard as they can. Ask them to stare so hard that their eyes want to close. Challenge them to keep staring and not lose concentration while you pass your hand in front of their eyes.

- **Blow bubbles** while children are lying in bed. Tell them to watch the biggest bubble and notice just where it pops. Children can count the number of bubbles or how long bubbles "live." They can imagine bubbles carrying away any upset feelings and pretend that every time a bubble pops, bad feelings disappear.

- **Pretending**. Have children pretend they are melting ice cubes. Ask what it feels like to melt and if they get warmer. They can also pretend to be napping kittens.

- **Breathing**. Hold a feather in front of children's noses and ask them to make it move with their normal breathing. They can make sounds and sighs as they breathe to see if that moves the feather more. Rest a stuffed animal on their tummies and ask them to make it move just by breathing.

- **Word association**. Tell children to say the first word that pops into their minds after you say a word. If you say *white*, they might say *black*. Use calming words like, *slow*, *still*, *peaceful*, or *silent*. Add your own associations to theirs. Take turns repeating and associating: *Calm-quiet, quiet-still, still-lake, lake-water, water-wet* .... Ask children to pick the word that makes them feel the most relaxed and to think that word every time they breathe out for 1 minute.

Going-to-Sleep Game

After regular routines of bathing and reading books, the following directions and script can help the most resistant children drift into dream sleep. Make it clear that after the bedtime routine, children can have their bedroom doors left open and nightlights on as long as they do not get out of bed or call parents for help. If they do leave their bedroom or pester parents, the door will be closed (or light turned off) for *only* a minute or two and then immediately opened. If children claim they do not care if their door is closed, open it anyway after a minute. They are probably trying to *act* brave, and the closed door will intensify anxiety.

1. **Side-to-side eye movements** simulate the rapid eye movements (REMs) that happen during dreams. Have children follow your hand, a small toy, or a plastic glitter wand while you move it from one side of their field of vision to the other for about 10 passes. If they are too young to track an object, alternately tap the outside of each eye. Say, *Follow my hand to help your eyes remember how they move when they dream.*

2. **Toe-to-forehead eye rolls** trigger automatic eye closure that aids deep relaxation. Have children hold their heads still while watching your hand or wand move over their tummies and past their eyebrows. Say, *Keep looking up at my hand until your eyes get so droopy that they remember to close all by themselves.*

3. Scripts for **Imagery focus and deepening**. *As soon as your eyes close you can find yourself at the top of a long staircase that leads to your special dream room. You begin to walk down those steps, and I don't even know how many there are .... Take a step down each time you breathe out and get a closer look at your dream door ....*

4. **Rag doll game for deep muscle relaxation.** Each time you mention walking *down* a step, pick up the child's leg and let it flop. Children should have experience with the rag doll game described earlier. Give several suggestions, like *One step at a time, down ... down ... so many steps before you reach the door of your dream room ....*

5. **Imagery focus to intensify observing**. Continue with the above suggestions. Say, *And now that you can see the door to your dream room more clearly, notice what it's made of tonight, what color it is, where the handle is, how big it is .... Will you have to shrink to fit in it or grow like Alice in Wonderland to reach the handle? Will you need a key? And when you're ready to go in the door, you can let your head nod so slightly ....*

6. **Script to stimulate dream sleep.** *And you go through the door to your dream place ... wondering where it will be and what you will do tonight .... Know that you can be anywhere and do anything that you love to do and not even know when your daydream ends and your sleep dream starts.*

CHAPTER 2

MINDFULNESS MATTERS

MINI INDEX TO CHAPTER 2

**THERAPIST'S
GUIDE TO
MINDFULNESS
MATTERS**

Help clients:

1. Collaborate with treatment by providing information about meditation (informed consent).
2. Practice basic skills: mindful breathing, body scan, witnessing thoughts, walking meditation.
3. Apply meditation skills in everyday life: moment by moment, choiceless awareness.
4. Describe concepts of witnessing and disidentifying to aid the understanding of meditation.
5. Apply meditation skills to specific problems of anxiety, hyperactivity, tics, memory loss, self-esteem, anger management, physical health.
6. Plan ways to help children with meditation.

Using the Handouts

- **Informed consent.** *Information About Meditation* meets the ethical obligation to provide clients information about meditation.
- **General literature.** *Information About Meditation, Mindfulness: Breath by Breath, Body Scan Appetizers, The Practice of Mindfulness, Mindfulness: Step by Step.*
- **Advanced meditative information and practices.** *The Witness Within, Mindfulness: Moment by Moment, Being Present: Choiceless Awareness.*
- **Scripts for recordings.** *Body Scan Appetizers, The Witness Within.*
- **Literature that addresses specific problems.** *Mindfulness: Step by Step* for hyperactivity; *Meditation in Mantra (Kirtan Kirya)* for memory improvement, hyperactivity, tics; *Loving Kindness Mantras* for self-esteem and anger management; *An Invitation to Yoga* for physical problems and calming the mind.
- **Literature for parents.** *Mini Meditations for Minors.* The exercises and explanations in this handout are an excellent way to introduce meditation to beginners.
- **Groups and presentations.** Setting up a meditation group offers a significant way to enhance your practice. An hour at breakfast or lunch is an ideal time. People can eat during the discussion following sitting for 30 minutes. Before meditating, review concepts of focusing on the breath, movement, or mantra and observing inclinations of the wandering mind. Afterward, allow each person to verbalize his or her experience round robin and normalize frustrations that are likely to occur.

Cautions and Comments

- **First, introduce meditation in the office** by giving clients brief experiences with mindful breathing, body scans, observing thoughts, walking meditation, mindfully eating a finger food, and so on. Use literature to reinforce home practice. Present one skill at a time. Very anxious clients may be able to do only three mindful breaths (p. 37).
- *Kirtan Kriya* **(p. 50) is a good introduction** to meditation because a mantra is easier for many people than mindfulness.
- *Mindfulness Moment by Moment* and *Choiceless Awareness* should come after people have acquired skill in breathing, sitting, and walking meditation. These two handouts work well together.
- **To model** *Choiceless Awareness,* do the Now I'm Aware exercise with clients (p. 48).
- *The Witness Within* provides cognitive input to help people realize the nature of pure presence and being in the moment. It is for clients who show a desire for more knowledge.

- **Have clients bring recording devices** for exercises that are best done as a guided meditation. Create a personalized recording for them in your office.

- *An Invitation to Yoga* is not a substitute for studying with an experienced yogi.

Sources Not Referenced in the Handouts

The Meditative Mind: The Varieties of Meditative Experience, by Daniel Goleman (Penguin Putnam Inc., 1988) clarifies the differences between concentration and mindful meditation approaches *and* explains various meditative paths.

Consciousness Speaks: Conversations With Ramesh S. Balsekar, by Ramesh S. Balsekar (Advaita Press, 1992) offers a fascinating discussion on nondualism and the concepts of the wandering mind and the awakened mind (not his terms).

The Wisdom of Yoga: A Seeker's Guide to Extraordinary Living, by Stephen Cope (Bantam Books, 2007) clarifies concepts and methods of meditation and the Self with personal examples.

Handout 2.1—Information About Meditation

Jon Kabat-Zinn, one of the leading teachers on meditation in this country, defines it as paying attention, on purpose, in the present moment, nonjudgmentally.[1] Concentration meditation focuses on an object like a flower, a flame, a prayer, or a repeated phrase (mantra). When attention wavers, the person brings it back to the single point of focus. With practice, the mind sinks into the object, and a sense of self recedes

Mindful meditation is a process of bringing awareness into the present moment. Focusing on the breath is the initial anchor for your attention. Soon a myriad of thoughts will appear, dragging people into the past or future. Once they move past the content of inner ideas and recognize jabbering thoughts as *thoughts*, they switch from thinking to witnessing. This *noticing* happens spontaneously and awakens people from commentaries on the past or future. The more stray thoughts are noted, the more they subside. The experience of detachment, clarity, and presence becomes increasingly profound, and the sense of self dwindles.

A Micro Look at Meditation[2]

Neurobiologists have used brain scans to study changes that happen during meditation. These changes explain the experience of focused calm, loss of sense of self, and the following benefits:

- **Increased activity in the left prefrontal cortex** (just above the eyes), which monitors the ability to stay attentive, alert, and focused on a task. The frontal lobes are also the seat of working memory.

- **Decreased activity in the right frontal cortex,** which is more stress-prone than the calmer left prefrontal cortex. This may reduce anxiety and depression.[3]

- **Decreased activity in the parietal lobes** (top and back of the brain cortex). This area helps orient people to their surroundings and creates a sense of self, space, and time.[3]

- **Increased activity in the thalamus** (in the center of the brain) proportional to the decrease in the parietal lobes. This structure relays incoming sensory information to many parts of the brain and communicates a lucid sense of reality to the frontal lobes.

- **Reduced activity in the amygdala** (in the emotional brain below the temporal [side] lobes) where the brain processes fear.[4]

- **Increased release of dopamine**—the pleasure hormone.

- **Asymmetry in the two lobes of the thalamus** during meditative and nonmeditative states, possibly causing a long-lasting change in outlook.

Benefits of Meditation

Dr. Herbert Benson first identified the relaxation response in 1975 as a change in people's physical and emotional response to stress. His research showed that meditation decreased blood pressure; levels of the stress hormones cortisol and noradrenaline; and the heart, pulse, and respiratory rate. Since then, physical, emotional, and spiritual benefits have been identified that are far too numerous to list here. The following give details of some of the more fascinating findings on the benefits of meditation:

Boosts Immunity. Twenty-five subjects who had participated in an 8-week training program in mindful meditation and 16 people who were on a waiting list were vaccinated with an influenza vaccine. People who had participated in the meditation training had a significant

---

1. Mindful meditation is thoroughly explained in Kabit-Zinn's book, *Wherever You Go, There You Are,* 1994, New York: Hyperion.
2. Andrew Newberg explains the neurobiology of meditation in *Why We Believe What We Believe,* 2006, New York: Simon & Schuster.
3. See www.project-meditation.org, ''Meditation Benefits,'' by Phil Pemberton.
4. See ''The Science of Meditation,'' by C. Barbor, 2001, *Psychology Today,* May/June.

increase in concentration of antibodies to the influenza vaccine compared with those on the wait list.[5]

Enhances Memory. Six patients who complained of memory loss were trained in a type of meditation called *Kirtan Kriya*. It required 12 minutes of practice a day for 8 weeks. The patients were given memory tests and brain scans before, during, and after the research study. After the training, the chief researcher, Dr. Andrew Newberg, described statistically significant improvement in the memory-test results and a dramatic increase in blood flow to a region of the brain linked to learning and memory. The posterior cingulated gyrus (where blood flow increased) is the first area to decline in Alzheimer's patients. Even though the initial sample is too small to be considered conclusive, the findings are promising.[6]

Decrease Risk of Heart Attack and Stroke. Sixty people with high blood pressure, at risk for cardiovascular disease, were assigned to a transcendental meditation group or a health education class for 7 months. The meditation group showed a marked decrease in the thickness of their artery walls, while those in the health education class actually had an increase in fat deposits on arterial walls (atherosclerosis). This condition leads to heart attacks and strokes. The improvement with meditation was comparable to results from using lipid-lowering medications. These findings were first published in the American Heart Association journal, *Stroke,* in March 2000.

Meditation Facts

- Meditation assumes that the natural state of the mind is calm and clear. The mind is trained to uncover its true nature. Insight into the process of thinking reduces reactivity.

- Meditation should not be confused with making the mind blank. It is the practice of experiencing reality as it is, without assumptions.

- Mindful meditation is generally devoid of all spiritual content and was popularized to enhance emotional and physical well-being. Conversely, most religions (Christianity, Judaism, Islam) use some form of meditation to strengthen spiritual practices.

- Like progressive relaxation and biofeedback, meditation has a calming effect. However, it has the added benefit of retraining attention.

- Both meditation and hypnosis produce a heightened state of internal concentration. The first produces clear, moment-to-moment awareness and loss of a sense of self. The second evokes or suggests nonordinary, desired responses for a specific purpose.

- Any activity can be meditation when people focus on their experience—the sensations in the feet while walking or feeling soapy water while doing dishes. Thoughts that occur during these experiences are observed—*I wish I didn't have to walk any further; I wonder if this soap is drying my skin.*

- When possible, meditation should be practiced daily. Three mindful breaths can produce instant calming. Ten minutes a day can begin to reverse some physical ailments. Fifteen to 30 minutes a day can help people achieve spiritual goals of deep connection with all that is.

- A teacher can be an invaluable aid to answer questions for beginners or people progressing to deeper levels. Meditating in a group provides a collective energy and focus.

---

5. ''Alterations in Brain and Immune Function Produced by Mindfulness Meditation,'' by R. J. Davidson, J. Kabat-Zinn, J. Schumacher, et al., 2003, *Psychosomatic Medicine,* 65, pp. 564–570.

6. ''The Biology of Belief,'' by J. Kluger, 2009, *Time,* February 12, p. 64. *Kirtan Kriya* is described in *More Brief Therapy Client Handouts* (p. 50), by K. Cohen-Posey, 2010, Hoboken, NJ: John Wiley & Sons.

Handout 2.2—Mindfulness: Breath by Breath

The focus of mindfulness is the breath. It is the current that connects your body and mind. Can you discover the boundary where air becomes breath? Breathing is a formless object that is an ideal target to observe because it can happen only in the present moment. When thoughts distract, it is easy to return to observing inhalations and exhalations, unless you have an inner *breathing critic*. Some biology basics will banish concerns and allow breath awareness to proceed freely.

A Word to the Breathing Critic

There is no right way to breathe. Rapid breathing is a normal reaction to a surge of adrenaline . It is expected after heavy exercise. Certain thoughts, emotions, low iron levels, or even allergens can cause an adrenaline spike, making the rate of breathing change suddenly. Trying to *catch your breath* by gasping for air worsens the situation. Too much oxygen can cause hyperventilation. Knowing that the brain will begin to neutralize extra adrenaline by releasing the calming neurotransmitter, gamma-aminobutyric acid (GABA), can help you understand that your breathing will return to its usual rate.

Aware Breathing[1]

The following steps will help you pay exquisite attention to your breath without changing a thing. There is no need to attempt deep belly breathing, cleansing breaths (inhale to the count of 3; exhale to the count of 6), or square breathing (inhale to the count of 4; and exhale to the count of 4). You only need to be aware of air coming into your body and breath going out. When breath becomes the object of attention (without judgment), it naturally regulates.

- Sit on a cushion or a chair with your head, neck, and spine aligned. Imagine a helium balloon attached to the crown of your head. Keeping your head upright will help your mind stay alert.

- Aim your attention at the beginning of the *in-breath* and sustain your awareness until you are ready to breathe out. Notice if there is a slight pause between the in and out breath.

- Aim your attention at the beginning of the *exhale,* and sustain it until you notice a pause or the desire to inhale.

- Each breath sets off a chain of occurrences. What do the muscles in your nose do to draw air in? Can you feel the hairs inside your nose shift direction with each in- and out-breath? How much does an exhale widen your nostrils? What is the difference in temperature between air going in and breath leaving? Do you use your sense of touch or smell?

- Where are you most aware of your breath—your *nose, chest, or belly*? Feel your lungs expand and the lovely sensations of your diaphragm moving down to push your belly out.

- Notice the *pauses between breaths*. Are they staying the same or lengthening?

- Establish air entering your nose as a focal point. However, if you are congested, notice the rising and falling of your belly. Whenever your attention wanders, come back to the breath.

- It is natural for your mind to wander. When you notice you have been sidetracked by thoughts, plans, memories, sounds, or sensations, go back to noticing your breath.

- If you lose your focus, note your breaths—*in ... out ... pause ... in ... pause ... out ... pause....* Notice if there is a rhythm and subtle changes.

---

1. This breathing exercise comes from *Empowering Dialogues Within* (p. 2.14), by K. Cohen-Posey (2008), Hoboken, NJ: John Wiley & Sons.

- Observe how you decide to stop this exercise. Do you think—*Okay, I get it.... I've had enough of this.... I want to find out what comes next.... I have other things to do....*

Three Mindful Breaths

There are numerous benefits to meditating for 20 to 45 minutes. But for many people the thought of such an extended period of time of nondoing is daunting. You can begin your adventure with mindfulness, three breaths at a time. Even such limited experiences can produce surprising results.

- Count three breaths, breathing all the way in and all the way out. Notice how you feel afterwards or any changes that take place in your breathing.

- Repeat the exercise again. Notice thoughts that occur or distracting sounds. Then go back to where you are in your breathing. Are you inhaling, exhaling, or pausing?

- Being sidetracked by sounds, sights, or thoughts is part of mindfulness! Having the awareness, *I'm thinking,* and then returning to the breath is a spontaneous act of noticing.

Take three mindful breaths whenever you think of it: before you start to eat, while driving the car, or when you are feeling tense. You can improve attention or become more relaxed, depending on the situation. Can you simultaneously be aware of three breaths *while* engaging in normal activities: reading this paper, taking a shower, washing the dishes? Use the sound of church bells, fire engines, or a dog barking as a reminder to take three mindful breaths. Take one or two mindful breaths before you answer the phone. Reminders to practice are limitless.

Make a special effort to take three mindful breaths when you are upset or obsessing about something. Notice what happens. Do you gain a moment's reprieve from disturbing thoughts? What do you think would happen if you made a regular habit of taking three mindful breaths?

Yah-Weh Breathing

An ancient Hebrew name for God is *Yahweh.* Its literal translation means *I am what I am* or *I will be what I will be.* The name should not be pronounced, but breathed: *Yah* on the inhale and *Weh* on the exhale. When first practicing aware breathing, it can help to *note* each inhale and exhale by thinking the words *in* and *out.* However, this can become confusing. It is far easier to *notice* or note the breath by thinking the syllables *Yah-weh.* If you prefer a more familiar word use *A-men,* which means, *truly.* Noting the breath can be especially helpful when you have racing thoughts.

- Take three mindful breaths, noting them with the syllables *Yah-weh* or *A-men.* It can help to stare intently at a spot while you are doing this.

- Become curious about your breath without trying to change it. Be with your breath just as it is. If it is tight, observe that; if it is gasping, just notice it.

- Follow with three more mindful breaths—simply focus your awareness on breathing. Again, pay attention to any subtle changes in your body and to the process of air becoming breath.

Easy Song Meditation

Breathe to lyrics that have a slow beat like "Amazing Grace" or "Let It Be." Inhaling and exhaling on each syllable will slow the breath down. If your breath is rapid, start with a song with a fast tempo and switch to a slower melody. Gradually, allow the syllable for the exhale to take longer and longer. If you find yourself racing ahead, return to your current syllable (the present moment). Refocus on your syllable if thoughts start to come:

Inhale	Exhale	Inhale	Exhale	Inhale	Exhale	Inhale	Exhale	Inhale	Exhale
A …	maz…	ing …	grace…	how…	sweet…	the …	sound…	that…	saved…

Handout 2.3—Body Scan Appetizers

Often, people do not realize the extent to which they have become distant from their bodies. When attention is focused on the territory betwixt your head and toes, your mind and body become one. Body scan meditations are important for beginners because they provide a systematic way to pay attention to the physical sphere, offer a method of being with any unpleasant sensations that may arise, and rehearse the first step of any mindfulness practice—settling into the body.

Preparation

- **Position.** Lie down on a carpet or mat. A bed can be used if you have discomfort. Let your legs fall open. A pillow under the knees can provide back support. Imagine your head pulling away from your feet and your shoulders pulling away from your ears.

- **Body focus.** Notice where your body makes contact with the floor or bed. On each out-breath, imagine that you sink deeply into the surface below.

- **Breath focus.** Bring awareness to the belly and how the breath pushes on the abdominal wall. Notice the expanding of the belly for three breaths and the sensations that accompany each exhale.

Body Scan Lying Down[1]

During this practice, attention will be focused in detail on every area of the body. This expedition through the physical sphere can take 45 minutes. Exploring even one limb in a session can bring a profound sense of calm stillness or a keener awareness of a particular discomfort and learning to contain it. Alternate between starting from the toes or head. If possible, have someone read the body scan to you and take turns leading each other in this meditation.

1. **Toes.** Bring the spotlight of your attention all the way down to the toes in your left foot. Focus on each toe in turn. Can you be aware of each one separately? What sensations do you discover—tingling, warmth, numbness, nothingness? Be with it.

2. **Breathing into.** On the inhale, imagine air passing down to the toes, and on the exhale, feel breath coming back up through the body and out the nose. If you notice any tension or intense sensation, breathe into those sensations. Be fully aware and let go on the out-breath. Continue breathing–letting go, breathing–letting go, and notice if sensations change.

3. **Foot.** Move your awareness to the sole of your foot—the ball, instep, and heel. Are the sensations there strong, weak, or neutral? Focus on the top of the foot and ankle. Capture the awareness of your whole foot, breathing into it and letting go.

4. **Calf and shin.** Pay attention to the angle at which your foot joins your ankle and then your lower leg. As you explore your lower leg, isolate your calf and your shin. Then, gain an awareness of all the sensations in your whole foot and lower leg: warm, cool, tense, strong, weak, or neutral. Notice your breath in the background.

5. **Knee.** Open your awareness to your knee, paying attention to how it connects the lower and upper leg. Be aware of any bony structures underneath or discomfort. Breathe into the knee, and breathe with any sensations you find. Expand leg awareness to include your knee.

6. **Thigh.** Move awareness into your thigh. Notice any sensations. Is there a difference between the inside and outside of your thigh? Breathe into your thigh and let go on the out-breath. Notice the wholeness of your entire left leg. Repeat steps 1–6 with your right leg.

7. **Pelvic area.** Widen awareness to your right hip. Imagine the bony structure underneath. Feel your right buttock cushioning your hip and making contact with the

---

1. A CD with a guided meditation for the body scan is found in *The Mindful Way Through Depression* by Williams, Teasdale, Segal, and Kabat-Zin (The Guilford Press, 2007).

floor or bed. Breathe into your right pelvic area and notice all the sensations that are there. Move awareness to the center of your pelvis and your genitals. Are the sensations strong, weak, or neutral? Breathe into your genital area and let go. Move awareness to the left hip and buttock as you did on your right side. Breathe into your entire pelvic region, notice any sensations, and let go. Carry an awareness of your entire body from the waist down.

8. **Lower back and abdomen.** Open awareness to your lower back. Notice how it curves away from the floor and how it supports your abdomen. Imagine all the organs lying in the abdominal cavity protected by a layer of muscle. Breathe with any sensations in your lower back and abdomen. Center your mind on a spot three fingers below your navel and two fingers behind it. This is the seat of spiritual energy. Breathe into this center for three full breaths.

9. **Upper back and rib cage.** Move awareness to your upper back. Feel your shoulder blades pressing into the floor. Allow awareness to flow around your ribs to your pectoral muscles or breasts. Notice everything you sense in this area. Is there any pain as your chest wall expands? Breathe into any sensations you notice. Hold an awareness of your torso and then of your whole body from your chest down.

10. **Shoulder and arm.** Scan both shoulders and arms in turn, paying particular attention to each area and joint as you did in steps 1–6. Start with an awareness of each finger, hand, wrist, forearm, elbow, upper arm, and armpit. Isolate your shoulder from the rest of your torso. Be aware of all the sensations in each area, breathe into them, and let go. Hold an awareness of your entire body from your collarbone down.

11. **Neck and throat.** Notice the natural curve of your neck and how it supports your throat. Do not suppress any need to swallow, but pay keen attention to it. Bring breath to your neck, noticing any sensations. Be aware of your whole body from your neck down.

12. **Face.** Allow your attention to flow to your jaw, chin, and cheeks. Notice if gravity is pulling your muscles away from your face. Has your jaw dropped? Notice the softness of your tongue and the hardness of your teeth. Is there tingling in your lips? Where does the roof of your mouth change from being soft to hard? Feel the wetness. Can you sense your whole nose and the hairs moving inside as you breathe? Do you breathe with both nostrils or one? Can you feel your eyelids resting? With your eyes closed, where are they focused—straight ahead or down? Let your attention go to your eyebrows, out to your temples, and up to your forehead. Is your forehead smooth or furrowed? Bring your breath to your forehead and let it flow down your face. Breathe with any sensations you notice in your face.

13. **Head.** Open your awareness to move around your entire scalp. Is it tight or comfortable? Feel the back of your head pressing on the floor and imagine energy moving out of the crown of your head. Breathe up into your head and let go.

14. **Whole body.** Notice the envelope of skin around your body. Breathe into the top of the head and out to the bottom of the toes. Sense your physical wholeness and the absence of distinction between limbs. If you cannot be conscious of this oneness, notice whatever sensations are there and imagine the idea of a whole body.

Seated Body Scan

Seated body scans are executed in a similar fashion to ones lying down but usually begin with awareness of the scalp. More attention is placed on the posture since the upper part of the body must support itself. Awareness is repeatedly brought back to the head being balanced on the spine, imagining someone gently pushing between the shoulder blades, and on the small natural curve in the lower back. Any slumping will increase feelings of pressure in the body.

Handout 2.4—The Practice of Mindfulness

Mindful meditation focuses on what happens *to* you and *in* you in each moment of perception. You may hear sounds and place your attention on raw auditory sensations. However, much of your interior landscape will be dominated by thoughts and their by-product, feelings. Before giving a step-by-step guide to meditation, it will help to understand the nature of thought.

Thinking About Thoughts

The thoughts that enter your mind can be divided into two main types—*working* and *wandering*.

Working thoughts are willed for the purpose of solving problems, planning events, and accomplishing a task. Wandering thoughts occur automatically. We seem to have no more control over them than over the dreams that dance through our minds at night. A person might be visited by such mental intruders as *I'm not good enough* or *He has no respect for me*. But by *observing* thoughts, a subtle shift takes place:

I'm not good enough becomes:	*He has no respect for me* becomes:
I'm <u>criticizing</u> myself.	I'm <u>reminding</u> myself that he has no respect.
The focus switches from the subject of the thought to the process of <u>criticizing</u>.	The focus switches from the subject of the thought to the process of reminding.
I'm not good enough decreases in importance, reducing reactivity.	The issue of respect decreases in importance, reducing reactivity.

This chart shows that whether thoughts are about yourself or others, in the moment of noticing them you witness what you are doing: *judging, comparing, analyzing, wondering, remembering, doubting, planning, rehearsing, or* just plain *thinking*. Recognizing thoughts for what they are is the mindful art of *insight*.

Witnessing thoughts can be tricky. Is the idea *This thought is stupid* an observation or a thought? It is an opinion based on personal perception. *I'm judging my thought* is, indeed, an observation that can turn any idea into a mental event that is neither good nor bad but simply the stuff of the mind.

Steps to Sitting Meditation[1]

Preparation

1. **Length of meditation.** Determine the length of your session before you begin so you will not yield to urges that you have done enough. If you are a beginner, start with a length of time that you can tolerate, even if it is only 5 or 10 minutes, and set a timer or look at your watch. This will give you the opportunity to practice noticing thoughts that try to resist nondoing. Practice meditating at the same time every day and gradually increase the length of your sessions to 30 or 45 minutes.

2. **Body position.** Take your seat mindfully, choosing your chair, cushion, and posture with intention. As the ancient Zen proverb suggests, sit as though you were with an honored guest.

3. **Head position.** Keep your head, neck, and spine aligned. Imagine a helium balloon attached to the crown of your head. Hold your head upright to help your mind stay alert. If you meditate lying down, lie flat on your back, with your head, neck, and spine in alignment.

4. **Hand position.** Notice how your hands want to fall. Palms down (containment), palms up (openness), and hands cupped (settled), index fingers pointed (focus).

5. **Eyes.** Do your eyes want to be opened or closed? If they are opened, focus on a spot. It is likely that they will close shortly. Simply observe this: Do your lids feel heavy? Do your eyes blink slowly?

---

1. Many of the steps for sitting meditation are described in Exercise 8, *Empowering Dialogues Within* (p. 2.15), by K. Cohen-Posey, 2008, Hoboken, NJ: John Wiley & Sons.

Focus on the Breath and Body

1. **Breathe with awareness**. Your focal point is air entering your nose or the rising or falling of your belly. Count three breaths and *pay exquisite attention* to how air moves in through your nose and lungs and breath moves out for the full duration of each inhale and exhale.

2. **Observe**. Notice where you find *the most vivid sensation of breathing*—the nostrils, chest, or belly. It may stay the same or change. Follow the rhythm of the breath—it regulates itself.

3. **Sense your body** as a whole, sitting and breathing. *Notice how you are supported* by the chair or floor by taking note of any pressure or contact. For a moment, be with your body.

4. **Expected arrivals.** The first few breaths can be easy to attend to and may produce a lovely calm quietness, but urges to move and thoughts are drawn to this stillness like moths to a flame. Honor these "guests" by observing them with *bare attention*. Then return to the breath.

Bare Attention

1. **Body sensations** may dominate awareness as they arise and pass away. If you notice an itch or need to move, do your best to focus on it and examine the urgency without yielding. This develops the ability to attend without desire. Often, itches go away, but if you become too distracted and scratch, notice the mechanics of how you do that.

2. **Sounds** may become objects of focus. Be aware of the sensory quality of sound—pitch, timbre, loudness, or duration without considering pleasantness, unpleasantness, or their source. Practice hearing sounds as they arise and pass in the moment. Listen for silence and return to the breath.

3. **Thoughts** are attracted to a still, clear mind. You may become uncomfortable if there is no chattering going on inside. *Observe* your thoughts and any impact they have—*planning*: excitement; *what if*: anxious; *questioning*: bored; *criticizing*: guilt; *judging*: anger; and so on.

4. **An emotional charge** can accompany a thought. If you feel excited, anxious, bored, or angry, notice where that feeling lies in your body. *Breathe into* the most intense part of the feeling. Continue to *breathe with* any sensations until they lessen, and *let go* of some of the emotion on the out-breath. There is nothing you can do about the issue at the moment. It is best to go back to your breathing focal point until your state of quiet, calmness returns.

5. **Thought metaphors.** Thoughts can be seen as clouds moving across the sky—sometimes dark and stormy or light and fluffy. They may fill the vista or clear out completely.

6. **Mind wandering** means that you are pre- or postoccupied with planning, daydreaming, or aimlessly drifting about. Noticing that your mind has been wandering means that you have reawakened to the moment. Quickly note where your mind went (*remembering, chatting, wondering, working thoughts*) and return to your breath. It is possible for your mind to wander 100 times in a 10-minute meditation, which means that you will have had 100 moments of spontaneous awareness. Congratulations!

7. **Doubts** about your skill, purpose, or the value of meditation are a sure sign that you are succeeding. They are evidence of your humility and can be noted with the words *doubting* or *thinking* before returning your attention to your breath. Asking questions is a good way to disarm doubts: *What part of me is questioning my ability? Who has had enough?* Inquire without expecting answers and enjoy the peace of silent responses.

8. **Impulses** to end a meditation session prematurely are common. Note your *impatience* or ask, *How do I know it is time to stop?* Continue to use bare attention until your timer rings.

Handout 2.5—The Witness Within

In mindfulness there are four spheres of attention: (1) body, posture, and movement; (2) physical sensations; (3) feelings and reactions such as being annoyed or pleased; and (4) mind objects that trigger a feeling (sounds or thoughts). When not using the focused concentration of meditation, people often become *identified* with one of these four spheres:

1. My body is disgusting.... I'm pretty.... I'm a runner.
2. I am tired.... I'm so hungry.... My body aches.
3. I'm worried.... I'm excited.
4. I'll never finish this project.... Maybe I'll be famous.

In mindfulness meditation, people focus on breathing, but inevitably they wander into zones of sensations, feelings, and thoughts. Then a surprising thing happens. The *realization* comes that they have *zoned out* and are no longer mindful of the breath. Here lies the ultimate question: What part of a person *notices* that his or her attention has wandered and *wakes up* to the awareness of what is happening in the present?

There is something inside of you that can observe your body, sensations, feelings, and thoughts. When that happens, you disidentify with mind-body domains and are no longer dominated by them. Instead of being tired, you can notice sensations of fatigue. Rather than being dissatisfied, the state of displeasure is observed. The idea *I have to make others happy* can run your life until you realize the desire to please people is controlling you. When you align yourselves with what ceaselessly watches, you are no longer a prisoner of pain and toxic thoughts. Roberto Assagioli, the originator of Psychosynthesis, formulated the following disidentification exercise that clarifies the distinction between the witness and the witnessed.[1]

Disidentifie-cation Meditation—Directions[2]

1. Pick one sphere of attention for your meditation (body, emotion, desire, or thought). Review the narrative.

2. Count three breaths and pay exquisite attention to how air moves in and out through your nose and lungs for the full duration of each inhale and exhale.

3. Close your eyes and repeat to yourself as much as you can remember about the zone of awareness that you have chosen.

4. Open your eyes and re-read the narrative. Take three more breaths and repeat in your own mind what you remember, ending with—*The vast free witness of them all.*

5. Review the affirmation at the end—*I am what remains*. Count three breaths, close your eyes, and repeat to yourself as much as you can remember of this statement to establish your true identity.

I have a body, but I am not my body.

- Sensations of pressure, warmth, tightness, heaviness, lightness, and pain come and go.
- My body is my precious instrument of experience and action, but it is only an instrument.
- Sensations come and go, but do not affect that which senses—the vast free witness of it all.

I have emotions, but I am not my emotions.

- Love, anger, fear, sadness, joy all arise, come and go, stay a bit, repeat, and pass.
- My emotions are neither right nor wrong, but reactions to events and thoughts.

---

1. Assagioli's original disidentification exercise is explained in *Psychosynthesis: A Collection of Basic Writings* (pp. 103–106), Amherst, MA: Synthesis Center, 2000/1965. Some of the wording is similar to Ken Wilber's witness exercise in *Grace and Grit* (p. 126), Boston: Shambhala Publications, 1991.

2. More about the disidentification exercise can be found in *Empowering Dialogues Within* (p. 2.18), by K. Cohen-Posey, 2008, Hoboken, NJ: John Wiley & Sons.

- I can feel my emotions but what is felt is not the feeler—the vast free witness of them all.

I have desires, but I am not my desires.

- Attractions, repulsions, dreams, and cravings can be steadfast or whims of the moment.
- My desires incite my body to take action in the world.
- I can feel driven, but my drives are not the driver—the vast free witness of them all.

I have thoughts, but I am not my thoughts.

- Ideas, doubts, memories, assumptions arise, come and go, stay a bit, repeat, and pass.
- My perceptions of events are recorded as accurate or inaccurate ideas.
- I know my thoughts, but what is known is not the knower—the vast free witness of them all.

I am what remains—an unmoved mover; a presence.

- I am a center of pure awareness and power, capable of observing and mastering movement, feelings, desires, and thoughts.
- I cannot doubt that the witness exists because the witness is there to observe the doubt.
- I am the simple witness of my ordinary I.

Pointers

Use different sittings to practice one of the four spears of attention. Eventually, review the entire meditation silently. If you tend to be intellectual, concentrate on *I have thoughts, but I am not my thoughts.* If you are emotional, begin with *I have emotions, but I am not my emotions.* You will know which zone of awareness you need to focus on most. Just a line from this meditation can be used any time by bringing attention to your experience:

SELF-TALK

- I am feeling afraid, but I am not my fear. My fear may come and go, but I am the constant, unmoved witness of fear.
- Even though I have just eaten, I still feel desire. I have desire, but I am not my desire. Desires come and go but do not affect what is constant and without need.

From Witness to Awake

The discovery of the witness offers a vantage point from which fleeting sensations, urges, and thoughts can be observed. As long as this concept helps you be less identified with your assumptions, doubts, and cravings, hang on to it. The truth is, there is no silent seer: there is only seeing and witnessing. The witness is the seed around which blooms the fruit of the *awakened mind*, an ever-expanding oasis that offers respite from the tedious *wandering mind*:

- **Wandering mind** works in the past or future. It dwells on memories and anticipates what is to come. Attempts to stifle the wandering mind is the wandering mind trying to suppress itself—*That thought is bad.*
- **Awakened mind** is concerned with the present moment. It concentrates fully on what it is doing. The *me* is not there, only the activity. Stored information is used to aid doing in the present, not to project into the future. Doing is done without concern about the outcome.

During meditation, awakened mind illuminates whatever crosses its radar screen: ever-present breath or attempts by wandering mind to steal the show.

Handout 2.6—Mindfulness: Step by Step

The tiger paces his trapped existence, expelling energy that has nowhere to go. Like these magnificent beasts, when our minds are agitated, we can be propelled to move in well-worn paths that prescribe the current cage of our existence. But when attention is transferred from thoughts to the very steps we walk, a shift occurs. Mindfulness is brought to movement and, in particular, to the point where the weight-bearing foot makes contact with the ground. Mindful walking is one of the oldest forms of meditation.

Preparation

- **Location.** Find a place where you can walk back and forth in a lane at least 20 feet long, or mark a square of similar dimensions. It can be indoors or outdoors, but should offer enough privacy to eliminate concerns about others and safety.

- **Attire.** Depending on your walking surface, you can be barefoot or wear thin-soled shoes.

- **Time.** Determine the length of your session before you begin so you will not yield to urges that you have done enough. If you are a beginner, start with 5 to 10 minutes. Eventually, you may practice this meditation for 20 to 30 minutes a day.

- **Grounding stance.** Position your feet parallel and hips-width apart. Exhale and bend your knees to feel the earth underneath you. Flex your knees slightly a few times and notice the weight of your body being transmitted through your legs and feet into the ground.

- **Alignment and body awareness.** Notice if your shoulders are aligned over your hips and ankles. Take a moment to scan your body from the soles of your feet to the crown of your head. If you observe any tension, just breathe into it.

- **Gaze.** Your eyes should stay focused on the ground about 3 feet ahead to avoid distractions.

Steps to Walking Meditation

1. **Left/right.** There are six components of walking, but at the beginning of your meditation, you may just want to focus on which foot is making contact with the ground—noting nothing more than right … left … right … left….

2. **Turning.** As you approach the end of the walkway, notice your intention to turn and how your body executes this action. You can stop for a moment and be aware of the alignment of shoulders, hips, and ankles before turning. Then notice the intention to walk again.

3. **Lifting/moving/putting.** Eventually, you will want to notice three main components to walking: lifting as you raise your foot, moving as the foot travels through the air, and putting as the foot is dropped to the ground. During each pass on your path, focus on just one of these aspects—lifting … lifting … lifting—until you fully gain a sense of it. Gradually, you can become aware of all three components.

4. **Shifting weight.** During another pass on your path, focus on the shifting of your body weight as each foot is put down. Noting is done mentally—shifting … shifting … shifting….

5. **Speed.** Notice the rate at which you naturally want to walk. Initially, you may want to walk quickly and will be able to mentally note little more than the movement of your right or left foot or shifting weight. Gradually, your pace may slow down, especially if you become more focused on the intricacies of movement.

6. **Six components (optional).** As you become more skillful, you will gain awareness of six parts to walking. The foot rises before it lifts. It pushes rather than moves through the air. Putting is composed of the foot dropping, touching the ground, and pressing. Use one span of your walk just to focus on each of these components. Then, mentally chant the six components as you walk—rising, lifting, pushing, dropping, touching, pressing.

7. **Shifts in consciousness.** Eventually, there will be no need to note lifting … pushing … dropping…. This will be replaced by bare awareness of movement through space. You should not seek this consciousness of movement, but allow any noting to fall away on its own. As awareness of pure movement becomes more pronounced, the sense of a me that is doing the walking or my foot will fade. This can take months or years.

Other Awareness

1. **Mental states and sensations.** As you walk, it is natural to have other awareness. Is your mind calm, busy, cloudy, or focused? Do you sense lightness, heaviness, hardness, softness, heat, or coolness in the motion of each step? Can you be conscious of your whole body as it moves through space?

2. **Widen your awareness.** Notice your breath as your body shifts weight. Observe how your heel and then the ball of your foot contact the ground.

3. **Feelings.** Are you having any emotional reactions to sounds that you hear? Do you feel annoyed by a phone ringing or happy at the sight of a puppy? Do you have an urge to smell a flower? Note any desires or emotions and return to your focus on the movement of walking.

4. **Thoughts.** The more automatic walking awareness becomes (with the ability to focus on lifting … moving … putting without even noting these components), the more likely other "guests" are to join the meditation—random thoughts. They are to be noted with such words as *remembering, wondering, criticizing, judging, planning,* or just plain *thinking.* Then return to your focus on movement. Picking up the pace of your walking while placing exquisite attention on movement can also keep thoughts from hijacking the meditation—roll the left foot up, … move it … place … feel … lift … move … place … feel….

5. **Turns** are an opportunity to realign your shoulders, hips, and ankles; to feel the weight of your body grounding into the earth; and to refocus attention to your body and movement if your mind has wandered.

Ending

1. **Outer focus.** Slowly ease out of this practice by noticing your surroundings—objects in your house, colors, grass, sounds, or the temperature.

2. **Aware standing.** Gradually come to a stop and become aware of the feeling of standing still again. Compare how you feel at this point with when you started.

3. **Ongoing practice.** Bring walking meditation into your daily activities. Practice it when you are walking to your car or for a few steps in a store aisle. While waiting in line, use the time to notice your body alignment and breathing. Feel the contact your feet make with the floor.

Walking Meditation Then and Now

Mindfulness was developed in approximately 500 BCE. Its originator identified several advantages of walking meditation. Practitioners develop stamina for long journeys—a necessity in an era when animals were the only means of transport. Walking became an important counterbalance to sitting meditation. Movement revives muscles and stimulates circulation for periods in which stillness is cultivated. It is an excellent meditation to follow meals. Digestion is promoted and drowsiness prevented. Walking followed by sitting meditation is a perfect combination to still the mind and bring greater awareness into everyday life.

Modern-day psychologists recognize that walking meditation is ideal for people who are hyperactive. Movement provides essential brain stimulation combined with a procedure for focused concentration. This is especially important for children and is a better alternative to time-outs that require sitting still.

Handout 2.7—Mindfulness: Moment by Moment

The image evoked by the word *meditation* is of an ancient yogi sitting pretzel style, gazing at his navel. Less well known is the cryptic meditative advice to *wash the dishes when you are washing the dishes*. This means to put full attention into the experience of dishwashing, rather than to wash dishes in order to make them clean. Thus, to be fully alive, people simply need to floss when they are flossing their teeth or pet the cat when they are petting the cat. This *choiceless awareness* starts with the present moment.[1]

Exercise 1—Self Narration

Narrate your activities and movements as they are taking place. This opens the doors of perception to ordinary event with a *beginner's mind*, as if for the first time. Notice all the mechanics that are involved in putting this paper down and picking it up: *I'm holding this paper in my hand. It is balanced between my thumb and my forefinger. I notice that it has very little weight. Now I turn my wrist to face it downward and rest it on my lap, withdrawing my hand. I pause to look at the back and slide my thumb underneath with my fingers on top, turn my wrist, bend my elbow, bring it toward my face until my eyes can focus and I find my place.*

Exercise 2—Waking Up in the Morning

Keep your attention on five full breaths—*I notice my slow and even breathing*. If you have any morning anxiety, locate where it is in the body and breathe into it. Notice your thoughts—*I have the thought, It's time to get up*, and another part of me complains, *I'm not ready*. Continue to narrate your actions—*I pull the covers down until my leg is free and I plant it on the floor. I push myself up with my hand and my arm in back for support. Now both feet are on the floor*. Notice the transition as your body moves from lying down, to sitting, to standing. Reverse this process when you go to bed. Bring your attention to your breathing for at least five full breaths.

Exercise 3—Drive the Car When Driving the Car

Frequently, narrate yourself while driving to increase attention. Before you switch on the engine, sit for a moment and notice three full breaths, letting go on the out-breath. Switch off the radio and experience the silence. Be aware of any tensions in your body—a knot in the belly, your hands gripping the steering wheel, or a clenched jaw. Say silently, *I am holding the steering wheel firmly; my foot presses on the gas; my eyes shift to the odometer to make sure I'm driving the speed limit.*

- Develop all-round awareness by using your rearview mirror as well as looking at what is in front of you. Notice the sky, trees, and other cars.

- Notice your attitude. Are you feeling competitive or rushed?

- Use cars passing you, stop signs and traffic lights as an opportunity to pay attention to your breath.

- After turning off the engine, sit for a moment and notice three full breaths.

Exercise 4—Eat When You Are Eating

Occasionally, narrate yourself while eating finger foods to relearn how to make each bite burst with flavor and satisfaction: Look at an apple as though you had never seen one before. Examine its color, where the light shines on it, and any unique features. Smell the apple and notice its flavor.

- Begin your self-narration: *I'm holding this apple in my hand and it feels hard, round, and cold. I have to open my jaws wide and use pressure to take a bite. I can feel a large chunk in*

---

1. Some of these exercises are adapted from *Empowering Dialogues Within* by, K. Cohen-Posey (John Wiley & Sons, Inc., 2008, p. 2.13).

my mouth and a delicious juice oozes out from one side on my tongue. Now I start to suck more juice out and then bite the chunk in half. I move it round and round with my jaw while pulverizing it with my teeth. All the while, there is a juicy, delicate apple flavor going over the top of my tongue, and I keep moving my tongue around, biting and chewing until that entire piece is gone.

- Detect your first intention to swallow as it comes up. This should be experienced consciously before you actually swallow. You cannot eat the apple until you have fully tasted the first bite. Notice whether you can stay with the experience and how it is different from your usual eating. Do not do this exercise with highly processed or sweetened foods.

Exercise 5—Listen When You Are Listening :[2]

A mindfulness basic is to note or narrate your thoughts, feelings, and sensations as they arise. When listening, put your full attention on other people and narrate or **name** their thoughts, feelings, or behavior: *You like to give <u>orders</u>; you're <u>guessing</u> that . . . ; you're <u>remembering</u> when . . . ; you're <u>disappointed</u> that . . . ; you're <u>suggesting</u> . . . ; you look <u>puzzled</u>.*

- Another way to listen is to *rephrase* what people are saying: *You're saying you think I stay awake at night planning ways to make you look bad. . . . You're not sure what I'm doing, but you believe I have an agenda to manipulate people.* When you can put your need to defend yourself aside while using what Taoism calls the mirror mind that reflects but does not absorb, you can remain surprisingly calm. Holding up a mirror to other people's erroneous thinking is far more corrective than offering endless explanations.

- Parents of young children have precious little time to meditate. Nondirective, nonjudgmental narrations of children's behavior during play are a powerful form of meditation called filial therapy: *It looks like you are digging a big chunk out of your Barbie doll's arm. Now you've cut off her toe and a chunk of her hair and you're writing on her leg.* This sort of play may seem extreme, but the parent (this author) knew her daughter had outgrown her Barbies. If she had not been a therapist, she might have referred her daughter to one. Sometimes the meaning of play does not become clear until years later—her daughter is now in medical school and intent on being a surgeon. One simply narrates.

Exercise 6—Wash Dishes When You Are Washing Dishes

Notice how you pick up the plate or utensil, the temperature of the water, and the pressure you use to scrub before putting it in the dishwasher or drainer. Notice any impatience to go on to your next activity and go back to washing dishes.

Opportunities to place your attention on experiences in the moment are endless. How mindful can you be when you wash your face, brush your teeth, or simply put on your shoes? In every instant that you become aware of what you are doing, you practice a fluid dance of being one with what is present. Wandering thoughts will return again and again, but gradually this tango of life can be learned until one moment flows into the next with exquisite grace.

Everyday Mindfulness

---

2. For a complete explanation of active and obedient listening and filial therapy, see *Making Hostile Words Harmless* (pp. 51–74), by K. Cohen-Posey (2008), Hoboken, NJ: John Wiley & Sons.

Handout 2.8—Being Present: Choiceless Awareness

Meditation is usually thought of as a gradual practice that fine-tunes the mind into a precise instrument that perceives the world as it really is. *Sudden approaches* claim that our minds are fine just as they are. We only need to *understand* the true nature of reality, revealed through certain underlying principles:

1. **Internal control**. We have little control over our body sensations, habits of thought (*I'm not good enough; they shouldn't act that way*), and resulting emotions and reactions.

2. **External control.** We also have little control over life events that attract, repel, and fool us.

3. **Source of being.** We cannot even take credit for our most inspired moments. Sometimes we are privileged to be vehicles of thoughts or actions that come from outside of us—from our interaction with the greater whole. We unwittingly synthesize an amazing amount of input from the universe.

4. **Acting without an actor.** In fact, a *me* that is a victim to or causes events does not exist. We are performers in a cosmic dance—playing parts prescribed by our physical endowments, temperaments, character traits, and life experiences. Any sense of pride in or guilt over our actions is a sign that we have identified with the part we are playing.

5. **Witnessing**. Understanding our impersonal role in the drama of life creates a sense of freedom. We can take the perspective of the audience and observe our fleeting feelings, thinking habits, sensations, emotions, temperaments, behavior patterns, and life events. These generate our attractions, repulsions, and reactions as they arise and pass.

6. **Nondoing.** As spectators of this grand show, we watch with curiosity and detachment.

7. **Consciousness**. Yet the very act of watching causes a subtle shift to occur. Any player in the performance who becomes *conscious* that the "surveillance camera" is on begins to slow down. He or she can continue to be *in* the play, but not be *of* the play.

Semiautomatic Enlightenment

Understanding precedes awakening. Once the above principles are thoroughly grasped, people are propelled to be *aware* of whatever is present without their usual repertoire of judgments and assumptions. Other schools of meditation would hold that this *choiceless awareness* is the end game. When attention is trained through single-pointed concentration on an object or single-minded breath awareness, people become more attuned to the present moment, without being pulled into the past or future by meddlesome thoughts.

A middle position may be closer to the truth. Experiencing what is happening internally and externally without choice or preference does not take years of meditation practice, but some basic understanding and intentional exercises are helpful. A bestselling book from the 1970s, *Awareness: Exploring, Experimenting, Experiencing,* by John O. Stevens (Real People Press, 1971), opens with an experiment in awareness that creates the perspective of the audience (number 5 in the list above) in a profound way.

NOW I AM AWARE

Experience can be divided into three zones of awareness : (1) *perception* of what you see, hear, smell, taste, or touch; (2) *sensations* of internal events—itches, tensions, pressure, tightness, and so on; and (3) *fantasy or mental activity*—explaining, guessing, planning, comparing, remembering, and **thinking**. Take some time to pay attention to your current experience. Voice your experience with statements that begin, *Now I'm aware of* .... Practice this exercise with a partner or in a small group to make it more powerful. The loss of privacy will bring up a wealth of thoughts to observe.

> ### Example
> *Now I'm aware of sitting in this chair . . . of feeling the hard surface on my back . . . of wanting to avoid looking at you. I'm aware of looking at you and of noticing your earrings. I'm aware of thinking they are pretty and wondering where you got them . . . I'm aware of hearing the air conditioner come on . . . of noticing a slight ache in my back . . . of wondering if I'm boring you . . . of noticing you smile . . . of deciding to stop for now.*

Consequences of Conscious Living

There are many opportunities to practice this exercise silently. Allow attention to drift without attempting to be still or return to the breath. Observation becomes the handmaiden of internal or external events: *I'm noticing that my pants feel tight, I'm relishing that conversation, I'm stewing over what happened.* . . . Some people have a sudden awakening to this *I-am consciousness;* others arrive at it more gradually. The more often you stay in the *I-am* place, the more subtle changes you will begin to notice:

- Emotions, thoughts, and desires still arise. They are neither willed to appear, nor suppressed. Your *watchful mind* notices what *is* without attachment or aversion.

- Observations become clearer when they are detached from assumptions and memories.

- All input (external and internal) is given the same importance. The separation between the observer and the observed dissolves, and connection is created.

- The fleeting nature of thoughts and feelings becomes more obvious. The quality of *my thoughts* or *my feelings* loses meaning as you approach the state of *no self.*

- Choiceless awareness brings pure presence and *connection* with what is happening into ordinary events. Super-conscious meditative states require *disconnection* from daily life. Bliss or utter peacefulness is often sought.

- This total involvement awakens your watchful mind that fully concentrates on what it is doing. Any me or sense of time is absent—only the activity. Stored information is used to aid doing in the present. Action happens without an actor or concern for an outcome.

Seeking a sudden awakening will only thwart it. When you know deep down that "enlightenment" is within, you will find yourself in the radical present. Any efforts to strive can be observed, along with other thoughts of being less than or better than. As Eckart Tolle states in his bestselling book,[1] " . . . the most significant thing that can happen to a human being . . . (is) the beginning of the separation process of thinking and awareness (of thinking)." He holds that a person's inner life purpose is to become aware of his or her thoughts.

A Methodless Method

Allow your attention to light like a butterfly on whatever is happening (internally or externally) and draw nectar where it will. But keep three things in mind:

1. Remind yourself that your only real existence is in the present.
2. In any given moment, notice the myriad activities going on *in* and *around* you.
3. Set an intention to have many moments of awareness (rather than making time to meditate)—chewing bread, holding a glass of water, making real (vs. mechanical) contact when you greet a friend, and so on.

Choiceless awareness avoids rules and procedures for meditating, as this would give people more about which to think, and thinking is the very adversary of being present in the moment.

---

1. *A New Earth: Awakening to Your Life's Purpose* (pp. 261–262), by E. Tolle, 2005, New York: Penguin Group.

Handout 2.9—Meditation in Mantra

In the ancient Indian language, the word *mantra* means advice or suggestion. Each word in a mantra has a sound pattern full of potent meaning. The mind immediately responds. When repeated over and over, the mind *transcends* the experience of unvoiced thoughts and arrives at the source of thought. Reciting a mantra is both one of the oldest forms of meditation (starting in India around 1500 BCE) and a well-known Western technique, due to the popularity of transcendental meditation (TM) in the 1970s.

The selection of a proper mantra for a particular individual is a vital factor in TM, and the practioner is cautioned not to reveal it to anyone. However, other words, phrases, or affirmations that have personal meaning can be used. They are first chanted out loud, then whispered, and finally mentally recited. Voiced words catch concentration and then the more subtle sound of subvocal thought draws the mind down. Often, people who use a mantra regularly find themselves intoning their chosen words or syllables spontaneously throughout the day. It is as though it becomes etched into the brain's neuro networks, where it is automatically summoned when the power of the concentrated mind is needed.

Kirtan Kriya: *Saa-Taa-Naa-Maa* Meditation

Kirtan Kriya is a 12-minute mantra meditation. A *kirtan* is a song. *Kriya* refers to spontaneous movements resulting from the awakening of *kundalini* energy (that lies coiled at the base of the spine). This meditation is basic to the Kundalini tradition. It came to the United States about the same time as TM, but remained a more esoteric path to enlightenment until recent scientific investigation brought it attention. Ancient yogis believed Kirtan Kriya had the power to break bad habits, achieve emotional balance, provide focus, cleanse the mind, and even heal the wounds of a broken heart. The meditation uses four sounds: *Saa, Taa, Naa, Maa*. They form the words *Sat Nam*, meaning "my true identity." It is made up of five primal sound currents:

- **Saa** is the beginning, infinity, the totality of everything.
- **Taa** is life, existence, and creativity that comes from infinity.
- **Naa** is death, change, and the transformation of consciousness.
- **Maa** is rebirth, regeneration, and renewal that leads to the joy of the infinite.
- **Aaa** is the creative vibration of the universe contained within the other four sounds.

Directions

1. Sit in an upright position on the floor or in a straight back chair with your spine straight. Rest your hands on your knees with palms facing upward.

2. Chant or sing *Saa Taa Naa Maa* to the notes *Mi, Ré, Do, Ré:*

3. "Play" the *Saa, Taa, Naa, Maa* sounds by touching the tip of your index finger to the tip of your thumb on *Saa;* touching the tip of your middle finger to the tip of your thumb on *Taa;* touching the tip of your ring finger to the tip of your thumb on *Naa;* and touching the tip of your pinky to the tip of your thumb as you chant *Maa.*

4. Press hard enough to keep yourself awake and aware of the pressure. Repeat a steady rhythm and hand motion throughout the meditation.

5. With each syllable, imagine the sound flowing in through the top of your head and out the middle of your forehead. Close your eyes and focus on the point between your eyebrows.

6. If you become aware of thoughts or emotions while chanting, simply notice them and return your attention to the syllable flowing out of your forehead. Do not try to avoid or control your experience—just be with it.

The finger movements are an unusual and vital part of this mantra. Fingertips touching the thumb are believed to stimulate nerve points that connect to specific areas of the brain. The index finger is related to knowledge, the middle finger to patience, the ring finger to vitality, and the little finger to communication. As an experiment, touch your thumb to your little finger when communication with someone becomes difficult and find out what happens. The qualities of tone and touch add to the effect of the mantra in creating balance and clarity.

Timing — 12-Minute Version

In traditional Kundalini Yoga, Kirtan Kriya is practiced for 30 minutes by singing, whispering, and silently repeating *Saa Taa Naa Maa*. Research on Kirtan Kriya in 2003 and 2006 used a 12-minute version of the meditation.[1] Results validated this briefer method. The first study with experienced meditators showed increased blood flow to brain structures that impact short-term and spatial memory and orientation. The 2006 study was done on people with mild cognitive impairment (MCI) who practiced 12 minutes a day for 8 weeks. Statistically, improvements in before and after memory tests hold promise. A CD with the following instructions can be ordered from the Alzheimer's Research & Prevention Foundation.[2]

- **Singing voice.** Chant *Saa Taa Naa Maa* ALOUD for 2 minutes (about 31 repetitions of all syllables).

- **Lover's voice.** Chant *Saa Taa Naa Maa* in a WHISPER for 2 minutes (about 31 repetitions).

- **Inner voice.** Chant *Saa Taa Naa Maa* SILENTLY for 3–4 minutes (about 62 repetitions).

- **Lover's voice.** Chant *Saa Taa Naa Maa* in a WHISPER for 2 minutes (about 31 repetitions).

- **Singing voice.** Chant *Saa Taa Naa Maa* ALOUD for 2 minutes (about 31 repetitions).

- **Move and release the energy.** At the end, inhale, hold the breath, and stretch your arms over your head, shaking your fingers wildly. Hold this position and exhale. Repeat once more. This helps move and release the energy in the body.

- **Exhale for three consecutive breaths**, hear the mantra, and experience energy moving in an **L** through the crown of your head and out a spot between your eyebrows.

The *Saa-Taa-Naa-Maa* mantra meditation exercise was chosen for its ease of execution and proven powerful results. The syllables that form the ancient Sanskrit word *Sat Nam* have little meaning for Westerners. But without realizing it, 12 minutes of this chant may bring a person closer to his or her true identity—clear in mind, present in the moment.

---

1. "Kirtan Kriya: Yoga for Age Proofing Postmodern Minds," by K. Roderick, 2005, *Yoga Times,* reported on the study by the Alzheimer's Prevention Foundation International (2003). Jeffry Kluger in "The Biology of Belief," 2009, *Time*, February 12, p. 64, reported on Dr. Andrew Newberg's study at the University of Pennsylvania (2006).

2. 6300 E. El Dorado Plaza Suite 400, Tucson, Arizona 85715; Online: www.alzheimersprevention.org/research.htm. Google *Kirtan Kriya* to find YouTube demonstrations.

Handout 2.10—Loving Kindness Mantras

It is well known that Eastern philosophy suggests the cause of all suffering is attachment to people and objects. It is less well known that aversion equals attachment as a cause of suffering. People have many types of aversion: fear, dislike, guilt, hatred, anger, jealously, and so on. These thinking habits can be systematically changed by replacing them with the opposite. Hatred dissolves if it is replaced with beliefs based on loving kindness. The purpose is not to turn you into a mushy, gushy moonstruck Pollyanna, but to break down divisions within your own mind and between you and others.

Loving kindness is made in the form of well wishing toward yourself and others—a beloved or respected person, a dear friend, a neutral casual acquaintance, or someone with whom you are have difficulty or think of as an enemy. Some version of the following phrases is repeated, inserting your own name and those of the four other people. A shortened form of each statement is shown in boldface. They focus on safety, mental health, physical health, and lack of struggle:

> **May** . . . **be safe** from harm.
>
> **May** . . . **be contented**, just as he or she is.
>
> **May** . . . **be healthy** and strong.
>
> **May** . . . **find peace** with life's ups and downs.

Wishing Yourself Well

For many people, acceptance of themselves is the most difficult part of loving kindness. It can help to visualize yourself the way God, your grandparents, or even as your pet sees you. It may be good to focus on wishing yourself well for a few weeks before addressing a beloved, neutral, or difficult person. Susan Salzberg, a well-known teacher of this practice, tells the story of her first attempt at loving kindness:

> I spent my first week repeating, May I be happy, may I be peaceful, over and over again with no obvious result. Then a crisis happened and I had to leave the retreat where I had been staying. As I hurriedly gathered my belongings, a jar dropped and shattered all over the floor. My immediate thought was, You're a klutz . . . but I love you. Then I realized I had benefited from the countless repetitions of loving kindness towards myself (p. 40).[1]

Directions

1. Sit in a comfortable posture. If necessary, use back support for a straight spine. Breathe in and out from your heart and allow your mind to rest in the chest area.

2. **Yourself.** Visualize a mental picture of yourself smiling back to arouse a feeling of loving kindness. Or reflect on any qualities you would like others to see in you.

3. Say the four mantra phrases several times. You can adapt them to suit yourself and use the first or third person: May I be safe; may I accept myself; may my wrist heal; may I be at ease.

4. Allow a full breath for each wish. Let the words spread through your heart, mind, and body.

5. Notice any positive feelings that arise toward yourself and focus on them. If they fade, return to visualizing yourself and repeat the mantra. It is not necessary for any positive feelings to emerge.

6. **The benefactor**. Move to the person who inspires feelings of respect, reverence, or caring, but not romance. It may be an elder, parent, grandparent, or teacher.

---

1. *Loving Kindness: The Revolutionary Art of Happiness* (Shamhala Publications, 1995) offers a complete guide to this practice.

7. Visualize your benefactor or think of all the ways he or she has helped you or contributed to the world. The person you choose can change over time. If possible, use someone living.

8. Start with the same phrases you directed toward yourself and use them for your benefactor: *Just as I am safe, may you be safe*. As with step 4, allow one full breath for each wish.

9. Don't struggle to manufacture feelings of love or judge yourself in any way. Mindless repetition will carve a canyon through whichever deeper feelings flow.

10. **Friend.** Move to a person you regard as a dear (nonromantic) friend—human or animal. Hold an image of him or her. What qualities make this being special to you?

11. Repeat the phrases again, breathing in and out from your heart center. If your mind wanders into stories or chatting, return to the mantra. Different friends may come to mind. Simply direct your attention to them. Be mindful of instructions 8 and 9 above.

12. **Neutral person**. This may be someone you see occasionally or do not know well, like a store clerk. Remember that, like you, this person desires safety, happiness, health, and peace. Repeat the mantra as you did in step 11 above.

13. A good way to practice loving kindness toward neutral people is when you are walking or driving. Instead of allowing your mind to wander, direct security, joy, strength, and serenity toward others in traffic jams, waiting rooms, airports, and so on.

14. **Difficult person**. Start with someone who is mildly annoying and work up to someone who causes you distress. Do not attempt to focus loving kindness on this person until you are comfortable directing it to yourself, teachers, friends, and acquaintances.

15. It may help to think of one good quality about this person or to imagine how they would benefit from being safe, accepted, healthy, or at ease. You might imagine the person as an infant, on his or her deathbed, or in a safe circumstance (behind bars).

16. Accept any feelings that come up. If grief or anger overwhelms you, go back to directing loving kindness to a friend, teacher, or yourself before returning to the difficult person.

17. It may help to use the wording, *To the best of my ability I wish that . . . may be . . . .*

18. Remember to follow steps 4, 8, and 9 above.

19. **All beings.** After the difficult person, begin to visualize or imagine all beings. See your heart as an ember radiating outward. Think of inclusiveness and complementary groups:
   May all males and all females be safe, happy, healthy, and free from struggle.

   May all those who are enlightened and living in ignorance be safe, happy, healthy, and . . .

   May all those who are suffering and those who cause suffering be safe, happy, healthy, and . . .

Growing Loving Kindness

Loving kindness grows in stages. The first glimmer of feelings may be friendliness or warmth, but be cautious of arousal or lust. Compassion can emerge as you begin to understand your own and other people's struggles. Be wary of the pity, which feels sorry for people instead of being with them and their distress. On the other side of compassion is appreciative joy that is glad for others' good fortune, without being jealous. The culmination of friendliness, compassion, and sympathetic joy is equanimity. Pleasure is fully felt without attachment; sorrow is experienced without aversion; a person's full presence is brought to neutral events without being bored. Loving kindness is quiet, but all-pervading.

Handout 2.11 — An Invitation to Yoga

The word *yoga* means to yoke or bind—possibly to restrain the stuff of the mind. Yoga is mentioned in early Hindu texts, but it was not written as a set of principles until the second century BCE in the *Yoga Sutras*. This text contains192 verses. Only three of the statements apply to assuming the poses that are now known as *hatha* (strong) yoga. Originally, these postures were a means to strengthen and temper the body/mind for extended periods of meditation. Holding a pose and moving from one position into another became a meditation in itself.

The Surprising Spine

The spine is the structural core of every movement you make. The secret of a healthy body lies in the flexibility of the spine. All yoga poses bring life to the spine and freedom of movement. The head, neck, shoulders, upper back, lower back, and pelvis come into balance. This frees the body's central support structure from being controlled by overworked muscles. Misconceptions abound about who can do yoga. People with stiff, rigid bodies or those whose backs are injured may benefit as much as long-limbed contortionists. Attention to alignment along with deep breathing and stretching has several benefits:

- The spine is massaged and toned, which benefits internal fluids, organs, and glands.
- Physical strength, flexibility, immunity, muscle tone, respiration, and circulation improve.
- Poses are a way of finding the *still point* at the center of muscle fibers as they extend and contract. They are both stabilizing and relaxing.

A Taste of Yoga

The spine has five movements and six positions. The following exercises are a tiny sample of how stretching, breathing, and sequencing can help you observe energy flowing through your body. Poses are ordered to take your body in the opposite direction from the previous one. This creates balance and eliminates resistance. They can inspire the uninitiated to find a teacher and offer students with some experience a better understanding of yoga's guiding principles. Positions should be practiced more than an hour after eating.

Positions→ Movements↓	Sitting	Kneeling	Standing	Lying Prone (Face Down)	Lying Supine (Face Up)	Inverted
Forward bend			Ex. 3			Ex. 3
Backward bend			Ex. 2			
Lateral bend	Ex. 4					
Twist					Ex. 5	
Extension			Ex. 1 & 2			

Exercise 1—Mountain Pose (Extension)

a. Stand with your back to a wall, one foot-length away from it. Your feet should be parallel, hips distance apart.

b. Distribute your weight evenly over the balls and heels of both feet. The toes bear no weight.

c. Your shoulders, hips, and ankles should all be aligned. Relax your shoulders downward.

d. Rather than simply hanging, feel energy moving through your arms and out your fingertips.

e. Take three breaths. Use a *whispering breath* [1] by breathing in through the nose and saying *Ha* on the exhale. This keeps the breath in the throat rather than the nose. Observe any sensations.

---

1. In his book *Emotional Yoga: How the Body Can Heal the Mind* (Simon & Schuster, 2002), Bija Bennett calls *Ujyayi* breathing the whispering breath (p. 71), which invigorates as well as calms the body.

Exercise 2—Standing Backward Bend

a. From mountain pose, inhale and stretch your arms out to the side and overhead into *Upward Hand Pose*. Reach your arms to the heavens with your shoulders relaxed downward, and imagine your feet pressing down into the ground. This stretches your arms and your torso.

b. Extend your back under your shoulder blades and reach your pointer fingers to the wall behind you. Keep your hips over your ankles. This stretches the upper and middle back.

c. Keep your chest open and pointed at the ceiling. Your ears should be even with your arms.

d. If you cannot raise your arms over your head, move your hands from their position in Exercise 1.d until your pinky fingers touch the wall. Make sure you are bending from under your shoulder blades and not the small of your back. If you need to, move closer to the wall.

e. Take three full whispering breaths in this pose and feel the stretch.

Exercise 3—Supported Forward Fold (Forward Bend)

a. Start with your bottom resting on the wall. Your feet are in the same position as in Exercise 1.a. People with lower back pain can keep their legs slightly wider than hip-width apart.

b. Fold your arms and extend your torso until you can melt over your legs. Move downward from your hip creases.

c. Take three full whispering breaths. With every exhale, see if you move more deeply into the bend. If you have insomnia, take 20 full breaths.

d. Notice where you feel the stretch in the back of your legs and your lower back. Can you feel your heart and mind slowing down and tension leaving your neck?

e. Roll up to standing, one vertebra at a time.

Exercise 4—Seated Waist Bends (Lateral Bend)

a. Sit in a chair with your feet hip-width apart. Inhale and lift one arm over your head. Let your other arm rest on your thigh or on the armrest. The seated position avoids back arching and knee locking.

b. As you exhale, feel your side body stretch, but make sure that your bottom does not lift off the chair and that you are not leaning backward or forward. Turn your head to look upward past your raised arm.

c. Take three whispering breaths and feel the stretch. Inhale, come back to center, and switch sides.

Exercise 5—Two-Knee Spinal Twist

a. Lying on your back, inhale as you bend your knees and lift your feet off the floor. Your thighs should be extending up to the ceiling and lower legs parallel to the floor.

b. Exhaling, open your arms out to the side in one straight line with your palms facing down for support. Take a breath and feel your core muscles holding your legs up.

c. As you exhale, slowly lower both legs to the left, keeping the feet and knees stacked. Knees should be at the level of the hips and the heels resting about a foot away from the buttocks.

d. Let your head turn to the right. Encourage your right shoulder to root down, maintaining the twist through the upper spine. Hold for at least three whispering breaths.

e. If the knees do not rest easily on the ground, place them on a large pillow, but make sure both shoulders are grounded on the floor.

f. Contract abdominal muscles to raise your legs to position 5.a. Then twist to the other side.

g. Finish by pressing both hands into the floor at shoulder level, contracting the abdominal muscles, lifting the knees up over the chest, and holding onto the shins or thighs with both arms. As you exhale, pull the thighs down into the chest.

Handout 2.12—Mini Meditations for Minors

Meditation offers children the same benefits that it gives adults: increased concentration, calmness, and confidence. The advantages of parent-led experiences are: caretakers can guide meditations, the parent-child bond deepens, and adults join their children for a few moments of calm stillness. Some guidelines are offered:

1. Children who are five-years-old and older can do some form of meditation. Younger children can gain much by just watching a parent's practice. They are natural imitators.

2. Allow children to sit or lie in whatever position is comfortable for them. Don't worry about squirming. Make it a part of the meditation by saying, *Notice how your body wants to move.*

3. After exercises, ask questions—*What happened when you followed your breath in and out of your lungs? Was it easy to remember to say your magic words? Did you have thoughts pop up? What did you hear or see? Do you think you could do this exercise on your own?*

4. It is not necessary to read an exercise verbatim. Once you have the gist of it, tell it in your own words. Do the exercises with your child and when possible share your own experience.

5. Help children pick their favorite exercises to do for a few minutes each day. Part b of Exercise 4 helps children who need to fidget. Tapping alternate shoulders balances and calms the brain.

6. Explain meditation in simple language. The description of the *watcher* is a definition that children can understand. Car rides, when children are a captive audience, or bedtime, when they want to hear the stories, are a good time to talk about the secret inside watcher.

THE SECRET INSIDE WATCHER

You have a secret watcher within that can see everything in your inside world and the outside world. It can spot a lucky penny on the ground, smell what is cooking, and know how something delicious tastes before it even gets in your mouth. It notices how air moves into and out of your body and where your clothes feel tight or loose. The secret watcher is so clever that it can notice when you're hurt without feeling the hurt; it can see anger or worries without feeling them; and it can watch you remembering and planning without doing the thinking.

Exercise 1—Draw

Draw a picture of how your secret inside watcher looks. You don't have to draw a whole person. You can make a sign to stand for the watcher or pick an animal to represent it.

Becoming Aware of Your Watcher.

The reason your watcher is so secret is that other thoughts try to be the boss of you. They also have inside voices that give orders and complain about what you or others are doing: *Don't say anything stupid! You look like a toad. Your teacher isn't fair!* If you have heard your watcher, it might have softly said, *You're giving yourself orders, calling yourself names, wishing your teacher would be different.* Your watcher is your true boss. It doesn't expect you to be "good for goodness sake!" It smiles kindly on all your experiences. The more you notice it, the better you will feel. Doing the following exercises will help you notice your watcher in tough times.

Exercise 2—Pillow Breath[1]

Lie down and put a small pillow or stuffed animal on your tummy. Take a breath all the way in and all the way out. Can your watcher feel the pillow move? Count five more breaths, noticing the pillow (animal) move. What else does your watcher notice about your breath and body? Do you take longer to inhale or exhale? Do you pause between breaths? Do your arms feel heavier, limper, or lighter? Do you feel more still or do you want to move?

Exercise 3—Thought Detectors

Do the pillow breath for five more breaths with your eyes closed. Feel the pillow or stuffed animal moving on your tummy. Keep counting your breaths until your watcher spots your first thought. Are you thinking about what you're going to have for dinner or what you will watch on TV? As soon as a thought turns up, go back to noticing your breath and picturing the pillow moving again. Practice catching one or two more thoughts and say "thinking" before returning to your breath. Your watcher will know when to stop.

Exercise 4—Word Magic

Most people have learned to say *supercalifragilisticexpialidocious* from Mary Poppins. Some lovely words from India are *Om Mani Padme Hum*. They mean: I bring caring and wisdom. Repeat the six syllables *Om-Ma-Ni-Pad-Me-Hum* over and over in your mind. This is like beating a tiny drum to create a soothing rhythm. It will be easier for your watcher to detect any thoughts, feelings, and even pain that tries to pop up. If a memory, worry, itch, or ache butts in, go back to repeating your six syllables.

a.   A good way to practice word magic is to beat the syllables like a drum. Alternately, pat the tops of your knees each time your say a syllable. If you are lying down, cross your arms so opposite hands reach your shoulders and make alternate taps. This can help you fall asleep.

b.   First, say and tap the syllables out loud at least 5 times. Then pat and whisper the syllables 5 times. Finally, think the syllables while you tap them about 10 times. Finish by whispering and then saying the syllables while you pat them.

c.   If you have a habit of repeating the same question over and over, make a deal that you have to say and pat *Om-Ma-Ni-Pad-Me-Hum* at least three times. Then take a breath and notice if you still need your question answered.

d.   For fun, chant these words in a group. Each person can lead a round and add two syllables: *Om-Ma-Ni-Pad-Me-Hum-Pea-Nut* (I bring wisdom, compassion, and a peanut).

Exercise 5—Picture Magic

The watcher not only sees what is happening in the outside and your inside world, but it can make its own images for the inside world like a waking dream. This makes it possible to go on many fun trips inside your very own mind.

a.   Close your eyes or stare at a spot until your eyes want to close on their own. Count three breaths.

b.   When you're ready, imagine a cord growing out of the bottom bone in your back all the way down through the floor, into the ground, and to the center of the planet. I don't know

---

1.   Exercises #2, #4, and #5 were adapted from *Sensational Meditation for Children* by Sara Wood Vallely (Satya International, Inc., 2008).

what the cord is made of, but you do . . . . Notice how well it anchors you to the center of the earth.

c. When you know you're really connected, you can begin to notice bits of energy moving from your head, down your backbones, and then all the way down the cord, disappearing into the earth. You might see this energy as pictures or thoughts coming out of your head. Does it make a sound? Feel it moving down one tiny backbone at a time . . . . Every time you breathe out, allow more energy to slide down the cord.

d. Remember, your watcher is in charge. It will tell you when the time is right for fresh energy to come back up the cord from the center of the planet. Each time you breathe in; feel fresh energy coming up the cord. Notice if any pictures or sounds are coming up from the earth.

e. When your watcher knows it's time to stop, notice how the cord disappears back into a magic place inside your body or mind, and slowly come back out to the room.

Exercise 6—The Doing Dance

The watcher has a partner called the doer. It takes ideas and information stored in your brain and turns them into action. It works without dreary thoughts like, *Am I doing this right? I know I'm gonna mess up . . . . What's odd Oscar doing?*

a. Think of an activity you like or one you would like to improve— your soccer kicks, doing math, paying amazing attention to your teacher, or raising your hand before your speak.

b. Close your eyes or stare at a spot until your eyes want to close, and count three breaths.

c. Picture doing the activity you chose. Notice how focused you are and how your body and mind work just right. This is good to practice for 10 breaths just before your chosen activity.

CHAPTER 3

SELF-DISCOVERY

MINI INDEX TO CHAPTER 3

THERAPIST'S
GUIDE TO
SELF-DISCOVERY

Help clients or clinicians:

1. Work collaboratively by providing information about treatment approaches that are based on self-empowerment (informed consent).
2. Organize information on the Self and subpersonalities into an attractive format for workshops.
3. Examine the concept of the Self through metaphors, imagery, and experiential exercises.
4. Identify and increase awareness of personality strengths and weaknesses.
5. Distinguish the wise, observant inner Self from personality parts, the outer personality structure, and personae.

Using the Handouts

- **Informed consent.** *Therapy for Self-Empowerment* meets the ethical obligation to provide clients information about this approach to treatment.
- **General literature.** *The Corporate Self* and *The Community of Self* explain the components of the Self through words and metaphor; *God and Goddess Personality Types, Personality Awareness* are nonthreatening instruments to help clients identify their dominant traits; *Pictures of Personality* help people have an experiential sense of personality traits; *Personae—The Masks We Wear* helps people understand the multifaceted nature of identity.
- **Literature that addresses specific problems.** *Connecting with Your Self* and *Aspirations and Abilities* helps people become more identified with their true nature; *Spiritual Guidance* connects people with the wisdom they have within, *Mandala: Symbols of the Self* offers creative expression of the Self's experience.
- **Groups and presentations.** *The Drama of the Subdivided Mind* is designed for group presentations. It could also be titled: Creative Cognitive Therapy. *Who Is the Self and Its Counterparts?* (3.2), and the Imagery Exercises in *Connecting with Your Self* (3.6) and *Turning Thoughts Into Parts* (5.4) are workshop handouts that can accompany the presentation. The *Self and Personality Parts* table (3.2) is a group think exercise in which participants call out names that go in the blanks. The *Self-Talk Case Study* (5.5) can be used to demonstrate how to use concepts of the Self and subpersonalities in therapy.
- **Small groups.** The exercises in *Spiritual Guidance, Aspirations and Abilities, Pictures of Personality,* and *Personae—The Masks We Wear* are excellent for small group settings.

Cautions and Comments

- ***Who Is the Self and Its Counterparts?*** is ideal for clinicians teaching psychology courses for a quick review of concepts of the Self in psychological literature.
- ***The Corporate Self*** is an appealing metaphor for clients in the business world and for those who have an understanding of chakras.
- ***The Community of Self*** offers a metaphor and diagram that show the central position of the Self and how it can calm domineering voices one by one.
- ***God and Goddess Personality Types*** and ***Personality Awareness*** offer two different approaches to increase awareness of character traits. The first instrument may appeal to mystical or literary people, while the second offers a scientific, research-based view.

Sources Not Referenced in the Handouts

The Climbing a Mountain Task, Fantasy Person, and Dwelling Visualization are adapted from an article by Hanscarl, Leuner, MD, "Guided Affective Imagery (GAI): A Method of Intensive Psychotherapy," *American Journal of Psychotherapy,* Vol. XXIII, No. 1, pp. 4–22, 1/69. It can also be found at www.synthesiscenter.org/articles/0340.pdf with directions on how to use and interpret the tasks in Leuner's *waking dreams.*

Psychosynthesis: A Collection of Basic Writings, by Roberto Assagioli (Synthesis Center, 1965/2000), offers the original ideas on the Self and subpersonalities.

Embracing Our Selves: The Voice Dialogue Manual, by Hal and Sidra Stone (New World Library, 1989), gives clear instructions for their psycho-dramatic approach to inner voices.

Internal Family Systems Therapy, by Richard Schwartz (Guilford Press, 1995), offers theory and a protocol for his approach to the Self and parts.

Handout 3.1—Therapy for Self-Empowerment

Several treatment approaches have made the Self and its counterparts the focus of their method. *Psychosynthesis* (1920s) was followed by a mushrooming of ideas 50 years later: *Ego State Therapy* (1970s), *Psychology of Selves* (1970s), *Internal Family Systems Therapy* (1980s), and more. These methods demystified the solitary individual and exposed subpersonalities revolving around a core Self. They have two basic principles:

Principles Based on the Self and Its Counterparts

- **A presence, being, or the faculty to observe** thoughts, feelings, and sensations (nonjudgmentally) rests within every person. It has been called our *(higher, supreme, core) self, hidden observer, awareness, spiritual nature, consciousness, conscience,* and more.

- **The specific agendas of mental chatter** are easily recognized by our observing faculty. *Inner critics, people pleasers,* and *controllers* of emotions have been called *complexes, ego states, energy patterns, subpersonalities, subvocal voices, roles,* and *parts.*

CASE EXAMPLE OF THERAPY FOR SELF-EMPOWERMENT

The following is a case example of *one type* of therapy that empowers the Self. Notice when the full capacity to compassionately observe personality parts and give guidance becomes present.

A client named "Bess" has obsessive-compulsive disorder (OCD) and genital herpes. She first became infected 7 years previously, but her only outbreaks were in the first 3 years after exposure. Her obsessions include confessing to any man she had sex with (prior to marrying 4 years ago) that she could have given him herpes, worrying about contamination, particularly when using bathrooms, washing towels *daily,* and so forth. She is currently pregnant. In past sessions she has (1) identified an OCD personality part and (2) learned that she has a *true Self* that can make observations and ask questions. The real work in this session started when Bess said, *I don't deserve to pray with the people at my church.* Mr. OCD had entered the room. [Note: therapist's and Bess's lines are lettered so they can be referenced under subtitle, Agreeing with Assumptions—Exerpts from the case example.]

   a. **Therapist:** Mr. OCD is saying, You don't deserve to pray with the people at church. Have your true Self go inside and ask him, Why doesn't Bess deserve to be at church?

   b. **Bess:** [Silently poses the question to Mr. OCD] He's saying, *Because she'll spread her STD to everyone.*

   c. **Therapist:** Have your Self tell OCD, *You've been tormenting Bess a long time; now you have new material.*

   d. **Bess:** I remember telling myself as a teenager that I might give people AIDS and I was a total virgin!

   e. **Therapist:** Have your true Self ask Mr. OCD, *Why did you start on her in the first place?*

   f. **Bess:** [After listening] He's saying, *She thought she was perfect* (seems surprised by OCD's answer).

   g. **Therapist:** Have your true Self ask Mr. OCD, *How did you think tormenting would help?*

   h. **Bess:** [After listening] He's saying, *My role is to help her stay perfect by making sure she hasn't hurt anyone by spreading a disease.* My gosh! What a vicious cycle. Mr. OCD is going in circles!

   i. **Therapist:** That's quite an observation. Where do you think that realization came from?

   j. **Bess:** From my true Self.

   k. **Therapist:** How does your true Self feel toward Mr. OCD?

   l. **Bess:** He's kind of pathetic. He's so mixed up. I feel sorry for him. How did he get that way?

   m. **Therapist:** It sounds like your true Self is curious. Why not go inside and ask Mr. OCD?

n. **Bess:** [Listens for a bit.] He's not saying anything and that's okay with me. The quiet feels peaceful.... What should I do if Mr. OCD comes back?

o. **Therapist:** What part of you might have asked that question? Was it OCD or another part?

p. **Bess:** No, that was my helpless, *Know–nothing* part. Here I am pregnant and I don't do anything without asking my mom.

q. **Therapist:** Go inside where you just felt some peace and have *Know-nothing* ask your true Self, *What should Bess do if Mr. OCD comes back?*

r. **Bess:** [Listens for a bit and smiles]: I just hear, *Ask ole OCD how he started thinking in circles?*

Additional conclusions can be drawn from the two basic principles about the Self and its counterparts. They are demonstrated in the case example. Note how strongly you agree with each assumption from 100% to 0% or mark (?). Review excerpts from the case example to clarify any uncertainty.

Agreeing With Assumptions

Assumption	%/?	Excerpts From the Case Example
1. Inner presence: In addition to making compassionate observations, our inner presence offers guidance in the form of insights, intuitions, dreams, and revelations. These give meaning and purpose to our lives.		The true Self observes that OCD is going in circles (**h**) and shows compassion by feeling sorry for it (**l**). The Self offers guidance by suggesting that OCD be asked how it began thinking in circles (**r**).
2. Finding presence *in the* mind: Observations and revelations can be distinguished from distressing thoughts. They are harder to detect in our mental chatter and emerge from a deep place in the body/mind when relaxed, falling asleep, and waking.		Silently posing questions to personality parts or the Self (**b, f, h, n, r**) induces a mini-trance that slows down thoughts and fosters finding presence *in the* mind.
3. Awareness of inborn ability: This presence or capacity to observe thoughts and receive inner guidance is innate and unlearned. With assistance, awareness of it can be increased.		The therapist increases awareness of the Self by pointing out that Mr. OCD is doing the talking (**a**) and *coaching* the Self to silently ask OCD questions (**a, e, g, m**) or make observations (**c**).
4. Subpersonalities: Automatic thoughts and beliefs are easier to notice when identified as personality parts (Inner *critic, people pleaser,* and so on).		Bess's automatic thoughts, *I'll spread my STD to everyone,* (**b**), *I have to be perfect* (**h**), *What should I do?* (**n**), are easy to recognize as *OCD* and *Know-Nothing* parts.
5. Disidentification: Giving our thoughts, assumptions, opinions, and judgments an identity and changing their subvocal grammar helps us disidentify from them.		The therapist changes, *I don't deserve to pray with the people at my church,* to second person: Mr. OCD is saying, ***You** don't deserve to pray with the people....*
6. Detachment: When thoughts are changed into parts, people *see* them more clearly and are less likely to cling to them. Likewise, parts are able to temporarily loosen their hold.		The comment, *Mr. OCD is going in circles,* shows clarity of insight (**h**). When OCD has no reply (**n**), it is a sign that it is detaching and losing energy.
7. Restoring the Self to its rightful role: An attempt is not made to rid people of their parts. When they are clearly seen and the meaning, origin, and purpose of their messages are understood, they are less dominant in a person's psyche.		The prominence of inner being is shown by OCD's silence (**n**) and the Self's humorous comment (**r**).

Empowerment therapies wed two well-researched methods into cutting-edge approaches: (1) *Cognitive therapy* is utilized to spot thoughts that unmask subpersonalities. (2) *Mindfulness meditation* brings awareness to the present moment. This promotes listening within and using questions to still the mind. Space is created for an innate wisdom and boldness to emerge that can clear life's hurdles.

Basis for Self-Empowerment Therapies

Handout 3.2 — The Self and Its Counterparts

The term *self* can be difficult to describe. The first three definitions in the *American Heritage Dictionary*[1] are: (1) the total essential *being* of a person; (2) the *personality*, character, or a person's unique individuality; (3) a person's awareness of his or her *identity*. Like an onion, you come to know your Self in layers.

- **Identities** provide an outer coating, made up of your roles as an adult, friend, and so on.

- **Personality,** with its unique traits and temperament, provides an unchanging structure.

- **Thoughts and feelings** are covert and fleeting.

- **Presence** permeates a person's beliefs, traits, and outer faces. This *Self*, from the Indian root *sva,* means "one's own." Like the word *svamin* or *swami,* the Self can be thought of as the master of thoughts, emotions, and behavior (personality).

The Self's Debut in Psychology

Although Freud may be considered by many as the originator of psychotherapy, he did little to fashion ideas about the Self. His *ego* was a mediator between basic *id* drives and internalized rules from society, the *superego*. Gradually, concepts of the layers of Self began to emerge:

1. Two of Freud's colleagues, Carl **Jung** (1912) and Roberto **Assagioli** (1927), did come up with models of a *Self* and counter parts in the psyche—*complexes and subpersonalities*.

2. The Self lay dormant as an idea for nearly 50 years. It almost surfaced in the 1970s when John and Helen **Watkins** began noticing that people have *ego states* that emerged under hypnosis and acted like semiautonomous personalities. One ego state always seemed to be present that was aware of and could understand the whole system.

3. In the next decade, the Self blossomed. Ken **Wilber** (1980s), a contributor to Transpersonal Psychology, offered a beautiful definition of the *Self* and other *inner voices*. Richard **Schwartz** was a major figure in the next generation of ego state therapists. He described a *Self* that led a family of controlling *managers,* distracting *firefighters*, and childlike *exiles*.

4. In the 1990s, interest in Eastern traditions and meditation began to interface with psychology. Following the ideas of J. **Krishnamurti**, a prominent speaker in the 1940s–1980s, Ramesh **Balsekar** and Eckhart **Tolle**'s ideas on *consciousness* and *ego* closely resemble concepts of inner voices, but may go beyond the Self into the territory of *no-self* and *nondualism*.

5. Finally, the work of neuropsychologists Andrew Newberg (2006) and Michael **Gazzaniga** (1980s) offers some biological correlates for concepts of the Self and its counterparts.

6. Most of the descriptions of the Self given on the following page are conceptual. Therefore, an empirical definition is offered that is based on common experience (Kate **Cohen-Posey**).[2]

Name the Theorist

The chart on the following page contains the basic ideas about the Self and personality parts of each boldfaced theorist listed above.

---

1. *The American Heritage Dictionary of the English Language,* 1969, Rockville, MD: American Heritage Publishing Co.
2. Kate Cohen-Posey is the author of *Empowering Dialogues Within,* 2008, Hoboken, NJ: John Wiley & Sons.

- Fill the blanks in the chart with the originator of each definition.

- More important, *choose the descriptions* of the Self and personality parts *that you like best*—the ones that give you the best understanding of your true nature and the voices that hinder you.

Self	Personality Parts
1. Self: Provides energy to create meaning, unity, and individuality and to fulfill one's potential. It is the organizing principle of the mind: _____	**Complex:** An emotionally charged cluster of *ideas* with a core issue at its center that attracts similar life experiences (inferiority complex).
2. Higher Self: A center of pure *awareness* and pure *will* capable of mastering, directing, and using the mind and body. It is both individual and transcends the personal Self: _____	**Subpersonality:** Parts of the Self containing fragments of what we *believe* we are, what we want to be, how we *think* we should appear, and internalizations of significant others that exist in various degrees of organization and refinement.
3. Hidden observer: An ego state that tends to be less emotional and wiser than other ego states and capable of giving guidance: _____	**Ego state:** Organization of behavior and experience into a (mental/behavioral) pattern that is separated from other states by a semipermeable boundary.
4. Transpersonal Self: Emerges from a universal dimension and can witness mental, emotional, and physical experiences and provide guidance for growth: _____	**Subpersonality:** Subvocal *voices* in one's inner dialogue that vie for attention and dominance. They vary in degree of detachment and need to control.
5. Core or true Self: Both an inner confident, compassionate leader and a boundaryless state of mind, which has been and is always present in an individual: _____	**Part:** A discrete and independent mental system with emotions, expressions, abilities, desires, interests, talents, temperament, worldviews, and possible associated ages.
6. Doing or "working" mind:[3] Focuses on the event in the present. Stored information is used to aid action. A *me* is absent. There is only activity: _____	**Wandering or "thinking" mind:** Dwells on memories or future predictions. Judges and compares from a personal point of view. Distracts the doing mind.
7. Consciousness: Essential being-ness or I-am presence that is aware, moment to moment, to witness and observe: _____	**Ego:** Repetitive thoughts, emotions, and behavior reactions with which a person identifies.
8. Selves: Mental processes (thoughts about thoughts) that observe and question distressing inner voices to produce clarity, calmness, and empowerment: _____	**Part:** Any subvocal message (*thought*) that creates distress in its attempt to manage the details of life.
9. Thalamus: Regulates incoming sensory information and *communicates* a lucid sense of reality to the cortex during focused, calm states. _____	**Mental modules:** Separate locations in the brain where experiences are processed and stored as sensations and images. *Verbal Self* in the left brain "watches" data stored by other modules. It spins a narrative to makes sense of the data. _____

The Need for Self-Understanding

Psychotherapy began with the *analysis* of free associations and dreams to bring unresolved conflicts into awareness. The current trend is to restructure irrational thoughts by *teaching* people to question their ideas and behaviors and to reach identified goals. When the Self is recognized, a source of wisdom beyond reason can be *experienced*. By learning to listen within, disturbing thoughts are witnessed with compassion. The focus is on an inborn faculty, not on disturbing automatic thoughts or inner conflicts.

---

3. Ramesh S. Balsekar talks about the *working mind* and *thinking mind* in *Consciousness Speaks* (pp. 117–134), 1992, Hermosa Beach, CA: Advaita Press.
Answers: 1. Jung; 2. Assagioli; 3. Watkins; 4. Wilber; 5. Schwartz; 6. Balsekar; 7. Eckart; 8. Cohen-Posey; 9. Newberg, Gazzaniga

Handout 3.3—The Drama of the Subdivided Mind

Following is a presentation script that illuminates how the mind works. It can be geared to client groups, the general public, or a professional audience. Information to enhance the workshop is shown in [brackets]. Choose volunteers to partake in the psychodrama. Give them each their lines (see Needed Materials). Instruct the *distressing* and *distracting voices* to take turns reading their lines. They will both focus on the *emotional being*. The distressing voice will start by saying a line and beating the emotional entity with a scarf or the soft end of a belt for dramatic effect.

Needed Materials

A bag filled with a chocolate bar, a small liquor bottle , and cigarettes; three sets of psychodrama lines; art materials for drawings; and a small riser. Wear a long scarf or a cloth belt.

Introduction

By a show of hands, who has used (heard of) such concepts as *irrational thoughts, cognitions, ego states, mindfulness,* or the *Self?* Our purpose today is to reconnect with your true Self:

- To distinguish the observant, calming Self from other inner voices.

- [Optional] To select definitions that describe the Self and personality parts and choose the ones that give you the best understanding of these concepts.

- To represent your own Self and other inner voices with images.

Psycho-Dramatic Demonstration

Traditionally, psychotherapy approaches people as a unitary whole. The following drama will give a new view of interior landscapes. It portrays a scene of intimate domestic violence. Three volunteers from the audience have been gracious enough to take part in this demonstration.

- First, we have_____, who will be playing the distressing inner voice whose aliases have been the *superego* and *parent ego state.* It is role centered because it internalizes society's rules and roles.

- The second player in an emotional being who is known as the *child ego state* or *inner child.*

- Our last player, the *distracter*, is exceptionally good at pointing us every which way but in [the distracter pantomimes pointing]. It is other-centered because it needs others for security, worth, or power.

Psycho Dramatic Script

Distressing voice: Talk to the emotional entity. Hit it with a scarf. Allow time for the distracter to respond to your comments.	**Emotional Entity**	**Distracting voice :** Frequently point at the audience or objects in the room. React to what the distressing voice is saying.
These people are going to think you're nuts. *They'll never want you to present here again!* *Don't clear your throat. It sounds disgusting.* *You should have (don't mess up your) PowerPoint!*	React naturally to other actors as though you were very vulnerable. You do not have a voice. Use facial expressions and body language.	*Here's a cigarette (chocolate bar). That should make you feel better.* *Well, they should have paid you more!* *Oh, I've got some booze that should work.* *If you don't get good evaluations, it's because these people are snobs.*

- Does anyone have a distressing voice or *inner critic* that makes you feel awful?

- Does anyone ever become wracked with anxiety or get a queasy stomach?

- Does anyone have a distracting voice that tempts him or her with food or booze or judges others? [Optional, explain: Object relations theorists in the 1950s began identifying inner representations of early caretakers that helped reduce anxiety by *impulsively* blaming, clinging, and avoiding.] For people who cannot tolerate anxiety, addictions and judging reign supreme.

- [Ask the emotional entity] How did it feel to be caught between the critical distressing voice, and the judgmental distracter?

- [Ask the distressing voice and distracter] What it was like to play your parts?

- How can we stop the chaos? Where would you start to intervene—with the distressing voice, the emotional entity, or the distracter?

Entrance of the Higher Self. Comforting the emotional part will be fruitless if the distressed voice does not receive help. One player is not on stage: the person's true Self. I will now assume that position.

[If possible, stand on a riser behind the players. Speak to the distressing voice. Ask the player to respond as the spirit moves him or her. The observation and question below begin a dialogue. Continue to speak in a compassionate way—pointing out warnings, orders, predictions, attempts to convince, and how these efforts make the person feel. End when the distressed voice seems calmer or has no responses.][2]

You're scolding [player's name] about PowerPoint.... What's bad about [...] not using PowerPoint?

- What did you see the Self do? Did it argue, disagree, or reassure? Or did it ask questions and make observations? Did the distressed voice change as dialogue continued?

- [Ask the distressed voice] How did you experience the Self's observations and questions?

Defining the Self and Personality Parts. [Optional: Pick a definition of the Self and personality parts in the handout ***Who Is the Self and Its Counterparts*** (3.2) that best describes the roles of the players, including the presenter, in the psychodrama. Go over information about names of theorists. Have participants call out answers for the *Self and Personality Parts* table interactively.]

Representing Your Self and Personality Parts. In small groups, discuss times that you've heard an inner voice that has helped you feel calmer when you were upset. It might have said, *You're giving yourself a hard time*, or *Do you need to be this angry?* What image could represent this voice—an all-seeing eye, a *Mona Lisa* smile, a searchlight that can brighten the dark corners of your mind?

- Draw an image or symbol for the still, small voice that can comfort controlling, critical, pushy parts. Draw images for upsetting voices as well.

- [Optional: Instead of having participants draw images, use the *Imagery Exercises* from handouts *Connecting With Your Self* and *Turning Parts Into Thoughts*. People can call out images they have drawn that represent their core Self and that depict their distressing thoughts.]

Time out

This scene could be going on in my head, but because of HIPPA[1] regulations, you'll never know. Did this drama sound familiar to anyone?

---

1. Health Insurance Privacy and Portability Act.
2. Many examples of dialogues with inner parts are found in *Empowering Dialogues Within,* by Kate Cohen-Posey, 2008, Hoboken, NJ: John Wiley & Sons.

Handout 3.4—The Corporate Self

What is your "Self"? It has been described in various ways: a center of pure awareness and will, capable of guiding your personality (Assagioli); the energy that creates meaning and individuality and helps fulfill potential (Jung); the *witness* of your ordinary I (Wilber). You may refer to your Self as your *reason, intuition, free spirit, calm center,* or *still, small voice.* Your Self has more to do with *knowing* than *thinking.* Beliefs are in the province of the personality.

Personality Components

Each person develops patterns of thinking, behaving, and feeling to cope with and react to everyday details of life. Thoughts, traits, and emotions are the three components of the personality that create an outer structure for the deep, innermost Self.

Distressing Thoughts. These thoughts attempt to manage and *direct* feelings but, at the same time, produce tension. They are acquired during developmental stages and from caretakers.

- **Controlling thoughts** help toddlers to be self-governing and control their bowels and bladder. The demands *You better not . . .* and *You should . . .* produce shame and doubt.
- **Protective thoughts** are needed when preschoolers take initiative to explore the world. *What-if* predictions that forecast catastrophes spawn guilt and fear.
- **Pushy thoughts** marshal industrious energy in school-age children to master skills and acquire information. Litanies of lists and *have-tos* generate feelings of inferiority.
- **Pleaser thoughts** will help teens find their role among peers and choose from various identities. The assumption *Others won't like you* causes confusion and foreboding.
- **Inner critics** record opinions from kin and culture in people of all ages. *You're at fault* or *not good enough* is the refrain that breeds shame and flawed feelings.

Traits. These are solidified mannerisms. They arise from imitating or complying with caretakers and are triggered by *distracting thoughts* that avoid angst by focusing on *others.*

- **Dependent, clinging/distancing, dramatic traits** avoid independence and are promoted by needy, desperate thoughts— *They have to be there for me; do it for me. . . .*
- **Bossy, rigid, suspicious, traits** avoid feeling worthless and are fed by boastful, perfectionist thoughts— *They're not as good as . . . ; they shouldn't . . . ; They can't . . .* [1, 2]
- **Shy, aloof, peculiar traits** prevent feeling humiliated and are fostered by avoidant thoughts—*Don't let others notice you; I don't need others; I have special powers.*
- **Defiant, shallow, stubborn traits** avoid feeling powerless and are fueled by self-centered thoughts—*Others don't matter; I can't count on anyone.*

Emotions. These are triggered by thoughts. They are energy in motion—fear retreats, sadness sinks, anger thrusts, love flows, happiness rises, tranquility moves inward. *Distressing thoughts* are most likely to produce fear and sadness, while *distracting thoughts* displace anxiety with anger, bitterness, and resentment that create interpersonal conflicts. When the Self regains its leadership of the personality, a wide range of feelings is experienced without being intensified by acquired thought patterns. Emotions are simply released and relief found.

---

1. **Carl Jung** and **Roberto Assagioli** were some of the earliest theorists in the new science of psychology in the 1920s. **Ken Wilber** is a modern day American philosopher, psychologist, and spiritual thinker.
2. Ideas about layers of Selves, personality components, and the flow chart are adapted from *Empowering Dialogues Within, 2008,* by Kate Cohen-Posey. Hoboken, NJ: John Wiley & Sons.

Although the Self is present from birth, it may not be able to assume all of its functions until intellect and verbal skills are sufficiently developed. The Self and its personality are similar to a corporation that can be represented by a flowchart:

Flowchart for the Corporate Self[3]

7. The executive officer is the link to the powers that be (creator, natural law, and so on). This *witness* can observe aches, emotions, and ideas without *feeling* distress or even *thinking*.

6. *Intuition* organizes experiences to provide inspiration, understanding, direction, and meaning.

5. *Reason* evaluates situations objectively, responds without reacting, and communicates to contribute ideas, not to convince others or to win approval.

4. The *center* works with the ever-observant witness to value agendas of personality directors, distracting traits, and emotional entities to bring compassion, harmony, and balance.

3. The personality *directors* of control, protection, pushing, people pleasing, and criticizing carry the standards of kin and culture. When ideas are too extreme, it is difficult to hear voices of compassion, reason, inspiration, and knowing.

2. Personality *traits* become hardened by overzealous distracters. They try to reduce pressure by focusing on other people or addictive objects.

1. *Emotional entities* are experienced as sensations and discharged tension (crying, laughing, striking out) triggered by the distressing messages of personality directors.

Board of Directors—Creates or establishes existence; determines corporate **mission**; **gives direction** and purpose; sets up **by-laws** (natural law), **offers guidance and inspiration**; and **ensures support**.

SELF: 7. Executive Officer—**WITNESS, KNOWER**
❀ **Purpose:** interface between the "Board" and the corporate officers.

6. Intelligence Officer **INTUITION**	5. Communications Officer **REASON**
△ **Purpose:** sees the big picture and below the surface; truth seeker.	◉ **Purpose:** communicate and express creativity.

4. HR Officer—**CENTER** (*Adult Ego*).
✿ **Purpose:** Initiates dialogue with corporate parties; finds balance.

PERSONALITY: 3. Directors (**Distressing Thoughts,** *Superegos, Parent ego states*)
▼**Associated with** domination and power. Attempt to suppress troublesome traits and emotions.

CONTROLLER Director of By-Laws Role: Rule-follower→ Convention master	**PROTECTOR** Director of security Role: avoid risks→ Stop all mistakes	**PUSHER** Director of Operations Role: keep on task →Taskmaster	**PEOPLE-PLEASER** Director of PR Role: affiliate & join→ Total Selflessness	**CRITIC, COMPARER** Director of Quality Control Role: Self-correction *Helps other directors.*

---

1. Driving Work Force—**EMOTIONAL ENTITIES** (*Id, Child EgoStates, Felt Sense*).	2. Inside Agitators— **TRAITS & addictions** (Distracting Thoughts).
☐ **Associated with** • Survival instincts—fight/flight, attraction/ repulsion • Bodily sensations related to upsetting memories recorded in the musculature	☽ **Associated with** gratification, sensation, pleasure. • Dependency: blaming, clinging, attention seeking. • Arrogance: boasting, controlling, suspiciousness • Avoidance: withdrawing, isolating, hoarding

---

3. **NOTE:** Numbers 7–1 correspond to the *Chakras* (energy centers) found in Yoga— ❀ △ ◉ ✿ ▼ ☽ ☐

Handout 3.5 — The Community of Self

The Self is usually defined by what it *is:* the essence of one's being, an inner leader, a center of awareness and will, the master of one's soul (from the Sanskrit word *svamin*—one's own master—or *swami*). In community, the Self is described by what it *does*—it meta-communicates or forms thoughts about thoughts that produce clarity, calmness, or empowerment. The Self is a higher order of thought processes than the trigger-quick distress recordings that play over and over in a person's mind.

The philosopher Martin Buber (1878–1967) had a vision of genuine communities in which all members have a common relationship to one central figure whose ability to value each person's uniqueness infuses the group with spirit and the ability to appreciate each other. All true communication emanates from this *center*.

Buber's idea of genuine community makes an elegant model for the *Central Self* at the core of a cacophony of thoughts: It makes mindful observations and poses compassionate questions to subvocal voices. During these inner dialogues, both parties are changed: (1) the Self is empowered as it separates (disidentifies) from personality parts by observing and questioning them; (2) runaway monologues of domineering voices are derailed and they relinquish attempts to dominate the psyche.[1]

Accessing the Self

There are three steps a person can take to access his or her core self: (1) identify distressing inner voices or thoughts and give them a name; (2) make nonargumentative observations and questions to clarify subvocal voices; and (3) silently listen within to responses from personality parts. Eventually, the third step will happen automatically as contact with the compassionate, curious Self deepens:

1. **Identify** distressing inner voices and, if possible, name them: *critic, blamer,* and so on.

   - **Directing thoughts** try to manage feelings and desires with *what ifs; shoulds; if onlys; pushy* reminders; and *critical*, disapproving lectures.

   - **Distracting thoughts** try to control people and objects with *shoulds, everybodies, nobodies,* blaming, orders, judging, boasting, and cravings.

2. **Observe and question:** Formulate nonargumentative observations of directing, distracting voices and ask questions to understand the meaning, origin, and intention of their messages. These should be stated in the *second person* to create space *between* the Self and the rambling monologues. The actual individual doing life is spoken about in the *third person* to make it clear that ultimate being is a compassionate, curious witness.

3. **Listen** within to hear any response. This strengthens the core Self's role as a compassionate listener:

   Inner critic: It was your fault that your friend died in the car accident. You had the bright idea to go to the beach.

   Core self: *You* are giving *her* amazing powers over life and death (observation).

   Inner critic: (Softer) Maybe it was destiny.

---

1. The metaphor of the Community of Self comes from *Enpowering Dialogues Within* (p. 5.6), by Kate Cohen-Posey, 2008, Hoboken, NJ: John Wiley & Sons, with permission of the publisher.

PERSONALITY PARTS are busy handling the details of life:

- **Distracters: (bold triangles)** blame, cling, boast, avoid, or isolate in order to manage others and objects
- **Directors (triangles)** try to control emotional energies **(bursts)** with sub vocal messages

The CENTRAL SELF is surrounded by a whir of personality parts. It is always wise and compassionate in tone and available to dialogue with any part in distress by:

- **Mindfully observing** the various types of thoughts and their consequences
- **Curiously questioning** the meaning, motive, source, and accuracy of ideas

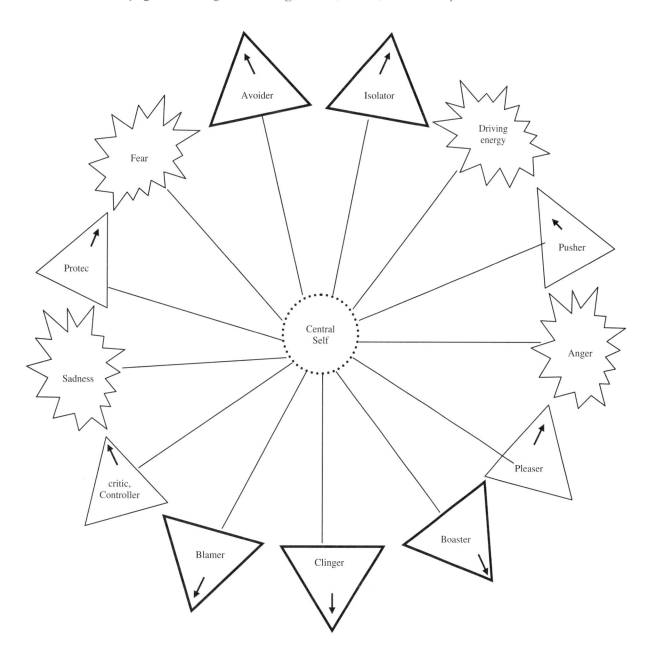

Handout 3.6—Connecting With Your Self

Deep beneath the outer layers of your Selves (the roles you play, your character traits, habitual thinking patterns, and emotional reactions) is the core of who you are. Because your identities, personality characteristics, beliefs, and feelings can be so prominent, you may have disconnected with the true nature of your being. It is a mysterious presence that sustains you in your darkest hours, is calmly aware of all your experiences, and has wisdom beyond reason. The following exercise is designed to reacquaint you with the qualities that make up your essential Self.

Directions

- Look at the images on the opposite page.[1] Check the ones that are most appealing to you. You can pick as many as you like, but notice the pictures and designs to which you were initially drawn.

- Pick a word or words that describe what you see in each image you chose—*freedom, security, peace, power*, and so on. Write any words that come to you in the box below.

> [ ]

- Using the words in the box above, create a name that gives you a handle for *your* inner presence. Common names are *Reason, Intuition, Knower*, and *Supreme Self*. The driving force within can be identified by a name that has special meaning for you—*At Ease, Transformer, Way Shower, Calm Self, Spirit Man. . . .*

- Write the name you would like to use for your deepest, innermost Self in the next box.

> [ ]

Imagery Problems

If you do not relate to art or designs, that is not a problem. An image for your true Self is a keyboard stroke away. The following are familiar emoticons created with just the right combinations of colons, parentheses, brackets, dashes, slashes, and so on. Choose one of the following or create your own. Then give it a name:

(-:0	:-D	8-)}{	8-)	

---

1. The first two rows of images come from the Rider Waite Tarot Deck and were retrieved from http://en.wikipedia.org/wiki/Rider-Waite-Smith deck on June 5, 2009. Three of the mandalas can be found in *Empowering Dialogues Within,* by Kate Cohen-Posey, 2008, Hoboken, NJ: John-Wiley & Sons. Thirdeyeman was retrieved from www.crysallinks.com on June 5, 2009, by permission of the owner. The *Hands of God and Man* is adapted from Michelangelo's original work.

IMAGERY EXERCISE

 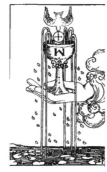   

 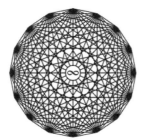  

Handout 3.7—Spiritual Guidance

Deep in the core of your being is a presence that is interwoven into the fabric of nature and has a connection to all beings. Ancient peoples understood this and sought direction from totem animals. This animal bestowed its unique abilities upon the clan and its people. In return, the tribe offered protection to their totem. In our society, many people feel a special bond with a certain animal, although it may never have occurred to them to adopt the wisdom that this creature can bestow. Follow the steps in the exercise to find guidance from a surprising source.

EXERCISE: TOTEM ANIMAL

- Imagine yourself in a wilderness, whether it be a forest, seashore, desert, jungle, or vast open plain. Take a moment to become familiar with your surroundings.

- As you look into the distance, you will notice an animal approaching. At first, you might not be sure what it is, but you can sense that it is an ally, a kindred spirit, or mysteriously connected to you.

- Allow it to approach in the way that is natural to its species, unless it beckons you to join it on a high slope or in the water.

- You can be surprised that contact can happen telepathically or by some other form of interspecies communication. It may begin talking to you by saying, *I am your totem animal and I am offering you my power of. . . . You will find it useful when. . . .*

- Listen to all it has to say and, in return, express your appreciation and plan to protect its kind.

- Imagine and journal your experience in the first person before reading the example below: *I am wandering in a deep forest. . . .*

EXAMPLE OF TOTEM GUIDANCE

I am standing in a vast plain, dotted by trees and filled with waving grasses. The sky is big around me and in the distance are low mountains. I see a bare speck in the clouds. I know it is approaching but I cannot make it out. As it glides effortlessly closer, I recognize a bird . . . a bald eagle. I reach out; he lights, wrapping giant talons gently around my forearm. With piercing eyes that seem to look down into my very soul, I know what he is saying:

I look at the world from great heights. Circling around above, I can see from all sides. What appears to be opposing forces are often two sides of one coin. To you I give my multiperspective view. This vision will help you in your work to know that there are ways of reaching an understanding in the worst battlegrounds, and when you see the rips and tears in the fabric of humankind, you will know where to place the stitches to begin mending souls.

Surprisingly, this majestic bird allows me to smooth its head and preen pin feathers that don't belong under his alabaster headdress. As powerful as he is, it seems he has exposed his vulnerability. I let him know I treasure his gift of involved neutrality and that, in turn, I will talk softly and move slowly around all of his kind so they will know there are islands of safety in the human sea.

Further Reading

Although, the imagery and intuitive guidance you receive in the above exercise are all you need, people seeking additional information on this topic may be interested in the book *Animal Spirit Guides: An Easy-to-Use Handbook for Identifying and Understanding Your Power Animals and Spirit Helpers,* by Steven D. Farmer (Hay House, 2006).

Handout 3.8—Aspirations and Abilities

The spirit of a high place is often needed to help people gain perspective and make contact with their observant Self. A mountain can be a symbol of life's journey and how connected you are to the resources you need to overcome obstacles in your way. Use the exercise to discover the dreams that draw you toward your future so you can strive with ease.

EXERCISE: CLIMBING A MOUNTAIN TASK

- Picture yourself in a meadow. Notice the length and color of the grass. Soon you will find a path that will lead through a forest into the foothills of a mountain.

- As the mountain comes into view, notice its height and appearance. You may know this mountain by name. It could be one you've been to before, one you've read about, or an unknown land mass waiting to be explored.

- Imagine yourself starting to climb the mountain by any possible means—by foot, by animal, or vehicle. How hard or easy is your journey. Does anything get in your way?

- When you have gone as far as you can go, whether you've reached the summit or are somewhere on the mountainside, take a moment to look at the view. Can you see all the way to the valley floor, or is something obstructing your vision?

- Imagine and journal your experience in the first person before reading the examples below: *I'm walking in a meadow. . . .*

EXAMPLES OF THE MOUNTAIN TASK

Example #1

It's night and I'm driving my car through the meadow and then a very thick, dark forest. As I come out the other side, I see a mountain looming before me. I manage to find the road that goes up it, but the grade is very steep. I've traveled around one or two bends in the road but the incline is getting worse and worse. It's like a nightmare. I cannot even look out. I fear I must turn back.

Example #2

There is a path through tall meadow grass. I can hear the bees working wildflowers. Soon, I see the mountain. I must be in Nepal because the mountain looks like Everest. I begin my climb. It seems like I travel by leaps and bounds, past other climbers. I'm at one of the rock faces and use my ropes to pull up. I've reached a low summit. There is still plenty above me, but the view from where I am is clear. The people at the start of the climb look like ants. I cannot believe how far I've come.

Comments

The woman in the first example had become involved in an affair despite what she said was a wonderful 7-year marriage to an adoring husband. Her new relationship is bringing her into uncharted waters and she feels torn by parallel lives. The young man in the second example is starting medical school. So far, he has succeeded in most everything he has done and has a clear view of his mental landscape. The next exercise can help you realize your true nature that effortlessly follows your dreams.

EXERCISE:
FANTASY PERSON   Quickly say a favorite name for a person of your own gender and picture him or her. List a few qualities that would describe the person's character. Jot down these words before reading the example.

EXAMPLE

My favorite female name is Audrey. She is classic, funny, and graceful. But I also like Angelina who is strong and would never let anyone walk on her. I guess my real Self is strong and has grace under fire.

Handout 3.9—Mandala: Symbols of the Self

The word *mandala* takes its name from the Sanskrit *manda,* which means "essence." The suffix *la* stands for container, making a mandala the container of one's essence or Self. The Self is constantly digesting and unifying everyday experiences. A mandala symbolizes our experiences by organizing perceptions, ideas, and physical sensations within a circle. These images reveal what state people are in at a given moment.

Many students of mandalas have observed a pattern to their designs that expresses a 12-stage life cycle. It repeats endlessly.[1] Before reviewing these stages, draw your own mandala, using the instructions on the following page. Then consider what your design is telling you about your current experience. This is an especially soothing activity to engage in during a crisis, an illness, or emotional heartache. Drawing a mandala is a type of meditation.

Understanding Mandalas

Mandala Designs	Current Experience
1. Void: Blank circles or vague forms, spider webs; dark or pale colors	**Fertile void (prebirth):** Waiting, patience, pain, ignorance, confusion, alienation, depression
2. Tiny scattered forms: Images of water, rays of sunlight, stars, small fish or plants; pastels	**Bliss (birth):** Passive enjoyment, rest, blurred boundaries, infinite possibilities, dreamy, drowsy
3. Labyrinth or spiral: Roads, stairways, maps, plants and vines, curving lines, spring colors	**Energizing (early infancy):** Searching, exploring, increasing energy, creativity, longing for growth
4. Small center form: Dot, circle, upward-pointing triangle, small boat, figure 8, curved lines, pastels	**Beginning (later infancy):** Dawning of a sense of Self, self-absorption, dependence on others
5. Target: Concentric circles radiating outward, bright or clashing colors	**Counterdependence (toddler's antagonism):** Vigilance, hostility, rituals, obsessions
6. Division of opposites (sky father/earth mother; dark/light, angel/devil, *yin/yang*): Landscapes with a solitary figure; opposite of nature colors	**Conflict and resolution (adolescence):** Passion, change, elation, excitement, and happiness, or alienated, fear, loneliness, and depression
7. Squaring the circle: Crosses, squares, flowers with four petals, straight lines, gold colors	**Self-governing (early adult):** Conflicts resolved, self-esteem, balance, striving toward goals
8. Power of man: Human figure reaching out, five-pointed stars, five-petaled flowers, four-armed swastika with center point suggesting motion	**Functioning (maturing adult):** Individual awareness, attainment of skills, ability to interact, active doing, readiness
9. Crystallization: Six-pointed stars, eight-petaled flowers, forms composed of even numbers > 4; variety of colors with contrast, autumn colors	**Fulfillment (mature adult):** Attainment of goals, creative activity nearing completion, satisfaction, harmony, enjoyment without attachment
10. Collapse: Spokes of a wheel, crucifix, prominent X-designs (facing a crossroad), downward-pointing triangle; dark colors, deep reds and blues	**Ending (crisis):** Completion of a project, time of surrender, retirement, relentless turning of life, turning toward Self, journey downward
11. Fragmentation: Sliced-up pie; crazy quilt with no order, no center; messy, dark, muddy colors or overly bright and psychedelic colors	**Breakdown (physical or mental):** Fear, confusion, uncertainty, chaos, profound loss, disorientation, guided by intuition and synchronicities
12. Upward focus: Chalices or other transformative vessels, infusion of light from above, birds in flight, contrasting of dark and light colors	**Transcendence (rebirth, sage):** Relationship to something beyond yourself, feelings of joy, harmony, reverence, unity with the world

---

1. *Coloring Mandalas for Insight, Healing and Self-Expression,* by Susanne F. Fincher, 2000, Boston: Shambhala Publications, gives the proper names of the Great Round of (12) Mandala Forms with 48 designs that can be colored.

EXERCISE:
CREATING
MANDALAS

1. Have a full range of colors and media—pencils, crayons, pastels, markers, and so on.

2. Use a plate to draw a circle or the *mandala graph paper* below.[2]

3. Draw from the center or edges of the circle. Allow an abstract design or a scene to appear.

4. When you are done, give your mandala a title. You may want to make this a daily exercise and date your work. It is natural to see progression and themes, but avoid overanalyzing.

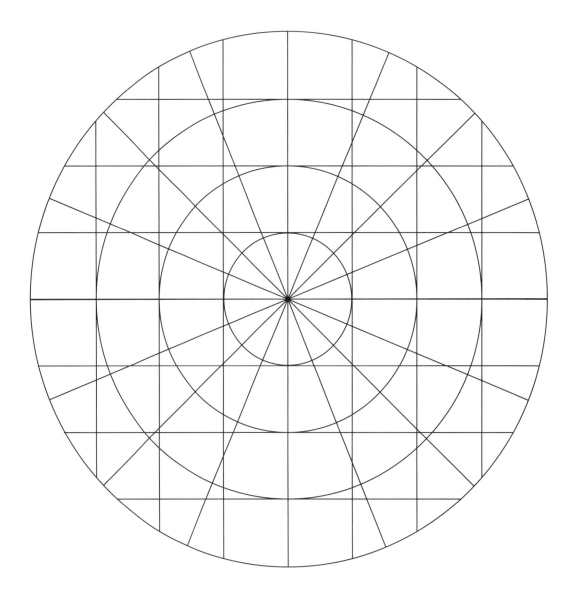

---

2.   The exercise for creating mandalas and mandala graph paper was taken from *Empowering Dialogues Within* (pp. 2.9–2.10), by Kate Cohen-Posey, 2008, with permission of John Wiley & Sons.

Handout 3.10—God and Goddess Personality Archetypes

Our true Self, noble, courageous, and compassionate, is shrouded by a mantle of personality traits. The basic characteristics that make up the outer shell of the Self were formed by imitating the people on whom we depended for survival. Temptations to classify personality types are ancient. The Greek and Roman pantheon of gods and goddesses was the first catalog of character traits that suggests archetypes for personal styles. This exercise can help you distinguish the constellation of traits that dominate your personality.

Mark 3 points for any type that strongly describes you, 2 points for types that somewhat describe you, and 1 point for types that possibly describe you. Leave blank types that do not apply.

EXERCISE: CHARACTERS OF THE GODS

Not all the descriptions need to fit for you to identify with a type (except for traits in **boldface**).

You may identify with only one character or several types.

Evaluating your character is like asking an eye to see itself. It helps to have friends rate you.

Type	Descriptions: You Are ...	Pts.
T-1	**Commanding**, in charge, decisive, ambitious, and/or unemotional. You value power, control, protection, discipline, reason, authority, initiative. Sex may be for conquest.	_____
T-2	**Relationship-oriented**, devoted, faithful, and emotional. Your partner's needs come first. You make excuses for your partner or endure hurtful actions, but feel angry.	_____
T-3	**Deeply emotional**, domineering (but lack power), impulsive, or spontaneous. You have a wild, untamed side and sexual urges. You may be unfaithful but are loyal to friends.	_____
T-4	**Nurturing,** generous, loyal, supportive, accepting, guilt prone, and protective. You can be critical and controlling, but do not show anger easily. You have close friends.	_____
T-5	**Reclusive,** self-sufficient, suspicious, shy, uncommunicative, cautious, and/or serious. You value a home, marriage, stability, and order. Tradition may be unimportant.	_____
T-6	**Open-minded**, receptive**,** flexible, creative, gullible, compliant, dependent, youthful, uncommitted, distractible, dreamy, and/or patient. You have many interests. Marriage can be deadening. With maturity, you become wise, mystical, intuitive, and/or psychic.	_____
T-7	**Goal-oriented**, objective, and/or unemotional. You are a leader, but not the top boss. You value reason, moderation, tradition, beauty, harmony, law, order, discipline, and compatibility, and you avoid conflict, communication, and intimacy.	_____
T-8	**Logical,** wise, go-getter, detached, skillful, problem solver, outgoing, stable, practical, and independent. You value strategy, diplomacy, tradition, moderation, and crafts.	_____
T-9	**Adventurous,** talkative, witty, charming, friendly (many acquaintances), quick, mischievous, open-minded, inventive. You guide others *or* test the limits.	_____
T-10	**Home-oriented,** quiet, peaceful, passive, detached but compassionate, restrained, attentive, organized, and tolerant. You like both solitude and visitors.	_____
T-11	**Aggressive,** protective, impulsive, loyal, passionate, and/or romantic, You value risks, physical power, action, male friends, masculine interests, and/or dancing.	_____
T-12	**Activist,** idealist, competitive, goal-oriented, persistent, adventurous, and independent. You value friends, the outdoors, protecting the downtrodden.	_____
T-13	**Creative,** artistic, sensitive, inarticulate, nonconforming or a misfit, intensely introverted. You value beauty, love, harmony, privacy, monogamy, and being faithful.	_____
T-14	**Loving,** seductive, sensuous, flashy, attractive, affectionate, approving, charismatic, outgoing, passionate, fiery, enthusiastic, intense, involved, spontaneous, creative, impulsive, youthful, and/or fascinated with others. You value soul connections.	_____
T-15	**Mystical,** interesting, alluring**,** sensual, erotic, and nonconforming. Prone to extremes (highs/lows, close/distant), altered states, having female friends, and wandering.	_____

Identifying Your Type[1]

If you have problems with social, family, or work relationships, the deities you favor may have become too dominant and need balancing by invoking the powers of others who sit on the pantheon. In ancient times, worshiping a particular deity was a means of acquiring its strengths. After identifying your type, consider any needed directions for growth.

Directions: Match the previous point values with the gods or goddesses that you most closely resemble. If one type does not clearly describe you or if you seem to be a combination of types, do not worry. You may have already achieved the right mixture of traits to deal with the daily details of life.

Type	Deities • Problems • Directions for Growth
T-1	ZEUS—*Sky God.* **Problems:** Grandiose, paranoid, abusive, corrupt. **Growth:** Usually needs a crisis to change and to experience humility and vulnerability.
T-2	HERA—*Goddess of Marriage and Fertility.* **Problems:** Possessive, jealous, vindictive, bitter, clingy. **Growth:** Put off relationships, resist jealously, and develop other goddess qualities.
T-3	POSEIDON/NEPTUNE—*God of Land and Sea.* **Problems:** Reactive, vengeful, moody, self-centered. **Growth:** Develop Apollo and Athena's objectivity. Express emotion through work.
T-4	DEMETER—*Goddess of Motherhood and the Harvest.* **Problems:** Depression, fatigue from inability to say *No*, resentment, unplanned pregnancies. **Growth:** Develop Athena's self-centeredness and learn to be self-nurturing.
T-5	HADES/PLUTO—*God of the Underworld.* **Problems:** Withdrawn, distorts reality, guarded. **Growth:** Develop Hermes/Apollo's expression. Find Persephone soul mate to relate to others.
T-6	PERSEPHONE—*Maiden who became Goddess of the Underworld.* **Problems:** Depression, self-doubt, indecisive, naïve, easy target. **Growth:** Develop Diana's fierceness, grow into the goddess who can guide others; develop Aphrodite for sexuality; let go of mother.
T-7	APOLLO—*Sun God.* **Problems:** Emotional distance, arrogance, poor communication, avoids conflict but not cruelty. **Growth:** Develop Dionysus's receptivity; learn humility through loss.
T-8	ATHENA—*Goddess of Wisdom.* **Problems:** Emotional distance, lacking empathy or ability to nurture, judgmental, selfish, flat, crafty. **Growth:** Find a mother; recover playful spirit.
T-9	HERMES/MERCURY—*Messenger god.* **Problems:** Impulsive, inconsiderate, immature; lacks commitment or a conscience. **Growth:** Develop Apollo's ethics and awareness of consequences; find a Zeus mentor; develop emotions and vulnerability through love.
T-10	HESTIA/VESTIA—*Goddess of the Hearth.* **Problems:** Emotional distance, loneliness, lacks social skills and boldness. **Growth:** Develop Diana's/Persephone's expressiveness and openness.
T-11	ARES/MARS—*God of War.* **Problems:** Reactive, abusive, low self-esteem, infidelity, lack of conscience, substance abuse, illegitimate children. **Growth:** Develop Hermes's communication, Apollo's discipline, Athena's reflection and good decisions. Find a mentor.
T-12	ARTEMIS/DIANA—*Goddess of the Hunt and Moon.* **Problems:** Emotional distance, rage, contempt for the weak, intense concentration. **Growth:** Develop Hera's relationship skills, Demeter's compassion. May need to experience a series of successes or failures to change.
T-13	HEPHAESTUS/VULCAN—*God of Fire and the Arts.* **Problems:** Misfit, low self-esteem, distorts reality, depression, bitterness. **Growth:** Develop Apollo's reason, Athena's strategic thinking, Zeus's ambition, Hermes's communication. Admit hurt; learn to value self.
T-14	APHRODITE/VENUS—*Goddess of Love.* **Problems:** Serial relationships, promiscuity, impulsiveness, obsession with men, loss of vitality when sexually denied. **Growth:** Develop Diana's/Athena's ability to focus; Hera's/Demeter's stability, Athena's emotional distance.
T-15	DIONYSUS—*God of Wine.* **Problems:** Substance abuse, poor self-esteem, illnesses, moodiness, distorted self-perception. **Growth:** Find a Zeus father figure; develop Hermes's facility to moderate highs and lows and Apollo's capacity for reason.

---

1. This exercise is based on Jean Shinoda Bolen's books *Goddesses in Everywoman: Powerful Archetypes for Women,* 1984, New York: Harper & Row, and *Gods in Everyman: Archetypes That Shape Men's Lives,* 1989, New York: Harper & Row.

Handout 3.11—Personality Awareness

Personality is a set of behavior traits, thinking patterns, motives, needs, and inclinations that are fixed by the time we reach adulthood. While this predetermined package of strengths and weaknesses allows little chance for change, there is hope. *Self-awareness* supplies the set of directions that informs us of our capabilities, motivations, and potential problems. The seat of awareness is deep within the brain and can be enhanced by certain practices. The TalentSmart study, which began in the 1990s, found that 83% of people who score high in self-awareness (in *all* personality types) were top performers in their various careers.[1]

Self-awareness requires people to have an understanding of their personal assets and liabilities. In 1928 William Marston, a Harvard psychologist, described a scientific model of healthy personalities. He created a graph with two axes that show a continuum of behavior traits:

DISC Personality Model

- **Vertical axis.** Responses to change vary from being *active* to *watching* how things develop.

- **Horizontal axis.** Being energized by engaging in *tasks* to enjoying interacting with *people*.

Each quadrant of the graph describes four basic personality traits: **D**ominant, **I**nterpersonal, **S**teady, or **C**onscientious. This came to be known as the DISC model in 1928.

Directions: Check off the characteristics in each quadrant that you believe describe you and write a score. For greater accuracy, average your score with the way a significant other would rate you.

Dominant (D)	ACTIVE >	Interpersonal (I)
Are: ☐ assertive, ☐ direct (to-the-point), ☐ competitive, ☐ determined, ☐ take-charge, ☐ independent, ☐ strong-willed Likes: ☐ power, ☐ control, ☐ influence Score : ____		Are: ☐ friendly, ☐ outgoing, ☐ emotional, ☐ entertaining, ☐ expressive, ☐ warm, ☐ understanding Likes: ☐ communicating, ☐ socializing, ☐ openness Score: ____
< TASK-ORIENTED		PEOPLE-ORIENTED >
Steady (S)	WATCHFUL >	Conscientious (C)
Are: ☐ persistent, ☐ patient, ☐ thoughtful, ☐ accommodating, ☐ undemanding, ☐ loyal, ☐ truthful Likes: ☐ routine, ☐ sincerity, ☐ honesty Score: ____		Are: ☐ cautious, ☐ compliant, ☐ precise, ☐ rule-follower, ☐ structured, ☐ organized, ☐ detailed Likes: ☐ etiquette, ☐ accuracy, ☐ tradition Score: ____

When the TalentSmart study began looking at what made people successful, they turned to Marston's widely used four basic traits. In their interpretation of the DISC model, the four components could be combined to yield 123,000 possible personality patterns. These were finally distilled into 14 distinct types—each one with its own strengths and weaknesses.

14 Distinct Personality Types

---

1. The information in the handout was adapted from *The Personality Code,* by Travis Bradberry, 2007, New York: G. P. Putnam's Sons. The official IDISC personality profile can be taken online at www.TalentSmart.com. Buying *The Personality Code* provides less expensive access to the test..

Directions: Use your scores from the DISC model to find a type that is similar to your mix of traits. If you have a *low dominant* (**D**↓) and *high conscientious* (**C**↑) score, you may have the **Detective** type of personality. The names are not meant to indicate an occupation, but are descriptive of the strengths and challenges of each type. Percents show how common each type is in the general population.

Types	Strengths and Problem Areas
I↑ S↑ C↓ Ally — 5%	**Strengths:** People skills, make lasting connections, good listener, accepting, teamwork, helpful. **Problems:** Working alone, speaking up,* handling rudeness.
I↓ S↑ Architect — 13%	**Strengths:** Completing tasks correctly, innovative, analytical, organization skills, attention to detail. **Problems:** Using intuition,* handling change.
D↓ I↑ S↑ C↓ Coach — 9%	**Strengths:** Helping, trusting, and affirming others; builds camaraderie and skills between and in others. **Problems:** Staying on task,* giving constructive criticism.
D↓ C↑ Detective — 9%	**Strengths:** Getting to the bottom of issues; accurate and logical, makes sound decisions. **Problems:** Admitting mistakes, self-disclosing,* working with others.
D↓ S↑ Diplomat — 9%	**Strengths:** Finding working solutions, tolerant, respectful, considerate, warm, inviting, modest. **Problems:** Gaining recognition* or speaking up.
D↑ S↓ Entrepreneur — 7%	**Strengths:** High achiever, goal oriented, can take things to the next level, independent, bold, forceful. **Problems:** Teamwork, patience,* showing restraint.
D↓ C↑ (I↑) Expert — 6%	**Strengths:** Knowledgeable, enjoy discussions/debates, quick learner, self-motivated. **Problems:** Considering others' ideas,* judgmental, perfectionist.
I↓ C↑ (D↑) Innovator — 3%	**Strengths:** Creative, visionary, want things done correctly, make new ideas work, multitasker. **Problems:** Impulsive, easily bored, unsympathetic, intolerant.*
I↑ S↓ Mobilizer — 3%	**Strengths:** Persuasive, friendly, interested in others, optimistic, confident, reaches goals. **Problems:** Gullible, dislikes routine, neglects data and facts.*
I↑ S↓ (D↑ C↓) Motivator — 13%	**Strengths:** Bringing people together, verbal skills, charming, people pleaser. **Problems:** Setting limits with others, managing time, getting discouraged.
D↑ I↓ (S↓) Opportunist — 2%	**Strengths:** Independent, innovative, determined; complete tasks on time; high standards. **Problems:** Teamwork, dealing with traditions, routine, and details.*
I↓ S↑ (D↓) Researcher — 4%	**Strengths:** Determined, complete tasks, logical, confident, independent. **Problems:** Showing emotion, trusting instincts, inflexible, appearing cold.*
I↑ C↓ Sponsor — 16%	**Strengths:** Many acquaintances, joiner, good networker and communicator, appreciative. **Problems:** Task completion,* setting limits, time management.
S↓ C↑ (I↑) Strategist — 1%	**Strengths:** Step-by-step action plans, leadership skills, trustworthy, considerate. **Problems:** Fearing failure, lacking patience, harsh tone,* moving too fast.

*Items indicate character flaws that can be managed by making efforts to change or relying on others.

Comments   You may have difficulty finding your unique combination of high and low DISC scores in the 14 types above. For instance, people with *high* **D** and **S** and *low* **C** scores do not have a clear match. If their **I** score is fairly low, both the *Opportunist* and *Researcher* types offered a revealing personality description. They need to take heed from (*) suggestions not to have the researcher's appearance of cool aloofness and know how to enlist the aid of others to give proper attention to details.

Handout 3.12—Pictures of Personality

Full concentration on objects in your surroundings can lead to a better understanding of your own makeup. Because a rosebush is a living thing, is it a perfect vehicle for understanding how you deal with change, relationships, frustrations, and meeting personal needs. These exercises create a waking dream that can help you discover what personal attributes are shaping your outer life.

EXERCISE: ROSEBUSH VISUALIZATION[1]

- Take a few breaths and allow an image of a rosebush to come to your mind. Begin to discover the details of this bush. What are its roots like? In what kind of ground is it planted? What are its stems and branches like? How old it is? Does it have blossoms? What color are they? How do you think this rosebush likes being a rosebush?

- Notice what is going on around the rosebush? What setting is it in—a field, a city, with other plant and animal life? What happens to the rosebush as the seasons change? Let your fantasy develop and notice if circumstances change the bush's experience of itself.

- Imagine and journal your experience in the first person before reading the examples below: *I am a rosebush and I am planted in . . .*

EXAMPLE OF THE ROSEBUSH VISUALIZATION

Example 1

I am a fairly small rosebush in the middle of a desert. Strangely, I have plenty of nourishment even though the soil is sandy and there is never rain. There is no other plant or animal life around. I have only two beautiful yellow blossoms at the top of my bush. My life in this environment is pleasant.

Example 2

I am in a hedge of rosebushes around what used to be an old monastery. We were planted to glorify the building and were cared for by monks. Now we thrive on our own, even though the building has been abandoned. Our blossoms are crimson with golden edges and are wide open. One side of the old building overlooks a cliff and a vast plain. I'm the third bush in, with a view of the vista. Some of my roots have broken through the side of the cliff. I enjoy looking at the wildlife on the plain. Even though my position seems perilous, I have no fear. This cliff has been here for a long time and will support me throughout my life. The summer warmth feels good. I dread the coming of winter and losing my blossoms.

Comments

The first example was imagined by a shy, quiet man. He likes to avoid social gatherings and is most comfortable with family and close friends. He lives alone with his wife. They are both independent but have a loving, harmonious relationship. Yellow roses indicate joy, friendship, and caring. A desert can mean disconnection from emotions, and this man is more aware of his environment than his internal life.

The second example was imagined by the man's wife. At one time she was dependent but has become self-reliant. A hedge suggests a protective function, and in her work she cares for others. Her fantasy shows that she is in a time of transition—she is now focused on the vista instead of the life inside the building. Red roses suggest love and passion. Is she afraid of losing this?

---

1. See *Awareness: Exploring, Experimenting, Experiencing,* by John O. Stevens, 1971, Boulder, CO: Real People Press, for the Rosebush Exercise. See *Empowering Dialogues Within* (p. 4.4), by Kate Cohen-Posey, 2008, Hoboken, NJ: John Wiley & Sons, for the first example of the Dwelling Visualization.

Dwelling Fantasy

The father of psychoanalysis considered a house to be a symbol of a person's personality. Basic traits can be projected onto the structure of a dwelling. One construction might show great ambitions, and another can symbolize a serious lack of self-esteem. Even the interior layout can reveal the forces at play in interpersonal relationships. Set this information aside to become fully involved in the next waking dream.

EXERCISE: DWELLING VISUALIZATION

- Imagine being in a meadow. Notice the color, length, and type of grass. Are there any other forms of vegetation or animal life? What time of day is it? What is the temperature?

- Begin moving through the meadow, and soon you will come to a dwelling or home. Even if it seems familiar, it will be unlike one you have ever seen. Notice how it appears on the outside. How is it made? What color is it? Are there windows? What kind and how many?

- How does the door appear? Does it have a handle or a knob? Is it hard to enter?

- What is the first room you see? If there is a kitchen, look in the cabinets or the refrigerator to find out if there is food. Is there furniture? How is it arranged?

- Are there bedrooms and bathrooms? How many? What kinds of beds do you find? Are there closets? What is in them? Is there an attic and basement? If so, find anything interesting.

- Imagine and journal your experience in the first person before reading the examples below: *From the grassy meadow I see . . .*

EXAMPLES OF THE DWELLING VISUALIZATION

Example 1

From the meadow I see a shack. As I get closer I can tell it's made out of wood with a front porch. It seems to be leaning. There is a living room but no furniture. The kitchen is to my right. The cupboards are empty, but there is a carton of fresh milk in the refrigerator. This seems strange because there is no electricity. The bedroom to the left has bare, double mattresses and a TV that does not work. The closets are empty. The second bedroom in the back of the living room has twin beds, neatly made up with brightly colored comforters.

Example 2

From the meadow I see a large stand of beautiful oak trees sheltering a stone home. Beveled glass windows are set into the stone. The door has a large handle, which is not locked. Inside is a great hall with high vaulted ceilings. Windows at the top let in streaming light. There is a kitchen in one corner with shiny appliances and lots of food. A bedroom is tucked behind a curving wall in the back corner. There is a walk-in closet with plenty of clothes. Most amazing is a stairway leading to a basement that turns into a cavern with underground springs, stalagmites, and stalactites that can be endlessly explored.

Comments

The woman in the first example thought her house showed how her entire family *leaned* on her for everything. Although she is highly successful, her family is always depending on her. In truth, she just wants to care for her much neglected niece and nephew.

The second example was envisioned by a woman with *deep* interest in scholarly pursuits. She needs to be cautious of wandering endlessly in the playground of her mind. The oak trees partially conceal her home and thick stone walls protect her from unwanted intrusions. However, her door is open to selected visitors. The great hall and kitchen amply supplied with food show confidence relating to crowds. Light streaming from above may suggest spiritual connections.

Handout 3.13—Personae—The Masks We Wear

The outermost layer of the Self is made up of the many masks we acquire to improve our chance of acceptance in a multitude of settings. We do not have one persona, or public-relations personality, but many personae. The personality you wear when you are relaxing with your family may be different from the one you assume as your professional self. It is important to become familiar with these adaptations or identities because you may be overvaluing some and neglecting others.[1]

**EXERCISE:
IDENTITIES**

DIRECTIONS: Write, I am a(n)... followed by a noun. Think of as many of your life roles as you can and list them:

- Your family positions (son, mother, grandfather, uncle, sister ...)
- Your occupation and avocation (artist, writer, coach, dancer...)
- Your nationality, race, ethnic group, family name, gender, sexual orientation, religion
- Your physical distinctions (red-head, physically challenged, senior citizen...)
- Your earned titles (veteran, friend, divorcee, survivor, felon, alcoholic, smoker...)
- Your interests (Red Sox fan, cat lover, movie buff...)
- Your hobbies (gambler, golfer, Trekkie...). Astrological sign, and so on.

1. *I am a(n)* _____

2. *I am a(n)* _____

3. *I am a(n)* _____

4. *I am a(n)* _____

5. *I am a(n)* _____

6. *I am a(n)* _____

7. *I am a(n)* _____

8. *I am a(n)* _____

9. *I am a(n)* _____

10. *I am a(n)* _____

11. *I am a(n)* _____

12. *I am a(n)* _____

13. *I am a(n)* _____

14. *I am a(n)* _____

15. *I am a(n)* _____

---

1. The information and exercise on personae is taken from *Empowering Dialogues Within: A Workbook for Helping Professionals and Their Clients,* by Kate Cohen-Posey, 2008, with permission of John Wiley & Sons, Inc.

16. *I am a(n)* _____

17. *I am a(n)* _____

18. *I am a(n)* _____

Evaluating Your Identities

After completing the exercise, put a check (☑) in front of the identities that are most important to you and a ☒ in front of the ones that are least important. Write a sentence with the roles that best describe you: *I am a single parent, Christian mother; I am an African-American, father, and physician.* Ask yourself the following questions to better understand the significance you place on your chosen persona:

- Do any of your identities seem to consume you so that you cannot drop a role when you are no longer in the appropriate setting?

- Did you leave out an important identity? Do you need to place more importance on being a spouse or a father?

- Was only one identity important to you? Do you need to develop more interests because being a one-persona person is making you dull and uninteresting?

- Are you having boundary issues because you are still being a mother at work, thinking about work at home, or using street language with your parents?

- Are you missing some personae and finding it difficult to adapt in social settings?

- Are you resisting changing your role as your children become adults or your parents become dependent?

Embracing Oppressed Personae

Review your list and make sure you have not left out any identities for which you feel ashamed. Although sometimes it is necessary, it takes energy to hide facets of ourselves. Even if you can only do the following exercise in fantasy, it will offer relief. It is even more powerful if done in front of a group of people that you trust.

EXERCISE: RECLAIMING IDENTITIES[2]

Part I

Imagine yourself standing in front of a large audience as you announce, "I am .... (a rape survivor, a Jew, a transsexual, a felon, ...)." You hear a thunderous applause. Then give this audience a talk about the three greatest advantages and disadvantages of having this title, what you want people to understand, and what changes society needs to make so you can be open with who you are.

Part II

If there are any activities in which you no longer want to partake, imagine confessing them to the same large audience and telling them your plan to stop smoking, shoplifting, or defeating yourself in some other way. Feel the group's compassion and goodwill pouring out to you.

The best way to fight oppression is by being visible whenever it is the tiniest bit safe to do so. If you are a person with a past, whether it be as a victim or as an offender, you have survived. Mentioning your experience casually at appropriate moments will help you reclaim yourself and open doors to the diversity in society for others. If possible, join a support group for people who have or have had a problem behavior that is difficult for you.

---

2. This exercise comes from Re-evaluation Counseling, which can be found at www.rc.org. It teaches a process whereby laypeople can learn to counsel each other (co-counsel) to free themselves from the effects of past distress experiences.

Section II

Thinking Mind

CHAPTER 4
HOW TO FIX FAULTY THINKING

MINI INDEX TO CHAPTER 4

Help clients or clinicians:

1. Collaborate with treatment by providing information about cognitive therapy.

2. Identify irrational ideas, automatic thought, and core beliefs.

3. Evaluate invalid and unhelpful ideas and restructure negative viewpoints.

4. Use several approaches to restructure negative thoughts and maintain helpful views.

5. Create statements that focus on desires and minimize doubts about making changes.

6. Use worksheets to practice acquiring adaptive, positive ideas.

Using the Handouts

- **Informed consent:** *Therapy for Faulty Thinking* meets the ethical obligation to provide clients information about a particular treatment orientation.

- **General literature:** *Identifying Irrational Ideas, Automatic Thoughts, The Power of Negative Thinking, Your Beliefs: Helpful or Harmful, Power Thinking: Beyond Affirmations.*

- **Specific problems**: *Angry Automatic Thoughts, Keep the Good Thoughts Rolling* (for solving problems and making decisions), *Be the Boss of Your Thoughts* (children's worksheet).

- **In-depth understanding**: *Pinpointing Your Beliefs, Restructuring vs. Refocusing.*

- **Visual aids to identify irrational thoughts and negative and positive cognitions:** Tables in *Recognizing Faulty Thinking* and *Your Beliefs—Harmful or Helpful.*

- **Forms:** *Power Thinking Worksheet, Thought Record and Evaluation,* and *Thought Changer Forms* are designed to practice rational or positive thinking as homework.

Cautions and Comments

- **These handouts are basic** to treating generalized anxiety and many other disorders.

- ***Angry Automatic Thoughts*** should be used after clients understand how to log thoughts with the *Automatic Thoughts* handout. It is helpful to compare these two handouts. *Angry Automatic Thoughts* can be useful with people who have Axis II tendencies and defend them themselves with blaming, clinging, boasting, and so on.

- ***Pinpointing Beliefs*** should be used with clients who are actively involved in therapy. The exercise at the end of this handout is valuable in restructuring core beliefs.

- ***Your Beliefs Help—Helpful or Harmful*** and ***Pinpointing Beliefs*** can be used in the assessment phase of the EMDR treatment protocol to identify disturbing material that needs to be processed.

- ***Be the Boss of Your Thoughts*** should be completed *with* children and not assigned as independent homework. Parents can be given this handout to teach their children cognitive therapy *and* to further reinforce concepts in their own minds.

Sources and Acknowledgements Not Referenced in the Handouts

Rational-Emotive Therapy, originated by Albert Ellis, formed the basis of *Recognizing Faulty Thinking.* This handout refines and reorganizes his basic irrational ideas.

Formulations for responsible, safety, and controlling cognitions are adapted from *Eye Movement Desensitization and Reprocessing: Basic Principles, Protocols, and Procedures,* by Francine Shapiro (Guilford Press, 1991, p. 430). Aaron Beck's helpless, unlovable core beliefs were adapted from *Cognitive Therapy: Basics and Beyond,* by Judith S. Beck (Guilford Press, 1995, p. 169).

The Dysfunctional Attitude Scale (Weissman, A. N., & Beck, A. T., 1978) was used to develop the table of attitudes and rules in **The Power of Negative Thinking**. It can be found online by doing a search for the *Acceptance and Commitment Therapy Measures Package* compiled by Dr. Joseph Ciarrochi and Linda Bilich, University of Wollongong, p. 54.

Handout 4.1—Therapy for Faulty Thinking

What causes people to be upset: the events in their lives or their thoughts about those events? In the early 1960s two psychiatrists, Albert Ellis in New York City and Aaron Beck in Pennsylvania, each reached the same conclusion. Their basic premise is the founding principle of what is generally now called *cognitive therapy*.

The Cognitive Principle

Our thoughts about our experiences and underlying core beliefs strongly influence our emotional and behavioral reactions. By extension, these reactions can include temporary feelings of sadness, fear, or anger or prolonged moods and habits.

Examples of the Cognitive Principle

When the above principle was presented at a convention of psychologists in 1960, it provoked more controversy than consensus. Now it is the prevailing wisdom in psychology. However, if this is your first introduction to this idea, you may have your own mixed emotions about it. The following examples will help illuminate how thoughts and beliefs can be so powerful.

Situation 1: Kay and Hal were raising their only child, Leila.	
Every time Leila got sick, Kay would become highly anxious. If asked what was going through her mind she might have said, *What if Leila never recovers?!*	Hal remained calm when Leila was sick. Kaye asked him how he managed this. He said he believed illness is normal and that there is a natural healing process.
Situation 2: Kay and Hal went away for a weekend trip. While they were gone their house was burglarized. The police recovered everything but Kay's heirloom jewelry worth several hundred dollars.	
Kay was a little sad about her loss but felt better when she thought, *It's only material stuff; no one was hurt.*	Hal was furious that his home had been invaded. He wondered, *Why do there have to be so many rotten people in this town?*
Situation 3: In their 60s Hal wanted to retire but Kay loved her work and could not imagine being unemployed.	
Kay often suffered from insomnia. She would wake up at night, bubbling with ideas about her next project. As a child she believed: *I will fail* (be a failure) *if I don't work extra hard.*	Retirement did not offer Hal an escape from what he thought was workplace pressure. His anxiety became full-blown. His need to be orderly made him believe, *I'm in control.* Now there was nothing to control.

The preceding three examples show how varied human responses can be to the exact same event. In an extreme case, two people may both deeply grieve the loss of a loved one, but one may believe he or she cannot bear the heartache, while the other has the firm conviction that life must go on.

- Reexamine your reaction to the cognitive principle. How strongly do you agree with it?
- Assign a number that denotes the degree of your agreement—100%, 60%, 15%.

Cognitive Therapy Practices

Cognitive therapy involves a partnership between counselors and clients. Any idea that the therapist will "fix" the person is quickly dispelled. Goals are identified at the beginning of treatment that provide symptom relief and resolve a person's most pressing problems. Regular sessions are not expected to last much longer than 3 months. Structure is provided in each session by reviewing progress, checking the client's mood, going over homework, setting an agenda, exploring issues, and deciding a direction for the next meeting. More specific elements of cognitive therapy follow:

1. **Current problems and specific situations** are discussed. Clients are helped to identify the ABCs of emotions and behavior. A is the **a**ctivating event, C is the emotional or behavioral **c**onsequence of the event, and B is the unseen **b**elief system that leads to that consequence.

2. **Automatic thoughts.** The first beliefs that clients are helped to identify are automatic thoughts. These are a part of the mental chatter that goes on in people's minds all the time. They are the rapid, first responders to a situation with perceptions and interpretations of what is happening—*She might not recover; people in this town are rotten.*

3. **Evaluating and changing thoughts.** Clients are taught a method for evaluating the accuracy and usefulness of their thoughts. Beliefs that are dysfunctional can be unlearned, and new reality-based ideas are developed and adopted. This is a skill that can be used independently of counselors to prevent problems in the future.

4. **Core beliefs.** As treatment progresses, people are helped to identify their core beliefs about themselves, other people, or the world. Unlike automatic thoughts that are situation specific, these beliefs are overgeneralized, rigid opinions a person has that can influence perceptions of events—*I'm a failure, I'm not in control.*

5. **Uncovering core beliefs.** Probing may be needed to identify core beliefs. A therapist might have asked Kay, *What will it mean about you if your daughter doesn't recover?* The response would have been, *I'm alone.* Interestingly, Kay had an irrational fear when she was 10 that her mother would die because her grandmother died when her mother was 10. Sometimes it is necessary to look at the past to understand the tenacious aspects of a core belief.

6. **Changing core beliefs.** Core beliefs are altered by formulating more practical, flexible ideas for clients to consider and test—*I have to be in control* becomes *I can respond to whatever happens.* A variety of techniques is used, including role-plays and behavioral tasks, to begin to transform beliefs.

7. **Homework** is a regular part of the treatment process. At the very least, this might include journaling any thoughts that occur during or after upsetting events or when a person's mood seems to change for no reason at all.

Effectiveness of Cognitive Therapy

Cognitive and behavior therapy easily merged into *cognitive behavior therapy* (CBT). Both focus on the here-and-now and symptom removal. Many CBT programs have undergone rigorous research for their effectiveness with positive findings. This places CBT in a prime position in the current health care climate that demands *evidence-based treatment*. Often, impressive results with CBT are based on comparisons to programs that use only medical care. Other research does not find significant differences between CBT and other types of psychotherapy. The following questions can help you decide if CBT is suited to your personal style:

- Do you like to think of yourself as a logical, rational person, or would you like to develop those qualities in yourself?

- Would you prefer a treatment approach that is structured, focused, and organized?

- Do you place a priority on solving your problems rather than on having a professional friend who can give you "objective opinions" or allow you to vent?

Handout 4.2—Identifying Irrational Ideas

It is natural to have *gut* reactions to certain life events. However, there are faulty thinking patterns that cause *shock waves* of fear, anger, and grief long after the initial tremor has struck. You cannot choose what happens to you, but you can *choose* the way you look at life's hardships. To have such options you need to recognize thinking patterns that hurt and opposing ones that help. Psychologists have identified several irrational ideas that wreak havoc in people's lives:[1]

1. **Externalizing vs. internalizing control.** Externalizing is the root of all other faulty thinking. It suggests that events and people cause distress. This implies that it is impossible to recover from past experiences. The more internal your sense of control, the less power outside events have to hurt.

2. **Awfulizing vs. observing.** Awfulizing exaggerates feelings about events and others' misfortunes. Instead, make a list of the three worst things that could happen. Decide that everything else is unfortunate or inconvenient, but not awful.

3. **Shoulding vs. understanding.** Judging focuses on how others *should* be and makes generalizations. This is frustrating because you can only change yourself. It is much easier to understand people you do not like. This will lessen your need to change them.

4. **Assuming vs. inquiring.** Assuming is a form of prejudging that creates a vicious cycle. The more you assume, the harder it is to understand others, and the easier it is to assume. This causes resentment and anger. Instead, simply ask questions to check the accuracy of your perceptions—*Did you do that because . . . ?*

5. **Expecting vs. responding.** Expecting goes one step further than assuming by pressuring others to change or to always meet your standards. This can cause people to rebel. Instead, make requests and give others the right to refuse. Reexamine your standards and make any needed responses when your expectations are not met.

6. **Judging vs. accepting yourself.** Although self-judging focuses inward, it is not freeing. It presumes failure, incompetence, or worthlessness if you have shortcomings or cannot solve every problem. Doing something wrong does not make someone inadequate, but failing to recognize, take responsibility for, and learn from mistakes is foolish.

7. **Passive vs. assertive thinking.** Passive thinkers give up having their needs met. They may appear independent but actually believe their environment has little to offer. This causes bitterness and constant complaining. Instead, make requests and set limits on how much you are willing to do.

8. **Limited vs. expansive thinking.** Limited thinkers believe they must be liked by everyone or that only certain (stronger) people can meet their needs. They think their feelings of dependency and disappointment cannot be helped. Instead, release temporary sadness for not having a desire met in a particular way and explore other options.

9. **Dwelling and dreading vs. affirming and acting.** People who dread think dwelling on worst-case scenarios helps prevent misfortune. *What-ifs* and *if-onlys* make it impossible to let go of fear and remorse. Instead, take well-thought-out chances. If the outcome is not satisfactory, try something else or accept your limits.

10. **Avoidance vs. responsibility.** The idea that freedom from responsibility and lack of commitment brings happiness is the ultimate fallacy. Structure, purpose, and rewarding self-discipline make life meaningful.

---

1. This list combines ideas from *A Guide to Rational Living,* by A. Ellis, 1997, New York: Wilshire Book Co., and *Feeling Good* (pp. 28–50), by David Burns, 1992, (New York: Avon Books).

Directions. Thinking patterns can be recognized by *mental grammar* in your mind and your viewpoints about life. (1) Mark ideas on the left side of the table you currently use that eliminate power and choice in your life. (2) Select options on the right that change faulty thinking:

Change Harmful Thinking Patterns . . .	To Helpful Thinking Patterns
1. *They make me feel . . . I can't . . .*	→ *When they . . . I feel . . . . I'm not willing to . . .*
❑ I am a victim of circumstances or my past.	❑ Events and people cause temporary upset.
❑ My past makes it hard or impossible for me to change, let go of anger, depression, etc.	❑ I can learn something from the worst situations.
	❑ Ideas are easier to change than events.
2. *This is awful, terrible, a catastrophe . . .*	→ *This is unfortunate, inconvenient, or reality.*
❑ When things go wrong, it is awful.	❑ Humor and good can come from bad luck.
❑ One should be very upset about others' hardships.	❑ I can manage or learn to accept what I cannot change.
❑ Every problem has a perfect solution.	
3. *She shouldn't . . . He ought to . . . They never . . .*	→ *The reason for this is . . .*
❑ People should always be at their best.	❑ In truth, people aren't consistently good or bad.
❑ When others do "wrong" things, they are wicked, rotten, or inconsiderate.	❑ There are reasons for the worst behavior.
	❑ If a person could act better, he or she would.
4. *She just thinks . . . He probably . . .*	→ *Are you saying . . . ? Do you feel . . . ?*
❑ I know what others feel without asking.	❑ The best mind readers make mistakes.
❑ If others don't meet my needs, they don't care or they're trying to hurt me.	❑ People don't have to put me first to love or support me.
5. *She better . . . He has to . . . or else.*	→ *I can respond to what others do.*
❑ I need to be in control of situations and prevent catastrophes.	❑ I can be flexible, take risks, and deal with whatever happens.
6. *I shouldn't have . . . I should be able to . . .*	→ *I'm . . . enough as I am.*
❑ I must be competent to be worthwhile.	❑ My worth is based on my efforts, not results.
❑ If I don't fix others' problems, find solutions, or keep them happy, I've failed.	❑ I can change my mind, disappoint others, and break rules (and experience the consequences).
7. *I don't need . . . I'm not important . . . can't get my needs met, so why try.*	→ *My feelings and needs count.*
❑ If I try to get what I want, I might be selfish.	❑ The only way to reach satisfying solutions is for both parties to express their wants.
❑ I shouldn't tell people how I feel if it will upset them.	❑ Telling others how their behavior affects me gives them the opportunity to change.
8. *I need . . .*	→ *I have . . . I can . . .*
❑ I need love and/or approval from everyone.	❑ I have my own self-respect.
❑ I need someone stronger than myself.	❑ I can depend on myself.
	❑ I can love others.
9. *What if . . . She might . . . If only . . .*	→ *So what if . . . I am . . . I can . . .*
❑ Fear of the unknown is unavoidable.	❑ When the unknown and responsibilities are faced, they become less difficult.
❑ It is best to avoid a difficult situation.	
10. *I can't wait until . . .*	→ *I have direction, purpose, and a mission.*
❑ I won't be happy until I'm free of responsibilities.	❑ My happiness comes from my interests, creativity, and desire to serve.

Handout 4.3 — Automatic Thoughts

Your heart never stops beating and your mind never stops thinking. But certain *automatic thoughts* in your stream of consciousness can cause undue or prolonged emotional reactions. That is because they misread situations in a way that causes overreactions or dwelling on events. However, you can learn to evaluate the *accuracy* and *usefulness* of these thoughts and adopt new reality-based ideas. The first step is to identify what is on your mind when you feel upset.

Thoughts and feelings are like chickens and eggs. Although it is thoughts that hatch emotions, you can use your feelings to tell you what you are thinking. Remember or imagine an event and the feelings you have about it. Then ask yourself one of several questions:

Identifying Automatic Thoughts

- *What was going through my mind when that happened?*
- *What is my best guess of what is on my mind when I have that feeling?*
- *What does this thought mean about me?*

The following example shows one way to use an upsetting event to log automatic thoughts. These can later be examined and evaluated for their accuracy and usefulness.

Bradley was excited about her new job clerking at a high-class clothing outfitter. . She had been at the store a month when a well-dressed woman sharply said, "I told you before, I don't like help when I'm shopping." Bradley was crushed, and after several days she still could not get the incident out of her mind. She began to dread going back to the job she loved and decided to log the automatic thoughts she was having on her *thought record*:

Thought Record

What was going through my mind when X happened? What does that thought mean about me?

Date/time	Situation	Automatic Thoughts(s)—% Believed	Feeling % Upset
6/25 1 P.M.	*Customer said, "I told you before, I don't like help when I'm shopping."*	1. *I should be more cautious about whom I approach to help in the store.* 100% 2. *I should be able to tell which customers want help and which ones do not.* 80% 3. *I've been enjoying myself too much on this job.* 70% 4. *When you enjoy yourself too much, you will always have a letdown.* 80% 5. *When people get mad at me, it means I've made a mistake.* 95%	*Angst 80%* *Tense 90%* *Worried 70%* *Scared 80%* *Sad 100%*

Pointers on Journaling Automatic Thoughts[1]

- Rating how strongly you believe a thought and the degree of upset it causes helps determine the importance of evaluating it.

- If a thought has no emotional charge, it is not necessary to journal or evaluate. Bradley wondered if she should have remembered the customer's face and quickly decided that that was unrealistic because of the volume of clientele in her store.

- Thoughts in the form of a question can be changed into a statement. *Should I be more cautious about which customers I approach?* becomes *I must be more cautious about whom I approach.*

- People often express thoughts as feelings—*I feel that I should be more careful about whom I approach*—is the thought: *I should be more careful about. . . .* Although this idea has some truth, it creates a fair degree of anxiety and, therefore, may not be a *useful* idea.

- Use feelings to identify key automatic thoughts. Bradley mainly felt sad about the incident with the customer, even though most of her thoughts were associated with anxiety and tension. She asked herself, *What does it mean if a customer is sharp or gets angry with me?* What went through her mind was, *That would mean I made a mistake.*

Evaluating Automatic Thoughts

Several questions can test automatic thoughts for their accuracy or usefulness and help formulate more adaptive perceptions of an incident:

- What facts do or do not support this idea?
- Is there another explanation for what occurred?
- What is the worst, best, or most likely outcome for this event?
- What would I want my friend or child to think in this situation?
- In what way is this thought helpful and harmful to me?
- What would be the effect of changing my outlook?

How rational is this thought? What thinking errors does it have.

☐ absolutes/imperatives (should, musts, always, nevers), ☐ assumptions, ☐ circular reasoning

☐ exaggerations, ☐ exclusions (of positives)

☐ mind reading, ☐ fortune telling, ☐ unrealistic expectations, ☐ overgeneralizations, ☐ polarizations (all or nothing thinking), ☐ personalizing (assuming you are the cause of other's misbehavior)

☐ labeling. ☐ other: _____

Once she had identified her thoughts, Bradley used the above questions to test their accuracy and usefulness. She was able to recognize several common fallacies in her perceptions of events and to consider alternative viewpoints. In some cases, just seeing her thoughts in writing made it easy to evaluate. The fifth idea (below) was so well engrained that she needed help from her counselor to construct an adaptive outlook. Finally, Bradley noted how much her new viewpoint reduced feelings of distress. Journal your own automatic thoughts and formulate more adaptive viewpoints to find relief from emotional reactions.

---

1. Ideas in this handout were adapted from *Cognitive Therapy: Basics and Beyond*, 1995, by Judith S. Beck. New York: The Guilford Press.

Automatic Thought	Fallacy	New Viewpoint—% Believed	Feeling % Upset
1. I must be more cautious about whom I approach to help	Imperative	1. I can be careful about whom I approach and learn from my mistakes. 99%	Angst 1%
2. I should be able to tell which customers want help and which ones do not.	Mind reading	2. This line of thinking might make me afraid to approach anyone and reduce my sales. 70%	Tense 20%
3. I've been enjoying myself too much on this job.	Exaggeration	3. Enjoying my work will make me a better sales person. 90%	Worried 10%
4. Enjoying yourself too much will always cause a letdown.	Generalization	4. Being careful not to enjoy myself will prevent me from being happy. 80%	Scared 10%
5. When people get mad at me, It means I've made a mistake.	Personalization	5. When people get mad at me, I can decide if my behavior deserves their ire or if they have issues. 90%	Sad 15%

Handout 4.4—Angry Automatic Thoughts

In truth, automatic thoughts are not angry, anxious, or sad. They are the ideas attached to mad, melancholy, or fearful feelings. However, irritating viewpoints deserve special attention and scrutiny. Ideas that raise your ire may actually create a sense of righteous indignation. The thought, *I made a mistake* (causing guilt), when turned on others becomes *They made a mistake* (producing annoyance). You may wonder, *If someone else is making me upset, why should I bother to examine my own thoughts, much less restructure them?*

Who Is Upsetting Whom— Identifying Thoughts

The basic cognitive principle states that it is our *thoughts* about events, not a person or situation that influences our reactions. The good news is that we are not at the mercy of every annoying character who crosses our path. The bad news is that we are responsible for how we react, even to exasperating individuals. You can begin to take charge of your emotions by asking yourself several questions:

- *What was going through my mind when that happened?*
- *What is my best guess of what is on my mind when I have that feeling?*
- *What does this thought mean about me?*

The following example shows one way to journal automatic thoughts that cause anger. Later, they can be examined and evaluated for their accuracy and usefulness.

Brad was excited about his new job at a high-class clothing outfitter. He had been at the store a month when a woman of obvious means sharply said, "I told you before, I don't like help when I'm shopping." Brad fumed. When he mentioned to his boss that that their clientele could be a bit snippy, he received the standard cliché: *the customer is always right*. Brad's blood started to boil. But he had lost jobs before because of his attitude, and he decided to journal the automatic thoughts he was having in his *thought record*:

Thought Record

What was going through my mind when *X* happened? What does that thought mean about me?

Date/Time	Situation	Automatic Thoughts(s)—% Believed	Feeling % Upset
2/06 11 A.M	Customer said, "I told you before, I don't like help when I'm shopping."	1. *She was being rude and disrespectful.* 100% 2. *She thinks just because she has money, it doesn't matter how she talks to others.* 85% 3. *She probably looks down on me since I'm only an employee in a clothing store.* 70% 4. *My supervisor should have been more supportive and understanding of me.* 80% 5. *I'll never get the appreciation and respect I deserve.* 95%	Annoyed 80% Angry 90% Shame 70% Angry 80% Sad 80%

Pointers on Journaling Automatic Thoughts[1]

- Rating how strongly you believe a thought and the degree of upset it causes helps determine the importance of evaluating it.
- Thoughts in the form of a question can be changed into a statement. *Is he looking down on me?* becomes *He probably looks down on me because …*

---

1.   Ideas in this handout were adapted from *Cognitive Therapy: Basics and Beyond*, 1995, by Judith S. Beck. New York: The Guilford Press.

- People often express thoughts as feelings—*I feel that he's looking down on me* is the thought: *He probably looks down on me because* . . .

- It is important to document the feelings that accompany automatic thoughts. Often, views that produce anger are masking more vulnerable emotions. As Brad continued to write his flow of thoughts, he finally came to an idea that hurts—*I'll never get the respect I deserve.*

Evaluating Automatic Thoughts

Several questions can test automatic thoughts for their accuracy or usefulness and help formulate more adaptive perceptions of an incident:

- What facts do or do not support this idea?
- Is there another explanation for what occurred?
- What is the worst, best, or most likely outcome, for this event?
- What would I want my friend or child to think in this situation?
- In what way is this thought helpful and harmful to me?
- What would the effect be of changing my outlook?

How rational is this thought? What thinking errors does it have? ☐ absolutes/imperatives (should, musts, always, nevers), ☐ assumptions, ☐ circular reasoning

☐ exaggerations, ☐ exclusions (of positives)

☐ mind reading, ☐ fortune telling, ☐ unrealistic expectations, ☐ overgeneralizations, ☐ polarizations (all or nothing thinking), ☐ personalizing (assuming you are the cause of other's misbehavior)

☐ labeling. ☐ other: _____

Once he had identified his thoughts, Brad used the above questions to test their accuracy and usefulness. He was able to recognize several common fallacies in his perceptions of events and identify alternative explanations for what occurred. However, people who focus other others' behavior to avoid internal anxiety or sadness can have difficulty adopting calming outlooks or giving up tendencies to blame. In Brad's continuing *thought record*, which new viewpoints seem particularly difficult for him?

Automatic Thought	Fallacy	New Viewpoint—Degree Believed	Feeling % Upset
1. She was being rude and disrespectful.	Labeling	1. She was stating what she wanted. I cannot control her tone of voice. 80%	Annoyed 30%
2. She thinks her money allows her to talk how she wants.	Assumption	2. There could be other reasons for her tone of voice. 60%	Angry 40%
3. She probably looks down on me since I only work in a clothing store.	Mind reading	3. If I respect the work I'm doing, I won't care what others think. — 70% I need to focus on self-respect. 65%	Ashamed 20%
4. My boss should have been more supportive of me.	Imperative	4. There are reasons why my boss cares about clients more than me. 80%	Angry 30%
5. I'll never get the appreciation and respect I want.	Exaggeration	5. Most of the customers like me. I can live without support from my boss all the time. 60%	Sad 30%

The concept of not having control over others (#1) and finding respect and support within (#3, #5) were new for Brad, so he continued to feel some annoyance, shame, and sadness. Equally challenging was the task of empathizing with others, making it difficult to consider various reasons for the wealthy customer's tone of voice (#2) or his boss's perceived lack of support (#4). Although anger and other feelings persisted, they were significantly reduced from their pre-self-examination levels. This is a remarkable achievement for someone who is ruled by anger. Log your automatic thoughts and construct more adaptive views to tame your temper.

Handout 4.5—The Power of Negative Thinking

Many people find themselves dominated by negative thoughts, particularly when they are under pressure. Stress hormones released during upsetting experiences actually cement other people's (or your own) perceptions of themselves into their brain! Ordinary experiences do not trigger strong biochemical reactions. For this reason, they are harder to remember, along with any positive information about yourself associated with those events.[1] Therefore, people who have *not* endured a trauma can have a collection of negative thoughts recorded in their minds. Being yelled at by a coach or relative may release enough adrenaline or cortisol to embed the thought: *I'm not up to this; I always make a mess of things;* or *I'll never be appreciated.*

Negative Distress Recording

Once planted in your minds, negative thoughts can fester and grow. This happens for several reasons:

- Any time pesky stress hormones are released, they can trigger negative automatic thoughts.

- Because negative thoughts carry doubt and shame, you tend to keep them to yourself. They are not open to scrutiny from others, who could point out how such ideas are flawed.

- The doubt and shame associated with negative thoughts makes you want to avoid thinking about them when you are feeling calm, rational, and capable of seeing how they are distorted.

- When negative recordings happen *automatically* (instead of being *intentionally* thought about and evaluated), they seem true.

- Because negative thoughts seem true, they become familiar to you, and they seem even more believable.

- Because negative thoughts can make you feel awful, they cause you to avoid doing things and being with people you enjoy. This allows more time to dwell on the very recordings that are causing the problem.

- The negative thought now acts like a magnet. Any information that supports the idea, *I always make a mess of things,* is recorded, and evidence to the contrary is ignored. The thought has now become a *schema* or a fundamental way of processing information.

Attitudes, Rules, and Assumptions

In addition to your thoughts, you can pick up certain attitudes and rules from society, particularly ones that are in sync with the negative thoughts that often pop up in your mind.

---

1. *Why We Believe What We Believe* (p. 187), by A. Newberg, 2006, New York: Simon & Schuster.

Check any of the following attitudes or rules with which you sometimes agree.

Attitudes	Rules
_____To be happy, a person needs to be thin, smart, and rich. _____ . . . or to have certain life experiences.	_____I need to do well all the time. _____I have to be as good as others.
_____If my job or a relationship ends badly, I've failed.	_____Asking questions makes me look stupid.
_____To be worthwhile, I have to excel at something.	_____Asking for help is a sign of weakness.
_____It is natural to be upset if you make a mistake.	_____Good people help those who are in need.
_____If people disagree with me, they may not like me.	_____It's selfish to put my needs before others.
_____If people knew the real me, they would not like me.	_____I can reach my goals without trying hard.
_____It's awful to be criticized by someone important.	_____If you avoid a problem, it will go away.

To connect the dots between any attitudes or rules you have adopted and the *assumptions* they give you about yourself, use the if . . . then test:

- If . . . I never marry, then . . . *I'm a failure as a woman.*
- If . . . I make a mistake, then . . . *I'm inadequate.*
- If . . . people don't like me, then . . . *I'm not likeable.*
- If . . . I get criticized, then . . . *I'm flawed.*
- If . . . I look stupid to others, then . . . *I am stupid.*
- If . . . I ask for help, then . . . *I'm incompetent.*
- If . . . I don't help people who are in need, then . . . *I'm heartless.*
- If . . . I have to work hard to reach my goals, then . . . *I'm not capable.*
- If . . . I face my problems, then . . . *I'll fail (be a failure).*

The Power of Unmasking Thought

Simply identifying trigger quick disturbing thoughts and assumptions at times when you are feeling reasonably calm is the first step to easing them. When you are not being flooded with stress hormones, thought fallacies can be obvious. Even if one or two people say you are stupid, it does not mean that you are unintelligent. You might further realize that anyone who is quick to judge you has issues of his or her own or that there are advantages of being underestimated. However, if negative thoughts are deeply embedded in your brain, just looking at them may stir a biochemical reaction. The good news is that there is a pleasure hormone that can counteract the effects of adrenaline and cortisol—dopamine.

EXPERIMENT—THE DOPAMINE BOOST

Brain-scan studies find that it takes less than 1 second for a word or phrase to trigger an emotional reaction (Newberg, 2006).

1. Review the inspiring quotes below and pick the one that you like best.

2. Read or say it silently to yourself 50 times for the next 2 minutes. Tapping a finger on each hand five times as you say the phrase can ensure completing the full 50 repetitions.

3. Notice how you feel after repeating the quote you chose. On a biological level, you have tuned out incoming sensory information, oriented to a positive thought, and triggered the release of dopamine.

4. Now, look at your negative attitudes, rules, or assumptions and find out how easily you can change them to a viewpoint that gives you a sense of well-being.

Inspirational Quotes

The journey is the reward.

—Chinese Proverb

Work like you don't need the money, love like you've never been hurt, and dance like no one is watching.

—Satchel Paige

Things turn out the best for the people who make the best of the way things turn out.

—Mark Twain

One's destination is never a place, but a new way of seeing things.

—Henry Miller

Courage is being scared to death, but saddling up anyway.

—John Wayne

The still small voice that brings calm and comfort is yearning to be heard.

—Susan Jeffers

Freedom is the ability not to care what the other person thinks.

—Seneca

I find the harder I work, the more luck I seem to have.

—Thomas Jefferson

He who asks is a fool for 5 minutes, but he who does not ask is a fool forever.

—Chinese Proverb

If you cannot convince them, confuse them.

—Harry S Truman

Handout 4.6—Your Beliefs—Helpful or Harmful?

It is common for people to have automatic thoughts in the endless parade of mind chatter that cause excessive or prolonged distressing reactions. Mixed in with these or masked by them are global, overgeneralized, absolute *core beliefs* acquired at a young age. How do these caustic self-assessments form?

When an upsetting event occurs, it is often hard to think clearly. Part of the brain may be overexcited, and information, images, and tension related to that incident become frozen in the nervous system. Sometimes, information like, *I'm not safe* or *I'm powerless* is accurate during a traumatic episode. However, feelings of fear persist after the event is over. Other ideas, like *I'm not good enough,* never had any truth and come from years of excessive criticism. Later fearful, inaccurate thoughts may be provoked by situations that are actually harmless.[1]

Identify Your Core Beliefs

Think of a situation or memory that is upsetting. Take a mental snapshot of it. Ask yourself, *What bad thought does this situation give me about myself? How does that person "make me" feel about myself? When I feel, ... I think, I'm ...* For example:

- When I feel guilty, I think, *I'm bad*.
- When I feel scared, I think, *I'm not safe*.
- When I feel sad, I think, *I'm lost, tarnished, incomplete, or alone*.
- When I feel angry, I think, *I'm not in control, a fool, or trapped*.

Feelings can be clues that help identify basic beliefs you have about yourself. The thought itself is often inaccurate or out of date. Use the table on the next page to identify any harmful beliefs you have. Highlight the ideas on the left that get triggered by a particular person, situation, or memory. Also, mark ideas that you think about yourself in your worst moments.

A negative thought is not always a core belief. To uncover any fixed, rigid assumptions you use to judge yourself, keep asking the question, *What does this thought mean about me?*

I should be more cautious. → *What will it mean about me if I'm not more cautious?*
If I'm not more cautious, **I'll make mistakes**. → *What will it mean about me if I make mistakes?*
If I make mistakes, it means **I'm a disappointment**.

Forming Positive Beliefs

Although negative beliefs can be overpowering, they offer clues to remembering and formulating positive thoughts. Look at the harmful beliefs you identify in the following exercise. In the right-hand column, mark ideas that contradict negative thoughts. Also identify beliefs that:

- You would like to have as you picture a difficult person situation or memory.
- You would need to feel safe, satisfied, confident, or calm.
- You already think about yourself in your best moments.

---

1. *Eye Movement Desensitization and Reprocessing: The Breakthrough Therapy for Overcoming Anxiety, Stress, and Trauma,* by F Shapiro, and M. S. Forrest, 1997, New York: HarperCollins, explains the role trauma plays in developing negative thoughts and core beliefs.

Change Beliefs that Hurt[2] ...	Into Beliefs that Help

Powerless/Helpless Beliefs →

❑ I can't, ... shouldn't have to ....
❑ I'm helpless, powerless, weak, or ineffective.
❑ I can't stand it or handle it.
❑ I'm inadequate, defective, or a failure.

Empowering Beliefs

❑ I can do something; I can take care of it myself.
❑ I have choices now; I can recover.
❑ I can stand it, handle it, or succeed.
❑ I'm adequate, effective, competent, or capable.

Unlovable Beliefs →

❑ I'm not good, smart, attractive enough ....
❑ I'm unworthy, unlovable, unlikeable, dirty, a disappointment, different, or unwanted.
❑ I don't deserve love, happiness, or to live.
❑ I'll be ruined, damaged, abandoned, or rejected.

Self-Accepting Beliefs

❑ I'm good, smart, attractive, enough ....
❑ I'm fine, loveable, likeable, desirable, worthy, unique, strong, or innocent.
❑ I deserve love, happiness, to live, to belong.
❑ I can survive, recover, belong, or heal.

Responsibility/Perfectionist Beliefs →

❑ I'm responsible for others or everything.
❑ I should have done something; known better.
❑ I did something wrong; I'm at fault.
❑ I have to be perfect, please everyone, control things, or fix it.

Reasonable Beliefs

❑ I'm only responsible for my part.
❑ I did my best or learned from it.
❑ I can make mistakes or I'm innocent.
❑ I can be myself or understand others (without having to fix them).

Safety and Vulnerability →

❑ I'm not safe; I'm in danger.
❑ I can't be trusted or trust my judgment.
❑ I cannot trust anyone or protect myself.
❑ I might (will) fail, get hurt, make a fool of myself, not get better, die, or be left.
❑ I cannot handle new, unfamiliar situations.

Affirming Beliefs

❑ I am safe now.
❑ I can be trusted; trust my judgment.
❑ I can trust some people and protect myself.
❑ I can succeed, recover, take a day at a time, or handle what happens.
❑ I can enjoy new, unfamiliar situations.

Control and Choice →

❑ I'm trapped; not in control.
❑ I cannot feel (show) emotions, or speak up.
❑ I'm not important; others come first.
❑ I have to be perfect or please everyone.
❑ I can't find caring, understanding, attention, approval, excitement, or a purpose.
❑ I cannot get what I want.

Active Beliefs

❑ I have choices; I'm in control.
❑ I can show emotion, ask, and set limits.
❑ I can decide what's right for the situation.
❑ I can be myself (make mistakes).
❑ I can find understanding, attention, excitement, meaning, and enough of what I (truly) need.
❑ I can meet my needs.

Journaling

Once you identify the negative beliefs and helpful thoughts that can contradict them, you can begin to build self-confidence. Start by keeping a journal of upsetting incidents. Ask yourself questions from the previous page and use the above table to identify the core beliefs that each situation triggered. Write a positive belief you would like to have in its place:

Upsetting Situation	Core (Hurtful) Belief	Positive, Helpful Belief
Boss yelling	I have to please him.	I only have to understand him.
Rude customer	I'm disappointing.	I'm worthy; he has issues.

---

2.   This list of harmful beliefs is a combination of Aaron Beck's major categories of *helpless, unlovable* core beliefs and Francine Shapiro's *responsibility, safety,* and *controlling* negative cognitions.

Handout 4.7 — Pinpointing Core Beliefs

Core beliefs act like weeds that have grown from painful life experiences. The more accurately you can pinpoint the beliefs that make you relive your past, the easier it will be to pull them out by their roots. The actual verbal recordings in your mind have four key features:

1. **They are recorded in present tense** even if they originated in the past. You may have concluded from the fact that you failed the second grade, *I am not bright enough*.

2. **They are generalizations** that delete specific situations from which they originated (failing the second grade).

3. **They are *self-referencing***. It may seem like you are bothered by the thought, *My child doesn't respect me*. Ask yourself, *What does this lack of respect mean about me?* to find out the painful thought about yourself: *I am not in control*.

4. **They are opinions** that you concluded from events and feelings. Thinking *I was powerless* may be an accurate description of your position during a past event. *I'm afraid* expresses your current feelings. *I can't protect myself* is an **opinion** based on an event and your feelings. *I was powerless* and *I'm afraid* are both **facts**.

Core Beliefs

Many core beliefs originate from childhood interactions and are seared in the mind by neurotransmitters released during painful situations. It is also possible to accumulate positive beliefs, but under duress, pesky (stress-related) brain chemicals will trigger your most bedeviling beliefs. You cannot change the events you have experienced, but the opinions about yourself that sprung from them can become unhinged. Instead of thinking, *I'm a fool* (because he cheated on me); you could believe, *I can trust myself* (to take any needed action when others are dishonest). Notice how each of the following feelings, perceptions of events, and comments about others are restated as the underlying beliefs that truly trigger distress.

	CURRENT AND PAST EVENT		CORE BELIEF
	Feelings, EVENTS, Comments About Others		Present Tense, Self-Referencing, General
(a)	I get upset when he makes jealous ACCUSATIONS. He should trust me.	→	I'm a failure (if I cannot get him to believe me).
(b)	I cannot trust her because she CHEATED on me.	→	I cannot survive (without her).
(c)	I'm unsure of myself because my teachers didn't GIVE ME MUCH HELP.	→	I cannot succeed.
(d)	Other people judged me because I MADE A MISTAKE.	→	I'm a rotten person.
(e)	I am bitter because my parents BEAT ME.	→	I cannot ever yield, give in, or relent.
(f)	Others cannot understand the heartache I feel from LOSING MY CHILD.	→	I cannot go on . . . . I'm alone.

Although events (a) and (b) are based in the present, there is a great likelihood that as children these people dealt with issues of having to defend themselves or with being abandoned. Event (f) is the ultimate anguish for any adult regardless of beliefs imprinted from early experiences. In the struggle to bear this sorrow, some people find nourishing beliefs they did not know they had.

Positive Beliefs

After pinpointing verbal recordings that cause distress, it is important to formulate positive belief to take their place. They are empowering assessments that contradict hurtful thoughts. In addition to being generalized, self-referencing conclusions, they have five other characteristics:

1. **They have an internal locus of control.** Although the statement, *People like me,* is self-referencing, it depends on others. Saying *I am likeable* is under your control.

2. **They contradict negative beliefs *as much as* possible**. If the statements, *I'm safe now* or I *can take care of myself*, seem too far-fetched, they can be modified to *I can learn to take care of myself. . . . The worst is over. . . .* or *I did the best I could.* Thus, a positive belief can start out in the past or future tense.

3. **They are valid statements and do not represent wishful thinking**. Statements containing superlatives like *always, never*, or *everyone* are often unrealistic.

4. **They avoid the word *not* and are stated as a positive**. This helps build self-esteem. Any negative words plant seeds of doubt.

5. **They are conclusions or rediscovered truths about yourself** rather than emotions. Feelings are fleeting and have little sustaining value.

When positive beliefs about yourself have the above characteristics, they have lasting value. Notice how each of the statements below have been reworded to form conclusions that would help sustain a calm, neutral, or confident state:

	UNREALISTIC, *Other-Dependent* Ideas or Feelings		Valid, Positive, Self-Referencing Beliefs
(a)	*He* will learn to trust me.	→	I can understand him (rather than make him trust me).
(b)	*She* will not betray me EVER again.	→	I can survive (regardless of what she does).
(c)	I am proud of myself.	→	I can succeed.
(d)	I'll NEVER make that mistake again.	→	I'm a good person (who did something foolish).
(e)	I do not let *others* control me.	→	I can (learn to) speak up for myself.
(f)	I can make *others* understand my pain.	→	I can find support. I can understand myself.

As upsetting as they are, hurtful thoughts hold the keys to their undoing. Sometimes just pinpointing a core negative belief and computing its opposite will give you relief. However, recordings that come from trauma or constant repetition can require a more intense approach. It may be best to do the following with a therapist who can guide you through distressing emotions that often surface: [1]

EXERCISE—LOOKING THROUGH ADULT EYES

- Pick a belief that often comes to your mind in your worst moments. Ask yourself, *When did I first get this idea* (such as, *I have to fix it*)?

- Allow a memory to come to your mind. Notice what room you are in, who is there, what is being said, and how you feel. Guess your approximate age. Take a mental snapshot of the worst part of the memory.

- Look at your younger self with loving eyes and give him or her any information that you know as a rational adult. Find out if the younger you accepts this information. Answer any questions from your younger self with the truths you now know as an adult.

---

1. Ideas in this handout were adapted from *Cognitive Therapy: Basics and Beyond*, 1995, by Judith S. Beck. New York: The Guilford Press.

Handout 4.8—Restructuring Versus Refocusing

When you become angry, anxious, or sad, the first step is to identify the *thought* that is causing the trouble. Once you have identified the bothersome idea, you can (1) *test* it to find out how much truth it has; or (2) *distract* yourself by using various concentration techniques. You simply need to know what to do and when to do it.

As long as your mind is not completely muddled or agitated and you still have some powers of reason, it is best to evaluate your thoughts. It is also important that your surroundings are not highly distracting. There are several ways to assess negative thoughts, beliefs, and images. Use these techniques to consider new ideas. Do not expect yourself to automatically adopt new viewpoints or suddenly feel good. You are embarking on a journey of changing thought patterns.

Test for Truth

EXERCISE 1—QUESTIONING FUNKY THOUGHTS

Question one of your upsetting thoughts or the suggested sample

Upsetting Thought

People will be shocked when they see how much weight I've gained. They'll think I have no self-control.

• Is this thought a fact or an opinion?	• Who do you know with a similar problem who would think differently about it?
• How true is it? (0–100%)	• What different thoughts could I have instead?
• How helpful is it? (0–100%)	• What is the worst, best, and most likely cause or outcome of this thought? (See pie chart)
• What facts do and do not support the idea?	• What would be the effect of changing my thoughts?
• Is there another explanation or possibility?	
• What would I tell my friend/child in this fix?	

New Viewpoint(s)

People will be more concerned about their own issues than calculating my weight gain. I might help those who do notice my weight feel good about themselves.

EXERCISE 2—THOUGHT FALLACIES

Review the list of thinking errors that your thought or the suggested example contains. Then restructure a more reasonable thought.

Upsetting Thought

I know it's my fault that my friend is upset with me because I'm guilty. I have to find a way to fix the problem

☐ **Discounting** any positive facts.	☐ **Magnify** the negatives and **minimize** positives.
☐ **All-or-nothing**, unrealistic thinking.	☑ Thinking you know what others are thinking (**mind reading**).
☑ Jumping to conclusions, exaggerations.	☐ Thinking you know the outcome (**fortune telling**).
☐ Predicting the worst-case scenarios.	☐ Thinking something is true because it feels true (**emotional reasoning**).
☑ **Absolutes**, imperatives (shoulds, musts).	☑ Supporting a statement by repeating it in different or stronger terms (**circular reasoning**).
☐ Using **labels** like loser, lazy, or hopeless.	
☑ Taking responsibility for others' behavior (**personalizing**).	

Reasonable Thought(s)

My friend could be upset because of her own issues, but it might help if I give her space and stop asking what is wrong.

**EXERCISE 3—
BEHAVIOR
EXPERIMENTS**

Sometimes the best way to test and restructure a thought is to conduct an experiment. Suppose you avoid going out in public because you think, *Everyone is looking at me* or *Everyone knows what happened to me.* Consider the easiest test you could do to challenge your belief. Walk to your mail box; spend 5 minutes in a store; or go to a restaurant and notice if people *are* looking at you. Make sure your eyes are not looking down and that you notice interesting things about other people: *Who looks more anxious than me?*

**EXERCISE 4—
PIE CHART
ANALYSIS**

Pie charts are a great way to graphically look at how the thought that has been dominating your mind fits in with all the possible outcomes or causes of a problem. The idea, *People will think my divorce is my fault*, can shrink down to nothing.

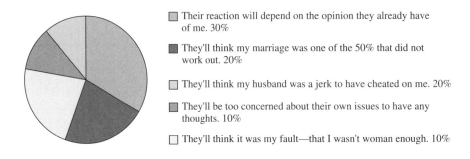

- Their reaction will depend on the opinion they already have of me. 30%
- They'll think my marriage was one of the 50% that did not work out. 20%
- They'll think my husband was a jerk to have cheated on me. 20%
- They'll be too concerned about their own issues to have any thoughts. 10%
- They'll think it was my fault—that I wasn't woman enough. 10%

**EXERCISE 5—
RESTRUCTURING
IMAGES**

Images can be more powerful than thoughts. In Exercise 1, the person could have imagined people being excited to see her, ignoring weight gain, and exchanging updates about their lives. This image can be practiced repeatedly. Conversely, the image of people being shocked can be played over and over. By focusing on details, often such images will change with repetition.

In addition to the preceding exercises, there are simple thought tricks you can use on yourself. Play **devil's advocate** and pretend you are convincing another person (who is in the clutches of your belief) that their idea is invalid. **Compare yourself** to a famous person who faced a similar problem—*Was . . . stupid because she did not realize her husband cheated on her.* Commit yourself to **acting as if** your faulty belief is *not* true for an hour.

Distract and Refocus

When you first start examining and restructuring your thoughts, you may need the help of a counselor. Refocusing is something you have probably already done *on your own* without realizing it. This skill is especially important when you are driving or engaged in an activity that makes evaluating thoughts tough or when a repetitious or grueling idea has a grip on your mind. It is still important to keep a written record of these thought demons for later evaluation and restructuring. In the meantime, when thoughts are bogus, just refocus. The following list can inspire you to be systematic and creative in ways to distract yourself from irksome ideas:

- Turn up the volume on music and pay attention to the lyrics or melody.
- Call someone on your cell phone.

- Describe what you see to yourself or out loud: There is an oak tree coming up on my right, a red car is at the crossroad, there's 10 feet between me and the next car, and so on.

- Count backwards from 100 by 9s or 3s: *100 ... 97... 94. ...* For an extra boost, stare at a spot as you do this.

- Count three breaths, thinking *ah* on the inhale and *men* on the exhale while staring at a spot.

- Recite the Pledge of Allegiance, inhaling and exhaling on each syllable: I ... pledge ... al ... le ... giance ... to ... the ... flag ... of ... the ...

- Count to 10 when you have angry thoughts *(How dare he ..., She should have ...)*. Use the added distraction of rubbing a small spot on the inside of your wrist under your little finger with each count. Press hard.

Handout 4.9—Keep the Good Thoughts Rolling

In the quiet calm of a counselor's office or your own home, you may be able to restructure upsetting thoughts and core beliefs. The trick is to maintain them during the hustle-bustle of life when stressors pop up like landmines. The ideas below will help you accentuate the positive.

Coping Cards

After identifying upsetting automatic thoughts and core beliefs, use standard questions to help restructure new viewpoints: Is this thought a fact or an opinion? Is there another explanation or possibility? What is the worst, best, and most likely cause or outcome? What would I tell my friend or child in this situation? What different thoughts could I have instead?

When you have identified the views you would like to have in situations that trigger distress, write them on a 3-by-5 card and keep it in a handy location. Following are coping cards for the thoughts, (1) *Everyone will be shocked when they see how much weight I've gained*, and (2) *I have to prove to people that I'm good enough.*

<table>
<tr>
<td>

- *People are too worried about them-selves to notice that I've gained 30 pounds.*
- *I'll make everyone else feel better about themselves.*
- *I've gained weight but I've lost my foolish pride.*

(1)

</td>
<td>

- *I can let other people think what they want.*
- *Everyone is not capable of recognizing my worth.*
- *Being underestimated can give me an advantage.*

(2)

</td>
</tr>
</table>

Positive Rein-forcement

There are many ways to reinforce sound reasoning. Once you have identified the thoughts and beliefs that cause you distress, start to pay particular attention to any positive thoughts that pop into your mind. They may come from a coping card or arrive unexpectedly like divine gifts—*It's fine for me to take the road where my mother had her car accident; I'll be perfectly safe.* To remain positive, make a mental note of each beneficial thought and, as soon as you can, tally the number of spontaneous, sound ideas you have had on a calendar or day planner. Even if you only had two impromptu, upbeat ideas, consider it an accomplishment. Seeing tally marks buildup is good visual reinforcement. Use the following exercise to reward yourself for encouraging views.

EXERCISE—BRAIN INSTALLATION[1]

Whether you are intentionally thinking of an idea from one of your coping cards or are visited by a lovely lucid thought, you can embed it in your mind by massaging the spot between your eyebrows with a gentle upward pressure. Use your index finger with your hands in a prayer position. Press a little more deeply with each exhale. To sink the beneficial belief even deeper, shift both of your eyes to the right and then to the left (on either side of your hands) about 20 times while thinking the thought. Later, just touching this middle eyebrow spot may bring the idea back to your mind.

---

1. This exercise makes use of ideas from three approaches: (1) The spot between the eyebrows is the Third Eye (Governing Vessel, 24.5) point in the acupressure system. It can calm the body and relieve nervousness. Moving the eyes to the right and left is a procedure in Eye Movement Desensitization and Reprocessing Therapy (EMDR) to process disturbing material and install positive cognitions. Neuro Linguistic Programming (NLP) pairs an *anchor* with a resourceful state (or thought). Eventually, the anchor can be *fired* and the resourceful state accessed just by touching the designated spot.

In addition to keeping tally marks of positive thoughts that spontaneously occur, make lists of any activities that you consider a tiny accomplishment or slightly enjoyable. These can also be kept on calendars and planners. This helps build the beliefs, *I'm competent; I'm capable; I can meet my needs.* These are not to-do lists, which can be discouraging for people who think it is taking them too long to mark-off designated tasks. Instead, at various times during the day or at the end of the day, write down what you've accomplished or enjoyed. Do not forget to include such items as staying calm while your coworker was being critical, writing the first paragraph of a paper that is due, or cleaning one corner of your bedroom.

Have-Done Lists

Problems arise when an obstacle makes it difficult to achieve a desired goal or purpose. The situation becomes more complicated when people make decisions too quickly (or too slowly) to resolve the issue. Sometimes a decision is not actually made and people simply act without thinking. Strong emotions are often the culprits that propel people toward impulsive action. Likewise, anxiety can paralyze someone from taking a chance when something must be done. A flood of feelings can create fixations on only one possible solution, which seems out of reach. If you are faced with the horns of a dilemma, there are several steps you can take to apply rational thought to the situation:

The Problem With Problems

- Define the problem: This situation makes it difficult to achieve this goal.
- Identify thoughts, rules, and beliefs that contribute to the problem.
- Compute a rational viewpoint that would help you achieve your goal.
- Generate a list of possible actions with the advantages and disadvantages of each one. Be sure to include incremental measures.
- Choose the latest possible deadline before you need to take your smallest step.

PROBLEM-SOLVING WORKSHEET

Problem: *My lack of feelings for my spouse seriously interferes with my ability to act pleasant or to want to spend time with her. We've tried counseling several times.*

Thoughts/rules/beliefs: *Divorce is wrong. I cannot let my child be hurt.*

Rational viewpoint: *Divorce is a choice. I cannot control my child's happiness, and she can also be hurt by seeing a dysfunctional marriage.*

Problem-Solving Steps	Advantages	Disadvantages
1. *Tell my wife the truth about my lack of feelings now and maybe in the past.*	*- I might resent her less, and she'll have a chance to make her own decision.*	*- My wife could be hurt or angry.*
2. *Spend less time with my wife and set limits on what she can do with me.*	*- I could find out if I truly miss my wife. This would also help my wife make a decision.*	*- My wife would be hurt and be especially angry.*
3. *Tell my wife I've had an affair, which the other woman ended.*	*- My wife would definitely end the marriage.*	*- It would cause my wife unnecessary hurt.*
4. *Stay married for the sake of our daughter.*	*- My 8-year-old daughter would not have to deal with a divorce.*	*- I'd continue to snap at my wife and just put off an inevitable divorce.*
5. *Get a divorce now or separate to find out if this is what I want.*	*- I wouldn't be leaving my wife for another woman; I'd be honest.*	*- I'd worry about my daughter.*

Deadline: *Complete step 1 before my next counseling appointment in 2 weeks.*

Handout 4.10—Be the Boss of Your Brain: A Workshop for Children

Here is a tricky question that many people do not know:
What makes you feel sad, mad, or afraid?

(a)   Other people and the things that happen to you.

(b)   The thoughts you have *about* other people and the things that happen.

If you guessed (b), GOOD JOB! When you have to deal with someone who is a pain or get smacked with a ton of troubles, you *will* feel upset. But a parade of *automatic* thoughts will also start marching through your mind.

Noticing Your Ideas

The first step to becoming the boss of your thoughts is to notice which ideas are popping up. In the exercise below, match the thought(s) that go with each situation:

THOUGHT MATCH

Situation	Automatic Thought
1. Your dad is often busy with work.	_____ I'll never be able to please her.
2. Your friend acts like you don't exist.	_____ I must be stupid. I'll never get it right.
3. Your mom reminds you to do your chore when you were just about to start it.	_____ I must have done something wrong.
4. You made a bad grade on your math test.	_____ Something bad could happen when I'm away from home.
5. You usually have a stomachache before going to school.	__1__ I don't matter. I need time with him for me to feel happy.

Answers: Noticing ideas—3, 4, 2, 5.

Noticing Thinking Errors

It not only helps to be able to notice which ideas are popping up, but also if those ideas have errors. In the exercise below, match the type of thinking error with the example on the right. More than one error can apply to some examples:[2]

THOUGHT MATCH

Thinking Error	Automatic Thought
1. Lousy labels	_____ I'll never be able to please her.
2. All-or-nothing thoughts	_____ I must be stupid.
3. Predicting the worst	_____ If I can't do it right, I should give up.
4. Unrealistic expectations —shoulds	__5__ I must have done something wrong.
5. Taking responsibility for others	_____ Something bad could happen when I'm away.
6. Mind reading and fortune telling	_____ I don't matter to him.
7. Blow up the bad; blow off the good	_____ He should spend time with me so I can be happy.

Answers: Thinking errors—3, 1, 2, 5, 6, 6, 7, or 4.

The biggest thinking error of all involves mistakes about what you can and cannot change. This brings up the next tricky question: What do you have the power to change?

(a) Other people

(b) The things that happen to you

(c) Your thoughts

(d) Your feelings

This time (c) is the right answer. It is hard to stop *feeling* afraid, when you *think* something bad could happen. Guilty feelings won't go away until you stop imagining that you did something wrong. You cannot change others. Instead of trying to make over family and friends, change your own thoughts.

Any person or situation can be looked at from a different angle. It is surprising how quickly your feelings change when you find a new viewpoint. Use the following questions to examine if your thoughts are true or helpful and discover new ways to see a situation:

Changing Your Thoughts

a. What facts do or do not support this idea?

b. Is there another explanation?

c. What is the best, the worst, and the most likely outcome or fact?

d. How does this thought help or hurt me?

e. What would I want my best friend to think if he or she had to deal with this?

f. What would I like to believe about myself in this situation?

After you have found the errors in the automatic thoughts, use the above questions to form more valid, helpful ideas. The letter for each question that helped change the thought are given. Fill in the missing words.

CHANGE YOUR THOUGHTS

Automatic Thought*	New Viewpoint
1. I don't matter to him. He should spend time with me so I can be happy.	My dad does other things that show he cares about me. I can find other ways to make myself _____. b,e,f
2. I must have done something wrong because my friend is ignoring me.	My friend could have her own _____. I've made new friends in the past and I can do it again. b,e,f
3. I'll never be able to please my mom.	It's okay for my mom to expect too much, because I know when I'm on _____. c,d,e,f
4. If I can't do it right, I should give up.	The more I practice, the _____ I'll get. b,e,f
5. I must be stupid.	Lots of _____ people get bad grades in math. a,b,e,f
6. Something bad could happen at home when I'm at school.	It's unlikely that something bad will happen when I'm at school; I can't _____ what happens anyway. a,c,d

Missing Words (New Viewpoints): 1. happy; 2. issues; 3. track; 4. better; 5. smart; 6. control.

Thoughts Cause Feelings

Now we are right back where we started. The *thoughts* you have about other people and events make you feel upset or calm. Which **automatic thought*** would make you have the following feelings? Write the number of the automatic thought(s) after each feeling:

Hopeless ＿＿, ＿＿, sad ＿＿, ashamed, ＿＿, worried ＿＿, guilty ＿＿, angry, ＿＿.

Notice how much better the new viewpoints make you feel. They will start you on the pathway to the **7Cs** —feeling **c**alm, **c**onfident, **c**urious, **c**aring, **c**ourageous, **c**onnected, and **c**lear. At first you may need some help to flip your thoughts. Once you learn some tricks, other people or events will matter less as you take charge of your mind.

Handout 4.11 — Power Thinking: Beyond Affirmations

Such titles as *Think and Grow Rich, The Power of Positive Thinking,* and *The Secret* suggest that thoughts emit positive and negative frequencies, which draw people and experiences with similar vibrations back to you. Likes attract likes. Therefore, by focusing on images and thoughts of what you want, you can bring more abundance into your life. These ideas can seem like pseudoscience to skeptics. However, the methods they suggest employ sound psychological principles.

Nix the Negatives

The underlying theme that runs throughout putting the law of attraction into action is to state things in the affirmative, rather than as a negative. This is a well-known hypnotic principle. If you tell someone, "Don't be nervous," all the mind hears is, *Be nervous.* The following are examples of how to change any of the DON'Ts you are thinking or saying into DOs:

I don't want to argue.	*I want to understand your point.*
No one is interested in me.	*Someone somewhere is interested in my life.*
I can't stop snacking.	*I can feel satisfied between meals.*
I don't have enough money to	*I have enough money for . . . .*

Employ positive language as you begin to practice the basic steps of the law of deliberately attracting what you want into your life.

Step 1: Know What You Want

Whenever you notice yourself thinking about what you do not want or like, ask yourself, *What do I want?* Spend only enough time thinking about the things that displease you to identify the change you would like to happen. Focus on one area of your life: your job, the way you eat, your relationship, your finances, and so on. List several things that are bothering you about this issue, and quickly write the change you want, avoiding negative words. The following examples are only beginning lists:

DESIRES	
IDEAL WORK PLACE	*IDEAL EATING HABITS*
~~People being critical.~~ → *People giving compliments.* ~~People don't like me.~~ → *People do like me.* ~~Feeling tense with people who don't like me.~~ → *Being comfortable with people who dislike me.*	~~Snacking often.~~ → *Satisfied between meals.* ~~Can't resist sweets.~~ → *Easily resist sweets.* ~~Eat large portions.~~ → *Eat optimum portions.*
IDEAL RELATIONSHIP — PARTNER …	*IDEAL FINANCIAL SITUATION*
~~Not interested in me.~~ → *Asks questions about me.* ~~Ignores my input.~~ → *Considers my input.* ~~Frequent arguments.~~ → *We both understand the other's point.*	~~Income too low.~~ → *Increased income.* ~~Pay bills late.~~ → *Pay bills on time.* ~~Too much debt.~~ → *Pay off debt in a timely manner.*

Step 2: Make Statements of Desire

Once you have identified what you want, the next step is to turn it into a statement. This is different than a standard affirmation, which is stated in the first person as a declaration of fact.

The affirmation, *I am satisfied between meals,* might raise doubts . Various phrases placed before an affirmation can make it more valid—*I love how it feels when I am satisfied between meals:*

- *I love knowing that . . . ; I love how it feels when . . . ; I love the idea of . . . ; I love seeing myself . . .*
- *It excites me . . . ; I'm excited at the thought of . . .*
- *I can find all the information I need to . . . ; The clues (people) I need to . . . will come to me . . .*
- *I've decided I am going to . . .*
- *More and more I am . . . ; I'm in the process of creating (enjoying, becoming, attracting) . . .*

STATEMENTS	
I've decided to pay particular attention when … *I notice coworkers saying nice things to me.*	*It's amazing when …* *I can be around sweets and not eat them.*
I love the idea that … *my partner will Considers my input.*	*More and more I can notice when …* *I have extra cash to pay bills.*

Often, people complain about being around negative people. Instead, use their constant fretting to practice thinking in terms of desires. When they whine, ask, "What would you like to happen?" This employs two important principles, one from assertiveness and the other from hypnosis.

When speaking to yourself or others:

1. Ask for what you want, rather than complaining about what you do not want.

2. Make suggestions as a statement of fact that is hard to deny—your hand can move or become still.

Step 3: Decrease Doubts and Limiting Beliefs

Even when statements of desire are stated factually in ways that are hard to deny, doubts are likely to surface. These limiting beliefs are easy to recognize with the words *That will never happen because . . . ; My partner will never consider my input because. . . .* Doubts and limiting beliefs block people from noticing any heartening changes that are happening. This prevents people from using the most basic psychological principle of all: Positive reinforcement increases the probability of a response's reoccurrence in the future. There are several ways to remove doubt from your mind and accentuate the positive:

1. Notice anything that approaches the change you want and acknowledge it: *I came close this time.* Use bad experiences to express more clearly want you want: *We did this part well. Next time I'd like it if we do. . . .*

2. Any time you get a fraction of the desired change you want, notice it, record it, and express gratitude: *This is really helping; I was able go without snacking for 2 hours; We talked a little at dinner; I'm grateful that I was able to . . . ; I appreciate that . . . happened.*

3. Instead of wondering why the change you want isn't fully present, use the expression, *Lots can happen in the next few days* (weeks, months, and so on).

4. Write an allowing statement in the third person. Is anyone doing or accomplishing what you want to do? How many people have done it today or yesterday? *Millions of people are . . . ; Everyday . . . happens; Hundreds of people are able to find extra money to pay their bills; Smart people are able to show their partners they understand what each other is saying.*

Handout 4.12—Power Thinking Worksheet

Life Issue: _____

Name an area of your life that is bothering you—your job, eating habits, relationship, finances, and so on.

Step I: A. What I Don't Like	B. What I Would Like
(What bothers you about this issue **Example:** ~~*Don't feel full after a meal.*~~)	(Write the change you want. Do not use negatives. **Example:** *Feel satisfied after my last bite.*)
	Cross out [A] as soon as you write [B].
1. _____	1. _____
2. _____	2. _____
3. _____	3. _____
4. _____	4. _____
5. _____	5. _____
6. _____	6. _____

Step II: Desire Statement

Write a desire statement for each item you listed in I.B. It should begin with such phrases as *I love knowing that I can . . .; I love how it feels when I . . .; I love the idea of . . .; I love seeing myself . . .; It excites me to think . . .; I can find all the information I need to . . .; I've decided to . . .; I'm in the process of . . . .*

Example: *It excites me to think . . . I can feel satisfied after my last bite of food.*

1. _____
2. _____
3. _____
4. _____
5. _____
6. _____

Step III: Decrease Doubts

A. **Allowing Statements:** Change thoughts like *This will never happen because . . .* into third-person statements that begin, *Hundreds of people can . . .; Every day more and more people are . . . .*

   Example: *Every day thousands of people stop eating before they finish all the food on their plate.*

1. _____
2. _____
3. _____

B. **Document Change and Express Gratitude:** *I came close to . . .; I'm grateful that . . . .*

1. _____	4. _____
2. _____	5. _____
3. _____	6. _____

Handout 4.13—Thought Record Form

		What was going through my mind when *X* happened? What does ... mean about me?			Adaptive Ideas		
Date	Event	Automatic Thoughts(s)—% Believed	Feeling % Upset	Thinking Errors	New Viewpoint—% Believed	Feeling % Upset
8/5	Doing school work/returning to school.	1. It's unacceptable for me to home school (If I'm too anxious)....I have to be normal.	Tense 90%	All-or —nothing	1. It would be OK for someone else with anxiety to home school.	Tense — 30% Accepting 60%
		2. It's not normal to home school.	Shame 95%	Exaggeration	2. I would not judge someone else who needed to home school.	Caring 70% 0%

FEELINGS: **afraid,** anxious, confused, doubtful, nervous, powerless, restless, shaky, suspicious, tense, terrified, threatened, timid, uneasy, unsure, worried; **sad,** alone, alienated, ashamed, despair, desperate, disappointed, discouraged, dismayed, empty, guilty, grief, heartbroken, humiliated, lost, rejected, tired, useless; **angry,** annoyed, betrayed, bitter, deprived, disgusted, dissatisfied, distrustful, enraged, frustrated, hostile, resentful, wronged.

THINKING ERRORS: absolutes (should, musts, always, nevers), assumptions, circular reasoning, exaggerations, exclusions (of positives), mind reading, fortune telling, unrealistic expectations , overgeneralizations, polarizations (all-or-nothing), personalizing (assuming you cause of others' misconduct), labeling.

HELPFUL QUESTIONS: What facts do/do not support this idea? Is there another explanation? What is the worst, best, or most likely outcome? What would I want my friend or child to think? In what way is this thought helpful and harmful? What would the effect be of changing my outlook?

Handout 4.14—Thought Changer Forms

Write one of your disturbing thoughts in the top row. Use the questions to evaluate it and write a new viewpoint in the bottom row.

Question-ing Funky Thoughts

Upsetting Thought(s):

Is this thought a fact or an opinion? How true is it? (0–100%) How helpful is it? (0–100%) What facts do and do not support the idea? Is there another explanation or possibility? What is the worst, best, and most likely outcome?	What would I tell my friend or child in this situation? Who do you know with a similar problem who would think differently about this? What different thoughts could I have instead? What would be the effect of changing my thinking?

New Viewpoint(s):

Write one of your disturbing thoughts in the top row. Check any thinking errors you have made. Formulate a more reasonable thought in the bottom row.

Thinking Errors

Upsetting Thought(s):

_____ Discounting any positive facts. _____ All-or-nothing thinking. _____ Jumping to conclusions. _____ Predicting the worst-case scenarios. _____ Unrealistic expectations (shoulds, musts). _____ Using labels like *loser, lazy,* or *hopeless.* _____ Taking responsibility for others' behavior (personal-izing).	Magnify the negatives and minimize positives. Thinking you know what others are thinking (mind reading). Thinking you know the outcome (fortune telling). Thinking something is true because it feels true (emotional reasoning). Supporting a statement by repeating it in different or stronger terms (circular reasoning).

Reasonable Thought(s):

(1) List all the possible outcomes or causes for a problem that have been troubling you. For example, *People will think my divorce is all my fault; people's reaction will depend on the opinion they already have of me;* and so on. Or, *I did something to upset my friend; My friend could have a problem and she's not ready to talk about it; Any mistake I made would not justify my friend rejecting me;* and so on. (2) Give a percentage rating of how much each factor contributes to your problem or how likely each outcome might be. (3) Use your percentage ratings to draw a pie chart that shows all possible causes or outcomes. (4) Title your chart: POSSIBLE REASONS FOR . . ., or POSSIBLE CAUSES OF . . . .

Pie Chart Analysis

___% **1.** _____

___% **2.** _____

___% **3.** _____

___% **4.** _____

___% **5.** _____

___% **6.** _____

CHAPTER 5

CONSTRUCTIVE SELF-TALK:

For Ego State Therapy, Psychosynthesis, Internal Family Systems Therapy, Creative Cognitive Therapy

MINI INDEX TO CHAPTER 5

Help clients:

1. Collaborate with treatment by providing information that shows how to use mindful observations and questions to create dialogues with personality parts.
2. Practice turning rambling mind chatter into constructive self-talk.
3. Compose self-talk in a written format for journaling.
4. Examine the concept of the personality parts through imagery and experiential exercises.
5. Organize information on self-talk and personality parts into a format for workshops

Using the Handouts

- **Informed consent:** *Creative Cognitive Therapy, Three Steps to Self-Talk, and Examples of Constructive Self-Talk* meet the ethical obligation to provide clients information about employing personality parts in treatment. *Therapy for Self-Empowerment* (3.1) provides a broader theoretical basis of the principles of the multiplicity of the mind understood by ego state therapists, internal family systems, psychosynthesis, and others.

- **General literature:** *Creative Cognitive Therapy, Three Steps to Self-Talk,* and *Examples of Constructive Self-Talk, Turning Thoughts into Parts.*

- **Specific Problems:** *How to Talk to All Your Parts: A Worksheet for Children.*

- **Forms:** *Self and Parts Record, Self-Talk Record.*

Groups and Presentations

- ***Turning Thoughts Into Parts*** can be used in conjunction with ***The Drama of the Subdivided Mind*** (3.3) and ***Connecting With Your Self*** (3.6) for a workshop on Creative Cognitive Therapy. Participants can name images that represent their *Directing* or *Distracting* thoughts.

- ***Self-Talk Case Study*** provides a means to demonstrate self-talk (ego state) therapies. There are several advantages to role-playing a case example over watching other types of demonstrations. (a) Video clips are not always audible; (b) the person in the video cannot be questioned about their experience; (c) role-players can comment on their experience, even though the enactment is not their own material; (d) attendees have a script to review and study; (e) prepared, thought-provoking questions can be asked about the script.

- ***Self-Talk Worksheet*** can be used in groups of twos and threes as a step-by-step guide to reword disturbing thoughts in the second person, name personality parts, identify the true Selves, and begin inner dialogues. It can also be completed individually for journaling.

- ***Fantasy Self-Talk*** is an excellent small-group exercise. It can be used when individual treatment is at an impasse or to help interpret dreams.

Cautions and Comments

- ***Self-Talk Case Study*** is based on an actual *ego state therapy* session. It was adapted for the ***Automatic Thoughts Handouts*** (4.3—Cognitive Therapy). It offers an excellent opportunity to compare these two approaches. When role-playing the case study, use the actual Rider Waite Tarot Deck, which can be ordered online. A queen of hearts doll can also be ordered online or a Queen of Hearts from an ordinary card deck can be used.

- **Self-Talk Journals** provides an example of the steps in the **Self-Talk Worksheet**. The **Self-Talk Record** is a form that simplifies journaling.

- **The Community of Self** (3.12) from chapter **3** offers a metaphor and diagram that illustrates the interaction between subvocal voices and the Self.

- **How to Talk to All Your Parts** is designed for children and should be completed *with* them (not independently at home). Parents can be given this handout to teach their children self-talk and to further reinforce concepts in their own minds. It can be paired with **Be the Boss of Your Brain** (4.10) to teach a creative approach to cognitive therapy.

- **Selves and Parts Record** can be used as a worksheet to help clients list their inner voices or it can be kept in charts to keep track of images and props clients have used for their ego states. This record is also helpful when working with dissociative identity disorder clients who have alters.

Sources and Acknowledgments Not Referenced in the Handouts

The Hidden Figure Exercise in *Fantasy Self-Talk* is adapted from an article by Hanscarl, Leuner, MD, "Guided Affective Imagery (GAI)," *American Journal of Psychotherapy,* Vol. XXIII, No. 1, pp. 4–22, 1/69; Also found at www.synthesiscenter.org/articles/0340.pdf.

Empowering Dialogues Within: A Workbook for Helping Professionals and Their Clients, by Kate Cohen-Posey (John Wiley & Sons, Inc. 2008), has many case examples.

Psychosynthesis: A Collection of Basic Writings, by Roberto Assagioli (Synthesis Center, 1965/2000) offers the original ideas on the Self and subpersonalities.

Embracing Our Selves: The Voice Dialogue Manual, by Hal and Sidra Stone (New World Library, 1989), gives instructions for their psychodramatic approach to inner voices.

Internal Family Systems Therapy, by Richard Schwartz (Guilford Press, 1995), offers theory and a protocol for his approach to the Self and parts.

Handout 5.1—Creative Cognitive Therapy—Informed Consent

Cognitive therapy begins by identifying the automatic thoughts that cause distress. A creative touch can be added by: (1) rewording upsetting ideas in the second person (*I'm not good enough* becomes *You're not good enough*) and (2) adding an image that could be voicing the disturbing belief. Turning thoughts into their original format—the opinions that came from caretakers, teachers, and peers—and representing them pictorially uses your creativity to distance from them.

Emoticon Images

Emoticons are the simplest way of representing your controlling, pushy, or critical beliefs and turning them into objects that can be observed and questioned. A sequence of colons, parentheses, dashes, and so on can turn an emotion into an icon—saying more with less.[1]

Directing Voices. The emoticons below are designed for broad categories of *directing* automatic thoughts that try to maintain control, prevent catastrophes, keep you on task, help you fit in, and avoid mistakes of any kind:

}:^[	(8-\	>8-[	~:- I	>:^<
Controller	**Protector**	**Pusher**	**Pleaser**	**Critic**
Don't think about it.	What if *you* have another panic attack?	*You* don't do enough.	*You* can't upset anyone.	*You* don't measure up.

Distracting Voices. Emoticons can also be designed for *distracting* automatic thoughts that attempt to control the world by blaming, clinging, avoiding, or tempting. This mental chatter is littered with third-person pronouns (*he, she, it,* and *they*) and requires no rewording for beliefs that treat loved ones and acquaintances as objects:

#:^0	IB'-( )	:-0	>:-)~
Judger/blamer	**Clinger**	**Withdrawer**	**Abuser**
He shouldn't curse!	*She* has to love me!	It's none of *their* business.	Smoking pot calms your nerves.

The Self. Distracting, distressing thoughts are only one side of self-talk dialogue. It also helps to have an image for the real you, full of awareness and wonder, that can calmly observe and question the most dismaying thoughts.

>:^<	**Critic:** You're a fool if you let anyone ever betray you again.
8-)	**Self:** That's a tall order (observation). *How does others' lack of integrity make you a fool?*

Using Emoticons

Emoticons and other types of feeling face images can be drawn on the lower half of a 3-by-5 card, folded in half, and stood upright. During self-talk dialogues, the distressing or distracting voice can be faced and have its message questioned—*Does giving yourself orders to keep others from betraying you provide an illusion of control?* Then listen within for a response from the troubled part. You can sense if the image of your calm Self needs more distance from a demanding thought or if it wants to move closer. Simply seek understanding of all inner voices.

---

1. These emoticon images were taken from *Empowering Dialogues Within,* by K. Cohen-Posey, 2008, Hoboken, NJ: John Wiley & Sons.

Your true Self is compassionate, calm, and curious. If you notice frustration or a desire to rid yourself of a cruel inner critic or a desperate people pleaser, this is the agenda of another personality part. Your witness within simply observes—*When you put everyone's needs first, another part gets mad and doesn't want to do anything for anyone*. If more than one personality part enters the dialogue, it helps to draw its image to keep track of all inner voices.

Other Props[2]

Emoticons offer a bare skeleton of a face. Many artists provide perfect images for personality parts and for the curious, observant center of your being. Edvard Munch's famous painting, *The Scream*, is ideal for protective voices that predict:

- *What if your boss thinks the new assistant is doing a better job than you?*

- *What if you have another panic attack?*

- *If you have a "bad thought," you might cause someone you care about to get into an accident.*

The standard Rider Waite Tarot Deck is full of pictures and symbols that can help people find attributes of their calm, peaceful center. A fifth-grader who had to take three steps backward anytime she had a negative thought about someone in her family found comfort in a Tarot image she called her *Secure Self* that could ask—*What is the chance of your thoughts causing a loved one to have an accident?*

Literary Characters

Tarot Card

Literary characters create powerful portraits for inner parts. Many people identify with the personalities that populate A. A. Milne's 100-acre wood. Eeyore is gloomy; Piglet is fearful; Rabbit is the clever critic; and Owl is arrogant. But what about Pooh? Pooh just *is* and offers the perfect model of not being bothered even if he gets stuck in the door to Piglet's house from eating too much honey. It is easy to find stuffed animals of these characters and use them to represent disturbing automatic thoughts. They can be faced with observations and questions, and a wonderful tactile dimension is added.

Piglet and Pooh can start a brainstorm of ideas for other household items found in toy chests or jewelry boxes that can stand for troubling thoughts and the observant Self. Thinking *I have to ...* or *I should have ...* identifies you with those thoughts. Visualizing the parts of your personality that are making disturbing comments and having them speak *at* you in second person—*You have to ...; You should have*—is a step toward disidentifying with them and becoming aligned with your true being that can reflect what is happening without absorbing misguided messages.

---

2. The copy of *The Scream,* first painted in 1893 by Edvard Munch and reproduced as a lithograph in 1895, was retrieved on June 6, 2009, from http://en.wikipedia.org/wiki/The_Scream. The tarot image (Ace of Pentacles) comes from the *Rider Waite Tarot Deck* (1909) and was retrieved from http://en.wikipedia.org/wiki/Rider-Waite-Smith deck on June 6, 2009.

Handout 5.2—Three Steps to Self-Talk

Random automatic thoughts are part and parcel of **monologues** that switch course and ramble indefinitely. Mental chatter like the following is typical:

I should have never called my boss and told him how slammed we are. Now he's going to send someone in from another office that actually has experience in corporate finance, and my accounting degree will look like a sham. He'll think I'm a complete fraud. I don't know how he could leave me in charge of this department when he went back to corporate ... and now I have to go back to the office and face everyone since our payroll got lost in the mail. I'm sure they all blame me. I think I'm going to get sick.

A runaway monologue can cause depression, panic attacks, phobias of all kinds, angry outbursts, and hopelessness. Life intervenes. Friends and family offer reassurance, and some people will adopt *internal allies* and talk to or debate themselves.

Debates

---

a. My boss is going to send someone in from another office that has real experience in corporate finance ... He'll think I'm a total fraud.

b. He knows you're a hard worker (encouraging) and you've been managing with an accounting degree. Maybe he's just trying to help (reassurance).

c. I just can't stop feeling uneasy. I'll always be playing catch-up to her.

d. Why would you think that? You excelled in school even though you were younger than everyone. Pull yourself together (ordering)!

e. And what about the payroll? People will chop my head off. What will they say?

f. It's not your fault some turkey lost the mail. Just ignore them (impossible demand)!

g. (Heart racing) Oh my God, I'm starting to panic!

Debates are an improvement over monologues and occur naturally, but they pose problems. Reassurance, suggestions, and demands create resistance. They come from a part of the personality that is trying to impose its position and force constructive action.

When a person (we'll call "Amy") is coached to respond to random thoughts with *observations* and *questions*, she can engage in genuine dialogue or constructive self-talk. The source of the ability to notice and query thoughts without any agenda is a person's *true Self*:

Dialogue

---

a. **Thought:** Your boss is going to send someone in from another office that has actual experience in corporate finance.... He'll think you're a complete fraud.

b. **Self:** You *assume* Amy's boss won't think she's good enough and you make her *feel inadequate* with your worries (o). How will that help her (q)?

c. **Worrier:** She won't measure up and she'll never stop worrying.

d. **Self:** You're the part that *compares* her to others and makes her *worry* (o).

e. **Worrier:** (Quiet, seems calmer).

Constructive self-talk is semihypnotic. Two features of trance induction are used: (1) **observations** reduce resistance: *You assume Amy's boss won't think she's good enough* . . . ; and (2) **questions** focus attention inward: *How will [assuming] help her?* The Self seeks the meaning of upsetting thoughts and listens with all its presence for responses to emerge. Although not the first to speak, it is the inner witness that initiates true dialogue.

Steps to Constructive Self-Talk[1]

Most mental chatter comes from thoughts or personality parts in charge of controlling emotions, preventing catastrophes, completing tasks, placating others, and self-correction. Occasionally, you have heard a *still, small voice* that understands, knows the meaning of events, and always brings a sense of calm. Your *true Self, inner witness,* or *core being* can be hard to hear when automatic thoughts are extreme in their efforts to control, protect, push, please, or criticize. However, when mental chatter is distressing, your true Self can use calming self-talk with three quick steps: (A) observe; (B) question; and (C) listen.

Inner critic: Your boss won't think you're as good as the new person he hires.

A. **Observe** the type of message a personality part is making. It can help to write an actual phrase that you hear in second person:

1. Starting with the word *you* or *your* provides distance from disturbing mental chatter.

2. Saying *I'm not good enough* keeps you identified with the distressing idea.

3. Ask what part of you is generating the upsetting thought—an inner controller, *protector, pusher, people pleaser, critic* (or any other name you like)?

4. Look at the upsetting statement. How would you label it?

5. Is it an order, demand, doubt, guess, or a reminder? Is it scolding, blaming or disapproving? The above inner critic is *assuming* Amy's boss won't think she is as good as the new person.

6. Make observations about the impact of specific messages. Cruel comments from friends and family hurt, but they are particularly painful when they come from within. Misguided mental chatter can cause pressure, fear, hopelessness, guilt, sadness, anger, insecurity, jealousy, tension, panic, and so on. The witness within can now observe:

Self: When Amy assumes her boss won't think she's good enough, she feels insecure.

B. **Question** controlling, pushy, critical parts to fully initiate constructive self-talk:

1. How will those assumptions (guesses, nags . . .) help?

2. What is the chance of . . . actually happening (1 out of 100, 1,000, 10,000, 1,000,000 . . .)?

3. Where did Amy first get that idea? Why are you bringing this up now?

4. What do you mean by . . . ? Can Amy ever be good enough?

5. Is there another personality part you're holding back?

6. Do you think you'll have no purpose if you stop being critical?

C. **Listen:** Turn inward to hear upsetting thoughts that come from subvocal doubters or people pleasers. Silence means you have found *peace of mind*, even if just for a moment. When a personality part attempts to debate, respond with another observation or question.

The Purpose of Self-Talk

The goal of self-talk is to engage distressing/distracting thoughts (personality parts) in a dialogue to better recognize their meaning, origin, and purpose. It is not necessary to restructure thoughts and beliefs. The less identified a person is with extreme messages (A.1) and the better they are understood, the less dominant they will be in a person's psyche.

---

1. These steps are fully explained in *Empowering Dialogues Within,* by K. Cohen-Posey, 2008, Hoboken, NJ: John Wiley & Sons.

Handout 5.3—Examples of Constructive Self-Talk

Thought patterns that scold, demand, and remind come from parts of the personality that try to keep wayward emotions and traits in check. In the process, they take on a life of their own and seem to have *subpersonalities*. Beyond your personality is the pure awareness of the *mirror mind* that reflects mental chatter without becoming absorbed in it. This *witness* persistently makes observations and asks questions in order to *engage* personality parts, rather than to change beliefs. The following example shows many features of self-talk that are often calming.

Stacy was molested by her uncle from the ages of 3 to 7 years old. While she does not always think about those early events, a critical part can torment her. In a recent journal entry, Stacy wrote, *I'm so cocky, but I don't know what I'm doing.* Her counselor helped coach her true Self to observe and question her inner critic so that it would no longer be the boss of her being.

a. **Critic:** You're so cocky, but you don't know what you're doing.

b. **Self:** Why do you think Stacy is cocky?

c. **Critic:** She acts like she knows it all and she doesn't.

d. **Self:** You have a horrible opinion of Stacy.

e. **Critic:** She always messes up and makes mistakes.

f. **Self:** Do you have trouble seeing her decent qualities, or do you not want to see them?

g. **Critic:** Both—nothing Stacy does is good enough. Even at her best, I can find flaws.

h. **Self:** You give her a hard time and you're awesome at it.

i. **Critic:** She deserves it because she does stupid things.

j. **Self:** What would happen if you stopped giving Stacy a hard time?

k. **Unnamed part:** She'd feel better.

l. **Critic:** No one asked you—if I don't give Stacy a hard time, she'd do more dumb things and make bad choices like she did . . . (stops speaking, withdraws).

m. **Self:** Are you thinking about the molestation? Do you think it was her fault? If you're hard enough on her, do you think you can stop other bad stuff? (Nods yes.) You've been around since Stacy was young and you're trying to keep her safe from her uncle.

n. **Critic:** Quiet, sense of relief.

The self-talk begins by changing the upsetting thought, *I don't know what I'm doing*, into the second person—*you don't know what you're doing* (a). Stacy's counselor coaches her Self to ask questions and make observations:

- Point (b) questions the meaning of the word *cocky*.

- Point (d) observes that the critic is stating an opinion.

- The Self asks a tricky question (f) to discern the purpose of pointing out flaws and stays connected to the critic by simply complimenting its viciousness (h).

- The next question (j) attempts to elicit any negative consequence of the critic's becoming less extreme. An unnamed part steps forward (k), but it provokes the core of the critic's fear (l).

- Stacy's counselor takes an active role (m) to help her Self verbalize the terror that triggers intense rebukes. These observations unearth truths that provide relief.

Dialogue Example for Distracting Parts

Stacy's Self had to question and observe degrading, anxiety-provoking ideas that would "magically" protect her from harm. Other people are dominated by traits that keep anxiety at bay with distracting thoughts. These can make them chronically clingy, bitter, wary, and prone to interpersonal problems.

> Vic fixated on the lack of professionalism that was causing him to dread going to work. Distracting thoughts were constantly complaining, *They should....* Vic prided himself on being logical. He did not realize he had wisdom beyond reason in the depths of his being.
>
> a. **Shoulder:** When I ask my supervisor the reason for some of our procedures, she should give me an answer instead of acting annoyed and saying *I don't know!*
>
> b. **Logical Self:** You wish Vic had control over the way his supervisor did her job.
>
> c. **Shoulder:** That will never happen.
>
> d. **Logic:** When you want Vic to have control and he doesn't, he feels stuck.
>
> e. **Shoulder:** It would be a big relief for Vic if they would tell him his next assignment.
>
> f. **Logic:** You're focusing on what they should do, not on what Vic can do to relieve his anxiety about the unknown.
>
> g. **Shoulder:** What can Vic do?
>
> h. **Logic:** You are wondering if there is a way for Vic to worry less about the unknown.
>
> i. **Shoulder:** (Quiet pause ...)
>
> j. **Wise Self:** What did seeking forbidden knowledge do to Eve?

This self-talk begins in the third-person—*she should* ... (a). Vic's overuse of the command *should*, earned his distracting part the name S*houlder.*

- Vic's counselor coached his Self to observe that his Shoulder's comment is a demand/wish (b).

- The next observation points out the emotional consequence of being unable to control others (d). A third observation patiently clarifies that Vic is focusing on others' actions instead of his own options (f).

- When the Shoulder turns to Logic for an answer, the only reply is further observation—*You are wondering* ... (h).

- In the void of not being given an easy solution, Vic's Self offered an amazing metaphor of what can happen to people who push for information that is (fairly or unfairly) withheld.

Practice

The best way to learn constructive self-talk is to journal mental chatter in a similar fashion to Stacy's and Vic's dialogues. When worries keep you awake at night, it is especially helpful to write thoughts as they occur and follow the self-talk steps:

1. **Rephrase first-person thoughts** (*I should* ...; *I'll never* ...) into the second person (*You should* ...; *You'll never* ...). Third-person thoughts (*They better* ...; *She always* ...) are natural for distracting ideas that focus on others. Use descriptive names for inner voices ("Shoulder," "Inner Critic," "People Pleaser," "Blamer," and so on) to begin your self-talk script: *Shoulder: She should give me an answer!*

2. **Respond** to distressing/distracting thoughts with:

   a. **Observations** that describe the type of thought—orders, wishes, reminders, doubts, and so on, or the consequences of a line of thinking—*Vic feels stuck when he doesn't have control.*

   b. **Questions** that clarify the meaning, motive, source, or accuracy of a thought—*What's bad about . . . ? How does it help to think . . . ? When did . . . first get that idea?*

3. **Name the inner witness** that observes and questions thoughts (Knower, Logic, Wise Mind, Self) to continue writing the script: *Logic: You wish Vic had control over . . .*

4. **Listen** for any reactions to observations and questions and repeat step two. Continue until critical, controlling voices become softer. It is fine to reach an impasse. Avoid attempts to reason, reassure, or explain that could cause a debate or resistance.

Handout 5.4—Turning Thoughts Into Parts

People often have trigger-quick (automatic) thoughts like *I sound stupid* or *I haven't done enough*. What two things are different about the following list of disturbing ideas from other lists of core beliefs?[1] Check any of the (inner) comments below that you "hear" in your *worst* moments:

DIRECTING VOICES

Controller Voice

☐ You cannot ... handle it, be trusted, stand it ...
☐ You cannot ... show emotions....
☐ You have to control things (yourself).
☐ You have to fix everything.

Protector Voice

☐ You're not safe.
☐ You're trapped.
☐ You cannot tell, speak up....
☐ You might (will) fail, get hurt.
☐ You cannot make a fool of yourself.
☐ You might get sick, die, make others sick....
☐ You could do something awful.
☐ You cannot handle new, unfamiliar situations.
☐ You're responsible for others, everything....
☐ You (your judgment) cannot be trusted.
☐ You cannot trust others.
☐ You are (will be) ruined, damaged....
☐ You have to be perfect.
☐ You cannot make mistakes.
☐ What if ... what if ... what if ...?

Pusher Voice

☐ You have to ...; You better...; You should. ...

☐ You haven't done enough!
☐ You have to get it (done) *now!*
☐ You have to have what you want now!
☐ You have to find excitement or a purpose.

Pleaser Voice

☐ You have to please everyone.
☐ You (your needs) are not important.
☐ Others come first.
☐ Others might not like how you look, act....
☐ You can't find love, caring, approval....
☐ You could be abandoned; or, alone....
☐ You're empty.
☐ You need others; you're incomplete....
☐ You have to make others love, understand, care for, approve of you.

Critic Voice

☐ You're worthless, defective, inadequate, a failure, different, weak, dirty, at fault....
☐ You're helpless, powerless, a fool....
☐ You don't deserve love, happiness, to live....
☐ You're not good, smart, attractive enough....
☐ You should have....

Distracting Voices

The distressing thoughts above cause tension by trying to *direct* life. If anxiety becomes too great, it can be avoided with automatic *distracting* thoughts about others—*They'll never understand me.* This replaces inner turmoil with *interpersonal* conflict. The anger that results is preferable to inner angst. Such ideas can also be reworded as though they are coming from an inner part: *They'll never understand you.* On the lists below, mark any familiar words of blame or judgment that target others or addictive objects.

---

1. (A) The automatic thoughts are stated in the second person: *You'll sound stupid; You haven't done enough.* Stating thoughts in the second person helps you disidentify from them because only part of you is voicing the harsh opinion. Roberto Assagioli said, *We are dominated by everything with which our Self identifies. We can control those things from which we disidentify.* This is different from dissociation, in which ego states or personality parts form alter identities that have no awareness of each other.

    (B) Automatic Thoughts are grouped in the order in which they are usually acquired: (1) *Controlling/Protective* ideas are obtained when toddlers and preschoolers learn to be self-governing and take initiative. (2) *Pushy* notions dominate the minds of school-age children. (3) Teens develop the *People Pleaser's* Voice as they try to fit in and form an identity. (4) People of all ages can absorb cruel comments from kin and culture and grow an *Inner Critic*.

- ❑ **Controller → Blamer**: They have no right to ...; They shouldn't be so ....

- ❑ **Protector → Prosecutor**: They can't be trusted; They won't handle it, get it right ....

- ❑ **Pusher → Demander**: They have to ..., better ..., should ....

- ❑ **Pleaser → Clinger**: They have to understand, love, pay attention to, be there for you ....

- ❑ **Critic → Judger**: They're disappointing, foolish, failures, weak, dirty, at fault ....

- ❑ **Addict Voice**: This will be the last time .... It won't matter if you ....

IMAGERY EXERCISE

Directions: Look at the *Directing* and *Distracting* thoughts you marked on the previous page. To give them added dimension, pick an image that depicts the source of messages.[2] The picture may help you give some of the most dominant voices in your mental chatter a name. The thought *What if you give everyone a disease!* could be uttered by an inner *screamer.*

2.   The first two rows of images come from the *Rider Waite Tarot Deck* (1909) and were retrieved from http://en.wikipedia.org/wiki/ Rider-Waite-Smith deck on June 5, 2009. The copy of the *Scream,* first painted in 1893 by Edvard Munch and reproduced as a lithograph in 1895 was retrieved from http://en.wikipedia.org/wiki/The_Scream, June 6, 2009. The pointing finger image courtesy of www.aperfectworld.org/ (metaphors) was retrieved on June 6, 2009. The puppet and puppy were drawn by Devon Collins; the Queen of Hearts was adapted from Sir John Tenniel's illustration in *Alice's Adventures in Wonderland* (McMillian, 1865).

Handout 5.5—Self-Talk Case Study—for Workshops

Self-talk begins by identifying inner antagonists who are raising issues that create distress. Once people have connected with faculties of curiosity and compassion that see beyond faulty thinking, their *core Selves* can be guided to engage difficult personality parts in dialogue.[1]

CASE STUDY

Bradley was excited about her new job clerking in a high-class clothing store. When she had been at the store a month, a well-dressed woman sharply said, *I told you before, I don't like help when I'm shopping*. Bradley was crushed, and after several days she still could not get the incident out of her mind. She began to dread going back to her job. She told her therapist, *I guess I should be more cautious about whom I approach to help*. Her therapist began to coach her to use self-talk. Stacks of pictures were used to amplify her experience.

Identify Self-Talk Participants

a. **Therapist:** A part of you is saying, *You should have been more cautious about who you approach in the store*. What picture could represent that part of you?

b. **Bradley: The Queen of Hearts.**[a] **She looks so disdainful.**

c. **Therapist:** (places the Queen of Hearts on a chair facing Bradley) The real you is filled with excitement about your job and has a love of helping. Other pictures can help you discover truths you don't know about yourself. Which ones appeal to you?

d. **Bradley:** (sorts through another pile of pictures) **I like the hand holding the budding stick**[b] **and the lady caressing the lion.**[c]

e. **Therapist:** What do you see in those pictures?

f. **Bradley: The stick is a sign of nature and new life. It looks magical. The lady shows power in beauty; strength in gentleness.**

g. **Therapist:** So your **real** Self is natural, coming alive, magical, and has power and strength. (Therapist gives Bradley those pictures to put in her lap.)

The Self Is Guided to Engage Personality Part(s) in Dialogue

h. **Therapist:** Let's go back to the disdainful voice that tells you, *You should be more cautious about whom you approach*. Have your strong, gentle Self silently tell the disdainful voice that it's lecturing. Ask if she's trying to help Bradley.... Let me know how the disdainful part responds.

i. **Bradley:** Now she is saying I should be able to tell which customers want help and which ones don't.

j. **Therapist:** Have your Self ask how Bradley can tell which customers want help and which ones don't.

---

1. The Queen of Hearts (**a**) was adapted from Sir John Tenniel's illustration in *Alice in Wonderland* in 1865. The Ace (**b**) and Knight of Wands (**d**) and Strength Card (**c**: lady and lion) come from the *Rider Waite Tarot Deck* (1909) and were retrieved from http://en.wikipedia.org/wiki/Rider-Waite-Smith deck on June 5, 2009.

k.   **Bradley:** (Looks puzzled) She just said I've been enjoying myself too much on this job.... She says if I enjoy myself too much, I'll always have a letdown.

l.   **Therapist:** She seems to like to switch the subject when she's cornered. How do you feel towards her?

m.   **Bradley:** I don't like her. She reminds me of the nuns in school. They were always so serious. I wish she would leave me alone.

n.   **Therapist:** That sounds like another personality part. How about using a picture of this friendly knight to represent it.[d] Your true Self is always compassionate, curious, and calm. Have your Self ask this *protective* part silently if it can trust Bradley's strong, powerful, inner being to handle the disdainful voice.

o.   **Bradley:** The knight feels unsure. It says the disdainful voice has been there for so long—since Bradley was a little girl. The protective part tried to shut out her mother's constant criticism. Bradley finished school and married her kind, caring husband. Then it was easy to hear the voice from within, gently guiding her. But her husband got a brain tumor and he became demanding and disdainful before he died (seems sad and sorrowful).

p.   **Therapist:** What is going on inside now?

q.   **Bradley:** I'm remembering how mad my husband used to get. The disdainful part is saying, *When people get mad at you, it means you've made a mistake.*

r.   **Therapist:** Have your gentle, strong Self ask the disdainful part, *How does Bradley know if it is her mistake or the other person's issue?*

s.   **Bradley:** The queen is finally quiet. It feels calm inside. (Bradley picks up the picture of the hand holding the budding stick and looks at it.) I had to come alive again after my husband died and rediscover my caring, compassionate Self that finally became strong after I left home.

1.   On which of Bradley's automatic thoughts does the therapist initially focus?

2.   How does the phrase *A part of you is saying* ... change the automatic thought (a)?

3.   Does putting the automatic thought in second person make Bradley less identified with it?

4.   Does *disidentify* mean the same thing as *disassociate*? [2]

5.   Did picking the disdainful queen image for the automatic thought, *You should have been more cautious,* help? If it did help, explain in what way an image or object is useful. (If the case was role-played, ask the participant what he or she noticed about using the image.)

6.   Other forms of therapy that do parts work object to representing the Self with objects or images because the Self is the seat of consciousness. *It is the place from which a person views and interacts with his or her parts.* Do you think the therapist's use of imagery to name qualities of Bradley's Self is helpful in this case example (e, g)?

7.   Do you think being natural, magical, powerful, strong, gentle, and coming alive are qualities Bradley has within her, or are they assets she wants to develop within herself?

Discussion Questions

2.   In disassociation, personality parts or ego states form alter identities that have no awareness of each other. Stating an automatic thought in the second person helps a person be less identified with it because only a *part* of him or her is voicing the opinion. Furthermore, research on journal writing by Campbell and Pennebaker cited in ''The Secret Life of Pronouns'' showed the more people varied their use of pronouns, the more their health improved. They theorized that pronouns offer a different lens through which people can see the world (*Psychological Science,* 2003, 14(1), 60–65).

8. Once dialogue is begun, the therapist repeatedly uses the phrase, *Have your Self tell or silently ask* .... (h, j, n, r); instead of saying, *Tell or ask.* .... Why is it important to summon the Self and to speak silently (not out loud) to the object or image?[3]

9. Do the observations and questions posed by the Self have an agenda to test the accuracy and usefulness of the disdainful part's ideas (as in cognitive therapy), or is it trying to gain a better understanding of this part's meaning and purpose (h, j, n, r)?

10. Many C words can be used to describe the core Self: compassionate, curious, calm, comedic, confident, and clear-thinking. What would it have meant if Bradley had said she was amused by the disdainful Queen's bait-and-switch tactics instead of saying she did not like her (m)?[4]

11. Why does the therapist have Bradley's Self ask the protective part if it can trust her inner being instead of having the protective part speak to the disdainful voice?

12. What question(s) finally helped Bradley align with her true Self (r)? Do you think the disdainful queen image could help critical thoughts be less dominant in Bradley's mind?

---

3. Calling on the Self to make observations and ask questions strengthens its voice (also see question 11). Using subvocal language mimics the way people naturally talk to themselves and it activates the frontal cortex, which becomes energized during meditation.

4. If Bradley said she was amused by the disdainful queen, it would mean she had connected with her compassion, comedic *Self.*

Handout 5.6—Self-Talk Worksheet—for Workshops or Journaling

1. A disturbing thought I often have is: _____ [1]

2. Reword this thought in the second or third person as though it is coming from a part of you (*You should . . . ; They have to . . .*): _____

3. Name the part of you that is voicing this thought: _____

Sample names of personality parts: Inner critic, people pleaser, controller, protector, pusher, judger, clinger, avoider, shoulder, gloomy voice, disdainful voice, mini-mom, mini-dad, needy part, inner terrorist, OCD part, fixer, angry part, punisher, small me, Rhonda rerun, and so on.

4. What image or object could represent this part of you? _____

Sample images or objects:1 Edvard Munch's *The Scream*, pointing finger, gloomy Eeyore, fretful Piglet, disdainful Queen of Hearts, emoticon (/:[ ), high mighty emperor, clingy king, barking dogs, charging knight, marching skeleton, exploding tower, pleasing page, distracted man, or other toys or objects—Barbie doll, crying baby doll, demon, witch, rubber chicken, rat, and more.

5. What quality(s) would you most like people to see in you? (a) _____
   (Optional) Pictures or objects can help you discover truths you do not know about your Self. Pick a picture, literary character, superhero, or object that appeals to you:

Sample objects or images: Toys or objects—Pooh Bear, wise owl, angel, eagle; Cheshire Cat, dove; Jesus figure; Stature of Liberty; lighthouse; hands of God and man; starburst man; emoticons (8)}}), hand holding a star, cup, word, or wand; peaceful priestess; powerful empresses; lady and lion; carefree man; man carrying a light; and more.

   Name all the qualities you see in this image/object: (b) _____ [2]

6. Name your core Self using qualities/abilities in (a) or (b):

Sample names for the Self: inner witness, logic, intuition, insight, consoler, knower, wise one, at ease, professional self, chutzpah, spiritual Self, real me, instinct, courage, guts, independence, conscience, source, magical Self, growing Self, and so on.

7. Rewrite your second- or third-person disturbing thought (#2) spoken by your _____ part.
   (#3)
   Part: "_____".

8.1 (First option) Have your _____ Self silently observe what the _____ part is doing: (#6)   (#3)
   You are (when you . . .) _____.

(Refer to yourself in the third person by using your name or the pronoun *she* or *her*.)

Identify Self-Talk Participants—Inner Parts

Identify Self-Talk Participants—True Self:

Observe or Question Personality Parts to Engage Them in Dialogue

---

1. Note any thought you may have checked or images you may have picked on the *Handout 5.4–Turning Thoughts Into Parts*, *More Brief Therapy Client Handouts*, by K. Cohen-Posey, 2010, Hoboken, NJ: John Wiley & Sons.
2. Note any images you have selected from the *Handout 3.6–Connecting with Your Self*, *More Brief Therapy Client Handouts*, by Kate Cohen-Posey, 2010, Hoboken, NJ: John Wiley & Sons.

Example (a)

Describe the personality part's thought process. Is it assuming, generalizing, ordering, reminding, lecturing, predicting, doubting, scolding, condemning, degrading, trying to convince, guessing, wishing, advising, comparing, criticizing, and so on—*you are warning Bradley.*

Example (b)

Tell the personality part it is causing feelings of sadness, frustration, fear, regret, guilt, hopelessness, helplessness, and so on—*you are making Bradley feel gloomy.*

Example (c)

Point out the consequences of the personality part's line of reasoning—*when you tell Bradley she is enjoying herself too much at work, she may have a harder time making sales.*

8.2   (Second option) Have your _____ Self silently question the _____ part
by: (6)   (#3)

Clarifying the Meaning of Vague Messages

- How do you think it helps … to … ?
- What is bad about … ?
- What would it mean to … ?
- What is the chance of … happening?

Clarifying the Origin of Misinformation

- From where do you think that worry comes?
- When did … first get that idea?

Clarifying the Purpose of Thoughts

- Why are you reminding … of … ?

- Why are you bringing this up now?
- Do you want control over … ?
- Does … have control over … ?
- What is the reason for … ?
- Why … instead of … ?
- What would happen if … did not … ?
- Is there another part you're holding back?
- Do you want the last word because you think you are being asked to lose power or disappear?

9.   Listen for a response from your _____ part. Write it. "_____
                                                     (#3)

_____.

10.   Continue to repeat steps 8 and 9 by listening for responses from personality parts and formulating observations and questions.

- Notice if new parts intrude. Ask, *What inner voice is speaking now?* Use steps 3 and 4 to identify and depict it. Any unnamed part that is ignored wields power.

- Eventually, the voices of inner parts will lose energy and become confused or quiet. This is experienced as a (temporary) sense of connection or inner peace.

Pointers

- **Silently speak** observations and questions by *going inside* to address inner parts. Use second-person you-statements— *You should be more cautious about whom you approach.* Refer to yourself in the <u>third person</u>—*You're lecturing <u>Bradley</u>. Are you trying to help <u>her</u>?*

- **Encourage the release of emotions**. The *Self* can say—*It is fine to cry; make noise; breathe; don't hold back.* Your *Self* can give you a hug as feelings are expressed by crossing your arms and alternately tapping your shoulders.

- **Personality parts do not need to change, integrate, or disappear**. The true *Self* is strengthened any time it identifies, observes, or questions individual facets. If a part continues a disturbing line of thinking, the Self can simply compliment its strength.

- **Notice negative reactions toward a part**. This suggests the presence of another subpersonality. Observing its thought processes and asking questions can make its identity clearer—*You don't like what the disdainful voice is doing to Bradley. Is there another part that is having difficulty trusting Bradley's inner being to handle the disdainful voice?* When the real Self is in charge, it will always feel compassionate, caring, or curious toward the most hostile subpersonalities.

Handout 5.7 — Self-Talk Journals

Any kind of journaling helps remove thoughts from your head and sets them into a tangible medium. In the process, thinking becomes less random and begins to take form, almost like sculpting a statue. Self-talk journals assume there are at least two parties participating in a dialogue. The conversation may begin with an upsetting thought worded in the second person, which is responded to with a question or an observation about the type of thought or its consequences. As the dialogue unfolds, the participants are identified (sometimes adding sketches to give characters dimension). The following example illustrates nine steps that can be used in self-talk journals.[1]

Aimee was still struggling with her self-esteem several years after her divorce from a difficult man. She used her self-talk journal to understand what made her feel uncomfortable when she tried to rekindle her social life.

IDENTIFY Self-Talk Participants

1. Aimee pinpointed an upsetting thought—*What will people at my new church think if they know I'm divorced?*

2. Written in the second person, her thought was: *What will people at your new church think if they know you're divorced?*

3. To represent the upsetting voice that was concerned about everyone's opinion, Aimee used a stuffed dog with pleading eyes. She named this part her people pleaser.[2]

4. The quality on which Aimee thought she could always rely was her intellect. She drew a rough sketch of *The Thinker* by Auguste Rodin, which had been her inspiration in college.

5. She named this aspect of her true Self her logic.

Observe or Question Personality Parts' Thought Processes to Engage Them in Dialogue

6. Aimee rewrote her second-person disturbing thought: People pleaser—*What will people in your new church think if they know you're divorced?*

7. She jotted down a question that quickly came to mind: Logic—*What will they think?*

8. Listening within, she wrote the next comment: People pleaser—*Sweet little Aimee graduated first in her class, went to church all the time, but failed at marriage. How could anyone want or stand to be around such a failure?*

9. She continued to listen within to notice if she heard the voice of her logic or people pleaser and to sense how her body felt. She wrote, *They wouldn't be so condemning . . . . No one would . . . . That's your own perfectionism. But if they did judge you, you wouldn't want them for friends.* Her logic had returned to its rightful position in her mind, and she felt a stoic strength that made her backbone straight.

Asking questions about the meaning, origin, or purpose of disturbing thoughts (*What would they think?* (7) draws out the venom of veiled ideas (*What will people think?* (6). Aimee was amazed by the degree to which she denounced herself once she saw the words on paper (8). With the image of *The Thinker* to help her muse on her harsh ideas, it is no wonder that her logic (9) was quick to realize the source of this line of thinking was her perfectionism—another personality part to be dealt with at a later date.

---

1. The nine steps for self-talk journals are further clarified in the *Handout 5.6–Self-Talk Worksheet*, *More Brief Therapy Client Handouts*, by K. Cohen-Posey, 2010, Hoboken, NJ: John Wiley & Sons. *Empowering Dialogues Within,* by K. Cohen-Posey, 2008, Hoboken, NJ: John Wiley & Sons, gives numerous examples of self-talk dialogues.
2. Stuffed animals are excellent objects to stimulate self-talk.

The more you realize that you have an inner presence that can offer amazing insight and guidance, the more easily journaling flows. It is not necessary to follow a step-by-step procedure. Simply *write* questions to your deepest, innermost Self. Often, it helps to start with the words, *Are you there?* The only participants in this self-talk might be your (small) *me* and your (deepest, innermost) *Self.* Two examples follow:

Free-Flowing Journals

ME: How do I find peace? Are you there?

SELF: Yes.

ME: How do I find peace about the email . . . sent to me?

SELF: Forgive her.

ME: I don't understand forgiveness. I'm not sure if I believe in it. What is forgiveness?

SELF: Overlooking.

ME: That sounds too simple.

SELF: Overlook her flaws even as she focuses on yours. You know she has much goodness. You want to ask her what she likes about you. What do you like about her?

ME: Her wit, her strength, her willingness to give. But should a parent point out a child's flaws or let her discover them? Don't parents have to teach their children manners?

SELF: It depends on the child. Are you afraid of her, or do you think she's too fragile? Is she a child or an adult? Is it time for her to learn from other teachers?

FEELING: Completely at peace.

The second example occurred prior to and just after a person testified in a legal case.

Pretrial

ME: Do I need to write to you?

SELF: Yes, you're too wound up.

ME: Why am I getting so involved in this case?

SELF: You like the drama. You like control. You like to scheme.

ME: Are you my true Self or an inner critic?

SELF: What do you get from being so involved? Does life and death depend on you? Does it make some part of you feel important? What part needs to feel important?

(Silence and peace—keep repeating the question, What part needs to feel important?)

Posttrial

ME: Do I have hope for sleep tonight?

SELF: Yes

ME: How?

SELF: You're indulging your fears and anger. It's quite dramatic. You're planning strategies and not trusting yourself to think on your feet.

PART: (Jumps in) You need to get hold of an attorney and get legal counsel . . . there's a good chance you'll be sued.

ME: Why is that part of me ruminating on this so much?

SELF: That part is terrified.

ME: Is it justified?

SELF: Not if everything is predetermined. Not if you're a pawn in a cosmic play .... Not if you're one player on the stage. Not if you can be in the audience and just watch the players play their parts.

ME: Just keep repeating, *Watch the players play their parts.*

Free-flowing journals can end with an unanswerable question or an almost incomprehensible statement. These have the effect of calming normal inner chatter, especially if the phrase or inquiry is repeated every time a new notion attempts to arise.

Handout 5.8—Fantasy Self-Talk

Self-talk usually begins by turning disturbing thoughts into a part of you. But personality parts can be elusive. Sometimes they emerge in dreams as symbols that wield more power than thought forms. The trick is to help these facets face each other and dialogue. The following waking dream exercise is a means to this end.

Exercise— Hidden Figure

- **Journey:** Picture yourself in a meadow. Notice the length and color of the grass. Soon you will find a path that leads to the edge of a forest or a cave.

- **Setting:** Listen for a sound that tells you something is coming out of the cave, forest, or even a pool of swamp water. Find a large tree to shield you and observe what appears.

- **Associations:** Notice the figure or animal that comes forward. Look at its features. Have you seen a similar facial expression? Is the feeling tone linked to any current life events?

- **Meaning:** Notice other details in its head, features, mouth, and teeth. Discover the message or meaning that the creature's existence conveys.

- **Confrontation:** It is important to neither run from nor struggle with this creature. The ancient art of staring into another being's eyes can cause change. It may become weaker, smaller, or transform into a gentler figure.

- Another practice for encountering a dangerous foe is to offer it food—enough to leave it well satisfied or make it sleepy. Hold your ground until you become comfortable.

- **Switch roles** with the creature to own its energy. What does it want to say to you?

- **Journal** or imagine your fantasy before reading the examples: *I'm walking in a meadow . . . .*

EVE IN THE BOG OF EDEN

Eve is 13 years old. She has unresolved feelings about her father's suicide when she was 4 years old. She is unable to forgive herself for being with her mother, visiting relatives on the weekend of the incident. Thinking her presence could have prevented her father's death is typical for Eve, who demands much from herself. At her young age, she is on an all-star basketball team and pushes herself academically. Her mother scheduled an appointment after Eve had a dream in which God was angry because everyone was a sinner. When she woke up, Eve found a knife and started to cut herself.

Her therapist asked if she thought she was a sinner. Eve readily agreed because sometimes she disobeys or talks about other students behind their backs.

a. Eve chose a marshy setting for fantasy self-talk. She saw an evil, homeless man coming out of the fog.

b. She would not look in his eyes because she thought he was too sinister, but she decided to offer him some food and concocted a baloney and cheese sandwich. Although this allowed her to look at his eyes, she said he was still too evil for conversation.

c. Eve was able to switch roles and be the homeless man. She explained that he lost his job when his car stopped working. Then his family refused to help him because he wanted to spend all his time with his friends rather than look for another job. He admitted that he made bad choices.

d. Acting out the critical part of Eve, her counselor stood up and shook her finger at this imaginary fellow and gave him a lecture on making poor choices.

e. Eve reported the homeless man was hanging his head in shame. She felt softer toward him. He no longer seemed evil.

It is no wonder that Eve has suppressed a part of herself that wants to be idle and carefree. She has taken on the enormous task of preventing catastrophes, and she has little time for leisure.

TRINA DREADS TRINIDAD

Trina was dreading a visit with her family in Trinidad. She relished the idea of an island holiday but recoiled at the thought of hints from her accomplished family about her ordinary work in the States. She decided to use fantasy self-talk to discover what part of her was creating the dismay.

a. Trina ventured into the forest and hid behind a large tree, where she saw a snake appear just at the opening of the cave.

b. Surprisingly, the snake was upright. It was green and brown with large white eyes.

c. Trina did not dare approach it, but felt the snake was as much afraid of her as she was of it.

d. She decided to offer it food and began eagerly cooking it chickens—curried, fricasseed, and barbecued. After finishing its tasty meal, the snake seemed satisfied and started to retreat into its cave.

e. Knowing she had not yet learned the reason for her dread, Trina switched roles and asked the snake how it felt toward the lady in the forest. The serpent replied that this woman had a nice smile, but even people who looked kind might want to kill it. Therefore, the snake said it stayed closed to the cave.

f. Trina asked the serpent to stay a little longer and to look into the lady's eyes to see if she could sense any danger and also to notice how it liked the full feeling in its stomach from all the delicious chickens.

g. The serpent reported that it was surprised at how calming staring was. She said it gave her a sense of control—she usually did not look at people, and the lady in the forest appeared kind.

h. Now Trina spoke to the snake as herself: *You are not an ordinary snake, no matter what others may think. You move vertically like a cobra, but you are not a cobra. I'll always be nearby to nourish your spirit, whether you are with coworkers or your arrogant family.*

This was a most meaningful exercise for Trina. She was a shy person and rarely initiated contact with coworkers because she did not know what lay behind their smiles. A snake in a cave seemed an appropriate symbol for the suspicious, fearful of part her. The shy part of her was able to look at people's eyes through guided imagery and become reconnected to her true Self.

Fantasy dialogues do not have to be dark. They can be filled with mythological figures, parents, friends, knights, goddesses, and so on—as the next example illustrates.

(MA)DONNA ESCAPES MOMMY LAND

Donna adored her two young children and, in spite of the fact that she had everything she wanted, she felt lonely. This was out of character for Donna, who had a knack for creating villages of friends wherever she lived. But being a stay-at-home mom and taking care of babies had definitely cramped her style, and she wondered if she had lost some vital part of herself. Perhaps fantasy self-talk could help her make contact with what was missing.

a. Donna went as far as the edge of the forest. She did not have to wait long for a band of 20 fairies to fly out of the woods.

b. It was hard to talk to any of them or even look at their faces because they were on fairy business—sprinkling dust to start springtime after a bleak winter and, then, off to people land to make mischief.

c. Donna did take the role of one of the fairies, who said that they always worked together as a team. It was a group effort to do fairy business and all the diminutive divas were generally cooperative.

d. This fairy then took note of Donna and said she looked lonely in the meadow by herself. She gave her a special star and said it would not be long before she would be back with her own band of friends.

Sometimes inner parts are not suppressed; they are just trapped by life circumstances. A troop of fairies was an appropriate image for Donna, whose genius for generating groups, being mobile, and visiting the city was not at all lost but relegated to her inner realm for the time being.

Handout 5.9—How to Talk to All Your Parts—A Worksheet for Children

Everyone has a quiet voice deep inside of them that brings them to their calm, cheerful, kind Self. It can help to have an image that reminds you of your true Self.[1] Pick a picture from the row below that gives you a good feeling:

Naming Your Real Self

Choosing a name for the voice deep down inside of you can help you find it faster. What would be a good name for each of the above images? Put a number before each name.

_____Wise Self	_____My thinker or knower	_____Inner strength
_____My spirit	_____Watcher within	_____Radiant Self
Make up a name for your own true Self: "_____"		

Personality Parts

Often, it is hard to hear your true Self that keeps you calm, cool, and collected. The parts of you that make you feel angry, afraid, or annoyed can be loud and pushy. It's good to pick out the *exact words* an upsetting part is saying. Then, think of an image for the part doing the talking. What picture goes with each of the words below?

_____ You sound stupid when you talk.
_____ You can't let your sister act so bossy.
_____ Maybe you did something that hurt your mom and will make her sick.
_____ You better make people stop calling you names.

_____ You're stupid 'cause you made a bad grade.
_____ Something bad could happen at home when you're away at school.
_____ You can't be happy without more time around your dad.

---

1. Images were retrieved on October 2, 2009, from the following sites: www.victorian-embroidery-and-crafts.com/free (angel, crying baby); http://www.dreamstime.com (bright idea and superhero); www.urbanthreads.com/designs/clip_art?category_id=86 www.urbanthreads.com/designs/clip_art?category_id=86 www.urbanthreads.com/designs/clip_art?category_id=86http://i-heart-god.com/ free_satan clip_art.htm; *The Scream (*Munch lithograph, 1895) was retrieved on June 6, 2009, from http://en.wikipedia.org/wiki/. The_Scream; The all-seeing eye was retrieved on October 8, 2009, compliments of http://www.urbanthreads.com/; The wise owl, flower, puppet, and puppy were drawn by Devon Collins (3/10); The Queen of Hearts was adapted from Sir John Tenniel's illustration in *Alice in Wonderland* (1865).

Naming your true Self helps you notice its quiet, calm voice. Naming the parts that upset you, shows that they are not the real you! Pick a name that could go with each image of a personality part. Put the number of the picture after each name.

Naming Parts

Miserable little me _____	Worrywart _____	Inner terrorist _____	Gloomy part_____	
Judger or Ms. Bossy _____	Inner critic, demon thought, or Miss Mad Face _____.			

Many people talk ugly to themselves. That is because a personality part is trying to be the boss of their brains. When you hear your real Self, its voice is sweet. The trick is to spot the part that is making cruel comments and let your true Self asks questions (q) or *point out* (po) what is happening. Match the sweet-talk response with the number of the ugly remark below.

Sweet-Talking When You Are Mad, Sad, or Afraid

Ugly-Talking Part	Sweet-Talking Self
1. You sound stupid when you talk.	_____ What will happen if you don't follow your sister's orders? (q)
2. You can't let your sister act so bossy.	_____ When you try to keep kids from calling you names, you lose control. That's what makes you look bad. (po)
3. Maybe you did something that hurt your mom and will make her sick.	__1__ Are other kids paying more attention to how you sound or worrying about how they sound? (q)
4. You better make people stop calling you names.	_____ Do smart people ever make a bad grade? Will calling yourself names help you work harder? (q)
5. You're stupid because you made a lousy grade.	_____ Are you stopping yourself from seeing who else you can enjoy (besides your dad)? (q)
6. Something bad could happen at home when you're at school.	_____ How did you get enough power to hurt your mom like that? (q)
7. You can't be happy without more time around your dad.	_____ What would the bad thing be? What is the chance of it happening? (q)

Putting Ideas and Images Together

After Eden saw her stepfather have a seizure, she began to worry that she would have one, too, and this idea was making it hard for her to sleep. She drew a picture to keep by her bed so she could remember how her guiding spirit calmed her inner terrorist. (Notice it usually takes more than one response to soothe a bothersome part, and there is no arguing.

1. **Terrorist:** You'll have a seizure, too!

2. **Spirit:** Why are you telling Eden things that are not true?

3. **Terrorist:** But it could be true.

4. **Spirit:** Do you think Eden's mom was telling the truth when she said more than 98% of kids *never* get seizures?

5. **Terrorist:** (Quieter) Yes . . . she was telling the truth.

6. **Spirit:** I know you are trying to help Eden be safe by coming up with worries, but are you protecting her from harm?

7. **Terrorist:** (Quiet—Eden feels calm and peaceful.)

Handout 5.10—Selves and Parts Record

Selves

Name	Image or Object	Calming Words
Examples: Higher Self; true or core Self; knower; reason; thinker; guiding spirit; watcher; still, small voice; consoler; inner peace; most adult ego state; hidden observer; and so on.	**Examples:** Dove, wise owl, Pooh Bear, *Thinker* statue, angel, superhero figure, Statue of Liberty, Mona Lisa, yin-yang symbol, Cheshire Cat, and so on.	**Questions—** How do you think it helps to …? What is bad about …? What is the chance of …; happening? When did you first get that idea? Why are you bringing that up? …. **Observations—** You are assuming, generalizing, ordering, reminding, lecturing, predicting, doubting, scolding, guessing, wishing, advising, comparing, criticizing, and so on.

Parts

Name	Image or Object	Typical Verbiage
Examples: Inner critic, people pleaser, controller, protector, pusher, judger, clinger, avoider, shoulder, gloomy voice, disdainful voice, mini-mom or dad, needy part, inner terrorist, OCD part, fixer, angry part, punisher, small me, poor me, worrywart, or name of any alter.	**Examples:** Witch, demon, rubber rat or chicken, Munch's *The Scream*, clingy king, high and mighty emperor, pleasing page, exploding tower, Knight of Swords, volcano, gloomy Eeyore, fretful Piglet, Barbie doll, crying baby doll, pointing finger, Queen of Hearts, emoticon (/:-[ ), and more.	**Examples:** You don't measure up; You can't upset anyone; You don't do enough; What if …; Don't think about it; He shouldn't …; She has to …; He won't think you're good enough; You don't know what you're doing; She should give you an answer; You should be more cautious; You have to convince people; You have to make people …; and more.

Handout 5.11 — Self-Talk Record

Disturbing Message From Personality Part	Calming Words From the True Self
(Controller, protector, pusher, people pleaser, inner critic, and so on)	(Higher Self, core Self, knower, reason, most adult ego state, and so on)
You don't …; You can't …; What if …; Don't …; He shouldn't …; She has to …; He won't …; You should …; You have to …; You can't …; and more.	**Observations:** You're assuming, reminding, lecturing, doubting, scolding, …. **Asks questions:** How does it help to …? What is the chance of … happening? ….
	Example
Inner critic: You can't remove the stain of abortion from your soul.	*Self: You're the part that won't let her forget. What do you get out of second-guessing her past decision?*

CHAPTER 6

BETTER ANGELS OF OUR THOUGHTS

Help clients:

THERAPISTS GUIDE TO BETTER ANGELS OF OUR THOUGHTS

1. Practice thinking and behavior patterns that reduce anger, eating disorders, grief, jealousy, obsessive-compulsive disorder (OCD), panic attacks, and trauma.
2. Formulate viewpoints that foster forgiveness, self-esteem, and happiness.
3. Identify disorders that cannot be addressed by changing thought patterns and behavior alone—attention deficit/hyperactivity disorder (ADHD), bipolar disorder, sensory integration dysfunction.

Using the Handouts

- **General literature:** *Knowing Peace Beyond Panic, Discovering the Me That Is Not OCD, Tempering Anger, Finding Life After Loss, Building Trust from Jealousy, Journeying to Forgiveness, Transcending Trauma, Thin Thinking, Not Thinking Too Thin, Raising Self-Esteem, Practicing Happiness*—these handouts offer a *bare outline* to approach the presenting problem and can help structure a treatment program.

- **Rating Scales:** *Distinguishing ADHD from Moodiness, Sensory Integration Dysfunction.*

- **Forms:** *OCD Exposure Practice, Anger Log, Daily Food Log.*

- **Groups:** *Thin Thinking* can be used to start a weight-loss group. At every meeting discuss a thin-thinking task, eat a snack with awareness, and weigh in.

Cautions and Comments

- ***A Tempered Mind Subdues Anger*** can be used with *Angry Automatic Thoughts* (4.8) and handouts in First Class Communication. Decide if clients have a greater need for a handout on anger, jealousy, or both. For anger at children, recommend *A Parents' Power Tools* (8.4).

- The ***Anger Log*** can be used with adults and children. Parents should log the trigger incident and the child's reaction. The child can be asked to think of a calming thought or strategy (when he or she is not angry) before engaging in a favorite activity.

- ***Building Trust from Jealousy*** can be used with *The Journey to Forgiveness* (6.14) and *Moving Beyond Betrayal* (8.20).

- ***Thin Thinking*** should be used with the *Daily Food Log. Automatic Thoughts* (4.8) or *Self-Talk Record* (5.23) should be used with clients who do a fair amount of emotional eating.

- ***Not Thinking Yourself Too Thin*** describes the beginning stages of treatment for eating disorders. Pages 170–171 address anorexia and page 172 for bulimia. These handouts give an idea of changes clients need to make with food rituals before engaging in more intense therapy (thinking patterns, self-talk, ego states, family relationships, etc.). The handouts will also help clients feel confident that you know how to treat eating disorders.

Note

Note that some of the tasks in *Thin Thinking* (6.8) are helpful for bulimics.

- The ***Daily Food Log*** can be confusing to first-time users. Make sure clients are not being too restrictive on daily calorie or food serving allowances. Help them circle the number of servings they want from each food group.

- ***Raising Self-Esteem*** can be used in conjunction with handouts in Chapter 5 (Constructive Self-Talk) to calm and paralyze the inner critic.

Sources and Acknowledgements Not Referenced in the Handouts

Chapters in ***Brief Therapy Client Handouts*** by Kate Cohen-Posey (John Wiley & Sons, 2000) were compiled into single handouts on panic disorder, OCD, and anger.

For additional information on John Bowlby's attachment theory, see ***Attachment and Loss: Loss, Sadness and Depression,*** *Vol. III* (Basic Books, 1980)—a readable and thorough treatment of grief and loss.

For a more in-depth understanding of the EMDR protocol referred to in ***Finding Life After Loss***, ***The Journey to Forgiveness,*** and ***Triumph Over Trauma,*** see *Eye Movement Desensitization and Reprocessing,* by Francine Shapiro (Guilford Press, 2001).

Handout 6.1—Knowing Peace Beyond Panic

If you have experienced a sudden onset of rapid heartbeat and shallow breathing, then you have known the pangs of a panic or anxiety attack. Your episode may have included some or all of the symptoms in the chart below. No doubt, you may have thought you were dying, going *crazy, or* making a fool of yourself. The truth is, all signs of panic are caused by only one thing . . . *a surge of adrenaline!*

False Assumptions

1. **Physical causes** are *not* related to heart conditions or some other grave physical issue. However, it is important to have a doctor rule out any medical problems. This is more for your peace of mind than to expose a mysterious illness. Once physical causes have been laid to rest, you can concentrate on understanding how adrenaline prepares the body for action by increasing blood flow and tensing muscles. This causes all the symptoms of panic.

2. **Mental breakdowns** *cannot* cause panic attacks. When people lose touch with reality, they have delusions (that people on TV are watching them, for example) and hear or see things that are not present. This is caused by too much of a neurotransmitter called dopamine. People who have panic attacks do not have enough of the neurotransmitters gamma-aminobutyric acid (GABA) or serotonin. They are overly concerned about reality, rather than out of touch with it.

3. **Looking foolish** is *less likely* than you would think. Although the symptoms of panic are intense, they are mostly internal. Anything that might be noticed by others can easily be explained as not feeling well. When you are ready, it will help you to tell people you are having a panic attack and teach them how to help you (see Attacking Panic Attacks on the following page).

Body Reaction	Cause Symptoms of Panic
Increased blood flow	☐ Rapid heartbeat ☐ hot flashes ☐ cold, clammy hands and feet
Tense chest wall muscles	1. ☐ Rapid breathing ☐ a sharp pain when inhaling 2. Too much oxygen (from rapid breathing) causes ☐ tingling or ☐ numbness
Tense arms or legs	☐ Shakiness ☐ faintness (tired muscles draw blood away from the head)
Tense throat muscles	☐ Difficulty swallowing
Tense jaw muscles	Inner ear pressure → ☐ dizziness ☐ blurred vision ☐ nausea ☐ diarrhea

The True Cause of Panic Attacks

Although it has already been stated that the symptoms of panic are caused by a surge of adrenaline, a question still remains: *Why do some people have these adrenaline spikes for no apparent reason?* One or a combination of the following conditions can be the culprits.

- **Physical predisposition** causes some people to *inherit* a body chemistry that makes them prone to anxiety. They tend to be hypervigilant, cautious, shy, reactive, and *overfocused on their body reactions.* Abuse of alcohol or drugs may be an attempt to self-medicate.

- **Stress and trauma** can cause a surge of adrenaline and panic symptoms. Constant conflict, doing things you dread, trying to accomplish too much in too little time, or thinking about an awful experience in your past may cause a wave of anxiety that seems to happen for no reason at all. Then, more adrenaline is triggered by the thoughts, *What's happening to me? Why is this happening? Will it happen again?* The vicious cycle of panic begins.

- **Feeling trapped** or cut off from your comfort zone. This may be in a car (particularly on freeways, crossing bridges, or when making left turns), in large crowded stores, going through checkout lines, or just being alone. Recognizing feelings of being trapped and trigger situations makes the mysterious onset of panic less frightening.

- **Emotional disorders** can produce the first or subsequent panic attack. People who are not able to engage in obsessive rituals to avoid germs or have everything in perfect order can be overwhelmed by anxiety. Socially phobic or shy people are at risk for panic when they are in situations where they fear they will look foolish.

- **Other physical problems** mimic the signs of panic and increase the likelihood of attack.

  - **Allergies:** Cause a surge of adrenaline during certain seasons or after eating particular foods.

  - **Anemia:** Heart and breathing rate is increased to help produce more red blood cells.

  - **High blood pressure:** Heart and breathing rate is increased to help pump blood through clogged arteries.

  - *Hyper***thyroidism:** Shakiness, palpitations, breathlessness, tension—with increased appetite *and* weight loss.

  - *Hypo***thyroidism:** Tension is due to fluid retention from reduced thyroid activity.

  - **Inner ear issues:** Sensitivity to fluorescent lights, steep hills, or cloudy days cause tension, nausea, etc.

  - **Low blood sugar:** Makes panic more likely on waking, a few hours after meals, or in the middle of the night.

  - **Premenstrual syndrome (PMS):** High levels of estrogen cause bloating, tension, jitters, and irritability.

  - **Mitral valve prolapse:** Dizziness, chest pain, faintness, and palpitations due to the mitral heart valve ballooning.

Attacking Panic Attacks

Once you have had a panic attack, the goal is to become an expert at dealing with symptoms—*not* to stop them. You can boldly tell panic to do its worst. This *flooding* has a reverse effect that reduces anxiety. *Distraction* is a more cautious but equally effective method.

1. **Stare at a spot** for starters. This spontaneously begins a gradual relaxation process. With your mouth closed, find out how far you can drop your jaw.

2. **Use mental activity** (while staring): Count backwards from 100 by 3, say the states in alphabetical order, recite song lyrics or a hymn, and so on. Refocus on anything that requires concentration *away from* anxious thoughts and hyperfocus on body sensations.

3. **Use physical activity** if preferred—walk, knit, shoot baskets, take a shower, phone someone.

4. **Use imaginary activity:** When people experience panic, they often want to run to a place of safety. You can do this instantaneously by imagining your bedroom, the woods, or the beach. Or picture yourself doing something you enjoy such as swimming or dancing. Make the details of where you are or what you're doing as vivid as possible. What time of day is it? What is the temperature like? What colors and shapes do you see?

5. **Notice your breath** *only* if it helps. *Do not* pressure yourself to perform a breathing technique just right. When breathing is rapid, inhale and exhale to the tune of "Jingle Bells" (Jin-gle-bells-jin-gle-bells-jin-gle-all-the-way . . . .). Your breath will gradually slow down. Then you can switch to "Amazing Grace" (one syllable per breath). If you are hyperventilating, breathe into a paper bag to reduce oxygen levels that are creating the problem.

6. **Dealing with driving**. It is completely possible to drive while having a panic attack. Use mental activities (#2) to refocus. Listen to the radio, look for your favorite cars, or name trees on the side of the road. If you find yourself wanting to rush to return to your place of safety, pull to the side of the road the first chance you get. Refocus and tell your panic you are not going anywhere until it settles down.

7. **Face trigger situations** that you may be avoiding once you know how to distract your way through panic. The greater your comfort zone, the less chance of attacks returning.

The more expert you become at handling panic, the shorter episodes will be and the less often they will happen until they seem to disappear entirely. However, a high-stress situation can trigger an attack and another cycle of episodes *unless* you look at it as an opportunity to review your understanding of panic, to practice refocusing, and to expose yourself to difficult situations.

Handout 6.2—Discovering the Me That Is Not OCD

Once you truly understand the title of this handout, obsessive thoughts and compulsive behaviors will no longer be a problem for you. When you feel the urge to call your loved one for the twentieth time to make sure he or she hasn't had a terrible accident or look at a knife and wonder if you might lose control and stab someone, you will say to yourself, *This isn't me, it's OCD.* The first step is to distinguish OCD ideas from everyday thoughts, or even your usual worries.

Identifying OCD

The major feature of OCD thoughts and behaviors is to prevent a (so-called) catastrophe from happening. This could be an illness, robbery, fire, being imperfect, or lacking a necessity. The following list shows how intense, repetitious OCD thoughts and behaviors can be.

	Repetitious Thoughts (Obsessions) and Behaviors (Rituals) Checklist
Contamination, Germs, and Dirt Rituals and Obsessions	• Avoid shaking hands, public restrooms, doorknobs, raw meat, cleansers, dirt, sticky substances, emptying the garbage, or changing kitty litter. • Avoid contact with radon, radioactive materials, toxins, insects, or animals. • Worry about diseases from my own saliva, urine, or feces. • Wash my hands, take long showers, or scrub countertops excessively.
Ordering and Cleaning Rituals	• Want my papers, pens, books, collections, or closets arranged just right. • I reposition rugs, pictures, and spend excessive time arranging my collections. • Must have my things in a specific order/pattern and notice if they are out of place. • Vacuum, dust, change sheets, or wash floors more than once a week. • Follow a set order during baths or grooming *and start over* if interrupted.
Checking Rituals	• Stop to check that I haven't (accidentally) hurt someone when driving. • Repeatedly check locks, stoves, or other things to prevent misfortunes. • Repeatedly search for news about any accidents caused by others or myself. • Repeatedly check for mistakes while doing bookwork and worry about it later. • Repeatedly check my body odor or appearance to make sure I'm acceptable. • Repeatedly ask or phone others for *reassurance* that I haven't made them mad, forgotten an appointment, or to find out if they are well.
Repeating and Counting **Rituals**	• Repeat activities such as combing my hair or going in and out of doorways. • Make sure I've repeated such activities above the "right" number of times. • Repeat "good" thoughts or words to erase bad ones or to feel safe. • Remember events in detail or make lists to prevent bad consequences. • Count floor tiles, books, nails in walls, my teeth, and so on to relieve tension.
Perfection Obsessions	• Worry that I won't say things just right or use the "perfect" word. • Worry about doing "the right thing" or being honest, fair, or on time. • Worry too much about hurting others' feelings or making people mad. • Worry about losing my wallet or unimportant objects, such as a scrap of paper. • Worry that part of my body is repulsive despite assurance to the contrary.
Aggressive or Sexual Rituals and Obsessions	• Fear harming myself or others with sharp objects or while driving. • Avoid sharp or breakable objects such as knives, scissors, or glass. • Worry that I will blurt out obscenities or insults, even though I never have. • Worry that I might (accidentally) steal something, even though I never have. • Get violent or sexual images that I would never act out; fear that I might be gay.

	Repetitious Thoughts (Obsessions) and Behaviors (Rituals) Checklist
Hoarding Rituals and Obsessions	• Save old newspapers, notes, cans, paper towels, and other useless items. • Have difficulty throwing things away for fear I may need them someday. • Worry excessively about saving money or food, even when I don't need to.
Bodily Rituals and Obsessions	• Repeatedly take my pulse, blood pressure, or temperature, or check for injuries. • Worry that I have an illness despite reassurance from doctors that I'm okay. • Worry how things feel or about body sensations and household noises.
Religious and Superstitious Rituals and Obsessions	• Pray for nonreligious reasons or have to pray ''the right way.'' • Need to confess to minor mistakes or things I never did. • Worry about having sinful thoughts, salvation, blaspheming, or other concerns. • Think saying or doing certain things can cause bad luck. • Avoid so-called unlucky numbers, places, or animals.

Brain Anatomy of OCD: Cortex ←→ Caudate ←→ Thalamus

Several studies suggest a physical cause for OCD. The *orbitofrontal* **cortex**, just above the eye orbits, is the first brain area to detect possible danger. It sends a *worry signal* to the **thalamus** in the center of the brain that determines the presence of actual danger. A man might get a scratch from a stray kitten and think, *I might get rabies*, but the thalamus (instantly coordinating information from everywhere in the brain) relays back to the cortex: *No real risk.*

The **caudate** lies next to the thalamus and acts like a gearshift. It helps the mind move on to the next thought. People with OCD have a slightly malfunctioning caudate that gets *stuck* on hot-button thoughts, causing a never-ending loop of worry signals to go between the cortex and thalamus. These physical facts clarify three falsehoods about OCD:

- People with OCD are overly concerned, not out of touch with reality. They are not psychotic or crazy.

- People with OCD tend to be high achievers. They are not weak or lacking in will power.

- People with OCD are overconscientious, not sinful. They worry the *most* about what they would be the *least* likely to do.

Defeat OCD With Refocusing, Relabeling, and Exposure

1. **Relabel** repetitive behaviors and thoughts as *OCD*. The table of obsessions and rituals helps identify typical patterns, but any *continuous habit* or *what-if thought* could be one of your hot buttons that jams the caudate, making it fire red alerts.

2. **Refocusing** is the all-important step that directly intervenes in the caudate's inability to shift gears. When people *do not* have OCD, high-level thought processes overrule distress signals and cause the caudate to switch off. When your brain's automatic gearshift is not working, you can create a manual override by intentionally refocusing on mental challenges.
   - Count backward from 100 by threes or sevens. Name the states north, south, east, or west of the one in which you live. List the presidents in reverse, all the way to JFK. Memorize and repeat a Psalm or a song lyric. Spell and then pronounce your name backwards.

   - Mental challenges help grow new neuron circuits to compete with and weaken the OCD-worry loop. The goal is to change the channel to a new activity (not to make feelings or urges go away). Refocusing thoughts or urges for even 3 minutes will begin to effect brain change. Mental challenges are quick and handy. They are a transition to other pleasurable activities (shooting baskets, talking on the phone, or working out) that prologue refocusing.

- Use physical challenges (like forward folds) that can be done quickly and require focus. Stand with your weight balanced on the heels and balls of your feet, fold your arms, bend from your hips, and let your head hang. Every time you exhale, notice how much deeper you go into the fold and where you feel the stretch. This releases serotonin into your brain.

3. **Exposure** helps when an OCD catastrophe is easy to imagine or recreate. Expose yourself to your disaster by intentionally placing your finger on your lips after touching a dollar, putting something out of place, or holding a knife in the presence of a loved one. As soon as you feel anxious, *refocus* on a mental challenge (above). Start with mild or imagined disasters and work up to more difficult ones. Doing exposure/refocusing with a partner helps.

Handout 6.3—Tempering Anger

Anger is a reaction to a real or perceived loss of power. Young people lose their temper because they must be taught to learn society's rules. Adults can feel a childlike anger when (1) they *give up* their power to people with no real authority over them; and (2) try to control people over whom they have no power. This renders them impotent. Log events that rouse your rage (see Anger Log Handout). Learn to temper your mind by applying the following strategies to infuriating incidents.

Anytime you explain or defend yourself, you may be treating someone as your superior. At the least, this is annoying, but it can lead to full-blown explosions. The following triggers will lose their punch when you know how to retain your power.

Giving Up the Ghosts of Past Authority

- **Orders from authority figures** are the only demands that require compliance. Even with them, you have some latitude in the *way* you respond. Focus on what you can do—*I can do ... as soon as I ...* Use the words *wish* and *and* —*I wish I could ... and I need to. ...*

- **Orders (O) from peers and subordinates** can be thought of as requests. Respond (R) with a question or by expressing your limits.

  - **O:** *You're not going to ...!* **R:** *I'm not?*

  - **O:** *Get me ...* **R:** *Maybe later.*

  Question demands to find out if they have any merit. If they don't, proceed with your plans—*Help me understand why you don't want me to go.*

- **Allow people to be angry and have attitudes** instead of trying to prevent a blow-up by doing others' bidding. Predicting how long someone will hold a grudge can have a reverse effect—*I imagine you'll give me the silent treatment for 2 days, 2 hours, or 2 minutes because I didn't ...* The other person will want to prove you wrong. Giving choices has a hypnotic effect. Be sympathetic—*I know it's hard on you when I don't ...*

- **Criticism and advice** can feel like an attempt to control but is really nothing more than an opinion. Agree with any part of the criticism that might be true, let people know you will consider their ideas, and acknowledge their feelings—*You sound disappointed (worried).*

- **Name-calling and rudeness** are intimidation tactics unless the focus is put on the *other person.* Act *as if* all is well—<u>*You say that like it's a bad thing.*</u> Ask questions—*Are you trying to upset me?* Restate hostile words—*Are <u>you</u> saying ...?*

- **Jealousy, prying, and other interrogations** reflect others' insecurities, *not* your honesty. Answering questions will encourage more queries. Log recurring questions and your responses to avoid unending quizzing. Respond to questions with questions or compliments—*What made you think of that now? That's sweet of you to be jealous.*

People are bound to behave in troubling ways. The more their conduct *truly* affects you, the more important it is to act. *Trying* to convince others avoids taking action and will increase your ire. Sometimes, no effort is needed. Recognize when a person's behavior has no real impact on you. The following triggers can help you decide when to act and when to relax:

Controlling Only What You Can

- **Dishonesty and betrayal** mean the person who has been deceitful is at fault. Thinking you are inadequate or foolish avoids placing responsibility squarely on the other person. The only action needed may be to *trust your self-worth* whether you stay in the relationship or leave, and to focus on what is going well as long as you remain with your partner.

- **Laziness and negligence** occur when people find others to do their bidding. Set limits on what you are willing to do. Ask for what you want, instead of complaining—*Would you ...?* Use a positive, future tone—*From now on ...; I know you meant to. ... Next time would you ...?* If people are still not following your house rules, put them out or have them evicted.

- **Conflicting opinions** trigger the desire to convince others. You may be imitating caretakers who tried to impose their views on you. When you feel yourself wanting to prove your point, immediately say, *We have different ideas on this*. Do not continue unless you are sincerely willing to consider the other person's outlook.

- **Conflicts of interest** require time to reach a win-win solution. Stay focused on the issue, but take breaks until answers reveal themselves. Make sure you have considered other people's ideas and are not expecting them to meet needs you could take care of on your own.

- **Undesirable behavior** can be maddening because people are not living up to *your* expectations. If you find yourself becoming outraged by the way people act on TV, drive their cars, or manage their children, remember you are trying to control something that is beyond your power. Ask yourself, *How important will this be a year from now?*

Types of Temper—

(A) Causes, (B) Characteristics, (C) Cures. If you have trouble adopting the previous strategies, it may be due to your biological temperament or learned traits. If your temperament predisposes you to be excitable and impulsive, but your upbringing has *not* caused you to crave perfection, security, adoration, or domination, your outbursts may feel out of character. Medication and anger management tactics can help you regain power lost due to one or more of the following types of temper:

High-Energy, Outgoing Temperament	(a)	Energetic, outgoing, bold, temperaments make people reactive to incoming stimuli both positively with passion and negatively with annoyance.
	(b)	Become upset about things others find trivial; difficulty self-soothing.
	(c)	When motivated, can master anger management; medication can also help.
Hyperactive Anger	(a)	Overstimulation and difficulty controlling impulses causing sudden outbursts.
	(b)	Anger can look scary but is short-lived and easily forgotten after the eruption.
	(c)	Medication for ADHD can give the person considerable control.
Bipolar Anger	(a)	During a manic high, the brain is overexcited, lasting days or weeks.
	(b)	As people become more manic, hostility, *or* need for control increases.
	(c)	Mood-stabilizing medication can markedly reduce or eliminate anger problems.
Premenstrual Syndrome (PMS)	(a)	Fluid retention puts pressure on some women's brains 2–10 days before menses.
	(b)	Agitation, explosions, and violence can occur during the 2-- 10-day window.
	(c)	Antidepressants and hormone treatment can be helpful.
Perfectionist (Obsessive-Compulsive Personalities)	(a)	Neurologically predisposed to focus on details, rules, order, and cleanliness, or raised by people with unrelenting high standards and rigidness.
	(b)	Frequent outbursts when others do not comply with demands to do it "right."
	(c)	Help from antidepressants or therapy may be sought in a crisis.
Erratic Anger(Borderline Personalities)	(a)	Caretakers were alternately rejecting or smothering, creating a long-term pattern of rapid mood swings, stormy relationships, and extremes in perception.
	(b)	Sudden outbursts from feelings of abandonment, suffocation, and victimization.
	(c)	Mood stabilizers, antidepressants, and anger management may help *over time*.
Narcissistic Anger	(a)	Parents may have been indulgent or not set limits, causing people to feel entitled.
	(b)	Rage is triggered by any lack of approval that threatens sense of self-worth.
	(c)	Fear of losing people or jobs that supply self-esteem *may* prompt desire for help. Mood stabilizers can reduce wordiness and help people engage in lengthy therapy.
Defiant Anger(Antisocial Personalities)	(a)	Never bonded with or developed trust in caretakers, causing rejection of authority and lack of internalized controls. Others are considered a means to an end.
	(b)	Rage from early unmet needs can be triggered anytime or on anyone.
	(c)	Due to lack of concern about others or rules, there is little chance of change.

Handout 6.4—Finding Life After Loss

Grief is an instinctual reaction to loss. A significant death triggers a response similar to what children do when separated from their mothers: they (1) protest and try to return to them; (2) despair of reuniting but remain preoccupied with them; (3) lose interest and emotionally detach. In theory, adults are like young ones seeking reunion with the deceased person. Any loss or change can cause a similar reaction, including:

- Death of a loved one or a pet, or a miscarriage

- Loss of health (your own or a friend's), a job, financial stability, a cherished dream, a friendship, safety after a trauma, a relationship due to a breakup

- Change in status due to graduating, retiring, leaving home

Responses to Loss and Change

If grief is based on the attachment instinct, why do individuals express the passing of a loved one so differently? As people mature, relationships become interwoven with connections to family, careers, religious traditions, and even to your innermost Self. People with many associations may recover faster from traumatic loss. Your attachment bond with your original caretaker will also affect how you grieve:

Original Attachment Bond	**Secure**	Children are comforted by parents but can separate. Adults may grieve intensely and then move on.
	Preoccupied	Children experience separation anxiety, but are hard to comfort. As adults, people are hard to comfort when a relationship ends.
	Avoidant	Children do not seek comfort or contact. As adults, people experience little distress when a relationship ends.
	Mixed	Children are both frightened and comforted by caretakers. Stormy adult relationships. Dramatic endings and grieving.

Finding a New Normal

If grief is simply an instinctual reaction to the loss of attachment, its purpose would be to rebuild the self-governing individual who can leave a lost loved one and find alternative connections. The survivor is brought to a new normal in a changed world. Other theorists believe that grief is a process of creating meaning and fostering bonds with the deceased.

- **Finding meaning.** Whether people realize it or not, they are constantly constructing and revising autobiographies to find meaning in their existence. There is a pull to believe life is predictable and unchanging, but a great loss forces people to write a new story. Questions must be asked to make sense of death, or it will be nonsense: *What does life mean? Why did death come at this time? What did this person mean to me? What was my role in the event? Was this death God's will or a tragic mistake? Is there free will or should God intervene?*

- **Fostering internal bonds.** Important people we have lost become permanent fixtures in our inner conversation. Mourners may be unaware of subtle connections, as suggested by the comment: *I never do that because my* (no longer living) *mother would be disappointed*. History gives precedent for persistent communion with the dead, rather than severing of all ties—surnames, memorials to war dead, and adopting causes of fallen martyrs. Perhaps the goal of grief is to reestablish a secure attachment to the deceased on a spiritual level.

The Dance of Grief

In 1969, psychiatrist Elisabeth Kübler-Ross described five stages of grief based on studies of patients facing terminal illnesses. Contrary to popular belief, you do not have to go through each phase in order to heal. Many people resolve grief without going through *any* of these stages or do not experience them in sequential order. However, it can be helpful to know what could happen:

- **Denial:** This can't be happening to me.
- **Anger:** This shouldn't have happened! Who is to blame?
- **Bargaining:** Make this not happen, and in return I will …
- **Depression:** I'm too sad to do anything.
- **Acceptance:** I'm at peace with what happened.

Usually, grieving is like a roller coaster. In the beginning, the lows are steep and long, but later become less intense and shorter. Even years after a loss, special life events can trigger sadness.

Accelerated Information Processing

There is a type of therapy that is especially effective in speeding recovery.[1] People focus on thoughts, images, and body sensations that intensify feelings while using eye movements that both compel relaxation and assist reprocessing of information. The following script from a partial session demonstrates the interplay of *disturbing thoughts* and easing of emotions. The mother's **comments** and *thoughts* are shown in bold or italicized fonts. They are elicited by the therapist's questions (TQ) or by tracking the counselor's hand to make eye movements (EMS):

A mother focuses on the image of her 14-year-old son's dead body in the hospital. He died 2 years previously when a car struck him. (TQ) → **I failed; I should have acted on my premonition that something bad was going to happen to him. … I feel devastated and tense all over.** (EMs) →

I feel nauseous. (EMs) → **I'm feeling a little calmer.** (EMs) → **I'm feeling a little calmer.** (TQ): **I still feel some distress.** (TQ) → *My son is not here.* (EMs) → **I blocked it.** The therapist asks her to focus on the thought that her son is not here during the next EM set.

The mother begins sobbing. Her therapist taps her shoulders (since she is crying too hard to move her eyes) and encourages her to make noise and breathe. **I'm angry … I feel it in my chest.** (EMs)→ *It shouldn't have happened.* (EMs) → *He took the wrong kid. … Other kids are abused. … He was happy. … He did well in school. … He was getting along better than his older brothers. …*

The therapist asks her to go back to the thought, *He took the wrong kid.* (EMs) → *He took the right kid.* (EMs) → *He's saying, 'I'm okay Mom.'* The therapist asks, "What does he mean?" **I'm afraid to ask.** The therapist suggests, "Focus on the thought; *I'm afraid to ask you about being okay.*" (EM) → *He is saying everything is going to be alright.*

(TQ) → **I'm feeling completely calm.** The therapist asks her to look at the original image of her son, DOA, in the hospital. (TQ) → **I feel calm … peaceful.** She looks entirely serene.

Boldface and italics are used in the case study to distinguish mother's spoken comments from thoughts that emerge during processing

---

This case story is an excellent example of recreating a healing bond with the deceased. You learn from all your relationships, even bad ones. A difficult breakup can make it hard to find meaning or foster internal connection with a lost love. The next case just focuses on the thoughts that people commonly experience when they grieve. As the acceleration of information proceeds, *negative thoughts* begin to alternate with *positive ideas.*

A young woman pictures her ex-lover and thinks: *I cannot do anything to get him back.* → *It's a picture, not a person.* → *It just captures a moment in time.* → *Who he was, wasn't what I wanted.* → *I miss him.* → *I don't want to completely forget him.* → *Holding on is safer than moving on.* → *What is the point of loving if I'm going to lose?* → *You can't go through life without experiencing things.* → *You love tea, but some blends don't taste just right.* → *Future relationships are a risk you'll have to take.*

Underline italics and regular italics are used in the case study to show how negative thoughts alternate with positive thoughts.

---

1. *EMDR: The Breakthrough Therapy for Overcoming Anxiety, Stress, and Trauma,* by F. Shapiro and M. S. Forrest, 1997, New York: Basic Books, has a chapter that shows how this powerful therapeutic tool can be used to lay grief to rest.

Handout 6.5—Building Trust From Jealousy

Jealousy is a complex feeling made up of all three basic emotions: an underlying *fear* of loss or *sadness* is expressed as *anger*. In the extreme, people become dominated by excruciating anxiety, rage, and even paranoia. Before jealousy can be properly addressed, the boundaries that define relationships need clarification.

Relationship Rules

Without any rules, couples have a nonrelationship. Seeds of distrust are planted where there were none. Overly strict rules choke the love out of a partner and the life out of a marriage. The following suggest guidelines. If you and your partner cannot agree, seek an expert opinion.

- **Privacy.** Each person should be encouraged to have a life separate from their partner, but not a *private* life. There is no reason to deny access to email, Facebook, or financial accounts.

- **Same-sex friends.** Activities may include fishing, hunting, line dancing, luncheons, dinner dates, engaging in church, sports, educational, or community activities, and so on.

- **Noticing people.** It is normal heterosexual behavior to look at striking people (without gaping or making lewd comments). This can be a pleasant pastime for couples to share.

- **Opposite-sex friends.** Avoid activities with friends of the opposite sex that are not work-related *unless* your partner is welcome. This includes phone calls and emails. Be especially wary when a friend is seeking solace for a troubled marriage.

- **Time frames.** Solitary outings should *not* be more than once or twice a month, or be used to avoid relationship duties. Rarely should an activity interfere with the couple's bedtime routine.

- **Courtesy.** Tell your spouse where you are going and when you will be home. Call if you might be late. Pepper your partner with information about what you did so he or she does not have to pry. This adds new blood into a relationship. Do not allow calls from friends to interfere with family time. Likewise, do not call or text your partner when he or she is out.

The Cause of Jealousy

It can be impossible to respect relationship rules when feelings of low self-worth and the need for attention feed jealousy. Most people try to soothe their angst with control tactics and end up feeling more powerless. To break this vicious cycle, a person must turn inward and discover his or her underlying concerns. Mark any of the following worries or fears that you have.

- ☐ Not being good enough (attractive enough) to hold on to your loved one.
- ☐ Being worthless without your partner or unable to find someone new.
- ☐ Not being able to survive on your own.
- ☐ The pain of loss, especially if you've had other losses.
- ☐ Being on the losing end of the relationship if your partner finds someone else.
- ☐ Being excluded from activities that don't involve you.
- ☐ Not getting enough attention.
- ☐ Being humiliated or looking like a fool if your partner is with someone else.
- ☐ Not being special, the most beautiful, or most important person in your partner's life.
- ☐ Being used and taken advantage of by everyone or anyone.

In addition to psychological factors, men and women have ingrained sociological patterns and biological differences that contribute to jealousy:

Jealous Males	Jealous Females
Historical purpose: Keeps a man from investing limited resources in raising another man's children.	**Historical purpose:** Kept mates from straying; protects commitments to the home and young.
Biology: Jealous thoughts activate subcortical brain regions rich in testosterone, which involve sexual and aggressive behavior.	**Biology:** Jealous thoughts trigger brain regions in the cortex that detect intentions, deception, trustworthiness, and abuse of social norms.
Behavior: Dominant, critical, on the outlook for hidden meanings, controlling about dress and social activities.	**Behavior:** Check whom partners talk to or look at; try to keep them at home with chores or by faking illness; make social arrangements.

Suggested Solutions

- The *less* you need your partner to ease your jealousy, the *more* you will feel assured.
- The *less* you accommodate your partner, the *more* chance for trust to be gained.

Whether jealousy is due to your imagination, frivolous gossip, or an actual betrayal, the above facts must be faced to recover from low self-esteem, suspicion, and competitiveness. People with trust issues need to admit their problem, *and* their partners must stop jumping through hoops to ease doubts. The following steps start to reverse downward spirals:

Jealous Parties	Targets of Jealousy
1. Admit you are jealous to yourself before you even have a chance to conjure up accusations.	1. Treat jealous attacks as if they are expressions of affection—*You really do love me. ...*
2. Identify the underlying emotion triggered by an event—feeling inadequate, abandoned, excluded, unimportant, and so on.	2. Ask questions directed at insecurities causing accusations—*What is it like for you when I ...?.*
3. Experience your emotions instead of avoiding them with accusations or asking for reassurance. Ask yourself questions instead of your partner—*Why am I tormenting myself with this idea?*	3. Become comfortable with your partner's distress. Do not try to reassure or fix him or her. It's fine to be sympathetic—*It must feel awful when you think I have feelings for someone else.*
4. Float back to your earliest memory of jealousy. Find the root of your insecurity. Seek professional help to address problems that dominate your life.	4. When you notice the opposite sex, do so appropriately, without gaping, and then give your partner a little extra attention.
5. Express underlying feelings with a statement that starts with ''I''—*I felt insecure (alone, lost) when you. ...* Do not interrogate, blame, or assume.	5. Express feelings provoked by jealousy as a simple statement that starts with ''I''— *I think you do not listen to me, when you ask me the same question I answered before.*
6. Make simple requests that will help relieve your feelings—*Would you give me a hug, call me when you're late, or introduce me?*	6. Ask your partner to rephrase your responses to ensure that he or she is listening—*What did you hear me say about why I did not call?*
7. Identify any unrealistic expectation you have—*If my partner notices someone else, it means he doesn't love me; If my partner finds others attractive, then she might leave me.* Discuss these with a professional. Do not expect your partner to make you feel better.	7. Keep a jealousy journal. Write every jealous question your partner asks you and record your response. Refer back to previous answers when questions are repeated. Do not address more than two questions in one talking session.
8. If your partner betrayed you, take responsibility for healing your wounded ego by changing beliefs that you are inadequate or stupid for not ''preventing'' the infidelity.	8. Switch roles. Act *as if* you are jealous and have your partner pretend to be trusting. Even if your partner will not agree to switch, shifting your behavior can alter a partner's pattern.
	9. If you have been unfaithful, you may need to end your affair *in front of* your partner and agree to have bank statements, phone bills, or email monitored for an indefinite period of time.

Handout 6.6—Journeying to Forgiveness

For many people, forgiveness is forced, superficial, or too difficult. The problem lies in a lack of understanding its real meaning. To forgive is to *recognize* what truly happened. Recognize means to reknow. In forgiveness there is a reknowing of events on many levels. This reknowing begins by recognizing the core (victim) beliefs you have that separate you from a source of power deep within you.[1]

A. Recognize the image, beliefs, and sensations that hurt you:

1. **Image.** If you took a snapshot of the event or person that hurt you, what would it look like? Put this in words *without attempting to be fair*. If it is too long a story to write, just name the person or form a mental image of him or her.

    > A.1:

2. **Core (victim) belief.** Ask yourself, "When I focus on the person or event in A.1, What does it mean about me?"—*I'm not enough; I'm powerless, helpless, trapped, unloveable, foolish, unimportant, alone . . . ; I'm not in control* . . . Write the belief in box A.2.a.

    > A.2.a:

    > A.2.b:

3. **Adaptive belief.** Now ask yourself a harder question: "When I focus on A.1, what would I like to believe about myself?"—*I am enough, loveable, important . . . ; I have power, I can do something, find support . . . ; I can respond to (learn from) this* . . . Write the belief in box A.2.b.

4. **Sensations and feelings.** Go back to focusing on A.1 and your victim belief (A.2.a). What sensations do you notice? Locate *where* you feel distress in your body. You may be able to attach a feeling to the sensation—hurt, anger, disapproval, inadequacy, anxiety, and so on.

5. **Releasing emotions that trap core beliefs.** Focus on the upsetting images (A.1), victim beliefs, and body sensations. Initially, this will increase your distress but eventually it will lessen. Ideally, this should be done with a therapist trained in helping people release emotions, but telling your story (A.1.) to a trusted friend may also help. *Real forgiveness does not happen without feeling the pain!*

B. Recognize repeating patterns:

1. **Core beliefs gain power in three ways.** They (a) are acquired during an early painful experience that attracts people and situations to reinforce them; (b) have little influence until a random event brings them to the forefront; (c) are superimposed on unrelated situations.

2. **Repeating core beliefs.** When you start to release emotions (A.5), earlier memories with the same core beliefs can surface. To avoid surprises in the presence of strong emotions, float back to the first time you had your upsetting thought (A.2.a).

    The first time I remember feeling trapped, powerless, helpless, alone, betrayed, lost . . . was:

---

1. Some of the steps in this handout were influenced by the protocols of EMDR. See *EMDR: The Breakthrough Therapy for Overcoming Anxiety, Stress, and Trauma* (Basic Books, 1997). The theories of *Radical Forgiveness,* by C. Tipping, 2002, Marietta, GA: Global 13 Publications, were revised to be more reflective of cognitive therapy.

3. **Understand your vicious cycle.** This will help you admit one or more of the following facts:

- Some of your discomfort comes from wanting another person or situation to change. The more you want others to change (even in your mind) the more they will resist change. Instead look inward to identify core victim beliefs.

- Being hurt *creates an opportunity* to identify your core beliefs about yourself (A.2.a).

- These victim beliefs can generate repeated upsetting experiences.

- Being hurt can also help you find strength you did not know you had or a new purpose in life (to prevent similar tragedies).

C. Recognize what you need to understand:

1. **Identifying your core beliefs** (A.2.a) creates an opportunity to change from a victim to a victor mentality—*I am good enough, loveable, . . .; I have power; I can do something, find support . . .; I can respond to (learn from) this. . . .*

2. **Others' behavior** is determined by their beliefs, backgrounds, character, and maturity level. If you choose to continue your relationship with them, look past their flaws and focus on their good qualities. Have compassion for the ignorance or pain that caused their missteps.

3. **Your difficulty was just painful enough** (you survived) to force you to look inside and find the core beliefs that contributed to your distress *or* a new meaning/purpose for your life. Decide how you can use your experience to help yourself or others.

D. For-give:

1. In **GIVING appreciation** to others **FOR** the part they played in helping you know and change yourself you FORGIVE them.

2. **Refocus** on the original situation (A.1) and notice what you feel. If you still detect distress, go back over steps in A–C.

3. **Realizations.** Make a statement about what you now realize about the part others were playing in helping you know and change yourself from victim to victor. *I now realize that when _____ did what he or she did (A.1), it brought up my deeply buried core belief that I am. . . . The more I release the hurt clustered around that belief, the more I will know that what I want to believe about myself (I am . . .) is true.*

E. Find your power:

1. **Inner source:** Listen inside for the voice that knows the truth about you—*I am good enough, loveable, important. . . . I have power; I can do something, find support. . . . I can respond to (learn from) this. . . .* Give the quiet calming voice a name—inner guide, knower, spirit. . . .

2. **Listen.** Ask your true Self what words of wisdom this experience offers you. What can you and what can you not change? *Forgiveness is not forgetting!* Do you trust your *Self* to respond to any future incidents? Can you stop pressuring your *Self* to *prevent* more pain?

3. **Reknow.** Ask this inner presence what it now feels toward the person who triggered the hurtful beliefs you had about yourself. Its voice will help you feel calm, confidence, and compassion—not tense or guarded.

4. **Learn.** Ask your true being what you will gain by knowing that the other person helped you discover (a) your core beliefs, (b) your new victor identity, and (c) the strength to take any future needed action.

Handout 6.7—Transcending Trauma—Informed Consent

A traumatic event is traditionally described as one in which people are threatened with death or serious injury or witnessed the same. People's ability to digest their experience may become disrupted. Such stress hormones as adrenaline and cortisol cement images, body sensations, and incorrect perceptions into memory networks—*It's my fault, I'm not safe, I'm trapped*. Because old information is not *processed* and *adapted* to current circumstances,[1] people may have three categories of symptoms lasting for more than a month or many years:

1. Reexperiencing (1+ of the following):	☐Intrusive memories; ☐flashbacks (reliving the event without awareness of the present); ☐nightmares; ☐panic attacks; ☐repetitive play (children)
2. Avoiding (3+ of the following):	☐Avoidance of thoughts, activities, or people related to the event; ☐poor recall of parts of the event; ☐feeling detached/numb; ☐reduced range of feelings; ☐decreased interested in usual activities; ☐future forebodings
3. Hyperarousal (2+ of the following):	☐Hypervigilance; ☐difficulty falling/staying asleep; ☐irritability or angry outbursts; ☐trouble concentrating; ☐exaggerated startle response

Wikipedia identifies and evaluates three main types of treatment for trauma other than medication. The following guide can help you find a therapist with whom you feel safe and consider any medication needs. The mechanism for change is *italicized* in each therapeutic method:

Therapy

Therapy and Mechanism of Treatment	Effectiveness
Exposure therapy (ET): Helps people repeatedly confront feared thoughts, sensations, and situations through imagination or actual contact. There is a change in evaluation of threat due to lack of expected harm. *A new, competing memory is formed.*	The success of ET has raised questions of whether it is necessary in the treatment of trauma. Some groups do endorse the need for exposure.
Cognitive behavior therapy (CBT) : *Changes the patterns of thinking and/or behavior* that are responsible for victims' negative emotions. In doing so, people change the way they feel and act. The goal is to understand how certain thoughts about trauma cause stress and make symptoms worse.	The *British Journal of Psychiatry* has recommended trauma-specific CBT or EMDR as first-line treatments. A comparison of EMDR and CBT found both protocols to have similar results.
Eye Movement Desensitization and Reprocessing therapy (EMDR): Alternately stimulates the right and left hemispheres of the brain with eye movements, bilateral sounds, or taps while people focus on disturbing images, body sensations, and thoughts. *The initial memory of the event is altered.* Imagery may fade or change, inaccurate thoughts adapt to current circumstances, and body sensations decrease in intensity.	The American Psychiatric Association, U.S. Dept. of Veterans Affairs, and U.S. Dept. of Defense have placed EMDR in the highest category of effectiveness based on research. Several international bodies have had similar conclusions.
Medications: Prozac, Lexapro, etc. (selective serotonin reuptake inhibitors—SSRIs) can help take the edge off of trauma effects; antianxiety medication (benzodiazepines—Xanax, Clonopin, etc.) are initially useful for disturbed sleep.	SSRIs help with reexperiencing and hyperarousal but not avoidance symptoms. Benzodiazepine dependence can hinder recovery from trauma.

Your therapist will help you learn self-calming tools to use when therapy becomes too intense or if symptoms surface between sessions. EMDR, in particular, has been shown to help some people with single incidents of trauma recover in 1–4 hours of treatment.

---

1. Francine Shapiro formulated the Adaptive Information Processing Theory to explain and predict treatment effects seen with the therapy she developed: Eye Movement Desensitization and Reprocessing (EMDR). It is explained in *EMDR: The Breakthrough Therapy for Overcoming Anxiety, Stress, and Trauma.* NY: Guilford Press.

Time Frames for Treatment

It is never too late or too early to treat the disturbing effects of trauma. People who suffer from intrusive memories of nightmarish events that happened 30 or more years in the past can completely recover.

In the first few weeks following highly charged incidents, some treatment approaches suggest waiting to see if trauma symptoms occur because many people do not develop disorders. Other theorists believe this is a fertile time for intervention. Separate points of disturbance have not knitted together into a cohesive whole. Therapy soon after an incident can help integrate memory fragments, prevent interference from negative thoughts, and find a positive meaning in the experience.

Distressing Life Experiences

You may not have experienced an event that threatened your life or safety, but still have symptoms of people who have suffered from bona fide traumas. Being ridiculed by a parent, failing a grade, or dealing with an unwanted pregnancy are situations that trigger stress hormones. The associated negative images, body sensations, and self-perceptions can be embedded into memory networks. Facing an authority figure may suddenly seem difficult even though the unsettling event contributing to distress happened years ago. Before working on a recent trauma or other current upsetting circumstances, it can help to list previous disturbing memories.

Directions: List your 10 most upsetting memories starting from age 4 or older. Rate how hurtful each memory was on a 0–10 scale, with 10 being highly disturbing. You can include memory fragments and adult memories, but you will probably address intact childhood (feeder) memories first.

	Rating 0–10
1. _____	_____
2. _____	_____
3. _____	_____
4. _____	_____
5. _____	_____
6. _____	_____
7. _____	_____
8. _____	_____
9. _____	_____
10. _____	_____

Whether you are working on a trauma or a distressing life experience, the way in which you approach events can vary. A woman who had dealt with workplace bullying first addressed the *earliest, worst,* and *most recent* incident in which she was harassed. Then she focused on *future* fears of facing coworkers. Another person focused on her panic attacks and the triggers for them in a similar order (earliest, worst, most recent, and future triggers). When thoroughly treated, trauma can be transcended with life-affirming insights.

Handout 6.8—Thinking Thin

Cognitive therapy is based on the idea that *automatic thoughts* cause all excessive emotional reactions. The surprising thing is that they also precede *all* food cravings. This creates an excellent opportunity to identify your **automatic food thoughts**. When you have urges to eat, ask yourself, *What was going through my mind just now?* The following list can help you identify your mental triggers for excessive eating:

Permission-Giving Thoughts

____ It won't matter if I eat this because . . .

____ I really want to eat that; I deserve this.

____ I can't resist this. . . . It looks so tasty.

____ I don't want to (I'm not ready to) stop eating.

____ It's a special occasion; I'm on vacation.

____ I'm hungry; I need to eat when I'm hungry.

____ I've lost weight, so now I can eat what I want.

____ No one can tell me what to eat.

____ I'll eventually eat it, so why not now?

____ I hardly ever get to eat this.

Catastrophizing Thoughts

____ What if I get hungry later?

____ It's not fair (I'll feel deprived) if I can't eat. . . .

____ Since I've blown my diet today, why bother?

____ I can't offend others by refusing what's offered.

____ I can't waste it. I have no will power.

____ It shouldn't be this hard; I can't keep this up.

____ This will never work; it's hopeless.

____ I'm too upset (bored) to have self-control.

Sabotaging Thoughts

____ I don't have to . . . (follow this part of my plan).

____ I don't have time to . . .

Minimizing Thoughts

____ These calories don't count (free samples).

____ It's just crumbs; It's not that fattening.

____ I'll make up for eating it later by . . .

____ No one will know if I eat it.

Use thin thinking to defy automatic food thoughts: *Is this thought true or helpful? How will I feel in 30 minutes if I eat this? Which is more important—a brief taste sensation or losing weight?* Thin thinking strengthens **resistance ability** and weakens **giving-in urges**. Distinguish between hunger and cravings. The first is experienced as an empty feeling in the stomach and rumbling sounds. Cravings cause tension in the mouth, throat, or body and desires for specific foods. The more you wait out cravings, the less intense or often they will be.

Must-Do Weight Loss Preparation Steps[1]

1. **Have a food plan.** Talk to your doctor or research several possible diets. An excellent Internet source is www.MyPyramid.gov. Base your plan on preset servings in each food group or on calorie intake. One mixed drink can have 400 calories. If you allow for alcohol, plan ahead how much you will drink. Follow drinks with no-calorie beverages.

2. **Design an exercise program** from a favorite activity. Exercise helps control appetite, increases commitment, burns calories, helps weight loss come from fat rather than muscle, and improves health. Start by exercising 5 minutes a day and then increase your time.

3. **List your goals.** *I'll have fewer cravings; I'll feel less guilty.* Other weight loss reasons may have to do with appearance, style, health, sex, or self-esteem. Make several copies of your list and place it strategically—on your computer, the refrigerator, and in your wallet.

---

1. The ideas in *Thin Thinking* are adapted from *The Beck Diet Solution,* by J. S. Beck, 2007, Birmingham, AL: Oxmoor House.

4. **Arrange your environment.** Put tempting foods where they are not easily seen or out of your house altogether. Use smaller plates. Tell others you share your living/work space with to help you keep enticing foods out of sight. Bring healthy snacks to work.

5. **Find a diet buddy** who is positive, good at problem solving, and motivating. His or her role is to hear your successes and help you plan ways to deal with setbacks or high-risk situations.

6. **Determine your initial weight** and set *only* short-term goals—5 pounds at a time.

THINKING THIN TASKS   **Directions:** Review your accomplishments every night and discuss them with your diet buddy.

Daily Tasks (items are helpful for people with bulimia)*

❑ **1. Plan what you are going to eat and monitor food intake.** Choosing a preset number of servings in each food group makes planning ahead easy. Tracking food intake on a daily food log (Handout 6.10) can be simple and rewarding.

❑ **2. Read your weight loss goals** at least twice a day. Pick scheduled times and read them again when dealing with temptation.

❑ **3. Mental credits.** Silently say, *Good job! Good going! Yes! I did it!* when you read your goals, pass up an urge, refrain from a second helping, ignore baked goods at work, and so on.

❑ **4. *Overcome cravings.** Put a tempting food out of sight or throw it away. The second you pull your hand back or take a step away, give yourself mental credit. Breathe into the area of tension. Use *Thin Thinking*. Cravings peak within in the first few weeks and then subside.

❑ **5. Practice hunger tolerance.** It is important to realize that hunger is not an emergency. From 20 minutes to 3 hours after a meal, *thoughts* of hunger are false. It is important to know you can wait until your next scheduled meal or snack to eat. When you feel hungry while waiting for food to be served or preparing dinner, tell yourself, *This is not a crisis!*

❑ **6. Prevent unplanned eating.** Stick to your food plan and make any food rules that will help, such as eating only raw vegetables while fixing dinner. You have other habits that are easy to follow like brushing your teeth and buckling your seat belt, so you can make *your* food rules a routine.

❑ **7. *Eat sitting down.** Eating standing up weakens resistance ability (6.18). Stop eating while cooking meals, putting away leftovers, or shopping.

❑ **8. *Eat slowly with awareness.** There is a lag of 20 minutes between your stomach's filling up and your brain's registering satisfaction. Eating slowly and noticing each mouthful gives your brain more time to realize fullness. Put your flatware down or take a sip of water every few bites.

❑ **9. *Recognize normal fullness.** Initially, this can be hard because your stomach may be stretched or you may have fears of hunger. Strictly measure your portions and let that be your guide. Move serving dishes to the side of the table and extra food to the side of your plate. When you finish your planned portions, put the handles of your flatware in the remaining food. Give yourself instant mental credit (#3) when you refrain from overeating.

❑ **10. Practice portion control.** Intentionally put more food on your plate than you are supposed to eat and shove the extra amount to one side. When you've finished your allowed amount, throw the extra away or save it for another meal. If you are tempted to gorge, practice overcoming cravings (#4), and give yourself mental credit (#3) as soon as your resist. Rehearse this prior to difficult situations.

Occasional Tasks

❑ **11. * Identify emotional eating.** Anger, sadness, anxiety, boredom, and even excitement can trigger emotional eating. Recognize the feeling and remind yourself that you can tolerate hurt just as you would any other craving. Make a NO EATING decision. Ask yourself how long the pleasure of food will distract you from your distress. Identify the thought triggering the feeling.

☐   **12. *Get back on track.** Having slips is normal and does not need to be a reason to go off your food plan. It takes 3,500 calories to gain 1 pound. Admit your slip and take a symbolic action to show you are back on the wagon. Read your weight loss goals, brush your teeth, touch your knees or toes, or take three breaths. Give yourself mental credit (#3) the second you step away from food— *Wow, I stopped that binge.* Don't try to make up for a mistake by reducing your calorie intake. Go over your mistake with your diet buddy and strategize what you could have done to prevent it.

☐   **13. *Deal with food pushers.** Which is worse—the resentment you feel if you take food from someone pushing it or the *possible* rejection he or she will feel if you say no? The easiest way to refuse persistent food pushers is to turn the tables and ask them questions: *Why is it important that I eat this now? Do you know how hard it is for me to turn down delicious food?*

☐   **14. Weigh in weekly.** Weigh at the same time of day in similar clothes. If you think you have had a bad week, the tell-all scale will renew your resolve. Expect to lose $1/2$ to 2 pounds a week. Plateaus in weight loss of 2–3 weeks are normal.

Handout 6.9—Not Thinking Too Thin

People with eating disorders are driven by fears of gaining weight. Self-esteem hinges on the number reflected on the scale. All or parts of their bodies seem grossly overweight and they may check scales and mirrors frequently. Thought processes are black or white: Foods are good or bad, bodies are fat or thin, they are in control or out of control. Men with the disorder may be perfectionists and low-fat eaters and hide behind an obsession with concerns about health or fitness. People who constantly compare their weight to others and are preoccupied with diet and food may have a disorder. The criteria below complete the clinical picture for anorexia and bulimia.[1]

Anorexia (Greek for loss of appetite)	Bulimia (Greek for ox hunger)
Criteria: 1. Body weight 15% below normal. 2. Absence of three consecutive menstrual cycles. 3. Calorie intake one-fourth that of a moderately active person. *4. Low self-esteem.	**Criteria:** 1. Binge episodes that cause guilt or out-of-control feelings followed by ritual to prevent weight gain (vomiting, laxative, fasting, or excessive exercise). 2. Binge/ritual cycle occurs two times a week for 3 months. 3. Weight is near normal.
Rituals: Religiously recording number of calories eaten, arranging food on plates, cutting food into specific number of small pieces, chewing a certain number of times, exercising to keep the body in a continual state of deprivation.	**Rituals:** Hiding binge-purge ritual, stealing food, digging through trash for food, looking for the nearest bathroom, *compulsive shopping (to fill unmet emotional needs). Long-standing preoccupation with eating/diet. Deny addictive potential of initial binge-purge episode.
Medical dangers: 5–20% have cardiac arrest due to electrolyte imbalances. Can lose heart mass and chamber size; heart rate slows down. Loss of hair on the head; growth of fine hair on the body. Low body temperature, low blood pressure. Delayed gastric emptying causes bloating.	**Medical dangers:** Imbalances in potassium, chloride, and sodium (electrolytes) lead to irregular heartbeat. Vomiting can cause choking, swelling of the esophagus, blisters, rotten teeth, and swollen salivary glands (chipmunk cheeks). *Exercise when body is depleted leads to dehydration.
Course: Can start in childhood or later. *Initially, raises self-esteem. Once a person's body weight reaches a starvation level, they will become preoccupied with food and need exercise and eating rituals to control food thoughts. In the later stages of starvation, people cease thinking about food. Many anorexics turn to bulimia.	**Course:** Starts in late teens or early 20s. Binges can be triggered by high numbers on the scale, eating something forbidden, taking one extra bite, difficult feelings, or just thinking about food. **Feelings:** *worthlessness* → *comfort* from a binge → *confidence* from a purge → *hope* that this is the last purge → return to *worthlessness*.
Causes: 1. Overbearing families, leaving home, a divorce, or death may trigger the *need to gain control* through anorexia. 2. *Food rituals are used to hide feelings of depression, anger, or rejection. 3. Clinical *depression and obsessive-compulsive disorder (OCD).	**Causes:** 1. Being thin is a way to please society and diet-conscious families. 2. Family histories with depression, addictions, eating disorders. 3. *Are often ideal children or people pleasers who fear criticism, failure, and conflict.
Effects: Gain a sense of power from low weight; *keep people at a distance until food becomes their sole relationship. *Even if they seem to be present in a conversation, their minds are on food.	**Effects:** During a binge, eating sweets and fatty food increases levels of endorphins; consumption of carbohydrates boosts serotonin. *An effective way to cope with difficulties through distracting rituals.
Coping with sexual abuse: A childlike body is a way to avoid intimacy. Rituals are used to control what does and does not go into the body. *Avoid risk of further abuse by only having a relationship with food. *Shift the focus from the trauma to intense preoccupation with food and weight.	**Coping with sexual abuse:** Eating and vomiting parallel act of forced oral sex. Stuffing down food stuffs down the anger and silences the voice that cries, *Don't do this to me!* Anxiety is numbed and physical needs denied. (*Rate of sexual abuse is a little higher than for women without eating disorders.)
*Items are true for both anorexia and bulimia.	

Recovery from Anorexia   One-third of anorexics fully recover. A second third reach maintenance weights, but still obsess over food. Treatment time is linked to the number of years spent being anorexic and to how low weight is when therapy is started. Medication is important when anorexics are depressed or have OCD. Hospitalization is needed if malnutrition is life threatening.

---

1. Information in these handouts came from *Anorexia Nervosa: A Guide to Recovery,* by L. Hall and M. Ostrof, 1999, Carlsbad, CA: Gürze Books; and *Bulimia: A Guide to Recovery,* by L. Hall and L. Cohn (Carlsbad, CA: Gürze Books, 1998.

Weight Restoring Tasks for Anorexia (*Items Also Help Bulimia)

☐ **Choose life.** Decide at a basic level that you want to live. Realize that what you think you are controlling is really controlling you.

☐ **Understand metabolism.** Your body has a *set point* or weight range that it fights to maintain. It is determined by your age, health, activity level, and genes. When your weight goes below your set point, your metabolism slows down. As your weight returns to normal, your metabolism will speed up, so you can increase food intake without gaining too many pounds.

☐ **Understand fluid retention.** Until your metabolism normalizes, you may feel bloated even after eating a small amount of food. This is a side effect of starvation and will normalize.

☐ **Increase food intake slowly** with the guidance of a doctor or nutritionist. Ice-cube size portions every 2–3 hours may be easier than three full meals. If you have severely restricted food intake, start with items that are easy to digest, and vitamin and mineral supplements. Work toward a balanced plan with recommended portions of protein, carbohydrate, and fat.

☐ ***Face fearful food thoughts.** Gradually introduce foods you consider forbidden. Expect intense anxiety. Set a timer for 10 minutes. Experience excruciating thoughts without acting on them—*I've made a terrible mistake; I'll get huge; I can't eat for the rest of the day; I need to get to the gym; Maybe I can vomit;* and so on. When the timer goes off, say out loud, "It's only food! I deserve to eat without fear!" Then, distract yourself with an enjoyable activity. As soon as critical food thoughts intrude, redirect your attention. Ask yourself, *Is my concern over this food an attempt to avoid other feelings?* Tell yourself, *Good job! Way to go!* when you do not use rituals to offset increased calorie intake. Initially, you may need a professional or a supportive friend present during this task.

☐ **Continue to face feared foods** until you become comfortable with a more varied diet. Eventually, you will not need to struggle against thoughts to restrict eating or exercise excessively.

☐ ***Recognize thinking errors.** People with eating disorders are especially good at **all-or-nothing thinking** (*Carrots are good, bread is bad; Why walk if I can run*); **magnifying negatives** (*It's all over if I gain a pound; If someone disagrees with me, they hate me*); **mind reading** (*other people are judging me*); and using **shoulds** (*I should only eat egg whites, I should not say anything negative*).

☐ ***Notice your feelings.** Facing food fears and recognizing thinking errors are designed to trigger feelings. Notice exactly *where* you feel tension in your body and if the location changes. Say to yourself, *I'm terrified, sad, ashamed.* Cry if you need to. Learn that feelings pass.

☐ ***Identify your inner critic** that constantly scolds you. Realize it is a part of your personality that came to believe being thin would help you manage your life better.

☐ ***Question the voice of your critic.** You can do this in writing or silently in your mind. Refer to yourself in the third person and talk directly to your critic: *What was happening in Kate's life when you gained so much power over what she could and could not eat? When did you start to place so much value on body image? Why do you compare Kate to women 30 years younger than her?*

☐ ***Discover your true Self.** Take a moment to wonder who is asking your inner critic questions. Is it a soft, quiet voice that has always been beyond the reach of parental demands and cultural expectations? When you engage in extreme eating behavior, you may have heard it quietly say, *This is not right*—but it never orders. Eventually, it will be important to follow its guidance.

☐ ***Challenge body image.** In the beginning, you may need to take radical steps: Stop getting on scales or looking in mirrors. Wear loose clothing. Tell yourself, *Good job!* every time you force yourself not to check how flat your tummy is. Talk to your critic. Be compassionate: *I know you still think Kate is too big when she is 10 pounds thinner than many women her age. It's hard to give up the false sense of confidence you get from being underweight.* Listen to how your critic responds.

☐ ***Write a new goal for each day.** Complete a meal, tell your feelings to a family member, eat with others, make a collage of people who are normal or above normal weight.

Recovery from Bulimia

Recovery from bulimia begins by changing binge-purge patterns. It then progresses to addressing obsessive food thoughts, improving relationships with parents, making more friends, handling conflicts, and becoming self-nurturing—not necessarily in that order. Many bulimics have found antidepressants helpful, but talk therapy is a must.

Healthy Eating Tasks for Bulimics (*Items Also Help Anorexia)

Preparation Steps

☐ **1. Decide to recover.** Although some people can stop bingeing cold turkey, a more realistic goal may be to gradually reduce overeating.

☐ **2. *Think of the reasons you want to stop**—to have more honest relationships, to save money, to arrest dental problems, and so on. Make several copies of your list and place it strategically—on your computer, the refrigerator, and in your wallet. Read it twice a day and when temptation strikes.

☐ **3. Have a food plan.** When you start to eat normally, listening to true hunger signals will be difficult. It helps to have a plan based on preset servings in each food group. Tracking food intake on a food log (Handout 6.10) can be simple and rewarding. Discuss with a doctor or nutritionist the number of daily servings you should have. An online source is www.MyPyramid.gov.

☐ **4. Decide between an abstinence or legalized approach.** Abstinence approaches avoid any addictive type of foods (high sugar or salt content or white flour). Legalized approaches differentiate stomach huger from cravings. People are taught to focus on the foods they want and to eat in moderate portions when they are physically hungry. Often, it helps to start with a structured plan and then move to one with more options.

☐ **5. Design an exercise program** from a favorite activity. Exercise helps control appetite, increases commitment, improves health, and can be used to avoid a binge. Start by exercising 5 minutes a day and then increase your time. Make sure you are not using exercise to compensate for overeating.

☐ **6. Arrange your environment.** Put binge foods where they are not easily seen or out of your house altogether. Tell others with whom you share your living/work space to help you keep enticing foods out of sight. Bring healthy snacks to work.

☐ **7. Make a list of binge distracters.** Brush your teeth, gargle with mouthwash, soak binge food in water, leave the room that is tempting you, call a friend, read a book, punch a pillow, touch your toes or knees, take three breaths, exercise, write what you're thinking in a journal, or write down the foods you want to eat and burn the list. Make copies of your list and post them strategically. Set a timer for 5 minutes and start a distracting activity. Commit to delaying the binge for 5 minutes at a time.

☐ **8. Buy a day planner and gold stars.** Initially, you may want to give yourself a star every hour you do not binge. Later, you can give yourself a daily star. Reward yourself when you reach goals.

Change Eating, Thinking, and Relationship Patterns

☐ **9. Mental credits.** Silently say, *Good job! Yes! I did it!* whenever you use a distracter activity (#7).

☐ **10. Stop a binge in progress.** This is a very powerful accomplishment. Set aside a couple of bites to eat while you destroy anything else that might tempt you. Give yourself mental credit (#9) the second you step away from food—*Wow, I stopped that binge.* Don't try to make up for mistakes by purging.

☐ **11. Analyze binges in a journal.** It is inevitable that slips will happen, and describing them in writing is a *necessary* consequence! What was the trigger? List *all* the foods you ate. What were you thinking before, during, and afterward? Did you try to do something else? Why didn't it work? What could you have done instead? How long did the binge last? Did you purge? Did you consider not purging?

☐ **12. Stop secrecy.** For many bulimics, secrecy is one of the most difficult obstacles to overcome. Make a list of everyone who already knows about your problem and another list of everyone close to you whom you will tell. Identify the order of disclosure and how you will make contact. Knowing that your significant others are aware of your problem will burn bridges to bulimic behavior when you are around them and open lines of communication.

☐ **13. *Start a relaxation practice.** Sit in a comfortable position with your spine straight for 5 minutes. Pay exquisite attention to your breath. Think *In* on your inhale and *Out* on your exhale. When thoughts come, say, *thinking*, and go back to noticing your breath. Work up to 30 minutes of aware breathing.

Handout 6.10—Daily Food Log

Consult your doctor to determine the best food plan for you. Web sites (such as www.mypyramid.gov) can help calculate calorie intake based on your height and goal weight. If you stick to the basic food groups, this log will allow you to count food servings rather than calories.

Daily Food Log | Date _____

Food Group	Servings Allowed (Circle your daily allowance)	Single Serving Choices (__ fill in # servings)	Other Choices Made
Grains (whole grains preferred) 1 serving = 70 cal.	4 = 1,200 cal./day 5 = 1,400 cal./day 5 = 1,600 cal./day 6 = 1,800 cal./day 6 = 2,000 cal./day	___ 1 slice bread ___ 1 cup dry cereal, $1/2$ cup cooked rice, pasta, cereal ___ $1/2$ hamburger bun, bagel, English muffin ___ 5 small, 2–3 large crackers ___ 1 small roll; ☐ other	
Vegetables 1 serving = 60–90 cal.	1.5 = 1,200 cal./day 1.5 = 1,400 cal./day 2 = 1,600 cal./day 2.5 = 1,800 cal./day 2.5 = 2,000 cal./day	___ 2 cups dark green, leafy, summer squash, tomato ___ $1/2$ cup beets, peas, winter squash, brussels sprouts ___ 1 ear corn; 1 baked potato	
Fruits 1 serving = 80 cal.	1 = 1,200 cal./day 1.5 = 1,400 cal./day 1.5 = 1,600 cal./day 1.5 = 1,800 cal./day 2 = 2,000 cal./day	___ 1 medium apple, orange, banana, grapefruit ___ 1 cup berries ___ $1/2$ melon ___ $1/2$ cup dried fruit ___ 1 cup 100% juice	
Dairy (fat free or low fat preferred) 1 serving = 90 cal.	2 cups = 1,200 cal./day 2 cups = 1,400 cal./day 3 cups = 1,600 cal./day 3 cups = 1,800 cal./day 3 cups = 2,000 cal./day	___ 8 oz milk, yogurt ___ 1 $1/2$ oz natural cheese ___ $1/3$ cup shredded cheese ___ $1/2$ cup cottage cheese	
Protein 1 serving = 80 cal.	3 = 1,200 cal./day 4 = 1,400 cal./day 5 = 1,600 cal./day 5 = 1,800 cal./day 5.5 = 2,000 cal./day	___ 1 oz lean meat, fish ___ 1 egg ___ $1/4$ cup dried bean ___ $1/4$ cup tofu ___ 1 tbs peanut butter	
Fat 1 serving = 90–120 cal.	No more than three servings	___ 1 Tbs. oil, margarine, butter ___ 10–12 olives ___ $3/4$ oz nuts	

Approximate number of times I let a craving pass today: ☐☐☐☐☐☐☐☐☐☐☐☐☐☐☐

Exercise today: _____ Minutes of ☐ walking, ☐ running, ☐ climbing steps, ☐ yoga, ☐ gym, ☐ other:

Notes

1. If you prefer a higher protein diet, you can switch meat and bread servings. For instance, someone consuming 1,600 calories a day might use 2 bread servings and 8 protein servings.
2. Beware of diets of less than 1,200 calories a day. They cause bingeing and other eating disorders!
3. If you have a considerable amount of weight to lose, start with a 2,000-calorie-a-day diet. Decreasing food intake slows down metabolism. A plateau in weight loss of 6 weeks or more means you need to decrease 200 calories a day and increase your exercise, or you may be at a weight that is ideal for your body.
4. Make 30 copies of this log and keep them in a binder to simplify monitoring your daily food intake.

Handout 6.11 — Raising Self-Esteem

People with good self-esteem have positive perceptions of themselves. They can say, *I'm as good as others and they are as good as me*. This means, *I'm as good as my counselor, my pastor, and even my favorite movie star*. Although everyone has unique accomplishments, we are all born into a particular position in life and have our own special struggles. Self-worth is based more on perseverance than achievement. To gain a sense of your own self-esteem, take the following quick assessment adapted from Morris Rosenberg's original scale (Princeton University, 1965):

SELF-ESTEEM RATING SCALE	**Directions:** In the past 3 months, indicate how much each statement represents the way you think about yourself: strongly agree (SA), agree (A), disagree (D), strongly disagree (SD)	

Scoring: 3 = SA, 2 = A, 1 = D, 0 = SD	Scoring: 3 = SD, 1 = D, 2 = A, 0 = SA
___ On the whole I am satisfied with myself.	___ At times I think that I am no good at all.
___ I can list my successes or good qualities.	___ I do not have much to be proud of.
___ I am able to do things as well as most people.	___ I certainly feel useless at times.
___ I'm equal to others and they are equal to me.	___ I wish I had more respect for myself.
___ Myself and others deserve the best in life.	___ I'm inclined to think I'm a failure.
___ I can forgive myself and others for mistakes.	___ I often compare myself to others.
___ I can accept criticism without feeling awful.	___ I frequently put myself down.

Interpretation: Normal scores are between 35 and 21. Scores below 21 may be a cause of concern.

Three skills needed to raise self-esteem are suggested by the rating scale: (1) learning to understand yourself—what hurts, needs, or beliefs influence your behavior; (2) admitting to facts about yourself (such as having panic attacks or trying to control others) *without judgment*; and (3) ceasing to dwell on past mistakes while strategizing ways to make any needed changes. A major obstacle to acquiring these abilities is the voice of the inner critic.

Take Charge of Your Inner Critic[1]

Your opinion of yourself is influenced by family, society, and your relationships. All of these factors form an inner voice that blames, compares, sets standards, calls names, exaggerates weaknesses, and thinks it can read other minds. The first step to keep your critic from dominating your mind is to simply recognize it. Change the thought, *I should have done more*, to *My critic is saying, "You should have done more."* Next, practice your first self-esteem skill by *understanding* your critic. Ask it questions to expose its backward attempts to help you:

1. Are you (my inner critic) telling me it's my fault that I didn't make my mother happy to keep me from feeling anger at her? (Some people find anger frightening and direct it inward.)

2. Are you trying to make me follow childhood rules to help me feel closer to my family?

3. Are you telling me I could have prevented my attack to give me a (false) sense of control?

4. Do you push me to do more, hoping I'll achieve the impossible and feel good about myself?

5. Are you telling me I'll never succeed so I won't risk the chance of failure?

6. Do you think that warning me in advance that people won't like me will make it hurt less if I'm rejected (even though you're overwhelming me with anxiety)?

---

1. The ideas in this handout mainly come from *Self-Esteem, A Proven Program of Cognitive Techniques for Assessing, Improving & Maintaining Your Self-Esteem,* by M. McKay and P. Fanning, 2000, Oakland, CA: New Harbinger Publications.

7. Do you keep reminding me that I'm bad to prevent me from committing the same awful act?

8. Will punishing me by rehashing my mistake or saying I'm immoral make me a better person?

Seeking, rather than finding, answers is calming and paralyzes your critic's efforts to berate.

Own Your Asset

Not only is it important to admit any of your human failings without judgment, but you also need to identify your accomplishments and good qualities. Some personality traits are mutually exclusive, but people will focus on their vices instead of their virtues. *Timid* people may not recognize their *caution* and heightened *awareness* as desirable. Other times, an asset is labeled as a liability. People who are *trusting* think of themselves as *gullible,* or *confident* people are told they are *conceited*. Use the following exercise to claim your innate resources.

ASSET BOX

Directions: In the box below, circle all the adjectives that describe you. Then complete the sentence:

I am a _____, _____, _____ person.

Consider this statement to be the seeds of a new opinion of yourself that values your unique qualities.

Bold alert	perceptive observant	confident modest	direct diplomatic
open discreet	accepting discerning	agreeable outspoken	influential tolerant
spontaneous structured	easygoing persistent	giving prudent	compassionate objective
logical warm	fair kind	organized creative	detailed concise
nurturing firm	peaceful protective	wise realistic	loyal flexible
decisive insightful	friendly independent	entertaining appreciative	other:

Manage Mistakes Realistically

The third self-esteem skill is to stop dwelling on past mistakes. A mistake is anything that you *later* wish you had done differently. A choice may turn out to be a mistake because you had no way of predicting the consequences; you forgot previous consequences under pressure; or you were not able to see all your alternatives. Sometimes you may have violated one of your personal rules. Notice how changing *shoulds* to *can-dos* offers relief from wrongdoing:

1. Rigid rules (include the words all, never, always, perfectly): *I should never make a mistake.* Flexible rules: *I can learn only by making mistakes.*

2. Foreign rules (adopted from family or society): *I should put others' needs first.* Acquired rules (personally examined): *I can decide whose needs come first in this situation.*

3. Unrealistic rules (absolute, global): *I should be a witty, fascinating conversationalist.* Realistic rules: *I can ask questions and get to know people.*

4. Restricting rules (demand the impossible): *I shouldn't get upset, be afraid, or cry.* Life-enhancing rules: *I can have a variety of emotions.*

5. Acquired/realistic: *I prefer not to yell at people or call them names.* Corrective action: *I can admit I'm wrong and write a note showing what I should have said.*

Having realistic rules, and being willing to take corrective action when actual mistakes are made, make the possibility of *undesirable* choices less daunting. In fact, it is important to label your decisions as *useful* or *unsuccessful*, rather than *good* or *bad*. An amazing statistic is that 3 out of 10 choices you make are likely to be dead wrong and several others are cause for doubt (McKay & Fanning, p. 136). While you are still responsible for your actions, you are bound to err. It is perseverance toward goals in the face of failure that is the backbone of self-esteem.

Handout 6.12—Practicing Happiness

Thomas Jefferson wrote in the Declaration of Independence that people have an unalienable right to pursue happiness. In Jefferson's time the word *pursue* meant "to practice a worthy activity," not to chase after joy. Before defining happiness and reading tried-and-true steps to becoming content, test your knowledge of how to grow gladness.

Mark *true* (T) or *false* (F) in front of each of the following statements:

___ To be happy, people simply need to do what brings them joy in the present.

___ To be happy, people have to engage in unpleasant activities for future rewards.

___ It is not possible to endure pain at times and still be happy.

___ The need for pleasure is greater than the need for meaning or purpose.

___ People with money, fame, or fortune are happier than those who are less fortunate.

___ Reducing your level of stress and tension is strongly related to happiness.

All of the above statements are false, as the rest of the handout will show. Happiness has been variously defined as an overall experience of pleasure and meaning, having positive emotions while pursuing goals,[1] and an inner state of peace and well-being.[2] According to Marci Shimoff (cited below), happiness does not come from getting what you want, but from learning habits that promote joy. Ninety percent of behavior is routine. When we think and act differently, the brain can rewire itself. It is important to make a habit of choosing activities that are both enjoyable and meaningful.

Thinking Habits

The most important prerequisite to happiness is to accept that you are responsible for any joy you extract from life, regardless of external circumstances. Considering the following questions may help you change your thinking patterns:

- **Look for lessons.** When a calamity occurs, ask, *If this were happening for a higher purpose, what would it be? What gifts have I gained from the bad things in my life? Is the universe here to support and teach me, or is it an obstacle course? Which idea helps me the most?*

- **Focus on solutions.** Do you focus on and complain about your problems, or do you think about what you could do to improve situations? Rate how distressed you are about a difficulty on a 1–10 scale. Start paying attention to anything that decreases your concern by 1 point, or think of a tiny step you could take to ease the problem.

- **Question your thoughts.** According to motivational speaker, Marci Shimoff (cited below) 80 percent of thoughts are negative. Ideas that bring peace and well-being are more likely to be true than ones that trigger anger and anxiety. Identifying and questioning thoughts can neutralize negativity. Byron Katie's Inquiry Method uses three basic questions.[3] If you think you do not deserve happiness because of some "horrible" past action, ask yourself: *Is it absolutely true that I don't deserve happiness? How do I feel when I think I'm undeserving? How would I be without this thought?*

- **Develop gratitude and appreciation.** What is the first thing that comes to your mind when you think, *I appreciate ...; I'm grateful for ...* Gratefulness brings great fullness to your being. Making daily gratitude/appreciation lists is known to boost happiness.

---

1. Found in *Happier: Learn the Secrets to Daily Joy and Lasting Fulfillment,* by T. Ben-Shahar, 2007, New York: McGraw-Hill.
2. Found in *Happy for No Reason: 7 Steps to Being Happy from the Inside Out,* by M. Shimoff, 2009, New York: Free Press.
3. Find out more about Byron Katie's work at www.thework.com/index.asp. Note that she is not a professional therapist and her method should not be considered a cure-all, although it may be a simplification of cognitive therapy.

Behavior Habits

Happiness is based on meaningful enjoyment. This invites the question: What is the meaning of *meaningful?* Humans require more than gratifying physical desires. They need to utilize their unique capabilities or serve an ideal beyond themselves. Having a sense of purpose intensifies pleasure. To identify joyful activities, ask yourself, *What made me happier 10 years ago, last month, or earlier today?* Use your answer as a guide to make a routine out of purposeful pleasure. This will require setting goals that lead to happiness. Goals inspire or put spirit in us.

- Goals need to be self-chosen, personally important, interesting, or meaningful, rather than directed by society. They can include anything from raising children to practicing medicine.

- Goals organize people and make them more efficient. Without a sense of direction, we may meander aimlessly and be pulled away from our true Self.

- Goals liberate us to enjoy the present by setting an objective and then making the most of where we are. The process of *striving* rather than *attaining* is crucial for happiness.

- Goals are best when the journey is enjoyable. They can involve growth, connection, and contribution, rather than money, beauty, or popularity.

- Are goals based on what you *say* you enjoy and value? Are you pulled off course by habits, fears, or others' expectations? What could you do to raise your happiness level three points?

Work Habits

Is your work a *job* or a chore that pays you; a *career* that focuses on advancement, power, and prestige; or a *calling* that uses your strengths for your interests and passions? Until you can find meaningful employment, the following tips can help make your job more of a calling:

- Change the question *Is my work meaningful?* to *What is meaningful about my work?*

- See your job in a broader context. How is your company or work a part of the greater good?

- Rewrite your *job* description as a *calling* description.

- Assume more responsibility at work. How can you contribute more?

- Do not equate work with suffering. There is a zone between over- and underexertion where people enjoy their best performance. Free time is wasted by freeing it of effort and meaning.

- Some mundane work is unavoidable. Whenever possible, find ways to inject mindfulness, passion, or pleasure into everyday activities. Happiness does not have to be constant.

Relationship Habits

Satisfying relationships are the only external factor that makes people happier. We do not need others for approval and praise but for sharing desires, fears, fantasies, and dreams. This is what makes connections happen between people. Such bonding is the glue of happiness. Relationships based on pleasure or for future gain will not last. Staying in a relationship to sacrifice for others leads to resentment for all parties. The more a relationship profits everyone involved, the more it will flourish. The following will help you foster deep connections with others:

- Discover your own passions and desires and admit your fears or sources of shame.

- Find support groups with whom to share these feelings until you can tell significant others.

- Make it your priority to *know* others' passions and hurts by rephrasing what they have said.

- Relate to *all* people as if they were your family. Make them feel special and appreciated.

- It is more important to cultivate current relationships than to find the right relationship.

- Engage in activities that are meaningful and pleasurable to yourself and your partner.

Handout 6.13—OCD Exposure Practice

OCD EXPOSURE PRACTICE

Objectives

1. List a variety of OCD-type fears and exposure/refocus exercises that build new brain circuits.

2. Stimulate ideas for exposure/refocus experiences that meet personal needs.

Use with Handout 6.2—*Discovering the Me That Is Not OCD.*

Catastrophic Fear	Imagined or Real Time Exposure	Refocus as Soon as I Feel Anxious
I'll get a horrible disease.	Touch a dollar bill and immediately place my fingers to my lips (or imagine doing it).	☐ Count backwards from 100 by sevens or threes. ☐ List the presidents in reverse—go back to JFK.
People will think I'm a slob or imperfect.	Put something out of place and stare at it until I'm less tense; delay nightly vacuuming for 1 hour.	☐ Name all the states north, south, east, or west of mine. ☐ Memorize and repeat a Psalm or song lyric.
The house will be robbed or burn down.	Leave the door unlocked (stove on) for increasing lengths of time (or imagine doing it).	☐ Do a toe touch, exhaling deeper into the fold.
Someone I care about will be hurt if I don't do my ritual.	Step on a sidewalk crack (or imagine doing it).	☐ Memorize and repeat the syllables: om-ma-ni-pad-me-hum over and over. Alternately tap my knees while repeating the syllables.
I'll do something dishonest, which would make me a horrible person.	Pay the incorrect amount for an item and risk the store clerk correcting me (or imagine doing it).	☐ Memorize and repeat the words: I have thoughts but I am not my thoughts. Ideas, worries, and fears all arise, come and go, and pass. I can know my thoughts, but what is known is not the knower—the vast, free witness of them all.
I'll stab my darling dog with a knife.	Imagine or hold a knife in the presence of my dog.	

Identify your own catastrophic fears, design exposure exercises, and choose a refocusing activity to build new brain circuits.

Handout 6.14—Anger Log

ANGER LOG

Objective: Recognize the repetitious pattern that incites my anger and plan strategies for the future.

Date	Incident or Trigger: Describe briefly	Reaction and Analysis: Temper lost by trying to (1) defend or explain myself or (2) control/change others	Calming Strategy that reduces rage by (1) changing my behavior or outlook or by (2) questioning myself
3/5 2 pm	Co-worker sarcastically asked me if I'd been put on probation yet.	I curtly remarked, "Ladies first!" (Attacking is a form of self-defense.)	I could have asked myself if being rude would have helped our relationship and responded with unexpected kindness by thanking her for her concern.
3/5 7 pm	My son kept asking to go outside after I told him it was too late.	I argued with him and explained that we had to get up early until I blew up (defending my decision or trying to change him).	I could have told my son I would not consider his question unless he put it in writing and wrote down my explanation (changing my behavior).
3/6 4 pm	Mom criticized the way I was helping her cut tile and told me to just let her do it.	I threw the tile and accidentally cut her back. I attacked (form of defense) because she took away my power.	I could have asked myself if she upset me by the way she corrected me or if I always need to do things just right.

Handout 6.15—Distinguishing ADHD From Moodiness—A Children's Rating Scale

ADHD vs MOODINESS   **Directions:** Check (√) column A or M to indicate what best describes your child or situation.

A	ADHD	Moodiness	M
	Family history of learning disabilities, underachievement, or hyperactivity.	Family history of depression, OCD, addictions, alcoholism, violence, or suicide.	
	Child separates easily from caretakers for his/her age.	Child has been clingy or had trouble separating from caretakers later than expected for his/her age.	
	May have trouble falling asleep but becomes alert shortly after waking up.	Sleeps less than normal for his/her age. Wakens often but may have trouble getting up in the AM.	
	Usually sleeps through the night.	Can awaken screaming from nightmares or sleepwalks; nightmares are particularly gory.	
	Is consistently distractible, hyperactive, impulsive, or restless when not medicated.	Has periods of distractibility, hyperactivity, restlessness, or impulsivity. May start the day sluggish but becomes irritable or excitable later.	
	Energy level consistently high.	Energy level varies—cycles of extreme low energy and extreme high energy.	
	May unintentionally blurt out inappropriate things.	Can say shocking, gory, morbid, and sadistic things or have a fear of death.	
		Excessive talk about death or suicidal comments, even at an early age.	
	Pokes, touches, and punches others but unaware of his/her strength.	Brags, bosses, or bullies peers.	
	May feel inept, inadequate, frustrated, clumsy, or different.	May feel worthless or no good or elated and special. Can act silly, goofy, or giddy.	
	Has frequent angry outbursts that usually happen when overstimulated or excited and last around 30 minutes.	Any limit setting can provoke a tantrum that can go on for several hours and/or several times a day.	
	Breaks things carelessly; unaware of consequences or danger.	Destructive, intentional risk taking.	
	Scrapes and scars from carelessness.	Intentionally hurts or cuts self.	
	Difficulty complying with requests due to inattention and distractions.	Oppositional: first response to almost any request is *No.* Can be cruel to animals.	
	Behavior worse in highly stimulating environments.	Behavior somewhat better when away from home.	
	Shifts from one activity to another; likes novelty.	Difficulty with changes in routine; lacks flexibility.	
	Difficulty completing tasks; may do many different things at once.	Can get obsessed with an idea or activity; may have special abilities.	
	Underreactive to sensations, pain, or getting hurt.	Overly sensitive or irritated by odors, tastes, textures, temperature, etc.	
	May become more hyper when consuming sweets.	Craves carbohydrates and sweets; may hoard food.	
	Appetite consistent.	Appetite varies; eats little for days and then binges.	
	Talks loudly or shifts from subject to subject.	Pressured, nonstop speech; talks to self; racing thoughts.	
	Mood stabilizers are not helpful.	Medication for ADHD or depression is not helpful or intensifies problems.	

Note: When column M is mainly checked, there is often a progression from an irritable infancy to separation anxiety, to night terrors or bed wetting, to distractibility, to poor attention, to hyperactivity, to restlessness, to obsessions, to defiance, to substance abuse, and to hypersexuality.[1]

---

1. This rating scale is based on information in *The Bipolar Child,* by D. Papolos and J. Papolos, 1999, New York: Broadway Books.

Handout 6.16 — Sensory Integration Dysfunction — A Children's Rating Scale

Difficulty processing sensations from sense organs, inner ear, muscles, and joints[1]

Oversensitive (Avoids Stimulation). May indicate OCD tendencies.	Undersensitive (Seeks Stimulation) May indicate ADHD tendencies.
Touch	
☐ Picky about how clothes or water feels. ☐ Avoids touching or being touched by objects. ☐ Dislikes being crowded or touched suddenly. ☐ Avoids touching others; may isolate. ☐ Likes pressure vs. light touch; hugs vs. kisses. ☐ Avoids getting dirty or messy. ☐ Doesn't like hair brushed, face washed, etc. ☐ Wears long sleeves, pants, and socks. ☐ Walks on tiptoe to avoid ground contact.	☐ Unaware of pain or temperature; underreacts. ☐ Doesn't mind getting dirty, muddy, or messy. ☐ Loves being touched; not ticklish. ☐ Craves roughhousing; bumps people. ☐ Likes to chew—collars, pencils, toys, gum. ☐ Rubs against walls, furniture. ☐ Seems compelled to touch certain surfaces. ☐ Likes tight clothes—belts, shoelaces, hoods. ☐ Treats pets roughly.
Movement (Inner Ear Senses)	
☐ Avoids moving or unexpected movements. ☐ Avoids swinging, seesaw, heights, running, climbing, sliding; earthbound. ☐ Poor balance, anxious when off balance. ☐ Has motion sickness in cars or elevators.	☐ Craves fast, swinging, rocking, spinning, bouncing, climbing without getting dizzy. ☐ Moves constantly, fidgets. ☐ Increased movement helps attention. ☐ Enjoys being upside-down; daredevil.
Sight	
☐ Overexcited when there is too much to see. ☐ Covers eyes, poor eye contact. ☐ Overreacts to bright light, prefers dim light. ☐ Vigilant, alert, watchful; often squints. ☐ Special talents—jigsaw puzzles.	☐ Misses important visual cues—facial expression, signposts, written directions. ☐ Difficulty discriminating shapes or colors. ☐ Uses touch vs. vision to learn; trouble visualizing. ☐ Writes up- or downhill.
Sounds	
☐ Complains about noises that don't bother others. ☐ Sensitive to background noise. ☐ Covers ears to block out noise or voices. ☐ Special talents—plays instrument by ear.	☐ Ignores voices; asks people to repeat. ☐ Misses sounds; ''tone deaf.'' ☐ Speaks loudly (doesn't hear him- or herself). ☐ Likes the TV loud; makes repetitive sounds.

(continued)

---

1. This rating scale was adapted from *The Out of Sync Child* by C.S. Kranowitz, 1989. New York: Berkley Publishing Group.

Oversensitive (Avoids Stimulation). *May indicate OCD tendencies.*	Undersensitive (Seeks Stimulation) *May indicate ADHD tendencies.*
Smells	
☐ Objects to odors like ripe bananas. ☐ Heightened sense of smell.	☐ Ignores unpleasant odors like dirty diapers. ☐ Sniffs food, people, and objects.
Taste	
☐ Strongly objects to certain tastes, textures, temperatures; picky eater. ☐ Gags when eats.	☐ Licks or taste inedible objects or toys. ☐ Prefers spicy, hot food, or extra sweet food. ☐ Likes most kinds of foods.
Body Position (Senses From Muscles and Joints)	
☐ Tends to be rigid, tense, stiff, uncoordinated. ☐ Holds objects too tightly. ☐ Excessive pressure when writing or erasing. ☐ Breaks delicate objects or toys. ☐ Trouble crossing the midline (switches hands to brush hair); trouble telling right from left. ☐ Poor hand-eye coordination.	☐ Slouches, poor posture, tires easily. ☐ Trouble balancing, hopping, tiptoeing. ☐ May prop head in hand or elbows on table. ☐ Clumsy, inaccurate, accident prone, trips. ☐ Messy dresser or eater; poor self-help skills. ☐ Difficulty using crayons, pencils, scissors, forks. ☐ Bumps into things, stamps feet, twiddles fingers.

Sensory integration (SI) dysfunction expresses itself in different ways: Children may not exhibit every characteristic and can be undersensitive in one area and oversensitive in another. SI problems may appear inconsistently—being clumsy one day and coordinated the next. The experience of being overloaded or deprived of stimulation, helps people understand SI problems.

Activities for SI Dysfunction

Occupational therapists (OTs) treat SI dysfunction. They find ways to improve nervous system functions that have been damaged or are inefficient. The younger children are when treated by a professional, the better chance they have for normal SI. In addition to providing activities on specialized equipment, OTs often suggest things parents can do to supply a balanced sensory diet that includes alerting, organizing, and calming activities.

Alerting Activities for Undersensitive Children	Organizing Activities to Regulate Responses	Calming Activities for Hyperresponsiveness
• Crunching popcorn, dry cereal, crackers, nuts, carrots, apples, ice cubes • Taking a shower • Bouncing a big ball • Jumping up and down on a mattress or trampoline	• Chewing licorice, dried fruit, cheese, gum, bagels • Hanging by the hands • Pushing or pulling heavy loads • Hanging upside-down, headstands, or handstands	• Sucking a spoonful of peanut butter, hard candy, popsicles • Pushing against walls with hands, back, bottom • Rocking, slow swinging • Cuddling, back rubs, baths

Any sensations that make a child happy tend to be integrating. However, young people can be gently introduced to stimulation that they find unpleasant. The following activities are only a beginning list to nourish individual needs for tactile, inner ear, and body position stimulation.

Tactile Integration

- Rub different-textured scrubbers, sponges, washcloths, and plastic brushes on child's skin in the direction of his or her hair.
- Play in a kitchen sink or washtub outdoors full of sudsy water. Use unbreakable pitchers, bottles, turkey basters, sponges, or eggbeaters.
- Finger paint with commercial paint or shaving cream, peanut butter, or pudding on a plastic tray. Encourage children to draw shapes, letters, and numbers.
- Draw shapes, letters, or numbers on the children's backs and have them guess what you drew.
- Cut a hole in the top of a shoebox to make a *feelie box*. Have children identify small objects (spools, marbles, plastic animals,etc.) without looking. Or put several objects in the feelie box and have the child find a specific one. This is also great to do in a sandbox.

Inner Ear Stimulation

- Wrap children up in a beach towel and roll them down a hill.
- Two adults hold opposite corners of a blanket (or use a hammock) and swing a child.
- Perching on a *sitting ball* while watching TV and other times. The ball's diameter should equal the distance between the child's fanny and the floor.
- Make a teeter-totter with a 1-by-3-foot piece of plywood over a 4-by-4-inch rail timber. The child can make the plywood balance or walk back and forth on the rail timber.

Body Position Integration to Stimulate Senses From Muscles and Joints

- It is good for children to carry heavy loads—soft-drink bottles, filled laundry baskets, or grocery bags from the door to the kitchen. Push strollers, vacuums, and heavy boxes.
- Have children hang by their arms. Get a chinning bar for bedroom doorways.
- Place a large beanbag on the children's backs and have them move around like a hermit crab.
- Give children yesterday's newspaper to tear into strips to make confetti.
- Sit two children back-to-back on the floor and ask them to link arms, stand up together, and sit back down.

Touch, Movement, and Body Position

SECTION III

BETWEEN MINDS

CHAPTER 7

FIRST-CLASS COMMUNICATION

For Communication Skills and Marriage and Family Therapy

THERAPIST'S GUIDE TO FIRST-CLASS COMMUNICATION

Help clients:

1. Distinguish fight, flee, and freeze reactions from flow responses.
2. Recognize four main types of responses that deescalate distressed people.
3. Execute a variety of deescalating responses with difficult people or families.
4. Name the elements of a backlash to a family member's expression of individuality.
5. Acquire effective, assertive speaking patterns.

Using the Handouts

- **General literature:** *Beyond Fight, Flee, and Freeze: Flow; Acting as If: The Art of Confirming; Asking Questions: The Art of Inquiry; Active Listening: The Mirror Mind; Talking So People Will Listen.*
- **Specific problems:** *Hypnotic Hints: The Art of Evoking* (advanced communication skills), *Surviving a Family Backlash* (for difficult families), *Hard-Core Bully Busting* (for teens).
- **Forms:** *Turning Disputes Into Discussions* (A Verbal Interaction Worksheet).
- **Workshops:** *Beyond Assertive Communication, Learned Responses, Verbal Arts Terms.*

Cautions and Comments

- ***Beyond Fight, Flee, and Freeze: Flow; Acting as If : The Art of Confirming; Asking Questions: The Art of Inquiry; Active Listening: The Mirror Mind;*** and ***Talking So People Will Listen*** can be used as a series when teaching communication skills or anger management classes. They can be used with families or other groups. The exercises in these handouts may be difficult for individuals and are best done by brainstorming as a group.

- ***Hypnotic Hints: The Art of Evoking*** might be reserved for more sophisticated clients and for workshops for professionals.

- ***Beyond Assertive Communication*** offers an excellent script for presentations. ***Learned Responses*** and ***Verbal Arts Terms*** are handouts designed to accompany this workshop. Read *Making Hostile Words Harmless,* by Kate Cohen-Posey (John Wiley & Sons, 2008) for extra preparation. Alternative workshop titles might be:
  - *Dealing With Difficult People*
  - *Hypnotic Language in Everyday Life*
  - *Hypnotic Tools for Parents and Teachers*
  - *Deescalating Anger*

- ***Surviving a Family Backlash*** can be used with individuals to help them adapt verbal skills with difficult families. Use this handout with the script in ***Beyond Assertive Communication*** for a workshop on family dysfunction.

- ***Turning Disputes Into Discussions*** is a good handout to use during volatile counseling sessions. People can identify the types of vicious cycles in their own families. Therapists can help people name the verbal patterns they are using on the interaction worksheet.

- ***Hard-Core Bully Busting*** has examples that teens often experience. Many instances from a young person's life can be role-played. The handout explains strategies used in role-plays and offers more practice. Use this handout with the script in ***Beyond Assertive Communication*** for a workshop on ***Empowering Students to End Vicious Cycles of Bullying***.

* ***Talking So People Will Listen*** provides a list of skills for confident, assertive communication.

Sources and Acknowledgments Not Referenced in the Handouts

Information on emotional operating systems can be found in *Affective Neuroscience: The Foundation of Human Animal Emotions,* by Jaak Panksepp (Oxford University Press, 1998).

Information on family systems therapy is found in *Family Therapy in Clinical Practice,* by Murray Bowen (Jason Aronson, 1978).

Chapter 1, Untangling Family Ties, from *Brief Therapy Client Handouts,* by Kate Cohen-Posey (John Wiley & Sons, 2000) contributed to *Surviving a Family Backlash* and *Turning Disputes Into Discussions* .

Handout 7.1—Beyond Fight, Flee, and Freeze: Flow

Fight and *flight* were originally considered our only defensive reactions. Now, the body's ability to *freeze* under extreme stress by tuning out is considered a type of flight. More recently, fight and flight have been described as complex *emotional* (rage and fear) *operating systems* that ensure survival. Fortunately, there is also a *seeking system* that is energizing and focusing. Attacks that fuel rage can turn fight or flight into *flow* responses that pursue contact and meaning.

Definitions and Examples

One of the easiest ways to turn fight into flow is to recognize when you are being attacked or on the offense yourself. Most of us are not likely to become physical, but we do verbal violence all the time by either making threats or by attempting to defend against an attack. In the following exercise, identify the type of attack or defense that is being described:

EXERCISE A

Definitions of Fight Reactions

Directions: Pick a word from the first row that fits each definition.

Verbal Attacks	Verbal Defenses
Accuse, blame, convince, criticize, disagree, lecture, order (*Note:* Complaining focuses on behavior—*You didn't ...*)	Explain, apologize, reassure
Blame: 1. To attack by making a claim of wrongdoing. _____: 2. To attack by finding fault or holding someone responsible. _____: 3. To attack by finding fault with or pointing out flaws. _____: 4. To attack by suggesting another person's ideas are wrong. _____: 5. To attack by telling someone what to do. _____: 6. An attack that tries to defeat others by argument or persuasion. _____: 7. A drawn-out attack that criticizes someone for personal failings, often using the word should.	*Apologize*: 1. To defend by taking responsibility for others. _____: 2. To defend yourself by giving reasons or pointing out logic. _____: 3. A defense that tries to ease others' distress.

Answers: 2. accuse, 3. criticize, 4. disagree, 5. order, 6. convince, 7. lecture; 2. explain, 3. reassure

The differences between types of attack s and defenses are subtle. Examples of each reaction follow.

Examples of Fight Reactions

Directions: Pick a word from the first row that fits each example.

Verbal Attack	Verbal Defenses
Accuse, blame, convince, criticize , disagree, lecture, order (*Note:* Complaining focuses on behavior—*You didn't . . .*)	Explain, apologize, reassure
Accuse: 1. You just want me to look like the bad guy.	*Apologize*: 1. I'm sorry I haven't done more to get my kids in line.
_____: 2. Stop making me look like the bad guy.	_____: 2. I promise I'll do more to get my kids in line.
_____: 3. You're a weak-minded meddler.	_____: 3. My kids don't behave as well as they could because you interfere when I do correct them.
_____: 4. It's your fault that your kid treats you like that.	
_____: 5. Your ideas on raising kids are all wrong.	
_____: 6. You <u>should</u> pull yourself together and make your kids do what you tell them instead of being so soft.	
_____: 7. If you read the Bible, you'd know you <u>should</u> not spare the rod.	

Answers: 2. order, 3. criticism, 4. blame, 5. disagree, 6. lecture, 7. convince; 2. reassure, 3. explain

---

Flee and Freeze Reactions

For some people it is more natural to flee or freeze than to fight when threatened. Backing away from a threat can be an instinctual reaction or a conscious decision suggested by the saying, *When you cannot think of anything nice to say, don't say anything at all.* Whenever a tense situation becomes too intense, often the best response is to flee or freeze. **Mark all the flee-freeze reactions with an *f-f* in Exercise C.**

EXERCISE C

Flee-Freeze (f-f), Flow (f) or Fight (a/d) Reactions.

Directions: Mark the responses below with an *f-f, f, a,* or *d*. Verbal responses are shown in *italics.*

a 1. You better change or …	___ 10. I'm glad you're trying to help by correcting me.	___ 18. Maybe I'm a precious meddler like gold.
d 2. My kids don't act right because …	___ 11. I'm pleased you think I'm involved.	___ 19. It sounds like you're disappointed in me.
___ 3. I'll make things go better.	___ 12. You give good advice.	___ 20. It's okay to feel …
___ 4. You should …, … and. …	___ 13. Stare.	___ 21. You have to realize that …
___ 5. I know you're wrong because …	___ 14. Avoid eye contact.	___ 22. It must be hard when …
f-f 6. Leave the room.	___ 15. Are you saying … ?	___ 23. I'm sorry that I …
___ 7. Drive away in your car.	___ 16. Make eye contact with soft eyes.	___ 24. It makes sense that …
___ 8. Stay quiet.	___ 17. I have been known to meddle.	___ 25. What's your reason for thinking … ?
f 9. I wonder why …		

ANSWERS: Exercise C: 3. **d** (reassure), 4. **a** (lecture), 5. **a** (disagree), 7. **f-f**, 8. **f-f**, 10. **f**, 11. **f**, 12. **f**, 13. a, 14. **f-f**, 15. **f**, 16 . **f**, 17. **f**, 18. **f** , 19. **f**, 20. **f**, 21. **a** (convince) , 22. **f**, 23. **d** (apologize), 24. **f**, 25. **f**.

The Flow Response

All mammals have a *seeking emotional operating system.* In animals it is used to find food, shelter, or a mate. Humans display *seeking* as curiosity, excitement, pleasure, and the desire for meaning. Seeking is driven by the neurotransmitter dopamine, which is the chemical twin of cocaine. This creates focused arousal, rather than aggression or fear. *Taoism* and the martial art of *Aikido* are a perfect expression of the seeking system or flow:

> **Taoism :** The way of creating harmony and balance through interaction with opposing forces; making life effortless by working with things as they are.

> **Aikido :** The way (*do*) of harmony or joining (*ai*) with an opponent's energy (*ki*).

A key feature of flow responses is to stay in contact with opponents by (1) *acting as if* all is well, (2) *asking* sincere questions, (3) *actively listening* to rephrase what people are saying and identify their feelings, and (4) using *humorous hints* that evoke desired changes in people. Return to Exercise C and **mark all the flow responses with an *f*.**

Review

After marking the *flight-freeze* (**f-f**) reactions and *flow* (**f**) responses in Exercise C, review the information on the fighting instinct (Ex. A). Decide if the remaining actions and examples are *attacking* or *defensive.* **Mark an *a* or a *d* in Exercise C.** While this handout does not explain all the details of how to create harmony and balance to disarm opponents, it does offer a glimpse into what lies beyond flee, freeze, and fight.

Handout 7.2—*Acting As If:* The Art of Confirming

Acting as if all is well is an advanced communication skill that confirms the best in people by treating verbal attacks *as if* they were harmless. Hostile people are thrown off balance because they are not given the resistance needed to continue an attack. It is important to understand that returning cruelty with kindness is not giving up. Contact is continued without fighting or fleeing.

There is a surprising number of ways to *act as if* all is well. Explanations follow, but a complete understanding is best gained by completing the practice examples:

Definitions

- **Agreeing** *acts as if* by agreeing in fact, theory, hypothetically, or with possibilities to rob opponents of a sparring partner.

- **Dramatizing** the logical extension of fault-finding plays out the worst-case scenario of an insult to *act as if* the exaggeration is fine.

- **Finding a golden nugget** uncovers something good and true in a verbal attack. Often, this requires probing with questions.

- **Reverse psychology** directs people to continue to be troublesome, *as if* it were a good thing, which places the behavior under the speaker's control.

- **Speaking what you want** uses *golden lies,* which suggest that people are acting in desirable ways (even if they are not) in order to evoke that behavior. This is suggested in the scripture Romans 4:17—*God who called those things that be not as though they were.*

- **Returning an insult with a compliment** responds to a verbal attack *as if* it were benevolent by complimenting, making a continued assault almost impossible.

- **Taking an insult as a compliment** reframes the meaning of an insult to make it sound *as if* it were a compliment.

Typical attack-defend reactions to the comment, *I'm not gonna do that,* might be: *Oh yes, you are* (disagreeing)! *You really need to do it because . . .* (explaining); *It won't be so bad* (reassuring). By thinking outside the box, a parent or teacher can make several surprising responses to defuse situations before imposing any needed consequences.

Teacher/ Student or Parent/Child Example

Directions: Place the letter of each type of *acting as if* response in front of the right example.
Comment: *I'm not gonna do that!*

a)	Agree in fact or theory or use reverse psychology:	*e* 1.	People who are picky about what they do make the best workers when they . . . *decide to buckle down.*
b)	Speak it as you want it (golden lie):	___ 2.	You must think I'm very patient to talk so boldly.
c)	Take it as a compliment :	___ 3.	I'm so glad you're willing to . . . *give it a try.*
d)	Return with a compliment:	___ 4.	Then you can't do it, even if it lowers your grade.
e)	Find a golden nugget of truth:	___ 5.	Maybe you'll forget how to say *Yes* and never agree to do anything again—like getting ice cream.
f)	Dramatize the worst outcome:	___ 6.	Refusing is the first step to making good decisions.

Answers: 2, **c**; 3, **B**; 4, **a**; 5, **f**; 6, **d**; *italicized* phrases are hidden suggestions.

Adult Relationship Example

The demand for total trust below might be made by a rigid person whose morals are above reproach. However, it was actually said by someone engaged in illicit activity who insisted on privacy. It is easy to retaliate to this type of attack by saying, *How can I trust you when* …? Or *It's hard for me to trust because.* … It is important to step away from the content of the message and not take the person's words as a demand. *Acting as if* responses validate the other person or yourself and flow around any commands.

Directions: Place the letter of each type of *acting as if* response in front of the right example.
Comment: *You should trust me without question.*

a)	Agree in fact, theory, or hypothetically:	*b* 1.	I'm so glad *you understand* my questions come from insecurity, not my doubts about you.
b)	Speak it as you want it (golden lie):	___ 2.	Thanks for your *confidence in my self-assurance.*
c)	Reverse psychology :	___ 3.	If I did that, it would eliminate many conflicts.
d)	Return with or receive it as a compliment:		
e)	Find a golden nugget of truth:	___ 4.	You're right. When I trust my Self, I won't need to question you … I'll just know what's what.
f)	Dramatize your worst flaws to turn complainers into consolers:	___ 5.	You should keep asking me to have absolute faith in you, even if it makes me more shaky.
		___ 6.	You're really asking a lot of an obsessive, paranoid freak like myself.

Answers: 2, **d**; 3, **a**; 4, **e**; 5, **c**; 6, **f**; *italicized* phrases are hidden suggestions.

It is more important to notice the variety of ways to stop resisting verbal aggression without fleeing the scene than to match the correct example with a particular type of *as if* response. In each scenario, choose the response that you like the most.

All-Purpose Confirmations[1]

Because validating or confirming the best in others with *as if* responses is such a new way of speaking, it helps to memorize some handy one-liners that can be used with almost any verbal assault:

a)	Agree in fact or theory:	*Absolutely! … Could be.*
b)	Take it as a compliment:	*Thank you.*
c)	Return with a compliment:	*You're a good mother (boss, sister, friend) who worries.*
d)	Reverse psychology:	*You might as well keep trying to … until it's not worth the effort.*
e)	Speak it as you want it:	*Oooh … You say that like it's a bad thing (implying that it's a good thing).*

Using these standard responses just a few times will naturally spark your creative juices and you may surprise yourself with how easily you can take the edge off a cutting remark:

Supervisor: Get your name tag on now like I told you to 2 hours ago!

Employee: You're so right. I don't have it on yet (agree in fact). You must be wondering what kept me from putting it on since *you like to understand* what goes on around here (give a compliment and a suggestion).

---

1. Adapted from *Making Hostile Words Harmless* (pp. 9–30), by K. Cohen-Posey, 2008, with permission of John Wiley & Sons.

Handout 7.3—Asking Questions: The Art of Inquiry

If you did not react to a verbal assault by fighting or fleeing, the most obvious alternative would be to ask a question—*Why are you pointing out that I've gained weight?* Interrogatives are one of four types of sentences (along with statements, exclamations, and commands), but to be genuine, they require that people put aside their agendas. The above query can be asked in a tone of voice that suggests the other person is rude *or* in a manner that seeks true understanding of why the observation about weight gain was made.

Although genuine questions do not have hidden agendas, they can have a hypnotic (calming) effect. This is because they evoke a focused inward search. Due to their hypnotic nature, most questions can be used to implant suggestions for desired change. Although this could be considered a covert agenda, the goal is not to attack or defend. Notice how questions vary from simple probes to complex messages:

Types of Questions[1]

1. **Genuine questions** change agendas to blame or accuse into quests for meaning and to identify the purpose of prying. They must be asked from a position of ignorance.

2. **Subtle questions** use the words, *I wonder ...* to pose questions in the form of statements. This eliminates pressure to respond and prompts silent or spontaneous replies.

3. **Questions that evoke inquiry** make queries that encourage others to respond with questions—*Do you want to know the reason why ...? Are you sure you want to know?*

4. **False choice questions (binds)** offer equally acceptable options—*Heads I win, tails you lose.*

5. **Forced choice questions (double binds)** compel agreement to a yes/no inquiry that assumes a desired change will or has happened—*Do you know how ... will happen?*

6. **Questions with underlying assumptions** link a time frame to a prediction of success—*Do you know when you will ...?*

Adults typically react to childish threats, attacks, or noncompliance by asking, *Why did you ...?* Young people are likely to act baffled, especially when the why question sounds critical. The genuine question below replaces *why* with *what*. Pay particular attention to the execution of queries that evokes choices and predicts success:

Teacher/ Student or Parent/Child Example

Directions: Place the letter of each type of question in front of the right example.
Comment: *I'm not gonna do that!*

a)	Open-ended, curious question:	_d_ 1. Do you know how ... *you will realize that doing this is in your best interest?*
b)	Subtle question:	___ 2. Do you understand the reason for my request, or is a concern of yours delaying your cooperation?
c)	Questions that evoke inquiry:	___ 3. I wonder why you don't ... *want to cooperate.*
d)	Forced choice (double bind):	___ 4. What is your reason for not wanting to cooperate?
e)	False choice question (bind):	___ 5. Then, what do you want to ask about the reason for this assignment?
f)	Underlying assumption (prediction):	___ 6. Do you know how soon ... *you'll decide to cooperate?*

Answers: 2, **e**; 3, **b**; 4, **a**; 5, **c**; 6, **f**; *italicized* words are hidden suggestions.

1. Adapted from *Making Hostile Words Harmless* (pp. 31-50) by Kate Cohen-Posey with permission of John Wiley & Sons Inc., 2008.

Adult Relationship Example

Although the demand for total trust (below) is commonplace, it is a curious request that invites exploration. Instead of asking, *What don't you like about being questioned?* it helps to use a multiple choice format to trigger insight. *I wonder* statements (subtle questions) that hide questions allow even deeper penetration into the psyche. Study the following examples to bring the the types of questions to life.

Directions: Place the letter of the correct example in front of each type of question.
Comment: *You should trust me without question.*

_f_ 1.	Underlying assumption (prediction):	a.	Do you think I'm doubting your character or that my questions mean I don't love you enough?
___ 2.	Open-ended, curious question:	b.	I wonder if deep love rids people of all queries or causes more concerns due to fear of loss.
___ 3.	Subtle question:	c.	What would you like to …*ask me about my doubts?*
___ 4.	False choice question (bind):	d.	Do you want to *feel more comfortable with my questions* or *understand the source of my anxiety?*
___ 5.	Forced choice (double bind):	e.	Do you know that …*you can become more comfortable when others question you?*
___ 6.	Questions that evoke inquiry:	f.	Do you know when …*you will be comfortable enough to answer some of my questions?*

Answers: 2. **a.** 3. **b**, 4. **d**, 5. **e**, 6. **c.**

Notice that the above series of questions flows from understanding the source of the demand for total trust to creating possibilities for change. Often, it is good to make *I wonder* statements without expecting any response. After musing, *I wonder …,* leave the room and hope that seeds have been planted for new ideas to sprout.

All-Purpose Questions

You will be most likely to use the first three types of questions. They are reviewed below. A kind of verbal assault not yet covered is prying—*Why did you and your boyfriend get back together? How much do you weigh? What did your therapist tell you today? Are you wearing any underwear?* Any unwanted question from nosiness to harassment can be undone by answering a question with a question: *How is that information important to you?* It will help to file the following four questions in your memory banks and practice them frequently:

a)	Genuine question:	*What is the reason you are …?*
b)	Subtle question:	*I wonder why …*
c)	Inquiry-evoking question:	*Do you want to know my reasons? Are you sure?*
d)	Prying prevention question:	*I'll gladly answer when you tell me how the information is needed.*

For extra practice, cover the responses below and think of a question that would focus on understanding the meaning of the remark on the left (rather than attacking or defending).

Verbal Attack	Question Response
Everyone thinks you're cruel to my kids.	*Why do you want me around them if I'm not nurturing?*
All you ever do is abuse me.	*How do you define abuse?*
How do you put up with your husband?	*I wonder if you've had trouble with men yourself.*
You never cared about me, just the sex!	*Are you trying to make me feel guilty or yourself feel bad?*

This handout ends by inviting you to go on your own focused inward search:

Do you know how this information *will help you* deal with difficult people in your own life?

Handout 7.4—Active Listening: The Mirror Mind

In the 1950s a type of counseling became popular that simply fed back the emotional content of what people said instead of giving complex psychological interpretations. This was soon adopted to teach parents and spouses an active form of listening that *showed* people understanding. But more than 2000 years ago, Chinese philosophy encouraged the sage to clean the dark mirror of his mind so he could reflect (others' words) without intent or absorbing (what he heard). The mirror mind can both subdue others' anger and protect one's self from personalizing insults:[1]

ER DOCTOR: I cannot believe it took you 45 minutes to get to this hospital to do a psychological evaluation. That is totally unacceptable and unprofessional!

PSYCHOLOGIST: It makes sense that you are distraught because you care deeply about your patients and want your ER to be well managed.

Definitions   These listening responses can be reduced to verbal formulae that are fairly easy to memorize. Rephrases, empathy, and narrating can be worded as statements or questions:

Active Listening Response	Verbal Formulae
1. **Paraphrasing** or **rephrasing** restates what others have said in different words as opposed to simply repeating:	1. You're saying … Are you saying…?
2. **Narrating** gives blow-by-blow descriptions of behavior or verbal patterns that feedback the *process* of what people do, not the *content* of what they say:	2. You are ____ing. Are you ____ing?
3. **Empathy** labels others' feelings with a word:	3. I guess you feel … Do you feel …?
4. **Validation** uses other people's *emotional logic* to explain to them how their felt experience makes sense:	4. It makes sense that you feel … because …
5. **Sympathy** adds compassion to labeling what others are feeling without taking responsibility for their emotions.	5. It must be awful when …

Teacher/ Student or Parent/Child Example

Taking a moment to show understanding calms adults and gives children an opportunity to switch gears and comply. But in many cases, all privileges still need to be withheld until the task is completed. Notice that rephrasing, empathy, validating, and sympathy all build on each other. It is not necessary to make all four of these listening responses. Just one or two will calm a situation. Narrating has the effect of heightening awareness and exposing any unwanted behavior—*Are you trying to … rush me; put me in the middle; ask for a free drink;* and so on.

---

1. Adapted from *Making Hostile Words Harmless* (pp. 51-74) by Kate Cohen-Posey with permission of John Wiley & Sons Inc., 2008.

Directions: Place the letter of each type of *active listening* response in front of the correct example.
Comment: *I'm not gonna do that!*

_e_ 1.	Narrate behavior or verbal pattern:	a.	You believe it would be impossible for you to even start to do it (purposeful exaggeration).
___ 2.	Rephrase or paraphrase:	b.	It sounds like you *resent* being asked to …
___ 3.	Sympathize:	c.	It makes sense that you *resent* being asked to … because …
___ 4.	Empathize—identify the *feeling:*	d.	It's really hard on kids to be asked to do things they dislike.
___ 5.	Validate emotional logic:	e.	For some unknown reason you're *rejecting* my request.

Answers: 2, **a**; 3, **d**; 4, **b**; 5, **c**

It takes tremendous powers of concentration to truly discern what is in the heart and soul of another person. Rephrasing buys some time to fathom the other person's feelings. Incorrectly identifying emotions helps others clarify what is bothering them—*I'm not offended. I just get annoyed when I have to repeat myself so often.*

Adult Relationship Example

Directions: Place the letter of each type of *active listening* response in front of the right example.
Comment: *You should trust me without question.*

___ 1.	Validate emotional logic:	a.	You'd like me to believe you and not ask any details.
___ 2.	Sympathize:	b.	Are you *offended* by my questions?
___ 3.	Narrate behavior or verbal patterns:	c.	It makes sense that you're *offended* by my questions because you think you've been fair and honest.
___ 4.	Empathize—identify *feelings:*	d.	It must be terribly taxing when I ask questions to put myself at ease.
_a_ 5.	Rephrase or paraphrase:	e.	It sounds like you're *telling me* how I should feel or act.

Answers: 1, **c**; 2, **d**; 3, **e**; 4, **b**

Do not use active listening in the hopes that others will show you empathy or consider your views. Its purpose is to empower your faculties of observation so you can deal with anyone under the influence of anger, anxiety, or ignorance. However, using listening skills will:

Advantages of Active Listening

1. **Promote listening.** The only time some people pay attention is when they are checking to see if someone is rephrasing them accurately.

2. **Encourage insight.** The person in the above example may become less demanding and more aware of the underlying issues causing him or her to expect undying trust.

3. **Help people control their emotions.** The difficult person has to either agree that he is distraught or contain himself (see ER doctor dialogue).

4. **Slow down a runaway monologue or lecture.** Use an explicative to interrupt (*Whoa! Hang on!*) and then begin with, *Did I get you right? …* If necessary, write what the other person is saying—*I'm having trouble getting everything you're saying; let me write it down.*

5. **Put the spotlight on the antagonist** and take it off of yourself.

Extra Practice   Uncover the right column as you think of your own listening response for the verbal attacks on the left. Emotions labeled by *empathizing* and *validating* are <u>underlined</u> and the process identified by *narrating* is shown in **boldface**. Any type of listening response can be used to reflect an attack without absorbing it. Use what is easiest for your own mirror mind.

Verbal Attack	Active Listening Response
Everyone thinks you're cruel to my kids.	Are you <u>hoping</u> I'll change if everyone is on your side?
All you ever do is abuse me.	It must be awful for you when you think I'm abusive.
How do you put up with your husband?	You're trying to **figure out** my strategy.
You never cared about me, just the sex!	When I said I'm leaving, you felt completely <u>rejected</u>.
You don't teach me! I teach you.	You feel <u>put down</u> when I tell you new things I'm learning.
Why can't you control your weight!?	It makes sense that you're <u>angry</u> about my weight because self-control is an important value for you.
Who were those guys you sat with in Spanish lab!?	Do you <u>worry</u> about any contact I have with other men because your worst <u>fear</u> is that I'll leave like the other important people in your life?

Handout 7.5—Hypnotic Hints: The Art of Evoking

A person may say, "Don't ever . . . *lie to me again!*" Or, "You can . . . *always tell me the truth.*" In either case, hypnotic language has been used to promote or discourage lying. Because it is easy to entrance people without realizing it, gaining command of this communication skill is especially important. Rather than thinking of hypnosis as deep relaxation, it may be more useful to define it as the evocation of involuntary experiences through unique language patterns. Several of these are defined below:[1]

1. **Embedded suggestions** slip an idea into the context of a sentence.

2. **Truisms** are statements of fact that are hard to deny—*You can, . . .* followed by an embedded suggestion.

3. **Utilization** directs people to continue an undesirable behavior in order to put it under the speaker's control, making the behaviors less likely to persist.

4. **Serial suggestions** identify an easy or currently occurring behavior and link it to a more difficult task—*While you're . . . you can start to think about. . . .*

5. **Implied directives** suggest easy, almost involuntary, behavior for people to make as soon as they are ready to comply with a request to change—*As soon as you . . . you can. . . .*

6. **Predictions** presume that something is going to happen and then speculates on all the ways it might occur—*Eventually you will . . . maybe in 2 hours, 2 years, or 20 years.*

7. **Paired opposites** describe a negative mind-set or behavior first to limit it and then focuses on the positive end of the polarity—*You may not want to <u>stop</u> . . . until you <u>start</u> to notice . . .*

8. **Power words** are hypnotic flourishes that block or promote the action following them, or discount preceding information—*Try, dare, but, now . . .*

9. **Random responses** disrupt the flow of content, catching the intentional (conscious) mind off guard. New behaviors or thoughts are accepted in order to fill the void.

The following examples show how hypnotic language tells the truth about or validates whatever a person is doing and then narrows his or her focus of attention with serial suggestions, implication, predictions, paired opposites, power words, or confusion. These verbal patterns increase an authority's repertoire. However, directives enforced by action (f.1) are still needed.

Teacher/ Student or Parent/Child Example

Directions: Place the letter of each type of hypnotic response in front of the right example.
Comment: *I'm not gonna do that!*

a.	Predictions with speculations of how change will happen	_b_ 1.	Sometimes people need to test limits and experience consequences that help them . . . *cooperate.*
b.	Truism —simple statement of fact	___ 2.	Don't <u>stop</u> complaining until . . . you're ready to start.
c.	Utilization —encourages more of the same; d. Paired opposites	___ 3.	After refusing to do what you're asked several times, you can figure out why it's important for you to do it.
e.	Serial suggestion—links a current action to a harder one	___ 4.	When you know . . . you can do what you're asked, . . . you can nod your head yes or no.
f.	Implied directive linked to an easy, almost automatic action	___ 5.	I wonder if you'll start to cooperate with subtle head nods, by saying "okay," or by just getting up and doing it.
f.1	Directive enforced by action (not hypnotic)	___ 6.	You can try to complain some more, but a part of you has the guts to . . . just do it.

(continued)

---

1. Adapted from *Making Hostile Words Harmless* (pp. 75–97), by K. Cohen-Posey, 2008, with permission of John Wiley & Sons.

| g. Power words —*try, but, dare:* | ___ 7. … And I'm not gonna screw in the light bulb. |
| h. Random response to disconnect: | ___ 8. Take your time, <u>but</u> when *you've done it*, I'll send in your paperwork. |

Answers: 2, **c/d**; 3, **e**; 4, **f**; 5, **a**; 6, **g**; 7, **h**; 8, **f.1**; *italicized* words are embedded suggestions.

Notes

(#2): Paired opposites ground resistance with a negative (*stop*) so the person can focus on the positive (*start*). (#6): The word *try* tends to block any action following it (*try* to complain). Words that draw and focus attention are dares that promote subsequent action (… *you [have] the* <u>guts</u> to *just do it*). The word *but* has the effect of negating anything that came before it.

Male/Female Relationship Example

Hypnosis presumes that people have the potential to change. Whether needed transformation is in one's self or others, nothing is forced. Hints are made about possible outcomes. Promising behaviors are described as they occur and unwanted habits are disrupted (f).

Directions: Place the letter of each type of hypnotic response in front of the right example.
Comment: *You should trust me without question.*

a. Truism —simple statement of fact	___1. You can <u>try</u> to make me totally confident, <u>but</u> it would really be <u>amazing</u> if *my questions stopped mattering.*
b. Implied directive linked to an easy, almost automatic action	*c* 2. Keep telling me to trust you completely, so *it will dawn on you* how hard that is for someone like me.
c. Utilization —encourages more of the same	___ 3. While you're expecting my undying trust, an idea might pop up that would *explain* why I'm concerned or why you want to be so private.
d. Serial suggestion—links a current action to a harder one	___ 4. When you figure out a way to *help me feel more secure,* you could tap your foot or sigh.
e. Power words—try, but, dare	___ 5. I wonder if *you'll* make a 180-degree turn and *deluge me with information* that will shut me up or if I'll gradually ask fewer questions as I get to know you better.
f. Random response to disconnect	___6. Automatic trust could be a good thing or a bad thing.
g. Predictions with speculations of how change will happen	___7. … And I should have been putting more money in my savings and trust account.

Answers: 1, **e**; 3, **d**; 4, **b**; 5, **g**; 6, **a**; 7, **f**; *italicized* words are embedded suggestions—promising behaviors.

Point to the Positive

This information is not offered with the expectation that you will make hypnotic language a part of your everyday speech habits. Several complex language patterns have been presented to drive home one point: *Telling people they are liars, cheats, or lazy will promote the very behavior you want to discourage.* Instead, when you feel yourself wanting to say something negative, just remember to point to the positive.

Verbal Attack	Hypnotic Language
Everyone thinks you're cruel to my kids.	It would be a <u>shock</u> if *we agreed on how to handle your kids.*
All you ever do is abuse me.	*You can be <u>strong</u>* and tell me when I mistreat you.
You never cared about me, just the sex!	<u>Trying</u> to make me feel guilty can help you *stop missing me.*
Why can't you control your weight?	I know you're <u>trying</u> your best to *help me* with my weight.
Who were those guys you sat with in Spanish lab!?	<u>Trying</u> to make yourself worry is tiring and you can be <u>stunned</u> to remember how to *feel calm.*

Handout 7.6—Beyond Assertive Communication—A Workshop

Following is a script for a workshop that goes beyond assertive communication skills to teach the verbal arts. Like the martial arts, the verbal arts disarm difficult people. This program can be geared to client groups, the general public, or a professional audience. Information to enhance the presentation and answer questions is shown in [brackets].

Three-by-five cards; four cards with the rude relative remark: <u>I can't believe your husband (wife) gave you a better Christmas present than me, his own mother!</u> Handouts: *Learned Responses; Verbal Arts Terms*. **Needed Materials**

Introduction

- Assertive statements tell people what you feel, want, or will and will not do. When dealing with people under the influence of anger, ignorance, or anxiety, special skills are needed to disarm and calm them. These are the verbal arts that, like the martial arts, use opponents' energy to join with them and unbalance or disarm them.

- The verbal arts make use of hypnotic language. How many people realize that they often use hypnotic language?

- Who knows what is hypnotic about that question? [It is a double bind because whether you say *yes* or *no*, you are agreeing that you use hypnotic language.]

- [Optional]: If you are a therapist, a good double-bind question to ask is: *"Can you say how this session helped you?"* Most often, clients will come up with a response.

- We often use hypnosis or embed suggestions in others' minds that promote misbehavior: You can say, "Don't ever *lie to me again*," or "You can always *tell me the truth*." One is a command that encourages the opposite. The second is a statement or a *truism*.

- Has anyone ever been bothered by a rude remark, unsolicited advice, or word pollution?*

- We are especially likely to make hypnotic blunders when we're the target of cruel comments. Which reactions do you commonly make? * [*See Instinctual Response Questionnaire on *Handout 7.7–Learned Responses*].

Our purpose today is to discover a new way of responding . . . to step outside your usual fight/flee/freeze reactions. When you leave here today, you will be able to: **Objectives**

- Distinguish the difference between instinctive reactions and learned verbal arts responses.

- List four types of verbal arts responses.

- Create your own responses to annoying comments.

Before we go further, write a cruel comment on a 3-by-5 card, as it was said to you. You can also add stage directions. Write as many comments as you like.

Verbal Arts Demonstration

- [Pass out the *rude relative remark* cards (see needed materials) to four volunteers from the audience. One by one, ask them to make the remark to you in the nastiest tone possible—*I can't believe your* . . .]

- [Use each of the following four responses in turn. Encourage the volunteers to continue badgering you if they can.] (1) It *is* unbelievable since you two are so close. (2) Do you think parents should be given better presents than a spouse? (3) Were you more *envious* or *surprised*? (4) Santa made him (her) do it—I have connections.

- [Ask the volunteers from the audience how they experienced your responses—Did they want to continue their veiled criticism; were they caught off guard, and so on.]

- Which of the four types of verbal arts responses were used? Did I combine different types of responses? Refer to *Handout 7.7–Learned Responses* handout to identify if I was *acting as if*, asking a question, active listening, or using humor or hypnosis. [Repeat each of your responses and encourage discussion. (1) *Acting as if* by agreeing with her feelings of disbelief and using a compliment—*You two are so close.* (2) Genuine question. (3) Actively listening by labeling feelings. Also using a forced choice question to help her focus on a less disturbing emotion. (4) Humor.]

- These four types of responses make up the acronym AAAH. They describe the feeling of *flow*, when a person breathes enlightenment into any cruel moment.

- What would your gut response have been to the remark—*I can't believe your husband (wife) gave you a better Christmas present than me, his mother?* Would you have been inclined to stay quiet, defend yourself, reassure her, or tell her she was one big bag of crazy?

Nonverbal Aikido Exercise

[Ask a member of the audience to stand facing you. Have the participant place the palms of his or her hands against yours at shoulder height with elbows bent. With only palms touching, encourage the participant to push you off balance while you push back. Give plenty of resistance and make eye contact. You should easily stumble. Repeat the exercise a second time but allow your arms to be flexible and follow the palms of the other person's hands wherever they move. Make sure your knees are not locked. The other person should quickly give up pushing.]

- What do you see happening? [Elicit the idea that resistance pushes people off balance. Being flexible and flowing while maintaining contact helps people stay centered.]

- What verbal reactions create resistance? [Defending, reassuring, convincing, blaming, and so on.]

- What response will keep you calm and centered? [All 4 (AAAH) verbal arts responses.]

- [Have participants practice the nonverbal exercise with their neighbors and share their experience as a group.]

- Suppose I had made an assertive statement: *If you're upset with your son (daughter), I'd like you to talk to her.* Would that be as effective one of the verbal arts responses? [Always be direct except when it does not work. Flow responses are designed for people under the influence of anger, anxiety, or ignorance and for people with personality disorders who are in the habit of blaming.]

Small Group Exercises— Handouts: Learned Responses, Verbal Arts Terms

- [Have four people demonstrate the learned responses from the handout—Use the instructions for **role plays**.]

- [Ask participants to break into small groups to practice making verbal arts responses without any sarcasm. Have the audience share their experience during the role-plays with the whole group.]

- Do you have any questions about the verbal arts responses? [Use the questions on *Handout 7.7–Verbal Arts Terms* handout to promote discussion on various types of responses.]

- [Ask participants to break into small groups to brainstorm verbal arts responses to an upsetting remark on the Response Worksheet. Use a cruel comment one of the group members wrote on his or her 3-by-5 card. If time is limited, each group can specialize in one type of the four types of responses.]

- [Ask a representative from each group to share responses with the entire audience].

Closing

- Does anyone have questions? I'd like to finish a question of my own: *Do you know how you will start to use the verbal arts or hypnotic hints in your own life* (or with your clients)?

- Do you need to know what was hypnotic about this question or will you just start to *act as if* to find the good in bad behavior, *ask questions* with heartfelt curiosity, *actively listen* to reflect and not absorb verbal abuse, and give *humorous hypnotic hints*?

Handout 7.7—Learned Responses— A Workshop Handout

Four types of neutral responses use language to absorb hostile words and render them harmless by being present with others and making contact with them in the worst of moments. Unlike attacking others or defending yourself, they do not come naturally and must be learned.[1]

Comment: I regret ever giving birth to you. Now you have a college degree and a husband; I have nothing.

1. **Act as if** (it is all good): Art of confirming	
a) Agree in fact:	I do have a husband and an education.
b) Agree in theory:	Raising me might have kept you from going places.
c) Speak what you want:	You never dreamed how your life could help mine.
d) Take it as a compliment:	I'm glad *you've noticed my accomplishments.*
e) Return with a compliment:	*You're a good mother* who sacrificed for her children.
f) Find a golden nugget:	*You are due* some sort of *an honor* for your sacrifice.
g) Dramatize the worst outcome:	My new house must make you feel even worse.

2. **Ask questions**: Art of inquiry **Comment:** *I regret ever giving birth to you. . . .*	
a) Genuine question (Socratic, curious):	Do you want to ever *stop regretting?*
b) Subtle question:	I wonder if *you could ever be proud of your kids.*
c) False choice question (bind):	Do you want to *stop regretting* or just *be glad for me?*
d) Forced choice (double bind):	Do you know how *you are going to become less upset?*
e) Underlying assumption (prediction):	Do you know when *you'll notice what you've done well?*
f) Questions that evoke inquiry:	Would you like to know a different way to look at this? . . . Are you sure . . . *you want to know?*

3. **Active listening**: Art of understanding **Comment:** *I regret ever giving birth to you. . . .*	
a) Rephrase, paraphrase, narrate:	You blame raising us on not having what you want in life.
b) Empathize—identify the feeling:	You feel sad when you think your life is empty.
c) Validate or sympathize— It makes sense that . . . It must be hard for you when . . .	It makes sense that you feel sad because you tried so hard to make your marriage work.

4. **Hypnosis and Humor** : Art of evoking **Comment:** *I regret ever giving birth to you. . . .*	
a) Truism; paired opposites ; dare:	You can *regret* what you missed and *suddenly*, for a moment, *be grateful for what you have.*
b) Implied directive:	As soon as you *remember one wonderful moment*, you can blink your eyes.
c) Utilization—encourage more of the same; serial suggestion:	Keep having regrets and being envious of me until you get worn out and find *they're not worth the effort.*
d) Power words—*try, but, dare:*	I know you're *trying* to be angry at me *but* you might be *shocked* to *realize what you really accomplished.*
h) Random response to disconnect:	I can forgive your regrets; the real tragedy of life is when people are afraid of the light (a play on Plato).
i) Humor—unexpected, irreverent connections that throw people off track:	Mom, I think this is the most expensive guilt trip you've ever tried to give me—thanks.

---

1. Adapted from *Making Hostile Words Harmless* by Kate Cohen-Posey with permission of John Wiley & Sons Inc., 2008, pp. 150-155.

- Check the responses that you like the most.
- Note the responses that would be easiest for you to make or come most naturally to you.
- **Role-plays:** The first person makes the comment: *I regret ever giving birth.* ... The second person responds, *I do have a husband and an education.* Then, the second person makes the comment, *I regret ever giving birth.* ... and the third person responds, *Raising me might have kept you from going places.* Continue round robin with each person making a comment and giving a response.

Instinctual Response Questionnaire

1. As an adult I have been bothered by: ☐ accusations, ☐ criticism, ☐ disrespect, ☐ insults, ☐ lectures, ☐ orders, ☐ rudeness, ☐ threats, ☐ unsolicited advice, ☐ other: _____

2. I usually respond to difficult comments by: ☐ staying quiet, ☐ apologizing, ☐ explaining myself, ☐ defending myself, ☐ reassuring others, ☐ trying to convince others, ☐ blaming others, ☐ attacking back, ☐ disagreeing, ☐ making accusations, ☐ lecturing, ☐ ordering, ☐ criticizing, ☐ threatening, ☐ giving advice, ☐ other: _____

AAAH Responses Worksheet

Directions: Write an upsetting comment in the box below. Make up various types of AAAH responses that could neutralize that comment without creating resistance. Use the examples from the previous page for help.

Upsetting comment: _____

		Responses
1.	**Act as if** (all is well): Art of confirming	
	a) Agree in fact:	
	b) Agree in theory:	
	c) Speak what you want:	
	d) Take it as a compliment:	
	e) Return with a compliment:	
	f) Find a golden nugget:	
	g) Dramatize the worst outcome:	
2.	**Ask questions**: Art of inquiry	
	a) Genuine question (Socratic, curious):	
	b) Subtle question (I wonder ...):	
	c) False-choice question (bind):	
	d) Forced-choice question (double bind):	
	e) Underlying assumption (prediction):	
	f) Questions that evoke inquiry:	
3.	**Active listening:** Art of understanding, mirror mind	
	a) Rephrase, paraphrase, narrate:	
	b) Empathize—identify the feeling:	
	c) Validate or sympathize—It makes sense that...; It must be hard for you when....	

4.	**Humor and Hypnosis:** Art of evoking		
	a)	Truism:	
	b)	Implied directive:	
	c)	Utilization—encourage more of the same:	
	d)	Serial suggestion:	
	e)	Paired opposites :	
	f)	Power words—*try, but, dare:*	
	g)	Random response to disconnect:	
	h)	Humor—unexpected, irreverent connections that throw people off track:	

Handout 7.8—Verbal Arts Terms— A Workshop Handout

AAAH: An acronym that captures the movements of the verbal arts that, like the martial arts, disarm difficult people: _Acting as if, Asking questions, Active listening_, and _Hypnosis_ and _Humor_.[1]

Acting As If

Acting as if all is well views an insult _as if_ it were a compliment or a harmless comment.

- **Agreeing** _acts as if_ by agreeing in fact, in theory, hypothetically, or with possibilities to rob opponents of a sparring partner.

- **Dramatizing** plays out the worst-case scenario of an insult to _act as if_ the exaggeration is fine.

- **Finding a golden nugget** finds something good and true in the worst insults. Often, this requires probing with questions.

- **Reverse psychology** directs people to continue to be troublesome, _as though_ it were a good thing, which places the behavior under the speaker's control (see **Utilization** —_Hypnosis_).

- **Speaking what you want** uses _golden lies_, which suggest that people are acting in desirable ways (even if they are not) in order to evoke that behavior. This is suggested in the scripture Romans 4:17: _God who called those things that be not as though they were._

- **Returning an insult with a compliment** responds to a verbal attack _as though_ it were benevolent by complimenting, making a continued assault almost impossible.

- **Taking an insult as a compliment** reframes the meaning of an insult to make it sound as though it were a compliment.

Asking Genuine Questions

Asking genuine questions changes agendas to blame or accuse into quests for the meaning of assumptions and the purpose of prying. They must be asked from a position of ignorance.

- **Asking subtle questions.** Use the words _I wonder . . ._ to pose questions in the form of statements, eliminating pressure to respond and prompting silent or spontaneous replies.

- **Asking false-choice questions (binds).** Present equally acceptable options to select.

- **Asking forced choice questions (double binds).** Compel agreement to a yes/no inquiry that is linked to an assumption that a needed change will happen—_Do you know how . . . will happen?_

- **Asking questions with underlying assumptions.** Link a time frame to a prediction of success—_Do you know when . . . ?_

- **Asking questions that evoke inquiry.** Make queries that promote asking questions—_Do you want to know the reason why . . . ?_

Active Listening

Active listening _demonstrates_ understanding of another person's experience by rephrasing, labeling feelings, validating _emotional logic_, and sympathizing.

- **Empathy** imagines others' feelings and labels them with a word—_I guess you feel . . ._

- **Narrating** gives blow-by-blow descriptions of behavior and verbal patterns. This heightens others' awareness of what they are doing, giving them a choice to continue or cease.

---

1. Adapted from _Making Hostile Words Harmless_ by Kate Cohen-Posey (2008) with permission of John Wiley & Sons Inc.

- **Rephrasing** restates what others have said in different words as opposed to simply repeating—*I hear you saying* . . .
- **Sympathy** adds compassion to labeling what others are feeling without taking responsibility for their emotions—*It must be awful to feel* . . .
- **Validation** uses other people's "emotional logic" to explain to them how their felt experience makes sense—*It makes sense that you feel* . . . *because* . . .

Humor disrupts habitual patterns with unexpected or absurd associations between the sensible and foolish, and the tragic and the commonplace.

Humor

Hypnotic language uses special language patterns and words to evoke change.

Hypnotic Language

- **Embedded suggestions** slip an idea into the context of a sentence.
- **Implied directives** suggest easy, almost involuntary, behavior for people to make as soon as they are ready to comply with a request to change—*As soon as you know* . . . *you can* . . .
- **Paired opposites** describes a negative mind-set or behavior first to limit it, and then focuses on the positive end of the polarity—*You may not want to <u>stop</u>* . . . *until you <u>start</u> to notice* . . .
- **Power words** are hypnotic flourishes that block or promote the action following them, or discount preceding information—*Try, dare, but, now* . . .
- **Predictions** presume that something will happen and then speculates on all the ways the desired outcome might occur—*Eventually you will* . . . *maybe in 2 hours, 2 years, or 20 years.*
- **Random responses** disrupt the flow of ideas, catching the intentional (conscious) mind off guard. New behaviors or thoughts are accepted in order to fill the void.
- **Truisms** are statements of fact that are hard to deny—*You can choose to* . . .
- **Utilization** directs people to continue an undesirable behavior in order to put it under the speaker's control, making the behaviors less likely to persist.
- **Serial suggestions** identify an easy or currently occurring behavior and link it to a more difficult task—*While you're* . . . *you can start to think about* . . .

Questions for Consideration

1. Which of the verbal arts focus attention on the antagonist?
2. What is the difference between agreeing in fact and in theory?
3. What is the advantage of subtle *I wonder* . . . questions?
4. How are evocative questions hypnotic?
5. Is the purpose of active listening to demonstrate an understanding of others' ideas and feelings or to protect yourself by reflecting others verbiage without absorbing it?
6. What is the difference between sympathy and an apology?
7. Why are truisms easy to accept?
8. How are implied directives and serial suggestions the same?
9. What is the fancy word for reverse psychology?

Answers

1. All the questions, active listening responses, and most of the hypnotic hints focus attention on the antagonist. Bullies try to put the spotlight on you.

2. Almost any remark can be agreed to in theory—"I *could* be nicer."

3. Subtle questions are actually statements and do not require a response. They are used to plant seeds or ideas in people's minds.

4. Evocative questions build impatience and focus attention—"Do *you want to know* what I think?" "Are you sure?" This is called a *hypnotic hook.* Opinions are not given unless there is a commitment to listen.

5. Both.

6. Sympathy puts the spotlight on the other person's experience. An apology takes responsibility for the other person's experience—"I'm sorry *you're* feeling . . ." vs. "I'm sorry *I made you* feel . . ."

7. They are statements of fact that are hard to deny.

8. Each links a hard behavior to an automatic one.

9. *Utilization.* This is an important skill for parents. Utilize your child's misbehavior: "Oh, you're doing that eye-rolling therapy that *will help you relax,*" instead of saying, "Don't roll your eyes!"

Handout 7.9—Surviving a Family Backlash

A family backlash is a strong adverse reaction to one member's taking a stand that is not in harmony with the family's current beliefs, values, or habits. This can happen to children in their nuclear family, to adults in their family of origin, to one person in a couple, or even in workplaces, which are recreated families. Before understanding how to survive a family backlash, it helps to be aware of powerful forces that exist in all groups:

- **Emotional reactivity** is expressed by gossip, threats, attacks, and triangles (two people in an alliance against a third). Name or describe groups of which you have been a part that routinely exhibit these characteristics: _____ _____

- **Togetherness forces** are expressed when members are alike in their beliefs, philosophies, values, and feelings. List groups or systems in which you have been involved with strong togetherness forces: _____

- **Differentiating force** arises within an individual to state what he or she believes or wants *without* imposing ideas on others. This is called the *I-position*. Describe a time when you (or someone you know) took the I-position: _____

- **Differentiated self** can remain neutral and connected to others in the midst of emotional turmoil. Name an example from your life (or a movie) of a time when you remained neutrally engaged during a conflict: _____

Expected Reactions to Taking a Stand

It is a common mistake for people to expect their families to be supportive when they express their differentness. Instead, they should anticipate a series of reactions:

1. The group will indicate that the person is *wrong* with expressions of surprise, hurt, anger, or labeling ideas and behavior as crazy, irresponsible, or immoral.

2. Efforts will be made to make the person *change back* or conform to the beliefs and behavior of the system.

3. *Consequences* will be threatened if the person does not change back, including threats that people will be angry or that the person will be cut off from the system.

4. Emotional turmoil will peak and then subside. The person taking the stand may be respected or appreciated *if he or she stayed on track without attacking or defending*.

These four reactions are so important that the only way of knowing if you have taken a step toward expressing your individuality is if (a) the group expresses a strong reaction to you; (b) you maintain contact with the group while under attack with casual responses; (c) you only take a stand for yourself, not for someone else or to win approval, and (d) praise from anyone is deflected—*I'm hurt that you think I was telling Mom off.*

The following example of taking a stand was adapted from *Making Hostile Words Harmless,* by Kate Cohen-Posey (2008) with the permission of John Wiley & Sons. It describes a hostile encounter between a married couple—Kate and Henry.

TAKING A STAND

On the spur of the moment, Kate and her friend Becky decided to take a road trip to Georgia to hear former President Carter teach Sunday school. Kate went to the bedroom and said to her husband, "Becky and I are going to Georgia tomorrow to hear Carter. Would you like to join us?"

"No," Henry shot back, "and you're not going either!"

"I'm not?" was Kate's baffled reply. She quickly left the room to make an online reservation. She returned in 15 minutes to inform Henry that she and Becky had a room in Americus, Georgia, the following night.

"You must be having a psychotic break," Henry countered.

"Well, that could be, but I usually only go nuts when I've gone more than 72 hours without sleep, and I'm well rested today. **Thanks for being concerned anyway."** Kate was undaunted.

"If you go, I'll be very angry!" Henry retorted forcefully.

"Of course you will be, Darlin'. You and half this county are *terrified* of my driving," replied Kate as she walked out of the room.

The next day, as she was carrying her packed bag to the car, Henry continued his pleas, order, and threats. Finally, Kate turned and said, **"You have a two million dollar life insurance policy on me. Should anything happen, you'll be a wealthy man."**

Her teenage daughter, overhearing this part of the conversation, jumped in asking, "How do I cash in on this?" And Kate made a quick get-away.

Two days later, Kate returned from hearing an inspiring message from a former U.S. president. Her mood was infectious, and her husband welcomed her with opened arms.

Decide if Kate genuinely took a stand by analyzing Henry's reaction. How did he try to convince Kate that she was wrong? What threat did Henry make? Most important, was Kate able to maintain contact with casual comments while under attack?

Casual Comments

When others overreact, it is important to *realize* that you are expressing your true Self, rather than *thinking* you have done something wrong. However, you will also need an arsenal of casual comments to disarm their attempts to pull you back into the herd. There are four main types of replies that can defuse attacks. Which of Kate's **boldface** responses is an example of each one?

Types of Casual Comments	Kate's Responses
Acting as if all is well views an insult *as if* it is a harmless comment. Agreeing in fact or theory and using compliments are types of *as if* comments that rob opponents of a sparring partner.	
Asking genuine questions that truly reflect not knowing or a desire to understand.	*I'm not?*
Active listening *demonstrates* understanding of another person's experience by rephrasing, labeling feelings, validating, or sympathizing.	
Humor and hypnotic language disrupts habitual patterns with unexpected associations between the sensible and foolish, and the tragic and the commonplace, or uses special word patterns to evoke change.	

Handout 7.10—Turning Disputes Into Discussions —A Worksheet

During a dispute, people give reasons to support their own strongly held convictions. Discussions allow ideas to shift because the pros and cons of a problem are considered. Some families or organizations are more prone to contentious debate than dialogue. There are several vicious cycles that create this disharmony. Mark the pattern(s) that is closest to your situation:

- ☐ Parents or the people in charge criticize, lecture, and blame. Children or subordinates are defensive, disagreeable, and sullen.

- ☐ Parents or people in authority have difficulty taking charge. They are defensive and argue with children or subordinates. Children or subordinates give orders, criticize, and blame.

- ☐ Mixed type: One parent undermines the other or tries to compensate for the parent that is "too hard." Children fear one parent and take advantage of the other.

- ☐ Certain people in the family or group have difficulty talking to each other and have to communicate through a middleman.

- ☐ One person tends to dominate discussions and others are afraid to voice their opinion.

- ☐ There are alliances in which two or more people regularly take sides against one person.

- ☐ One person is targeted and blamed for most of the family or group's problems.

- ☐ The focus on one person may be masking a problem between other people.

- ☐ The family or group endorses one "right" way to approach a problem. Differences of opinion result in criticism, lectures, advice, defensiveness, and even illness.

- ☐ The family or group is overconcerned about some members' behavior and allows few independent decisions in order to prevent mistakes.

- ☐ The family or group is underconcerned about some members' behavior and places few or no limits on independent decisions or consequences for mistakes.

- ☐ Feelings are invalidated—*You shouldn't feel . . .* Or, *You have no right to feel . . .*

- ☐ One person is emotionally cut off and tunes out the family.

Changing Vicious Cycles

There are three common problem-solving approaches: (1) fault finding; (2) understanding the reasons for difficult behavior; (3) focusing on solutions to change unproductive patterns. The first tactic is certain to perpetuate vicious attack-defend cycles. The last two approaches help people *stop* playing the blame game and *start* seeking understanding and solutions. It takes only one person to transform the interaction pattern of the entire group. Use the *Verbal Interaction Worksheet* as a guide to be the change agent in your family or organization by:

1. Following every statement made to you or others with a listening response that rephrases, empathizes, sympathizes, or validates.

2. Instead of criticizing and complaining, either (1) seek understanding by asking, *What was going through your mind when you . . .* or (2) focus on solutions by clearly identifying what you want: *Next time, would you . . .*

3. Identifying and complimenting positive behaviors on the part of other people.

4. If you are in a position of authority, use consequences instead of nagging, explaining, and lecturing: *You won't be able to . . . until your grades come up (you say that differently, your clothes are picked up,* etc.).

5. When you state an idea, opinion, or memory, preface it with the words, *My idea (opinion, memory) is . . .* This will make others less likely to correct you or disagree.

6. Being concise. The more words you use, the less you will be understood. Others may need to rephrase your ideas until you make your point.

Verbal Interaction Worksheet

This worksheet is designed to increase your awareness of the verbal patterns you use. It is likely to slow down the pace of a discussion, which will reduce tension and prevent disputes. Have an experienced person or professional present who can:

- Model the frequent use of listening responses.
- Help identify the verbal patterns being used.
- Gently correct statements that might promote disputes.
- Point out positive interaction.

Directions: After making any comment or response, check the type of language pattern you used in the small boxes. Do not monitor anyone else.

Solution Seeking	Understanding Seeking
1. State a feeling *I feel … when …* ☐☐☐☐☐☐☐☐☐☐	1. Empathize *Do you feel …?* ☐☐☐☐☐☐☐☐☐☐
2. State a specific desire *I would like …* ☐☐☐☐☐☐☐☐☐	2. Narrate *Describe action/thought* ☐☐☐☐☐☐☐☐
3. State limits ☐☐☐ *I'm willing … not willing …* ☐☐☐☐☐☐☐	3. Rephrase *Are you saying …?* ☐☐☐☐☐☐☐☐☐☐
4. State a memory *What I remember is …* ☐☐☐☐☐☐☐☐☐	4. Sympathize with *It must be hard when …* ☐☐☐☐☐☐☐☐
5. State viewpoint or idea *What I think/ believe is …* ☐☐☐☐☐☐☐☐	5. Validate *It makes sense that …* ☐☐☐☐☐☐☐☐
6. State an opinion *My opinion is …* ☐☐☐☐☐☐☐☐	6. Question *What is the reason for …? I wonder why …?* ☐☐☐ ☐☐☐☐☐☐☐
7. Statement of fact (truism) *You can tell me the truth, or not.* ☐☐☐☐☐☐	7. Agree in fact or theory/admit *You're right; Could be.* ☐☐☐☐☐☐☐☐☐
8. Evoke inquiry *Do you want to know my idea?* ☐☐☐☐☐☐☐	8. Use a compliment *Thanks for …* ☐☐☐☐☐☐☐☐☐☐
Blaming comments	**Defensive comments**
1. Accuse ☐☐☐☐☐☐☐☐☐☐	1. Answer for someone else ☐☐☐☐☐☐☐☐☐
2. Blame *It's awful … your fault …* ☐☐☐☐☐☐☐☐	2. Apologize *I'm sorry that I …* ☐☐☐☐☐☐☐☐☐☐
3. Convince *It would be good if …* ☐☐☐☐☐☐☐☐☐	3. Disagree ☐☐☐☐☐☐☐☐☐☐
4. Criticize *Finding fault or flaws* ☐☐☐☐☐☐☐☐☐	4. Explain /defend *It's just because …* ☐☐☐☐☐☐☐☐☐☐
5. Fake question *Criticize with a question* ☐☐☐☐☐☐☐☐☐	5. Interrupt ☐☐☐☐☐☐☐☐☐☐
6. Lecture/advise *You should/shouldn't….* ☐☐☐☐☐☐☐☐☐☐	6. Reassure *It's okay that …* ☐☐☐☐☐☐☐☐☐☐
7. Order /demand/command *You have to …* ☐☐☐☐☐☐☐☐☐☐	7. Take sides *I agree with …* ☐☐☐☐☐☐☐☐☐☐

Handout 7.11—Hard-Core Bully Busting—For Teens

When people are caught off guard by a stinging comment, they usually act out of habit. Think of a remark or action that made you mad. On the off chance that no one has ever upset you, consider how you would react to the following:

You barely bump into someone, and he or she says, *Get your ugly self out of my face!*

Would You:

1. Attack back: *Hey toad, watch who you're calling ugly.*
2. Threaten: *Meet me after school and we'll see who gets out of whose way.*
3. Lecture: *You don't have to get so hyper.*
4. Physically attack: Forget words and just smack him or her.
5. Indirectly attack: Plan for revenge with harassing phone calls or by spreading a rumor.
6. Gossip: Say little, but complain about what a jerk the person is to your friends.
7. Defend yourself: It *was just an accident.*
8. Apologize: *Gosh, I'm so clumsy.*
9. Flee: Just walk away and not tell anyone because it would be too embarrassing.
10. Act as if everything is cool and say: *Hey man I like your style.*

Bullies and Targets

The first seven reactions show how easy it is for people to attack when under fire. If you are likely to react in one of those ways, it does not mean you are a bully unless you (1) think you have to win, be tough, or be in charge; (2) are not concerned with others' feelings; or (3) believe things are always the other person's fault.

People who retreat from conflicts often have reaction 8 or 9. This can be good, but if you feel anxious and awkward around others, give in easily, and do not have friends to help you with difficult situations, you may frequently find yourself the target of bullies. Everyone gets an occasional shove and, even more often, is put down. However, some young people feel like the school punching bag. This is even more likely to happen if your feelings are easily hurt.

Bully Busts [1]

Neither being tough nor ignoring rude remarks works well. One provokes more verbal violence and the other makes bullies think they have won. Not many people would use the tenth response after an insult: *Hey man, I like your style.* Giving someone a compliment after a cut takes guts or a sense of humor. Responding without attacking others or defending yourself will make you feel powerful! The following exercises show how to unbalance a bully with surprise comebacks.

A—*Acting As If*. Pretending an insult is harmless by **agreeing** (a) with it, using **compliments** (c), or **dramatizing** (d) and exaggerating the worst part of it.

---

1. See *How to Handle Bullies, Teasers, and Other Meanies,* by K. Cohen-Posey, 1995, Highland City, FL: Rainbow Books, to help younger children.

ACTING AS IF

Directions: Put an _a_, _c_, or _d_ next to each response to show if _a_greeing, _c_omplimenting, or _d_rama was used.

Remark	Response
That's quite a zit farm you've got.	____ Last time I counted there were about 57 little buggers.
Kiss my a**.	____ Which cheek?
You're such a geek!	____ Thank goodness you're not.
You stupid idiot.	____ I can't help it. I get smarter every day.
You overweight heifer.	____ And it's always grazing time—got any snacks?
What's with those wacko noises?	_a_ You mean my vocal tics? Be glad you don't have them 24-7.
Someday I'll kill your fat a**.	____ I think you're way too classy to do that.
Trailer trash.	____ I hope it still counts if I live in a double wide.

A—Asking Questions. This strategy puts the spotlight back on difficult people with **curious** (c) questions that try to understand how rude people think, **hidden** (h) questions that conceal inquiries in statements, and **suggestive** (s) questions that present acceptable or false choices.

ASKING QUESTIONS

Directions: Put a _c_, _h_, or _s_ next to each question to show if it was _c_urious, _h_idden or _s_uggestive.

Remark	Response
So-and-so said you're a *itch.	____ Do you think I should fight everyone who talks trash about me?
You dress like a hoochie.	____ Why are you concerned about the way I dress?
Give me your test! I'm copying it.	____ When will you realize _you can't make people do what you want_?
Here comes the incredible hulk.	_s_ Are you saying I'm incredible or getting too muscular?
You overweight heifer.	____ I wonder why you like to point out people's weight.
Get out of my way, little man.	____ How soon _will you_ use your size to _put people at ease_?
You're corrupting my sister with your crap.	____ What do you think I said to her? …
Don't say anything! Just be quiet.	____ I wonder why you wouldn't want to _hear both sides_.
Did you buy that from Goodwill?	____ Are you looking for bargains or worried about my cash flow?

A—Active Listening. This will reflect cruel words without absorbing the content by **rephrasing** (r) what was said, **empathizing** (e), or labeling the person's feelings and **sympathizing** (s).

Directions: Put an *r*, *e*, or *s* next to each response to show if *r*ephrasing, *e*mpathy or *s*ympathy was used.

Remark	Response
So-and-so said such-and-such.	____ You seem *excited* that so-and-so said such-and-such about me.
Are you wearing any underwear?	*e* You seem mighty *curious* about underwear.
I know you're lying.	____ You're convinced that I'm holding out on you.
Other people said what you did.	____ You're in a bind—either believe the others or what I say.
I can't stand liars.	____ It would be awful to have a friend you can't trust.
Just say how your story is true.	____ You want me to keep explaining so you can figure this out.
Well, what am I supposed to do?	____ You think your only choice is to figure out what really happened.
Maybe I'll say, *Don't tell me any more BS because I wasn't there.*	____ So you figured out another choice that would get you out of the middle and out of the rumor mill.

H—Hypnotic Hints. By sneaking **suggestions** (s) into a response, use what people are doing to **reverse** (r) behavior, or add **confusion** (c) to disconnect people from what they are doing.

Directions: Put an *s*, *r*, or *c* next to each response to show if it is a *r*everse, a *s*uggestion, or adds *c*onfusion.

Remark	Response
Who would ask you out?!	____ You can try to be more discouraging, but *it's not worth the effort.*
You're due to get your face hit.	____ So my face is overdue, not my library books.
You're a little sl*t.	*s* It will be amazing when you … *stop calling people names.*
Your momma's a hog.	____ When you *get your momma off your mind*, just say, "Whatever."

It is more important that you think about each response than that you correctly identify what elements it contains (agreeing, rephrasing, suggestions, etc.). For this reason, answers are not given. The four types of responses make up the acronym **AAAH:** the sound of a refreshing pause that breathes kindness into life's cruel moments.

Handout 7.12—Talking So People Will Listen

Do you talk to interact with others or to give and receive information? The first goal focuses on building relationships and bonding. When your purpose is for other people to attend to your opinions, desires, or data, certain skills will help you make your point.

Seven Habits of Highly Effective Talkers

1. **Listen first** by *rephrasing* what others are saying. This will: (a) clarify if there is an actual difference of opinion that needs to be addressed; (b) model listening skills; (c) motivate others to pay attention and make sure you are accurately stating their point; and (d) help you reframe your opinions in a way your audience can accept.

2. **Agree before you disagree.** Listen intently to find some common ground or mutual interests before expressing your ideas. Whatever thoughts you need to say will come to you after your full attention has been on the other person.

3. **Commit others to listen to you** by asking, *Do you want to know what I think* (. . . *my opinion, what I remember*, etc.). This helps people change gears from talking to listening.

4. **Make your statements for the record,** not to persuade or judge others. True dialogue does not require people to justify their feelings, desires, and information with long-winded explanations. Tell your views or story gradually, allowing others to interject their thoughts.

5. **Announce the type of statement(s) you are about to make:** *My thought (opinion, memory, belief) is* . . . ; *I have two problems with what you are saying.* This clarifies that you are stating your own ideas, not facts that need to be proved and defended.

6. **Be concise.** Announcing the type of statement you are going to make will help you get to your point. If you notice that you are talking for too long, tell others you are losing your point and ask them to tell you the gist of what you have said.

7. **State what you want,** not what you do not want. Complaints and orders shut down people's brains, making it harder for them to listen when you do make a clear request. Saying, *Can you* . . . *I'd like you to* . . . or . . . *needs to be done,* is less direct than asking, *Would you* . . .

The Art of Asking

First, you need to know what you want and why you want it. Are you seeking cooperation, approval, or agreement? Then, ask for what you want *out loud*. Other people cannot read minds even if you give daily reminders. Everyone's priorities are not the same as yours. Improve the chances of others listening to your requests with the following steps:

- **Break the problem into small, achievable objectives**. What is the first thing the person could do to accomplish your goal—*Would you hang up your clothes before you talk on the phone?*

- **Ask with one short question** followed by the word *because*—*Would you let me get on the computer for a minute because I have to leave early for class.*

- **Make specific (multiple-choice) requests**. Instead of *I'd like you to care more,* say, *Would you ask about my day, give me a hug, or wash my feet?* Choices and absurd requests help.

- **Practice accepting *No* gracefully** by making some unreasonable requests so you can simply say, *That's okay* . . . *no problem.*

- **Do not require others to *want* to do what you ask**. When their initial response is to grumble, remember that they're in the first stage of considering your request. Listen quietly and trust them to work through their struggle.

- **If people forget** to do your bidding, ask again without making a fuss—*I'm sure you meant to* . . . *Would you do it tomorrow?* When others do what you ask, show appreciation!

- **When others refuse to do something**, ask once more, with only one reason why your desire is important, or simplify your request. Then, if they decline, accept *No* gracefully. If you're in a position of authority, use leverage—*You can do this after you've done that.*

Everyone Has an Opinion[1]

In spite of the old saying, your opinion is not smelly. In fact, you have an inalienable right to express your views. Your thoughts deserve attention, but you cannot express them if you are doing more than your share of listening. To reverse this pattern:

- **Catch people's attention** by saying their name, pausing, and waiting for them to look at you. Other clever attention-getters can be used, but people love to hear their names spoken.

- **Use a confident posture** and, if talking in a group, stand up. Make your voice firm and strong. Emphasize important words. Reinforce words with hand gestures—I have three points (hold up three fingers). Talk loudly enough and not too fast. Dramatize what you are saying with your body. Look directly at people.

- **State your opinion** rather than giving the pros and cons of an argument. If you are asked what you want to do, make a decision! Responding with the proverbial, *What do you want to do?* makes you look mindless and wishy-washy.

- **When interrupted**, look firmly at the person and say, *I'll be happy to continue when you finish.* If people are going on too long, do not hesitate to interrupt. Say, *Whoa . . . time out . . . hang on. . . . Let me see if I understand what you've said so far.*

- **Do not turn statements into a question** by raising your inflection at the end of a sentence. Do not tag statements with a question—*Don't you agree? Shouldn't we?* This shows a lack of confidence in your opinion.

- **Do not use qualifiers** that suggest uncertainty—*I kind of think . . . We probably should . . .*

- **Do not apologize.** Frequent *I'm sorries* make you look clumsy, half-brained, and at fault (when you're not).

The Devil *Is* in the Details

Do you speak in sentences or paragraphs? If you habitually use two or more sentences, you are likely to lose your audience. Do not blame others for glazed eyes, fidgeting, and wandering attention. Learn to be concise.

- **Present the highlights and stop**. People can ask follow-up questions if they want to know more. Giving too many details at once deprives others of the chance to dialogue.

- **Prioritize details**. Use the standard rule of thumb: *need to know, nice to know, don't need to know.* If you barely have other's attention at need-to-know, do not go on to nice-to-know.

- **Stick to the issues**—*I want to make three points. . . . I have two problems with what you're saying.*

- **When telling others about your day**, start with the funniest, most unusual, or demanding thing that happened. If they ask questions or share their own stories, you can go on.

- **Resist the urge to give advice.** The less guidance you give, the more it will be listened to when you do offer counsel. Save your wisdom for key issues.

- **Fewer words are more with children.** Instead of saying, *You need to wash the dishes because blah blah blah, . . .* say, *Dishes . . . now!* Then *withhold* valued activities until the chore is done.

---

1. More ideas on self-expression and speaking concisely can be found in *How to Talk So Men Will Listen,* by M. K. Woodall, 2001, San Jose, CA: Writers Club Press.

CHAPTER 8
RELATIONSHIP REMEDIES

MINI INDEX TO CHAPTER 8

Help clients:

1. Practice steps that decrease conflict and increase cooperation and bonding in relationships.
2. Identify indicators of affairs, codependency, and emotional abuse and change vicious cycles.
3. Make wise decisions about divorce, dating, and step-parenting.

Using the Handouts

- **General literature:** *A Parent's Power Tools, Relationship Fundamentals, Cures for Common Couple Problems, Acts of Love That Renew Romance, The Science of Dating*
- **Specific problems:** *Surviving the Taxing Teens, Surviving Picky Parents, Analyzing Affairs, Moving Beyond Betrayal, Undoing Dependency, The Bait-and-Switch Trap, Divorce Dilemmas, Blending Families*
- **Exercises:** *Can We Just Talk? The Tale of the Tiger's Eye Treasure*
- **Workshops:** *The Tale of the Tiger's Eye Treasure* can be used with families or for a presentation on enmeshment, resolving conflicts, living in the present, unity in the workplace, and more. The fable can be read with participants acting out the five major parts:

  The first person to look for the stone was a cautious man. . . . [The volunteer acts cautious] . . . *He was always careful and on the lookout for danger.* . . . [The participant pantomimes looking out for danger]. . . . He debated within himself [Participant reads two sentences of script]. . . .

  After the dramatic reading, participants can break into small groups. The discussion questions can be changed slightly, depending on the audience. A representative from each group can report their answers to the whole group.

Cautions and Comments

- ***A Parent's Power Tools*** and ***Surviving the Taxing Teens*** should be read by both parents. They can be used as a guideline for parents to reach agreements on their own policies and can be supplemented with handouts on anger (Handouts 6.3, 6.14).
- ***Surviving Picky Parents*** contains skills that some adolescents can acquire, but considerable coaching will be needed. This handout is important if parents are resistant to treatment.
- ***Relationship Fundamentals*** provides a bare outline of the Gottman approach to marriage counseling. ***Can We Just Talk?*** is meant to supplement his first step of creating *Love Maps,* and ***Cures for Common Couple Conflicts*** offers strategies to reach compromises for solvable problems. Handouts in Chapter 7 also address

Gottman's concerns regarding *harsh start-ups*, criticism, contempt, (Handouts 7.1, 7.10, 7.12) and learning ways to repair conflicts (Handout 7.4).

- ***Acts of Love That Renew Relationships*** will require guidance to help people identify their partner's love language and understand the benefits of giving.

- ***Analyzing Affairs*** helps people decide if they want to continue their relationship. If they choose to remain together, ***Moving Beyond Betrayal*** offers pointers for treatment.

- ***Undoing Dependency*** and ***The Bait-and-Switch Trap*** are both about the use of control tactics. In *Undoing Dependency*, codependents try to control and fix their loved one's problems. *The Bait-and-Switch Trap* shows how misogynists control and belittle their spouses to avoid abandonment. Both handouts offer a series of tasks to change patterns of caretaking and victimization. They are also excellent to use in groups.

- ***Divorce Dilemmas*** helps ambivalent clients make decisions about their marriage, but, even more important, it encourages them to analyze their part in marital problems.

- ***The Science of Dating*** is excellent to use with young adults who have not been in a serious relationship or for people venturing into the singles scene after marriage. Emphasize that it is never too late to change self-destructive patterns.

- ***Blending Families*** can be supported with other handouts in this section. The ideas from *Divorce Dilemmas* can help couples work through unresolved issues from previous marriages and *Relationship Fundamentals* and *Acts of Love* can strengthen the step-couple bond.

Handout 8.1—A Parent's Power Tools

A parent's power comes from action, not his or her voice. Infants have as much vocal clout as their caretakers. A slightly altered version of Job's words (1:20–21) offers the key to parental leverage . . . a *parent* **gives** *and a parent* **withholds** *(blessings)*.

Withholding

Withholding is a simultaneous stick/carrot action. A reward (the carrot) immediately ends an aversive consequence (the stick). This is different than *taking away* what children want: the TV, computer, cell phones, toys, going outdoors, going to a special event, and so on. Taking away privileges takes away your power. *Withholding* what young people want until they have executed a desired task places them in control of how long the punishment part of the consequence lasts. There is a special grammar for withholding:

- *You can . . . when you have . . .* focuses children on the incentive and motivates them.

- *You can't . . . until you have* (done) *. . .* is discouraging. Some children stop listening after hearing *You can't . . .*

- Nagging reduces the power of withholding. Do not give reminders. Just start to withhold privileges when it is time to start a chore or task.

Blessings

A parent's *blessings* are any privileges, coveted items, or events young people desire. How you use them depends on if children are (1) *not* complying with requests or (2) breaking a rule.

1. **"Sins of omission."** Withhold *everything* the child wants until the job has been completed.

   - Give a 5- to 15-minute warning before you start withholding privileges. Use a timer as a reminder to turn off TVs and computers or make children come inside.

   - Do not threaten to take something away the next day or week. There is usually something children value that can be withheld immediately.

   - Set deadlines for tasks to start prior to something young people enjoy. Leaving dishes or baths to be done before bedtime does not give parents anything to withhold.

   - If withholding everything does not motivate children to start a task, use aversive action: tickle, shadow, hug, or sit on them until they are ready to start.

   - There are times when a child has to do something immediately and parents will not have any incentives to withhold. Be ready to physically guide them when it is time to leave or move small children's arms like a puppet to help them pick up toys.

2. **"Sins of commission."** Do not take all of a child's rights when he fails to follow rules or meet expectations. You will need some privileges or items to ensure that daily tasks are done.

   - A student with *poor grades* may not be allowed to go out on weekends until she has a B or better in all subjects, but she may still have limited phone calls or computer time, so these can be withheld if she does not do her chores.

   - **Essays** require children to explain in writing (a) why a rule is important, (b) what they were thinking when they violated it, and (c) how they plan to keep from breaking it in the future. Depending on the degree of the infraction, the child may need to write the essay more than once or several nights in a row. Younger children can copy a sentence.

   - **Basic training** is a way to have children practice desirable behavior at times that are inconvenient for them: (a) Before a favorite TV show, a child may have to put on his pajamas and practice getting dressed and ready for school as a consequence for *morning tardiness*. (b) Write down *disrespectful comments* a young person made. Tell her she must calmly disagree with you or gracefully accept your decision, *using the right words and tone of voice* (several times), before talking on the phone or using the computer.

- **Time-out** interrupts disruptive behavior. Have children sit where they can be observed—a minute or less per year of age. Hold beginners in the time-out spot until they are ready to comply and ignore fussing as long as they stay where they have been put. Hyperactive children need time-out that requires muscle action: slow marching or modified push-ups.

Giving Rewards

Rewards are any specialty items that go beyond a child's routine privileges. Some things that children are used to receiving can be given *only* when they are earned (by performing desirable behavior)—candy, sodas, or pocket change. Giving rewards requires a parent to catch their child doing something good—admitting the truth, having chores done before the parent comes home, being ready for school on time, hanging up a bath towel, putting dishes in the sink, and so on.

- Use the easiest method possible to give rewards—put beans in a jar, stickers on a calendar, or points on a chart. Points can build toward buying something special. Tic Tacs are handy candy that you can carry in your pocket.

- A stopwatch is one of the most powerful tools a parent can use. They are found on many cell phones. Challenge children to race against time while picking up their toys.

Special Situations

- **Dinnertime.** When a child dawdles while eating, put food in the refrigerator when the family is finished eating. He can heat it himself, have it cold later, or wait until the next meal to eat. When children do not like what the family is eating, allow them to fix a simple meal themselves. A child can survive on SpaghettiOs every night of the week.

- **Car problems.** When a child misbehaves in the car, pull to the side of the road at the first opportunity, get out, lock the doors, and stand with your back to the car for about a minute. Give only one warning before pulling over. If it is raining, pull under a bridge.

- **Public places.** Immediately take a child to the car for time-out. Cars are amazingly soundproof. You should not have to repeat this many times.

- **Tantrums.** Either send the child to her room or ignore her as much as possible. Use a stopwatch or clock to time the tantrum. Make a bar graph of how long each meltdown lasts and give her a reward whenever a tantrum is shorter than all the others. When she is feeling good, log the anger trigger and what she needed to *think* to stay cool.

- **Arguments.** Children cannot argue without help from parents. When they push your buttons, make a neutral response: *Good try; Be nice if it worked; Could be; Sorry you feel that way; I know.* If a child repeatedly asks the same question, tell him you will answer only if he writes what you say. Give children a little reward if they can explain why you are saying no (instead of repeatedly answering *Why-can't-I* questions).

- **Sleeping alone.** Prepare yourself for 1 to 4 nights of screaming. Children need to cry it out until they learn to put themselves to sleep. If the child leaves the room, physically return her to bed without discussion and hold the door closed for 3 minutes. Agree ahead of time that the door can be open a crack if she stays in bed. Give her a special reward every morning she wakes up in her own bed until sleeping alone becomes a habit.

- **Also see poor grades, tardiness, and disrespectful comments under "Sins of commission."**

Handout 8.2—Surviving the Taxing Teens—For Parents

The terrible twos are similar to the terrible teens. Two-year-olds are learning to internalize basic rules of living and regulate body functions, while adolescents are facing actual separation from parents and raging hormones. The biologically driven adolescent agenda has five parts:

1. Teens literally repel parents because being near them creates repugnant feelings of dependence. To take parental advice can feel like defeat. The more dependent the teen (or parent), the more intense the struggle. Boys avoid confrontations and withdraw, while girls tend to argue. This, at least, gives girls some contact.

2. The need for closeness and intimacy with peers is a priority during this period of separating from parents. Friends are equated with security and self-worth. How a boy dresses indicates with what group he identifies. How a girl dresses is equated with status. Her looks take on extreme importance.

3. Parents are seen as flawed people who have somehow managed to function. This eases the threat of independence while provoking extreme embarrassment.

4. Teens want trust even though they lie to cover up wrongs or manipulate. They think lying to parents doesn't count. Trust is equated with independence.

5. Development of conscience begins with internal arguments with rules and exaggerating parental criticism. Some teens drive themselves beyond adult expectations or give up on (self-imposed) demands. Teens rarely feel the blame for anything.

A Parent's Mission (Impossible)

The task for parents is to let go while setting limits, making demands, and loving teens in spite of their reactivity. Parents are stripped of their active parenting role at the exact time when the risks children face are greater. Today's teens have more of a sense of entitlement than in the past. Parents feel the need to respond to misbehavior but have no idea of the best way to take action.

STRATEGIES FOR DEALING WITH TEENS

Directions: Decide if you agree with the following strategies and regularly rate yourself on how often you can execute them: (O) often, (S) sometimes, (R) rarely.

___ 1. Do not battle for control. The best parents will get is imperfect control, and that is enough. Teens do not want to overthrow the system; they just want to get around it. If teens think they can get away with something, they will usually try.

___ 2. Consider a teen's input on decisions unless it is ridiculous. There is a difference between having no curfew and changing it for a special night. It is fine for rules to be amended if the parent makes the change without being bullied. There should always be rules, even if they are changed or broken.

___ 3. Confront teens with broken rules or irresponsibility. Emphasize that the behavior is not acceptable, and declare that the rule is still valid. After the confrontation or stating a consequence, walk away! This forces an internal debate that helps develop a conscience.

___ 4. Avoid arguing. Do not get into fights to demand that rules be obeyed before they are broken. Often, teens have outbursts because they are not getting their way, but they will comply (somewhat). Prolonged arguments with parents delay internalization of rules.

___ 5. Do not demand obedience to the letter of the law. Young people often do not comply as a show of independence. There is a difference between being 15 and 50 minutes late. Mild offenses can be handled with confrontation (#3) that builds a conscience and internal controls.

____ **6.** Focus on rules and responsibilities rather than lying. Confront teens with their deceit and communicate its effect on you without making it a disaster or taking it personally. When teens lie, a sacred trust has *not* been broken. Parents are better off not trusting teens in every area.

____ **7.** Focus on rules and responsibilities rather than disrespect or cursing. These are teen tactics to keep arguments going and avoid rules and responsibility. When attitudes cannot be ignored, it is enough to simply state that you do not like what is happening and that you will resume contact when your child can find an acceptable way to make his or her point.

____ **8.** Give teens a 5-minute warning to start a chore, but do not wait too long, or the task will never get done. Set a timer to ensure that you will give a final reminder and then withhold all privileges until the task is finished. Most teens will not do what is asked of them without reminders! Their priorities often look like laziness to parents. If teens act listless, shadowing them provides excellent motivation.

____ **9.** *Briefly* state your views for the record. Lectures help parents feel better, but they are counterproductive with teens, who are masters at tuning out or arguing. Even if teens seem to totally reject your ideas, an internal debate is begun that registers opposing views. Discuss difficult issues during neutral times, but be ready to accept that such talks usually will not work out as you wish.

____ **10.** Resist the urge to give advice. The less guidance you give, the more credence your views will have when they are given. Save your wisdom for key issues or for when it is solicited.

Additional Pointers

- **Restrictions** can be given for defiance, but they will work only if the teen still buys into the system of parental control. The more mild the restriction, the better the parent's chance of enforcing it. Even if young people break the same rule as soon as they are off restriction, parents have still met their responsibility by responding with a consequence. Constant restrictions will only turn parents into jailers.

- **Corporal punishment** can have a devastating impact on teens because physical contact with one's parents has sexualized undertones. If teens break the taboo and hit parents, immediate help must be sought from outside authorities.

- **Reversal of nights and days** is common with teens but bad for their health. Require teens to get up at a reasonable time in the morning, regardless of how late they went to bed. Here are some options: Spritz them with water, rub ice cubes on their feet or backs, hold a cotton ball soaked in ammonia under their noses, pull off all their blankets, or sing opera to them. Take the computer mouse and disable the TV when you go to bed.

- **Poor academic performance** warrants increased parental supervision. Withhold some (but not all) privileges until grades show signs of improvement. Most schools provide online access to grades daily. Instead of nagging, restrict computer time or weekend activities until grades are at an acceptable level.

- **Poor conduct reports** do not necessarily require punishments over and above the school's consequences. Parents can do little more than support these and express disappointment. Withhold important privileges while a teen is suspended from school.

- **Involvement in sex, alcohol, and drugs.** The more sense of purpose young people have for achievement, extracurricular activity, or future goals, the less likely they will be sidetracked by risky behavior. When parents suspect children are endangering themselves, they should seek outside help. If a young person is so out of control that they are threatening the family, they may have to leave home. Defiance of rules, in itself, may not be a cause for leaving. Parents should continue to express their views. Teens will be able to consider concerns based on possible risks more easily than parent belief systems.

Handout 8.3—Surviving Picky Parents—For Teens

If your parents are between 35 and 65 years old, they may be suffering from **Middle Age Mania** (MAM). *Not my problem*, you say. Oh, but it is. Although MAM is not recognized by doctors, its effects on offspring of the afflicted have several glorious titles—oppositional defiant disorder (ODD), bipolar disorder (moodiness), and even attention deficit/hyperactivity disorder (ADHD). If you want to avoid being labeled, your best chance is to recognize MAM in your parents and learn strategies to ease their suffering. If your caretakers exhibit *any* of the following symptoms, they may have MAM:

☐ **Attempting to control your choice of music, friends, or future goals.** They are examining their lives and experiencing failed dream syndrome. Their regrets and memories of childhood struggles are turned into misguided efforts to manage your life.

☐ **Correcting your flaws in order to grade themselves as parents.** They think they will earn an A+ if you are perfect or share their beliefs and interests! You either need to be an extension of their success or make up for their failures.

☐ **Thinking they are *entitled* to automatic obedience and appreciation.** They believe they have done more for you than anyone. Often, they feel attacked, ignored, misunderstood, taken for granted, and abused *by you* (of all people)!

☐ **Thinking you expect too much**—to give you rides any time or any place, to buy you a car or the latest electronic device, to be as fair as your friend's parents, and to give you too much freedom. And all this time you thought they were expecting too much of you!

☐ **Thinking it is their job to worry.** They do this for two reasons—either they do not remember what they did as teens or they remember too well what they did. They may worry about your friends, hair, posture, clothing style, and types of food you eat. It is enough to make you wonder if you have any brain cells left.

☐ **Hold certificates in worrying.** This means that they have an actual diagnosis of obsessive-compulsive disorder (OCD). They may alphabetize vegetable cans, disinfect countertops, and make sure the stove has been turned off 10 times.

☐ **Thinking you have all the freedom and they have all the responsibility.** While you may consider yourself a prisoner in your own home, they think you are a carefree creature who does not have to pay bills, please a grouchy boss, or worry about health issues. Tons of homework, testy teachers, and everyday dramas do not meet their standard of stress.

The Teen's Challenge

Your task is to be the mover and shaker in your family. You may think it is a parent's job to fix problems, but rigidity is an underlying feature of MAM. All your attempts to help by doing your share of yelling or refusing to talk to anyone will only intensify parental mania and land you a lowdown label. Your parents need shock therapy. The following list will give you a start.

SHOCK THERAPY FOR MIDDLE AGE MANIA (MAM)

Directions: Decide which strategy you are willing to use first, second, third, and so on. After executing each action a few times, rate how helpful it was on a scale of 1–10.

____ **Close the communication gap.** Set a goal of telling your parents three bits of information a day—*Fred's hair caught on fire in chemistry; I think Mrs. Fox has PMS; Freida's parents are getting a divorce.* Be conversational and stay away from risky topics that promote *I-hope-you-don't-do-that* or *What-did-you-do-to-cause-it* remarks. Likewise, show interest in your parent's lives—*What project are you working on? Did you ever experience peer pressure?* Doctors with a good bedside manner are rarely sued, and teens who converse with parents get fewer restrictions.

_____ **Give your parents 30 minutes of quality time (QT) a day.** Eating meals together does not count. Even if your room is your haven, parents with MAM need attention and hugs. You need to venture into their living space. Giving parents QT has been known to markedly reduce adult mania, although it cannot cure middle age. A problem parent needs extra TLC.

_____ **Build your trust fund.** Being trustworthy is a habit. It involves consistent honesty, keeping promises, doing what is right, using good judgment, and keeping secrets. Parents with MAM are prone to paranoia, but deceptive escapades will get you in lock-up, not them. To gain trust *and your freedom,* you need **documentation**. Tell your parents you are starting a journal to help you be a better person. Every time you do something right, write it down and have your parents initial the entry—*Admitted I broke the teacup; Told Billy Jean she couldn't come over till you got home; Did not tell a lie today.* As long as there is no evidence of dishonesty, they may initial the last one.

_____ **Recover from mistakes gracefully.** Even if you are Honest Abe, mistakes are bound to happen. Focus on a sincere, heartfelt apology—not defending yourself or making excuses: *I'm sorry I was 2 hours late because I fell asleep at Angie's. You must have been so worried. I'll give you the mouse to my computer at 9 P.M. every night this week to make sure I get to bed on time.* Naming your own *logical* consequence can keep your parents from coming up with a harsh penalty.

_____ **Start a savings account.** Make deposits by helping parents without being asked. Even though you will be accused of wanting something, you must *not* commit random acts of goodness for that reason! Remember, you are saving for a rainy day when you do need something. Writing parents poems, making them a gift, and saying *Thank You* download quick currency into your account.

_____ **Ask so you will receive.** Timing is everything. It's best if you have points in your savings and trust accounts. Work in the long-forgotten word *please.* Be brief. Give one reason and consider your parents' concerns. Do not pressure them: *Can I go to the dance at South End because I brought up my grades? I know the neighborhood is not great; I'll give you the chaperon's telephone number. Please take 10 minutes (2 hours, 2 days) to think about it before you answer.* If the answer is *No,* accept it gracefully. This may earn you a *Yes* next time.

_____ **Train parents to stop nagging.** This involves radical steps. Tell your parents they can withhold (not take away) all your privileges and goodies until you have completed required tasks—then you get everything back. The deal is, they cannot remind you to do homework or chores until the agreed-upon time for starting them. (You may have to go along with their deadlines.) While this sounds like a scary strategy, teens who have tried it say it reduces nagging and yelling by 72%.

_____ **Disarm out-of-control parents.** When the noise level is rising and parents are calling you names (lazy and disrespectful are all-time favorites), *do not* yell back or roll your eyes. *Do:*

- Look alert, make eye contact, and utter *uh-huhs.*

- At the first opportunity, rephrase what was said and name feelings—*You're furious that my girlfriend was here when you weren't home. You believe that I'm old enough to remember to . . .*

- Use the magic phrase *You're absolutely right* if you are in the wrong. This trashes most tirades.

- Name your own feelings to respond to heartless comments—*I feel devastated when you say . . .*

- Lecture yourself first to avoid lectures: *Boy, did I do a dumb thing. You've told me a million times not leave my tuba on the sofa, and now Charlie sat on it and the keys are stuck. I'm going to have to work a lot of extra chores to pay to get that fixed.*

- There will be times when you may feel yourself pulled into the blame game. Instead, say, *Can I do time-out in my room until we can talk calmly?* If you make it sound like your bad, you might be able to get away until the emotional tsunami has passed.

- Give up on lost causes. Save your strength for important issues when you must persevere.

- Do not even begin to argue over your beliefs and other things that parents cannot control.

You do not need a medical degree to administer parental shock therapy. Just shove your pride aside and find the will and wisdom deep inside you to turn your family on its fanny.[1]

---

1.   For serious cases of MAM, read *Bringing up Parents,* by A. J. Packer, 1992, Minneapolis, MN: Free Spirit Publishing.

Handout 8.4—Relationship Fundamentals

Whether relationship problems have been building to a crescendo or springing up from nowhere, people tend to focus on specific issues and get caught on minute details of daily life. In truth, dysfunctional behavior patterns develop when relationships are missing basic ingredients.

As a result of studying hundreds of couples over several years, a psychologist named John Gottman claims he can predict divorce with 91% accuracy. However, there are many myths about relationship red flags.

Predictors of Relationship Failure

DISASTER DETECTORS

Directions: Mark any of the behavior patterns below that you think are signs of troubled twosomes.

____ 1. The inability to resolve conflicts and a lack of important communication skills.

____ 2. Partners avoid conflicts altogether.

____ 3. A partner(s) has emotional or personality problems.

____ 4. Partners have different values, goals, and interests.

____ 5. A partner makes complaints about tasks that were not done—*I wish you had . . .*

____ 6. A partner blames or criticizes—*You are so . . . ; What's wrong with you?*

____ 7. Discussions start off with criticism, sarcasm, or contempt (*harsh start-ups*).

____ 8. A partner expresses contempt with name-calling, eye-rolling, sneering, and hostility.

____ 9. A partner defends him- or herself with explanations, excuses, and reassurances.

____ 10. One partner *stonewalls* the other's attempts to talk by looking away, acting deaf, or leaving.

____ 11. During disagreements, one partner becomes physically *flooded*—heart races or sweats.

____ 12. Negative thoughts about partners outweigh the positive.

____ 13. A partner(s) has mostly negative memories of dating, their wedding, or first year together.

Fortunately, the first five patterns are common in many good relationships. Most marital conflicts do not get resolved. While skillful communication can come in handy, it cannot save a marriage. A couple may avoid conflicts or be prizefighters, as long as they have similar styles for handling disputes. Mates can accommodate each other's eccentricities when they make their quirks mesh and not clash. Values, goals, and interests can be different, but partners need to know and support each other's pursuits.

If a relationship meets certain basic criteria, it can weather the storms of character flaws, knock-down-drag-out fights, and even withstand an affair. Dr. Gottman identified seven fundamental requirements in successful marriages. They are summarized as follows:[1]

Steps to Successful Relationships

1. **Build your bond.** All relationships begin with an attachment bond—whether that is between parents and children or spouses. The source of attachment is knowledge; self-disclosure is the glue of intimacy. The acronym OPEN suggests ever-deeper levels of self-disclosure: Observations, Perspectives (views), Emotions/Experiences, and Needs.

---

1. Adapted from *The Seven Principles for Making Marriage Work,* by J. M. Gottman and N. Silver, 1988, New York: Crown Publishers.

Make trivial pursuit questions for each partner that increase knowledge of each other's friends, family, missions, philosophies, fears, and secret desires.

2. **Focus on positives.** All people have quirks and annoying habits. The reason that happy couples tolerate them is that their positive thoughts about their partners and their relationship outweigh the negatives. Their marital cup is half full—not half empty. Remember what first attracted you to your spouse. Describe her the way a compassionate higher being would. Pick three positive words to describe her. Turn weaknesses into strengths—a messy person may be creative. Remind yourself of her good qualities often, especially when you are feeling fed up.

3. **Connect in little and big ways.** Asking for a hug, going for a walk, pointing out what the dog just did, and (of course) having sex all count as connecting. The ritual good-bye and hello kiss are all important. *How was your day?* yields more details if asked: *What happened at the meeting? Tell me something good the kids did before the bad news.* Choose good times to talk. Be sure to take your partner's side when he is venting and refrain from giving advice. People have varying needs for connection and independence. If you and your partner have major differences, discuss how to make little changes to adapt to one another.

4. **Share power with your partner.** Men who do not share power have an 81% chance that their marriage will self-destruct. Women often complain that men do not do their share of chores and childcare. However, some men are people pleasers, and the woman is the decider. Sharing power means considering your partner's feelings and opinions before making major decisions. Accepting a spouse's influence strengthens friendship. Learn to yield to win—consider ways to meet your partner's request. Evaluate yourself: *Are you interested in your spouse's opinions? Do you learn from your spouse? Can you find things to agree with in your partner's position?* Acknowledge any problems accepting influence. Have your partner gently point out times when you are dominating or disrespecting her (or him).

5. **Solve solvable problems.** Only 31% of a couple's problems are solvable. This means they are due to a difference of opinion or a temporary situation, and can be resolved through compromise. Steps to solving problems:

   (a) **Soften *harsh start-ups*** by complaining and not blaming (*I wish you had* . . . vs. *You are so* . . .); avoiding the words *never* and *always*; and making specific requests— *Would you* . . .

   (b) **Make ongoing corrections** kindly—*Let's get back on topic, not lecture, lower our voices, take a break, hang in a little longer.*

   (c) **Self-soothe** if someone gets flooded (see disaster #11) by separating for 20 minutes and using calming distractions—exercise, read, work puzzles.

   (d) **Reach a compromise** (eventually) by focusing on areas of agreement, brainstorming options, and identifying what you can each give up.

6. **Work with perpetual problems through dialogue.** Some conflicts are due to core differences in personalities, temperament, and backgrounds. Your heart's desire is a part of your identity. When differences are viewed as dreams, judgment is removed. A Nancy Neat longs for cleanliness and order; Mr. Messy craves a safe haven from rules. Clashing goals require partners to (1) understand underlying dreams; (2) validate desires or traits; and (3) support aspirations. Then, the issue can be discussed peacefully without being resolved. The problem is identified; nonnegotiable areas are stipulated; areas of flexibility are defined; temporary compromises are reached; and the ongoing conflict is returned to periodically.

7. **Build shared meaning.** As two people become a *we*, they accumulate stories of their struggles, victories, and family histories; create rituals for mealtimes, daily partings, birthdays, holidays, and entertainment; define unique pursuits and common passions; and decide who does what. Their partnership develops a distinct identity. This additional glue holds them together in troubled times and keeps them from becoming two ships passing in the night.

Handout 8.5—Can We Just Talk?

When couples are on the edge of divorce or mired in conflicts of interest, making small talk becomes a big problem. Other twosomes drift apart, lead parallel lives, and can barely say a syllable to each other. The secret to strengthening good relationships or repairing ones on the brink of disaster lies in talking about topics that do not invite trouble. The following conversation openers will keep you apprised of your partner's activities, interests, joys, memories, feelings, beliefs, and sexual needs.

COUPLES TRIVIA PURSUIT

Directions: Have your partner pick a category and number. Ask the corresponding question. Adapt questions to make them appropriate for your partner. If your relationship is rocky, start with inquiries at the beginning of the alphabet that have low numbers.

A. Current Events	B. Interests
1. What was the most interesting, challenging, or fun thing you did today?	1. Who are your two closest friends, and when did you last talk to one of them?
2. What annoyed you or got on your nerves today (other than me)?	2. What do you like most about one of your close friends or relatives?
3. Who helped you do something today?	3. Who is your favorite star, athlete, or performer? What do you like about him or her?
4. What one thing are you grateful for today?	4. What is your favorite TV show, song, reading material, book, movie, restaurant, sport?
5. Who did you enjoy talking to most/least today? What did you enjoy doing most/least today?	5. What was the last thing you read, watched, enjoyed?
6. What is your biggest pressure or worry?	6. What's your favorite kind of animal/pet? Why?
7. What important event is coming up in your life? What are you looking forward to?	7. What president or person from history do you most admire? Why?
8. What would best describe how you felt today—confident, important, bored, left out, frustrated, involved, misunderstood, excited? Why?	8. If you could travel to any state or country, where would you go?
9. Who did you smile at, hug, or show love to today?	9. What kinds of exercise do you like most/least?
10. When was the last time you noticed the sound of your own breathing?	10. What do you like most/least about your work or duties at home?
C. Joys and Secret Desires	**D. Memories**
1. What is your favorite salad dressing, food?	1. Who helped you most as a child?
2. How do you like your steak cooked? Coffee served? What is your favorite beverage?	2. Who was your best friend? What did you like most about him or her?
3. How do you most like to relax or spend time?	3. What is your earliest childhood memory?
4. What do you like to happen on your birthday?	4. What is/was your best childhood memory, experience, or vacation?
5. What is your favorite holiday or season? What do you like about it?	5. What pets did you have as a child? What pets did you wish you could have had?
6. What would you do with a million dollars?	6. What childhood memory (used to) makes you most angry?
7. What do you consider your greatest success?	7. What was the hardest thing for you as a child?
8. What would you do differently with your life if money and health were not an object?	8. What person helped you the most in your life?
9. What is one thing you have not done that you want to do? For what would you like to be remembered?	9. What subjects or extracurricular activities did you like best in school or college?
10. What would you like to be different in your/our life in 5 years, 10 years, 20 years?	10. What was your most passionate, alive, spiritual, or transcendent moment?

(continued)

E. Emotions and Concerns	F. Opinions and Beliefs
1. How did people express emotions in your family?	1. How old would you be if you did not know how old you are?
2. Who intimidates you, or whom do you consider an enemy (outside the family)?	2. Does free will exist or is life predetermined?
3. What is something you were upset about 5 years ago that does not bother you now?	3. Do things happen for a reason or is life full of random events?
4. What would you most like to change about or improve in yourself?	4. Which is more important: good deeds or the right beliefs?
5. What or who helps you the most with your worries and concerns?	5. Can you really know what is truly good or evil?
6. How do you feel about getting help from others when you need it?	6. In what way have you challenged the things you currently believe?
7. Which emotion is easiest for you to express?	7. How have your beliefs changed over time?
8. What makes you feel best about yourself?	8. Are you worried about doing things right or doing the right things?
9. What is your biggest fear?	9. Are bad deeds always punished, or do some people get away with evil?
10. What has been your biggest heartache?	10. What do couples or families need to succeed?
G. About Us	**H. Romance and Erotica**
1. What was I wearing when we first met?	1. What is your idea of a perfect date night?
2. What first attracted you to me?	2. Do you believe in public displays of affection?
3. What did you like doing most when we first started seeing each other (other than sex)?	3. How are infatuation and love different?
4. What is the best time we had as a couple or family? What was our best vacation?	4. How are sex and making love different?
5. What is one thing we planned together?	5. What gets you in the mood for intimacy (sexy clothes, help with chores, deep discussions . . .)?
6. What do/have you liked about our relationship?	6. What is the most romantic thing you/we have ever done?
7. What do you like most about me? What do you enjoy doing with me the most?	7. How often would you like to have sex? What time of day? Which days are best?
8. Describe a time when I helped you feel better.	8. What are your two most erotic body parts?
9. Describe a conflict we worked out.	9. What do you secretly wish I would do or say during sex that I'm not doing?
10. What (nonsexual) things do you wish I would do?	10. What is your secret sexual fantasy?

Suggestions

- Use these trivia questions during car rides, dinners, commercials, and when just hanging out.

- Cut each section of questions out, laminate them, and make them into cards for handy use.

- Take turns asking questions. Each person does not have to answer the same question. One person may choose a topic from Interests and the other from Emotions.

- At later sessions, questions can be reversed to "test" knowledge of each other. *What pets did you have as a child?* becomes *What pets did I have as a child?*

- You may want to limit each session to two questions and start with Current Events inquiries.

- Milk each question for all it is worth. Ask partners to elaborate on their answers with gentle prodding—*What makes you think that? When did you first get that idea? How would you feel if others knew?* Make listening noises—*Uh huh, hmmm.* . . . Use rephrasing to understand what your partner is saying—*Are you saying . . . ?* Tune into emotions—*Do you feel . . . ?*

- If a question brings up a problem, switch subjects! The point of this exercise is to talk about anything but touchy topics. Likewise, beware of criticism, lectures, and defensiveness.[1]

---

1. This exercise was inspired by John Gottman's concept of Love Maps (pp. 4760) in *The Seven Principles for Making Marriages Work*.

Handout 8.6—Cures for Common Relationship Conflicts

There are many common problems couples face. Once the nature of the task and underlying conflict is understood, strategies can be identified to minimize problems. This is especially true when differences result from a lack of information and one or both people have the flexibility to change viewpoints and behavior.[1]

Daily Stress

Task: Create a safe zone apart from the daily demands of life.

Conflict: He handles stress by putting his mind on something else, watching TV, getting on the computer, exercising, or being left alone. She handles stress by talking, complaining, and expressing feelings.

Compromise

1. Don't try to talk as soon as one or both of you walk in the door or while the kids are fussing.

2. When one person seems moody, give him or her time to work it out first.

3. Schedule a daily debriefing that is best for both of your schedules. Depending on your couple communication style, this may take from 5 to 60 minutes. If your approaches differ, compromise or set the maximum amount of time that the nontalker can tolerate.

4. Make listening noises (*uh-huh, hmmm*), look alert, and sound empathetic—*You must have felt so* . . .

5. Always take your partner's side first and refrain from giving advice unless it is solicited.

6. If your spouse is a nontalker, use other sources or types of destressing (talk to friends, exercise, journal, or meditate) before debriefing with him. He still needs practice connecting in small doses.

Relations With Relations

Task: Establish a boundary as a couple; separate from your family of origin and in-laws.

Conflict: One spouse gets caught in the middle between his partner and his parents or family.

Compromise

1. Recognize if you are still trying to get approval from your parents or other family members.

2. Admit if you are forming an alliance with your family to gain support for your position in an ongoing conflict with your spouse.

3. If your family addresses your spouse with contempt, sarcasm, or criticism, point out what they are doing in a nonargumentative way: *You're disappointed in* (horrified by) *the way Jack talks to me* (the kids). *If you cannot be neutral or see Jack's good points, please refrain from making any comments.*

4. Family members may bully a spouse when you are not present. Bring her and the offending party together to show that you and your spouse talk and that you are going to question any rudeness: *Kerry told me that you said you don't think much of her line of work. Are you trying to make her feel bad?*

---

1. These areas of concern and some of the strategies were adapted from Coping with Typical Solvable Problems (pp. 187–216) found in *The Seven Principles of Making Marriage Work* by John Gottman.

5. Family members may try to undermine decisions your spouse has made or other routines you are forming. Make it clear that you are on your partner's side: *I cannot take any telephone calls after 7 P.M. because that is our family time.*

Financial Conflicts

Task: To balance freedom and power with security and trust.

Conflict: Couple has differences on how they value types of entertainment, education, and needs for clothing, housing, savings, and so on.

Compromise

1. Make a list of everyday expenses. Prorate who will pay what bills based on earned income.

2. If your long-term financial goals are different, open three savings accounts, two to meet each of your separate needs and one for joint endeavors—retirement, children's education, and so on.

3. If one person is a shopaholic, he or she may need to be put on a daily cash allowance and surrender access to credit cards and checkbooks. Agree that any purchase over $100 must be a joint decision.

Sexual Needs and Preferences

Task: Physical expression of love, appreciation, acceptance, and biological release.

Conflict: Difference in needs and desires.

Compromise

1. The person with the lower libido needs to set the maximum amount of lovemaking a week (hopefully at least one time, at a time that is best for her). This will eliminate pestering and nagging that has been lowering her drive.

2. She needs to be guaranteed that other forms of cuddling or nonerotic touch will not increase the agreed-upon amount of sex. This will bring sensuality back into the relationship.

3. A variety of sexual contact should happen—slow, brief, or intense. This also decreases pressure that intimacy has to be an orgy every time.

4. Understand what your partner needs to climax but do not make having an orgasm a must. Many women cannot have orgasms during intercourse and sometimes they cannot have one at all, but can still enjoy sex.

5. Men with concerns about potency are helped by focusing on their partner's pleasure.

6. If a woman has her orgasm first (with or without her partner's help), it reduces pressure on the man to maintain his erection and can excite a man with a low libido.

7. Show your partner verbally or nonverbally what you want during sex.

Housework

Task: Working as a team; balancing power and influence.

Conflict: Different standards for neatness; different cultural roles.

Compromise

1. Make a list of all the domestic tasks you and your partner do on a daily, weekly, or monthly basis. Hopefully, this visual aid will help you negotiate a more equal distribution of tasks.

2. If your partner is willing to rise to your standard of neatness, remind him of what he needs to do or make a Honey-Do list. People can be trained.

3. Ask an objective outsider if your standards are too high. Be willing to lower expectations or choose your battles.

4. Learn how to let go of problems. If your partner does not pick up his belongings, shove them out of sight. If he does not put his clothes in the hamper, let him do his own laundry.

Discipline and Childrearing

Task: Including children in your lives in a way gives that each parent a connection to, responsibility for, and influence over young people.

Conflict: Different behavior standards create polarization in what parents expect of children.

Compromise

1. Consult an expert or read a book for guidelines on what to expect from children and how to handle discipline.

2. Make general agreements on basic rules and consequences, but do not get picky on differences in style. Children can adjust to different personalities.

3. If parents can quickly resolve differences, it is fine to disagree in front of children so they can learn how to negotiate. Otherwise, settle conflicts without children present.

4. When a child is defying one parent, do not take over for her. This undermines her influence. Ask the other parent if she could talk to you for a moment and give her some pointers to help her gain control.

5. If you think your partner is being too lax, do not automatically jump in. Have a quick consult to find out why the behavior is not bothering him. Decide who should take charge and in what way if you both think action is needed.

Handout 8.7—Acts of Love That Renew Romance

Mother Teresa said that countless people in the world are dying for a piece of bread, but many more are dying for a little love. Yet, we do not know how to speak the languages of love, let alone understand this mystifying emotion. It is often mistaken for infatuation, in which we will do and be anything for that special someone whose flaws elude us. This legal form of insanity lasts an average of 2 years, until little by little our individual desires and thoughts reassert themselves. Then we can chase another hot romance with a cold end or pursue real love.

Real Love and Five Ways to Show It

When you want *what is good for* another person, you know real love; when you want the other person, you are lovesick. Falling *in love* is not a choice, and what you do for your beloved happens effortlessly (or obsessively) without conscious decision. Real love requires (1) identifying the other person's unique needs and (2) being willing to expend energy on his or her behalf. When you commit *acts of love* to enrich your partner, the wealth of your relationship improves. But knowing which love acts will replenish depleted emotional reserves is a must. There are five kinds:[1]

1. **Words of affirmation** include appreciation, encouragement, kindly worded requests, and forgiveness. To be verbally supportive:

    *   Censor any criticism and harsh words for 1 week.

    *   Give your partner one or more compliments or appreciative words a day and record them in a log. At the end of the week, review your log with your spouse.

    *   Leave appreciation or love sticky notes in surprising places.

    *   Compliment your partner in the presence of family or friends for extra credit.

    *   Think of your spouse's strengths and point them out to her regularly.

    *   Buy or make a card that expresses your gratitude or appreciation.

2. **Quality time** involves giving someone your undivided, fully focused attention; listening sympathetically to understand his or her thoughts, feelings, and desires; and engaging in quality activities. To practice giving quality time:

    *   Talk every day about one thing that happened to you and your partner and describe how you each felt about it. Turn off cell phones and do not interrupt each other.

    *   Have a history night once a month. Each person has to come up with a question about each other's past—Who was your best/worst teacher? Name a mistake your mom made. Get ideas from stories of famous people.

    *   Go on a walk and talk about the flora, fauna, houses, or people you see.

    *   Make surprise dates for lunch or dinner. Talk by candlelight or in the hot tub.

    *   Make the bed, cook, garden, or clean up together.

    *   Ask your partner for a list of five activities he would like you to do with him. Do one each month. Remember, even if you do not enjoy the event, you are giving an act of love.

3. **Gifts** are visual symbols of love. They show your partner that you think about her when you are apart. If she has been critical of your presents, gifts may not be her primary love language. Being present during a crisis is the most important gift of all. To offer gifts:

    *   Give your partner a small present every day for a week—a flower on her pillow, her favorite juice from the grocery store, a pair of warm socks in the winter, and so on.

    *   Keep a log of gift ideas. Take note any time your spouse mentions something she likes, ask friends and relatives for ideas, or look through catalogs together.

---

1. Find out more about the five love languages in Gary Chapman's book, *The Five Love Languages,* 1992, Chicago: Northfield Publishing.

- Watch for nature gifts—unique stones, sticks, or feathers that your partner might like.

- Make your spouse a present or enroll in a class for the purpose of crafting him a gift.

- Give your partner a book and read it yourself so you can have a discussion.

4. **Acts of service** provide routine or surprise assistance that your partner appreciates. These can be requested, but are not acts of love if they are forced. To show love through service:

- Ask your spouse to make a list of four things she would regularly like you to do. Choose which requests you can honor. As you become better at serving, regularly add a new act.

- Make a list of all your partner's recent requests and do one a day or a week, depending on your schedule and the nature of the request.

- Give your partner a love note accompanied by an act of service.

- Take care of a chore your partner dislikes when she is away. Say, *Surprise! I love you,* as she walks in the door.

- Ask your spouse to give you reminders to train you to do the little things that please him—closing drawers, wiping hairs out of the sink, putting your shoes away, and so on.

5. **Physical touch** is the way sensual people show love. Although a man may be very sexual, if he does not enjoy nonsexual contact, touch is not his love language. To give love touches:

- Put your hand on your partner's shoulder, brush against his body, sit close while watching TV, kiss good-bye and hello, make toe contact while eating, hold hands, and do not forget to give three hugs a day.

- Learn the art of massage if your partner is sensual, and do not forget fore- and afterplay during sex at least sometimes.

- Holding your partner when she cries may be important even for nontouchers.

- Making physical contact with your partner in front of family or friends earns extra credit.

Discovering Your and Your Partner's Love Language

Asking questions is the easiest way to identify your love language: What would your ideal partner do? What do you most often ask your partner to do for you? Ask your spouse, *What can I do to be a better partner for you?* More multiple choice questions follow:

Love Language Questions	Affirmation	Quality Time	Gifts	Service	Touch
1. How do (have) you and your partner like to express caring?	Praising, thanking	Spending time together	Giving gifts	Performing tasks	Touching
2. What hurts you or your partner the most?	Criticism, harsh words	Being ignored	Never getting gifts	Not getting help	Physical distance
3. What means the most to you or your partner on birthdays?	The note in the card	Doing something nice	Thoughtful gifts	Breakfast in bed	Massages

Love is something you do *for* someone else, not what you do for yourself. Performing acts of love that do not come naturally are the greatest expression of devotion. When people's emotional reserves are on empty, they cannot give. Offering the type of caring they need may improve their moods enough that you can begin to make requests to fulfill your own heart's desires.

Handout 8.8—Analyzing Affairs

Only 3% of mammals are monogamous, and humans are among them. People who are in contented, vibrant relationships are protective of their bond unless one of them has a personality disorder or addictions to drugs or alcohol. There are certain times in the lives of emotionally healthy couples when marital bonds are more easily broken. Therefore, when infidelity occurs, it is important to examine your relationship, the transgressing partner, and life triggers.

You and Your Relationship

After years of research, a psychologist named John Gottman identified seven essentials for relationships to work. Problems are not an excuse for straying, but infidelity is an opportunity to correct issues that may have weakened your bond. When these are not addressed, affairs happen to avoid conflicts, fulfill unmet needs, or to end a crumbling marriage.

Directions: Take an honest look at your relationship prior to the affair. Seek professional help if one or more of the following was missing.

_____ 1. Did you *know and understand* your spouse's successes, aggravations, interests, and beliefs?

_____ 2. Did you have more *positive thoughts* about your partner than negative?

_____ 3. Did you have routines, chitchat, or mutually desired sex that kept you *connected*?

_____ 4. Did you allow your partner to *influence* you on decisions that affected both of you?

_____ 5. Did you resolve *some* of your conflicts without blaming, contempt, defensiveness, or withdrawing?

_____ 6. Did you *tolerate* your partner's *shortcomings* and find ways to work with them?

_____ 7. Did you share *common ground* on core values, styles of conflict resolution, *or* desires for individual pursuits and togetherness?

Traits of Transgressors

People who repeatedly disregard marital boundaries have personality, emotional, and substance abuse problems. In these cases, it is important to stop blaming yourself or your relationship, understand the devil with which you are dealing, and find out if it can be fixed.

- **Narcissists** stray outside the marriage to find someone who enhances his or her grandiose self-view and supply needed adoration. While they are easily hurt, they lack compassion for partners and are unlikely to be helped by counseling unless in extreme pain.

- **Borderline personalities** switch from glorifying to condemning people. They are prone to infatuations due to frequent fights with mates and tendencies to idolize (and then despise) others. High-functioning types (with jobs) can benefit from long-term therapy and medicine.

- **Sociopaths** may be successful businesspeople, athletes, and politicians. Their impulsivity, thrill seeking, risk taking, and immunity to remorse and anxiety make affairs routine. Nothing short of a jailhouse conversion is likely to change their behavior.

- **Substance abusers** have lowered inhibitions and access to available partners. Borderlines and sociopaths are frequent substance abusers. Sex, itself, can be an addiction when spouses have many erotic demands or *replace* partners with pornography, masturbation, or sex with strangers. People who *want* to give up their addictions can be helped.

- **Bipolar disorder** is a chemical imbalance that can be corrected with medication. When people are on an emotional high, they can become hypersexual, show poor judgment, and engage in behaviors that put them at risk for affairs. An inevitable depression will follow, and they will feel terrible remorse about what they have done.

People often bring an equitable exchange of goods and services to the marital market. When one spouse experiences an abrupt change in fortune, the other mate may need to nurse her wounded pride or find ways to feed his inflated ego. Workplace philandering is the greatest challenge to fidelity. An accidental affair can be an unplanned one-night event or a passionate romance. Circumstantial wanderlust is especially likely when a spouse poacher is on the prowl.

Spotting Spouse Poachers. You would not blame your child for being abused by a molester. Likewise, there may be little your husband can do to escape the clutches of a skilled mate poacher. She may be a plain Jane who has overcome ordinary looks by perfecting social and sexual skills. Unlike their openly aggressive male counterparts, *femme fatales* are subtle, devious, and patient. She will enchant a man by stroking his ego, flashing sexual wares, and ignoring all cost to you and herself. Consider forgiving your husband if he has fallen prey to this deadly diva.

- **Commitment phobics** want adventure, romance, and good times. She will have her way with your husband and then move on—possibly leaving him broken-hearted.

- **Narcissists** see your man as a source for attention, adoration, and praise. She believes she is his equal (even if her achievements are minimal) and feels entitled to him. Her nonstop talking takes pressure off a quiet man, especially if you fret over lack of communication.

- **Borderline personalities** are willing to do anything sexual to find someone to take care of them. Initially, they appear intense, mysterious, and appealing to men who are rescuers or people pleasers. They then get sucked into the borderline's demanding, chaotic world.

- **Sociopaths** want instant gratification of sex, money, or power. She is incapable of loving but skillful at lovemaking and has no remorse. Although beautiful and charming, she will use intimidation and extortion to get what she wants, which may be your family's bankbook.

People have traumatic reactions to a discovery of infidelity. Common emotional stages are anger, depression, shame, embarrassment, despair, hypervigilance, mourning, and, finally, a ceasefire. At some point you will need to regroup, put your feelings aside, and use reason to make sense of what happened. Consider the following points to keep your brain chemistry from causing you to do something you will regret:

- Don't make decisions while in a state of emotional turmoil. Wait until you understand the meaning of betrayal. Was it a symptom of a relationship problem or an unresolved traumatic event? Did your spouse fall prey to a mate poacher, or is he the one with the character flaw?

- Is your partner remorseful, admitting responsibility, or minimizing? Did he repeatedly deny the affair before it was proved? Is he willing to end all contact, possibly in your presence?

- Are there enough redeeming factors in your relationship to make it worthwhile despite a transgression (kids, stability, financial security)? Do not ignore violence and substance abuse.

- People who divorce due to cheating have greater postdivorce distress than from other types of marital ruptures, and remain emotionally connected to their spouses. Eighty percent of those who part due to infidelity regret their divorce—both the betrayer and the betrayed.

- Ignore cultural advice that *all* affairs are punishable by divorce. Sometimes this guidance is given by potential mate poachers or people who have led sheltered lives.[1]

---

1. For more information, see *You Can't Have Him—He's Mine,* by M. H. Browne and M. M. Browne, 2007, Avon, MA: Adams Media.

Handout 8.9—Moving Beyond Betrayal

Taking a clue from the philosopher Friedrich Nietzsche, anything that does not destroy a marriage may make it stronger—even infidelity. Decide if your mate is fatally flawed or has redeeming value. Even if your spouse cheated in the past, his moral compass can change with age. Your response to an affair can build a marital fortress that can withstand outside foes or maintain misguided patterns that contributed to problems in the first place. Proceed with caution.[1]

Immediate Measures

1. If you need to rant, do so with friends or counselors. Find professional resources to manage any depression, stress, or bitterness. Seek meaning from your circumstances—what were you meant to learn? Your husband cannot be your therapist on this issue!

2. Present yourself as the wounded, graceful spouse. Ask, *How did we get to this point?* Let him know he can talk to you about his relationship concerns so he will not talk to others.

3. It is very damaging to demand the gory details of transgressions. Keep a written log of your questions and the answers your spouse gives. This avoids needless repetition.

4. Teach your spouse the facts of love. Infatuation is a temporary dopamine effect—nature's amphetamine. Only 1 out of 10 men weds his mistress, and 60% of these unions fail.

5. Fight dopamine with oxytocin (the bonding hormone), which reduces stress and increases potency. It is produced by nurturing companionship and loving touch. *Talk about other things than the affair!* If you are comfortable, it is fine to have sex.

6. Use guilt to insist on counseling and new relationship rules: No contact with members of the opposite sex unless you are invited or get a newsy debriefing when you cannot be present.

7. There is little point in contacting the mate poacher. She will try to upset you by making herself look good and telling lies. If you need to, write a letter, but keep it a few days before mailing. The written word lasts forever.

8. Staying with your spouse and being as pleasant as possible makes a mate poacher demanding. The more she pushes, the more your partner will feel annoyed. You can take the understanding role that she once had.

9. If the other party continues to be bothersome, file harassment or stalking charges with the local police. A wise man will go to his human resources office to ask his employer to intervene before a wounded female coworker makes charges against him.

10. Forgiveness involves recognizing that the transgressor's actions were unacceptable and *making a choice* to bear no ill will. It is a gift. See the person for who he is—a good person who made a mistake or a flawed character who needs to be eliminated from your life. Desires to retaliate and nurse rage are futile attempts to avoid pain and reclaim lost power.

Keep the Marital Hearth Warm

11. Review information on how to improve your marriage and how you might be falling short. See a counselor for sexual problems. Make five positive statements (compliments, validation, humor, and appreciation) for every negative one (blame, criticism, or sarcasm).

12. Offer regular, casual reminders of what is good about your relationship, how you met, and exciting events in your past. Make your man feel good about himself.

---

1. For more information, see *You Can't Have Him—He's Mine*, by M. H. Browne and M. M. Browne, 2007, Avon, MA: Adams Media.

13. Identify your assets and flaunt them. Flirt and let him know you are still attractive. Keep him focused on your vital signs—your humor, companionship, devotion, and shared values.

14. Keep him busy with activities he enjoys. Accompany him to the gym. According to Browne and Browne (cited below), engaging in exciting, even risky, activities together enhances bonding.[1]

Marriage Protection Policies

After your partner has cheated, it is easy to think you are (or look like) a fool. This is your pride talking. Anyone can be deceived! An affair can happen in the best of marriages, and it is good not to put blind faith in any person. Once your eyes are opened to the fragility of marital bonds, there are steps you can take to protect against future intruders:

1. Expect fidelity from your spouse even if you've been wronged. Let your partner know you believe he is capable of being trustworthy. Telling someone he is a liar and a cheat will encourage him to be one.

2. Encourage your husband to discuss temptations with you without reprisals. This keeps you in the loop and ensures all-important open communication. Having a fantasy of a crush during sex is not infidelity! Due to the well-studied process of sensitization, any arousal he feels will become associated with you and make you more attractive.

3. React quickly to other women who make you uncomfortable. Let her know you are on to what she is doing—*Why are you staying after work with my husband when you're not being paid? You have a knack for asking for computer help just when Sam and I have alone time.*

4. Belittle your rival but compliment your husband—*She's putting you in an awkward position, but I know you like to do the right thing.*

5. Consider anyone a potential rival: friends, sisters, neighbors, husband's coworkers, old flames, or new cyber buddies. Be wary of single-and-looking fiends.

6. Show up at your husband's workplace occasionally and make acceptable demonstrations of affection—hand on his shoulder or kiss on his cheek. Put family photos in the office, especially a glamour shot of yourself. Lay your claim.

7. Accompany your husband on as many work functions and business trips as you can. Show up unannounced at a conference. Mention that a friend or associate (by a strange coincidence) will be staying at the same hotel where his meeting is located.

8. Confront your mate about any covert contact with females and tell him you want to be invited to or given a newsy report of future contacts. If he is apologetic and welcomes your request, the other woman may be a friend. If he is defensive, angry, and wants his own space, make relationship rules and see a counselor if necessary.

9. Confront unusual changes in behavior quickly before relationships start. Men often fall in love faster and harder than women and suffer longer after the breakup. Consider the following warning signs and seek professional help with or without your spouse:

Emotional Distancing
Little interest in what you say or do, or in your ideas.
Does not fight back.
Makes excuses to be alone.
Forgets significant events.
Reduced participation in family activities.
Slow reduction in frequency of sex (unless due to illness, depression, or anger).

Habit Changes
Increased work hours, duties, business trips.
Computer history cleared.
Visits singles or porn sites.
Sets up private email.
Wakes up to get online.
Buys a new cell phone.
Unexplained disappearances, jewelry receipts, hang-up calls.
New interest in appearance.

Financial Changes
Reroutes mail away from home.
Opens separate bank account.
Reroutes checks to his account.
Changes way of paying household expenses.
Transfers assets without asking.
Wants a large amount of cash for himself.
Chooses to be unemployed or underemployed.

If you choose to remain with a cheater due to various benefits (financial security, status, the children's welfare), do not make a career of trying to change him or you will end up in codependency land. Take responsibility for your decision and live a full life!

Handout 8.10—Undoing Dependency

The term *codependency* was first used in substance abuse circles. It designated a person who was dependent on someone who was dependent on alcohol or drugs. Today, its meaning suggests an obsession with controlling other people's behavior or trying to fix their problems. In the quest to micromanage others, codependents lose sight of how to change the most important person in their lives—themselves. The first step is to *become aware* of how you focus on others.[1]

CODEPENDENT
CHECKLIST

Directions: Mark any characteristics that describe you. There is not a required number of traits to be codependent, but you will recognize if you fit the profile.

Caretaking	Dependency
____ Feel responsible for others' well-being.	____ Look for happiness outside yourself.
____ Do more than your fair share of work.	____ Feel threatened by the loss of what you think is providing your happiness.
____ Have a compulsion to help accompanied by anger when that help is not effective.	____ Seek love from people incapable of loving.
____ Resent that others do not help, but feel guilty about or reject any assistance that is offered.	____ Do not consider if others are good for you.
____ Need crises and needy people to feel worthy.	____ Focus on relationships, not personal success.
____ Feel unappreciated and used; blame others.	____ Worry about abandonment; wonder if you will find love.

Low Self-Esteem	Obsession and Control
____ Think you are different, guilty, or defective.	____ Try to control people and events with advice, threats, domination, or helplessness.
____ Afraid to make mistakes and decisions.	____ Worry incessantly about others and lose sleep.
____ Blame yourself for everything but get on the defensive when criticized.	____ Try to catch people misbehaving.
____ Reject compliments and praise but get depressed from a lack of appreciation.	____ Cannot take care of your own business due to taking care of others.
____ Help others live their lives because your own is not worth living.	____ Think you know best how things *should* turn out or how others *should* act.

Denial	Poor Communication
____ Pretend circumstances are not that bad.	____ Blame, threaten, coerce, beg, bribe, or advise.
____ Distract yourself with busyness, shopping, eating, and work.	____ Have trouble getting to the point, making requests, or voicing an opinion.
____ Believe lies; lie to yourself; lie for others.	____ Frequently apologize or degrade yourself.

Weak Boundaries and Lack of Trust	Miscellaneous
____ Tolerate behavior you say you never would.	____ Come from troubled family but may deny your family's dysfunction.
____ Cannot say *No*; trust untrustworthy people.	____ Are victims of emotional, physical, or sexual abuse, neglect, or abandonment.
____ Become totally intolerant and lose faith.	____ Did not feel love and approval from parents.
____ Are afraid of your own and other's anger.	____ Find it hard to feel close to people and have fun.
____ Feel safer with anger than hurt feelings.	____ Are passive and helpless or dominant and angry.
____ Have sex to take care of others or to find love.	
____ Refuse to enjoy sex out of anger.	

1. For more information, see *Codependent No More*, by M. Beattie, 1987, Center City, MN: Hazelden.

The opposite of depending on, controlling, and taking care of others is helping yourself. **Self-Care** If you believe you are responsible for yourself, it follows that others are accountable for **Basics** themselves. Acting on this simple idea is not easy. The art of self-care can be broken into several steps.

Detach. Notice when you are worrying, obsessing, and intervening. Ask yourself if these actions or thoughts give you an illusion of control. Are they making the situation better or worse? Can you teach the other person more than she can learn by experiencing her own consequences? Are you greater than the powers that be? Have you ever learned from your own mistakes? Do you love someone enough to allow her to experience a cruel consequence? Do not expect to let go all at once. Learning to detach is a habit that builds little by little.

Act, Do Not React. When you feel *compelled* to say or do something, that is a reaction. You always have a choice how to think, feel, and behave, but you cannot exercise your options until outrage, anxiety, or rejection pass. Ask yourself, *If I were certain I was not responsible for this person's behavior, what would I do?* The answer might be as simple as ignoring a comment and not talking until attitudes change or as extreme as not paying bail.

Accept Reality. Facing the truth helps upsetting feelings pass. Reality includes accepting your current circumstances, who you are, your lost dreams, and that you have no control over others. If you are living with a troubled person, this will mean facing many sudden changes. Acceptance is not tolerating. It is a platform from which you can decide what you need to do.

Control Yourself, Not Others. When you try to control others with lectures, begging, monitoring, ordering, and so on, they will resist you or double their efforts to prove you cannot manage them. What would you be doing if you were not trying to fix this person's problem? Concentrate on playing your part well (on the stage of life) and not performing others' parts.

Stop Rescuing. If God helps those who help themselves, how can you do more? Say *no* when you do not want to do something. Refuse to anticipate or guess what people want. Do not try to prevent problems and allow consequences to happen. If others are disappointed in or angry at you for not taking care of them, you have succeeded. Congratulations! Acknowledge their frustration kindly—*I know you're used to me ironing your uniforms.*

Practice Independence. People have varying needs for contact with others, but these do not have to be met by just one person. Begin to develop your own interests, activities, and support system. Gradually increase the amount of time you enjoy by yourself. Do not avoid fearful or sad feelings that arise from taking risks. They will subside.

Deal With Feelings. Feelings are energy and indicators that something is amiss. Acknowledge the sensation and move on to the next step. Examine any underlying thoughts that may be causing an overreaction. Discuss distress with a support person and make a plan of action. If you are feeling angry with someone, identify what you might want from him and make a specific request.

Meet Your Needs. Ask yourself, *What do I want?*, not *What should I do?* Does what you want interfere with your responsibilities to your children, spouse, or other family members? Get a second opinion if you have doubts. Do not hesitate to make requests for help from others. If they will not give you what you want, find another way to have your needs met. Turn other desires into goals that will give you direction and purpose.

Learn to Love Yourself. This may sound like a tall order, but all you have to do is identify the voice of your *inner critic*. It may have taken over your psyche when you were young by copying a cruel caretaker. Question your critic by asking if its lectures are helpful. Think how life would be without its cutting comments. What is the statute of limitations on your past mistakes, and what action do you need to take to correct recent ones? Underneath this loud critic is the still, small voice that loves you just as you are. You will hear it in surprising, quiet moments.

Handout 8.11—The Bait-and-Switch Trap—For Emotional Abuse

Are you in a relationship that started with a romantic whirlwind but now flips from hot to cold at a dizzying pace? Do you find yourself apologizing much of the time just to keep your relation-ship afloat? If so, you may have become caught in the bait-and-switch trap. The players in this drama need to be identified before exposing how the snare is set.

Man	Woman
• Initially showers partner with promises, presents, or compliments—*You're not like all the other women who failed me.*	• Initially may have been independent, lively, and even a trophy girl—the perfect woman to meet this man's impossible needs.
• Has a history of financial, substance abuse, gambling, work, or relationship problems.	• Feels flattered by partner's idealization of her but is upset that she cannot meet his desires.
• Expects partner to be loving, giving, strong, and unquestioning; has extreme nurturing needs.	• Experiences an intoxicating ''high'' from the good times in the relationship.
• Says he loves his spouse but acts hateful—yelling, insulting, constantly criticizing.	• Will tolerate a great deal of abusive treatment in order to get this relationship high.
• Uses special weapons: cruel remarks about looks or sexuality; compares her to others.	• Rationalize unacceptable behavior—*He's under a lot of stress. People don't understand him.*
• May feel no or very brief remorse for incidents.	• Comes to accept that she is to blame for partner's shortcomings—*He's just trying to help me be a better person.*
• Denies, revises, or blames spouse for incidents.	
• Angered if partner is upset by his tirades—she should be more understanding or less sensitive.	• Believes that she can help him be more loving by finding the right way to act.
• Triggers for tantrums are unpredictable.	• Looks for or makes up tiny signs of hope for change.
• Can be charming and loving between outbursts, as though nothing happened.	• Starts to become dependent, giving her partner an increasingly important role in her life.
• Controls when and what happens during sex—partner seen as cold or demanding.	• Depends on his mood to feel good about herself, making her fear withdrawal of his love.
• Controls how his partner thinks, feels, and behaves, and her social circle and family life.	• Fears physical harm, loss of financial support, or living independently.
• Controls finances: either denies access to money or squanders wife's earnings.	• Unconsciously agrees to be compliant and renounce her needs and wishes.
• Can vie with children for attention, attack wife's parenting, or try to turn children against their mother.	• Can develop physical illnesses and depression due to having her feelings censured.
• Physical battering is unlikely, but can be triggered by alcohol abuse and stress.	• Has covert cultural beliefs that men are entitled.

Family Background	
• Overcomes hidden fear that loving a woman will destroy him by making his partner weak and dependent on him.	• Early caretaker(s) taught her that she was inadequate, worthless, or unlovable.
• Family of origin: passive father/smothering mother; tyrannical father/unprotective mother; abusive or reject-ing mother.	• Driven to repeat childhood circumstances and make them turn out better.
	• Father made her feel wonderful *and* terrible.
	• Identification with a needy, helpless mother.

Setting the Snare

- **The bait** is set for this tyrannical relationship during a rapid romance that keeps a woman from seeing her partner's true nature. He will know the right words, deeds, or gifts that make her feel loved. Both parties crave fulfilling nurture needs and try to fuse into one. There is a sense of desperation and purposeful blindness during this dreamy time.

- **The switch** happens early on when a disappointment causes the man's temper to flare. However, explosions do not become a way of life until there is talk of commitment or the future. Love always follows bouts of abuse.

- **The trap** operates like a slot machine. The woman expects the payoff to come any minute. The return to romance happens enough to keep hopes high and she ignores anything that does not fit her passionate picture. Waiting for the good times creates tension and excitement.

If you have been caught in a bait-and-switch trap, it may mean that you are married to a woman hater (misogynist). This can be a shocking revelation. By focusing on yourself, your life can become livable. This list of liberating steps can be followed at your own pace:[1]

Springing the Trap

1. **Observe your reaction** to your partner's attacks. Add the words, *How interesting!* Think, *Every time Max belittles me I feel ..., ..., and. ... How interesting!* Note how long each feeling lasts in a log: fear—2 hours; hurt—3 days.

2. **Continue your usual responses** to your partner's attacks but first silently say to yourself, *I choose to apologize, defend myself,* or *explain what I did*. This will help you observe your own behavior and change your *reactions* into *actions*.

3. **Make a label list** of all the insults your spouse has given you—*nonnurturing, careless, frumpy,* and more. Taunts are control tactics and attempts to destroy self-esteem. They are often the opposite of the truth. Make a second list that turns accusations into assets: *caring, busy,* or *tasteful*. Think of good words others have said to you.

4. **Use guided imagery** to picture yourself as a castle with a protective wall around it. On the parapets of the wall, place your positive labels. See the castle under attack with arrows bearing your partner's slur and slights. Watch them hit the wall and fall feebly into the moat.

5. **Picture a beloved friend** being targeted by your partner. Realize that his behavior has more to do with how he feels toward women than you. Would you want anyone you love to receive this treatment? Allow yourself to feel anger instead of your usual hurt.

6. **Picture your partner behaving irrationally.** Ask yourself, *Is he looking for an excuse to attack me? Is he avoiding taking responsibility for something that is his fault? Does anyone have the right to act this way?* Ask these questions any time you start to doubt yourself.

7. **Do not target yourself.** When you face the truth about your partner, you may think you were stupid to fall for him. This is your inner critic talking. Remind your inner critic that enough people in your life have verbally abused you and you do not need a voice in your own head scolding you. Any time you hear it, say, *Scolding!* This keeps your real Self in charge.

8. **Care for yourself.** Make a list of 10 things you would do to comfort someone in pain and do them for yourself. Find someone to talk to, say nice things to yourself, and so on.

9. **Identify hurtful memories from childhood.** Work with a therapist to release the hurt and anger from those experiences. Grieve the loss of the nurturing parent you never had and hold on to anything that is good about your family. Write a letter to the hurt little girl inside of you. Tell her all the loving things she wanted to hear when she was little.

10. **Set limits with your partner.** Say, *I'll discuss this when you are calmer. Screaming won't work anymore. I know you're upset, but I'll leave if you yell.* **Do not** apologize, plead, defend yourself, or try to convince him. Expect him to be outraged, and trust yourself to withstand his fury. Show appreciation anytime he is kind and loving.

11. **Make specific requests** once your partner shows some self-control in response to limit setting. Work on making one tiny change at a time, and do not expect a personality overhaul.

---

1. For more information, see *Men Who Hate Women & The Women Who Love Them,* by S. Forward, 1986, New York: Bantam Books. See *Making Hostile Words Harmless,* by K. Cohen-Posey, 2008, Hoboken, NJ: John Wiley & Sons, for more ways to handle verbal abuse.

Handout 8.12 — Divorce Dilemmas

Divorce ultimately needs to be a time for finding in yourself what you could not find in another person. Hopefully, divorce is not a doorway into another relationship. When you put thought into a marital dissolution, it can lead to new self-identity, fulfillment, and freedom.

Making the Decision

How do you know if you are on a down slope in the marital roller coaster or if you have reached rock bottom? You will never know for sure. However, if remaining betrothed is breaking your spirit and one* or more of the following criteria apply, it may be time to untie the nuptial knot:

- ☐ You are going through the motions of married life.
- ☐ You are putting up walls and have no desire to share everyday events or deep, dark secrets.
- ☐ You or your partner no longer cares about each other's expectations or feelings.
- ☐ You or your partner seeks opportunities to avoid each other.
- ☐ You or your partner use criticism, blame, and accusations to batter each other's egos.
- ☐ You and your partner disagree on everything.
- ☐ You do not have the energy or goodwill to reach compromises or deal with differences.
- ☐ Your children witness and absorb daily battles or bitter silence.
- ☐ Your partner's drug or alcohol use affects your marriage, and she refuses to make changes.*
- ☐ Your partner is in love with someone else and has no plans to end the relationship.*
- ☐ Your partner is physically abusive, making an immediate separation a must.*

Premortem Changes

It is important to examine and modify your usual responses to the opposite sex before coming to a final divorce decision. Remedies for the four most common marital mistakes follow. Consistently altering your behavior can breathe new life into relationships. Or, as you grow stronger, you may feel more ready to leave. If making change is too tough, it may be time for new ventures.[1]

- If you criticize and find fault by attacking your partner's personality or character, make specific requests for what you want and show appreciation for the tiniest positive changes. Adults are never too old to be trained.

- Do you show contempt by attacking your partner's sense of self-worth with name-calling, sarcasm, or eye-rolling? Did you learn your attitude from culture or kin? Catch insults before they leave your lips. Say five kind words to your partner for every cut.

- If you defend yourself against your partner's criticism, lectures, or accusations, stop! Do not explain, make excuses, disagree, or say *yes-but*. Instead, sympathize or agree in theory—*You sound disappointed. It must be hard to worry so much. I'll consider your ideas.*[2]

- If your partner has distanced from you with stony silences, monosyllabic mutterings, and spending time away from home or in cyberspace, *build you*r own life. Find friends and interests. *Some partners who have distanced will start pursuing when the roles are reversed* or you will become ships passing in the night. Regardless, your life can be more tolerable and you will find other sources to meet your needs.

---

1. For more information about divorce, see *He's History: You're Not*, by E. Manfred, 2009, Guilford, CT: Globe Pequot Press.
2. To stop being defensive, see *Making Hostile Words Harmless*, by K. Cohen-Posey, 2008, Hoboken, NJ: John Wiley & Sons.

There is nothing wrong with a long, drawn-out, dramatic divorce. Like witnessing a loved one dying from a debilitating disease, you may be more ready or even grateful for the end when it comes. If you are the person doing the leaving, it is important to take steps to protect yourself. But if you suspect your spouse may be planning a future exit, you also need to prepare:

Divorce Preparedness

1. Consult with an attorney to find out how you will stand financially after the deed is done: What kind of child support or alimony will you have to give or be receiving? What will you need to do to protect yourself against your partner's debt? Do this before disclosing your plans to your partner!

2. Ask around before choosing an attorney. Make sure others have been satisfied with his or her services. Is he or she more interested in settling your case or looking out for your interests?

3. Do not make your lawyer your teacher or therapist. This wastes precious legal time. Stick to the facts of your case and do not go off on tangents. Use the Internet to become familiar with laws in your state about alimony, no-fault versus fault divorce, marital property, equitable distribution, dividing retirement funds, or protecting your inheritance.

4. Uncover hidden assets before going to an attorney, if possible. Filing a joint tax return entitles you to your own copy from the IRS that will show all interest-bearing accounts. Many cash business transactions suggest shady dealings. Hinting to call the IRS may give you leverage. Get a grasp of cash flow by checking credit card statements.

5. Do not be done in by guilt. If you believe you partner will be emotionally devastated by your divorce, remember that you still have the right to your fair amount from your marital union. Allow the courts to make financial decisions, rather than your bleeding heart.

6. Do not use a mediator or a divorce package, unless the playing field is level between you and your spouse. This may be cheaper in the short run, but mediators tend to push the person who is most likely to agree. If you partner has money, a lawyer may take your case on contingency and charge your spouse court costs.

7. Train for a viable occupation while your marriage is ailing. Being able to earn your keep is more reliable and better for your ego than alimony.

There are no memorial services to mark the end of a marriage and, unlike losing someone to death, your ego may be crushed and your pride wounded by betrayal. If you were the one who was left, allow yourself to grieve:

Mourning the Loss of Marriage

1. **Cry yourself a river.** Tears can get you into heaven when prayers cannot. The more you cry in the beginning, the less you will need to in years to come.

2. **See a therapist.** Figure out what hurts the most—the idea of being alone, fears of not finding someone else, thinking you failed. Learn to question the gloomy, critical parts of you.

3. **Do a postmortem (if you did not do a premortem) on your marriage.** Identify if you made one of the four common marital mistakes—chronic criticism, contempt, defensiveness, or isolation. Were you a user or pushover? Did you insist on having your way? Surprisingly, the more responsibility you take for the demise of your marriage, the less bitter you will feel.

4. **Find new friends and keep your old ones.** There are tons of support groups and fellow travelers who know what you are experiencing. Find them!

5. **Write a good-bye letter** listing all the things you will miss and what you are glad is gone from your life.

Handout 8.13—The Science of Dating

In your dating history, have you ever had any of the following thoughts: *Love is all that matters. I'll just follow my heart. I want to find my soul mate.* The truth is that soul mates can become cell mates. Endorphins (your body's natural pain killers) released during infatuation suppress activity in the areas of the brain that control critical thought. Dr. John Van Epp, a dating expert, states that by learning a few important facts, you can teach love to think.[1]

Dangerous Dates

Anyone can have annoying qualities, but certain traits are particularly damaging for relationships. This is especially true when a date denies possessing these qualities or lacks any desire to change. Often, partners can keep flaws hidden for the first three months of dating. Therefore, it is important to remain attuned to any of the following deficits in potential partners:

- **A lack of boundaries.** Players love to love and can carry on several romances at once. Or they may have an insatiable appetite for attention. Space Invaders believe that what is yours is theirs. They feel entitled to your attention, money, time, and support.

- **A lack of empathy.** These people cannot see things from others' viewpoint. They are self-absorbed blamers. If you are a natural giver, you may quickly forgive and overlook their self-centeredness, minimize shortcomings, and give second chances.

- **A lack of emotional control.** Initially, this person is the life of the party. Fun-loving Larry becomes overreactive and explosive and you become a part of his chaotic world. Easygoing Ellen is later cold, detached, and shows few emotions. You feel empty and unloved. Some dangerous dates can swing from exciting and explosive to cool and detached.

Dangerous Relationship Patterns

Many healthy people are in danger of becoming involved with a dangerous date. They often give, accept, and overlook too much. It is not a relationship that changes a person, but the person in the relationship who changes him- or herself. Three patterns blind people to potential problems:

1. Idealization is a habit of avoiding feelings of disappointment. Such people only see the good in others, ignore flaws, and are adept at turning frogs into princes or princesses. Eventually, they have to deal with the loss of having never been shown the love they deserved.

2. Identifying with a quality in others that you suppress in yourself is a way of trying to correct your own emotional imbalance. A shy person may connect with someone who is chatty to dodge the burden of carrying on a conversation. The talker avoids having to learn to listen. In healthy relationships, people can have differences that complement each other. An extrovert can encourage her partner to be more outgoing, and he can help her develop independent interests. A deep and mutual appreciation of differences develops. However, if you have traits that are outside the norm, it is important to learn to find balance within yourself.

3. Recreating dysfunctional patterns from your childhood in a current relationship is a misguided attempt to change the past. Until you recognize the wounds you suffered with caretakers in the past and grieve unmet needs, you will be driven to reenact them over and over in the hopes of living happily ever after.

Love Potion Number Five

Dr. Van Epp lists five factors that build the bond of love. For love to last, each element needs to be introduced at the proper moment. One component serves as a foundation for the

---

1. For more dating data see *How to Avoid Falling In Love with A Jerk* by J. Van Epp, 2007, Columbus, OH: McGraw-Hill.

next. They are listed here in reverse order. When the final ingredient comes first, love is put under pressure, making it fall flat.

5. **Sexual touch.** Sexual knowing increases passion and chemistry in a twosome. Predetermined stopping points help couples slow down the pace of intimacy or abstain from intercourse until marriage. Boundaries need to be resolved when sexual activity is not happening. Any sex beyond kissing should not happen until *commitment* has been discussed.

4. **Commitment.** The willingness to please each other even when it requires sacrifice, a sense of belonging to someone, and a declaration of not having outside relationships all convey faithfulness. Commitment does not have to include a promise to marry. To gain a sense of how well your partner can commit, observe how he or she honors obligations to other people and family. A couple cannot truly make a commitment until they know they can *rely* on each other to meet their needs.

3. **Reliability.** Depending on each other is a huge source of bonding. Give and take needs to be reciprocal. Some couples are lucky—what their partner wants is what they like to give. However, it is good to stretch yourself to meet your partner's needs and become more than you would have been on your own. Watch out for (1) pillars of strength who are ruggedly independent and resent neediness; (2) dependent people who are always in need; (3) caretakers who want to cater to your every whim; or (4) people who are self-absorbed. Reliability grows gradually from meeting each other's superficial needs and then moves to deeper levels. Experiences that foster *trust* help partners rely on one another.

2. **Trust.** Confidence in your partner provides feelings of security and closeness. Trusting someone you just met is based on preexisting stereotypes (of cheaters, users, or abusers), reminders of persons you have known, and ideal hopes for the best. The assumptions made after the first encounter are revised as behavior patterns become more obvious. Notice if your date can put others' interests first, be flexible, keep promises, see him- or herself from others' viewpoint, speak his or her mind, and enjoy making others happy. Does she desire companionship? Find out what your date is like when he is angry at you and how he handles your anger. Your level of trust should always be lower than what you *know* about your new partner.

1. **Knowledge.** Knowing someone requires self-disclosure and seeing him or her in action over time. In-depth, nonstop sharing (often done in cyberspace) creates intense intimacy without the test of being together. A focus on fun activities that lack meaningful discussions also offsets the balance of talking and togetherness. You need date data in five areas: (a) similarities in work ethics, intelligence levels, talking and listening, views on male/female roles, and other values; (b) relationship styles that show respectful treatment of strangers, friends, and family; (c) history of complaints from ex-mates—ask delicately and note any minimizing; (d) a secure attachment to at least one family member; (e) evidence of a conscience—the ability to delay satisfaction and admit wrongdoing, adherence to a moral code, respect for others' views, productivity, and responsibility. A conscience is the best predictor of healthy relationships! Resist the temptation to make your date act right or you will never know his or her standards.

Dr. Van Epp's dating disclaimer: The good doesn't always last and the bad usually gets worse. Differences that bother you during dating will become magnified in marriage. Changes need to be worked out before nuptials. They are easier to accomplish while you have leverage.

Handout 8.14—Blending Families

The blending of two families can be a chaotic time with a cascade of characters: stepparent (SP), biological parent (BP), stepchildren (SCs), biological children (BCs), and ex-spouse (XS). The good news is that within 4–7 years people adjust to their new environment and feel like a traditional family. The challenge is to juggle multiple demands of virtual strangers. This will happen naturally as you accomplish certain step-coupling tasks.

Focus on Being a Couple

- Subsequent feelings of estrangement are normal after the honeymoon. Talk every day—in person, on the phone, and text. Develop personal rituals and find common interests to make up for differences in values.

- Cooperate and find solutions instead of blaming your spouse for problems. Ask, *Do you want to fix things between us or do you want to be right?*

- When your relationship is loving and supportive, other challenges can be faced more easily.

Form Realistic Family Expectations

- Do not expect yourself to bond with your SCs just because you love your spouse. It is difficult to have the same love for an SC that you have for a BC. Focus on knowing your SCs as individuals, understanding them as people, and appreciating their positive qualities.

- Expect the bond between the BP and BC to be deeper than the one between the new couple. Work toward an ever-deeper relationship between partners and between the SP and SCs.

- Do not expect children to tolerate public displays of affection, but do model a healthy relationship between two loving adults.

- Expect a full range of feelings from children about being in a blended family. The transition to remarriage is harder than divorce for young people. During divorce, both parent and child experience loss. With remarriage, as parents gain, children may reexperience grief. To help children mourn, encourage them to verbalize the emotions behind their behavior.

- Be careful about including an XS in family events. Seeing both biological parents together can make children uncomfortable and bring up the painful loss of family togetherness.

- Expect that you and your children will be safe and treated with respect. But do not expect your new mate to fulfill your every need or cater to all of your children's caprices.

Learn to Handle Insecurities and Resentments

- Be open with your mate about feeling left out. The BP needs to be responsible for including the SP in relationships with children and to gently help young people acknowledge the SP.

- Be flexible about your terms of inclusion. If you feel insecure about your place in the family, SCs may fear losing another adult in their lives and be less willing to include you.

- The BP needs to loosen the parent-child tie to create space for his or her new partner while remaining close enough to meet his or her child's needs for comfort and reassurance.

- SPs can reduce resentment by eliminating unnecessary child care. This can be supplied by the spouse, an older sibling, or grandparent. Instead, go on optional, fun outings with SCs.

- SPs can share feelings about SCs by using *I* statements: *I feel . . . when . . . does . . .*

- Do not demand desired behaviors from SCs. Model positive behaviors you would like to see returned by your SCs. Do not take rude and rejecting behavior personally.

- Ask your spouse to remind you of what he or she loves about you. The more happiness you find in your relationship, the more tolerance you will feel for your SCs.

- When you don't like SCs' music, style, or friends, try to listen without giving your opinions. Find one positive characteristic about your SCs. Come to know SCs as individuals.

Develop a Working Discipline Plan

- The SP should gradually take the role of a coparent. Initially, he or she can provide physical care or be an adviser. This is especially true for teens, who may ignore an SP's preliminary attempts to guide. An SP needs to bond before taking corrective action.

- The BP can appoint the SP as the acting authority when he or she needs to be away. Review the ground rules that will be enforced before leaving.

- If the BP and BC are arguing, an SP can help clarify each person's point without taking sides.

- Have the best relationship you can with your SCs, even if their behavior does not improve. Use written notes instead of nagging. Do not complain constantly to your spouse. Offer suggestions only when asked. Listen sympathetically and applaud your partner's successes.

- SPs need to detach from SC's problem behavior so the BP can deal with it. If you get too upset, the BP has to focus on you instead of dealing with his or her child. Did you marry your mate to straighten out his or her children? Refuse this role!

- Find a middle ground between different parenting styles. Autocratic parents order, lecture, and may use corporal punishment. Permissive parents plead, fuss, wait for change, and settle for the way things are. Read parenting materials that teach how to *withhold* privileges until tasks are completed and use logical consequences for breaking rules.

- If your partner has higher expectations than you for young people on duties and rules, hold your children responsible for the most basic ones. Tell them they may not like your decisions, but you believe in what you are doing. Different standards can enrich a stepfamily.

- Value conflicts between partners may be the root of distress over children's behavior. When your values about education, thrift, generosity, work ethics, honesty, coupling, and responsibility are different, work at understanding rather than changing each other's viewpoint. Do not make children the victim of your differences.

- Reach agreements on allowance, monetary rewards, and spending money. Although it is easier to give your BCs a monetary handout, be as fair-minded as you can with SCs.

- Be careful of labels—*troublemaker, helpless,* or *nice.* Labeling puts kids in rigid roles.

Master Dealing with XSs

- You cannot control your XS's lifestyle or child-rearing rules no matter how much you dislike what they do. Provide balance in your home to offset other experiences.

- You may let your child know his or her BP's home life is different from what you want to provide, but you are not condemning it. Establish limits and standards for your home.

- Evidence suggests that children benefit from experiencing different lifestyles. This gives them a broader perspective from which they ultimately make their own choices. Even when children are exposed to a consistent value framework, they often stray from it.

- Energy you put into anger at an XS creates a false bond and interferes with your new relationship. Your XS is not there physically but rules your life emotionally. Say, *You're right. She is awful but let's not spend our time talking about her. I want to be with you.*

- Too frequent contact with an XS can interfere with your partner's development as an SP. Coparenting with an XS takes time away from your current marriage. Too much contact may be due to guilt or other emotional ties. Negotiate new limits on the amount of contact.

- Allow the children to have a relationship with their BP. As they grow, they may discover the good, bad, and ugly parts of that parent. Accepting that your partner has a former spouse and that your SCs have a BP takes time.

- If an XS is present at a special occasion, ask for extra attention from your partner. You may need to stretch your comfort zones to include new people and ways of doing things.

Handout 8.15—The Tale of the Tiger's Eye Treasure—A Fable for Family Discussions

In the time of long-ago, there was a village that was being stalked by a fearsome tiger. It was said that this tiger was the guardian of a treasure—a stone of priceless beauty called the *Tiger's Eye Treasure*. The spirit, strength, and mystery of the tiger were said to be contained within the stone. As long as the gem lay hidden in the forest that surrounded the village, the tiger would continue to haunt the people, taunting them to capture its jewel.

The first person to look for the stone was a cautious man. He was always careful and on the lookout for danger. He debated within himself—*Although there are risks, if I could find the Tiger's Eye Treasure, I would never have to be afraid again. I could draw on the power of the stone for protection.* He was walking carefully through the forest when, lo and behold, he spied the tiger! The tiger began to chase him, and the man soon found himself on the edge of a cliff. He stood there paralyzed. He could see the tiger's open jaws looming toward him, ready to swallow. As the man backed up to the edge of the precipice, he slipped but was able to grab a root growing out of the side of the cliff. There he cowered, hoping that the tiger would leave and he could sneak home. Sure enough, after several hours the tiger disappeared. The man was able to pull himself up and creep back to the village. He warned the people of his plight and told them he had learned *it is better to be cautious and safe than to risk danger when the reward is uncertain.*

The second person to look for the treasure was a kind man. He thought, *I would love to find that stone. Surely its power could bring good fortune to the people in my village and I could help them with their problems.* Soon after he entered the forest he also came face to face with the tiger. He was chased to the edge of the cliff, and, like the cautious man, he slipped and found himself clinging to the root that grew from the side of the ridge. The kind man knew that he was not the only one to walk those woods, especially now that many were searching for the treasure. Sure enough, he soon heard people in the distance and called for help. A party of hunters rescued him. He returned to the village and told the people he now knew *that one can always count on the kindness of friends for help in times of trouble.*

A woman in the village was becoming increasingly angry as she heard tales of her countrymen being tormented by the tiger. She was as strong as she was beautiful and was known for her skills in battle. As her rage boiled, she pondered, *I must protect the people of my village. If I find the Tiger's Eye Treasure, I will join its power with my strength and become an invincible shield for my people!* She prepared herself with bow and arrow to stalk the tiger and steal its jewel. But the tiger snuck up on the fierce woman. She had no time to draw her bow and had to flee for her life. In her haste, she stumbled over the edge of the cliff but was able to cling to the root. The woman gathered her wits and while hanging by only one arm, she loosened sticks to carve out niches for her feet and was able to draw her bow. Just as she took aim, the tiger vanished into the darkness of the forest. She returned to the village filled with adventure and spirit, telling the people they must gather their courage. She said she understood that *one must not back down from a challenge—life must be faced ready to do fierce battle!*

Another woman in the village had been intently listening to the stories of those who had sought the tiger and its treasure. She was a seeker of truth, and she thought, *I cannot believe that the tiger has come to my village to teach simple caution, kindness, or courage. I know there must be a deeper lesson than these.* She began her search. The woman walked through the forest deeply engrossed in thought when she realized that the tiger was upon her. Like the others, she was chased to the edge of the cliff, slipped, and found herself clinging to the root. As was her practice, the seeker of truth began to pray. God answered and told her that she must let go! Although she was frightened, she knew this was a test of faith. She loosened her grip and was amazed to discover that she had fallen onto a ledge only a few feet below. The seeker could not wait to return to the village to tell the people her good news. She crawled as quickly as possible along the ledge until she came to a tunnel that entered the side of the cliff. She started to run toward a dim light and fell on a rock that crossed her path, twisting her ankle. Undaunted, she made her way through the passage and limped home to tell the people that her faith had been confirmed and that *they could always find answers through prayer*. But the people laughed at her, telling her there had been no miracle or divine communication, only a lucky coincidence.

There was a person in the village who seemed untouched by the stories of the tiger and the treasure. This person, Pat, found great pleasure in the simplest tasks of life. At first, Pat listened to the story of the Tiger but decided to leave that quest for others. Pat had pursuits and loves that filled life with meaning and passion, allowing little time for this difficult search. Pat dearly loved the forest and knew it well. While walking one day, Pat encountered the tiger and was also chased to the edge of the cliff and grabbed the root that had held the others. As Pat wondered what to do, the thought came to let go. Pat had not heard the story of the seeker of truth, so the idea seemed strange. But Pat was used to trusting intuition. Like the seeker, Pat discovered the ledge a few feet below. Pat studied this new path carefully and discovered the tunnel. Pat felt a way through the darkness toward the dim light in the distance.

A rock seemed to be in the passage that did not belong. As Pat carefully moved it out of the way, a soft light filled the tunnel, banishing the darkness. There was a large stone that seemed to glow from within. In daylight, this glow was barely visible and the stone seemed ordinary. But in darkness its light was sure and steady. Pat sat in wonder before the stone. Was this the acclaimed *Tiger's Eye Treasure*? It was not as that jewel had been described—beautiful, powerful, inspiring. In fact, its appearance was beyond description. A sense of peace and awe fell over Pat. Unsure of the lesson, Pat did not seek out the villagers and returned home instead. The stone filled Pat's home with its steady glow and Pat never slept in darkness again.

Epilogue

Years passed, and Pat seemed to have less time for previous pursuits. Visits from the villagers became more frequent and Pat enjoyed their company. Surprisingly, few people asked about the stone. Even after dark, people seemed to take for granted the glow that filled Pat's home. But there were those few who did notice the unusual rock and Pat would say:

I cannot answer your questions. I only know that when others discover the stone and wonder about it with me, it is even more radiant and I feel a special bond and love that I feel with you now. At first I tried to point out the stone to visitors, but they did not appreciate it unless they found it on their own. I am always grateful for visitors, such as you, who notice the stone during their stay in my home so we can cherish it together.

Pat would chip off a tiny piece of rock for the visitors, cautioning them not to lose it or forget it. Strangely, no matter how small the chip, it glowed as intently as the mother stone.

Pat eventually left the village to start a new journey. No longer needing the stone, Pat crushed the remainder into tiny pebbles and scattered them throughout the forest that surrounded the village.

And what had become of the tiger? No one had seen it since the seeker returned to the village and some began to believe her message of faith. But, the *Tiger's Eye Treasure* remained a mystery. The legend of the tiger grew and was passed down from generation to generation. Since the legend was incomplete, each teller added his or her own slant. It was used at various times to prove that caution, kindness, courage, faith, or some other belief was *the* way. However, there were some people in the village who simply enjoyed the legend for its mystery. They found pleasure in the simplest tasks of life and especially loved walks in the forest, even at night. Often, they discovered the pebbles and wondered if they had found the *Tiger's Eye Treasure*. Not sure what to believe, they would be filled with awe and peace. They would take the pebbles home and place them in the most obvious places and wait for others to take note and share their joy.

Study Guide to the Fable

Directions: (a) Read the fable together with your partner or family. Long car rides are an ideal time for reading the story and discussing the questions. (b) Take turns asking questions and considering answers. (c) When answering questions, think on the level of the fable and on a personal level. How does the topic apply to you, your relationship, or your family? (d) Do not answer a question for your spouse or someone else who is taking part in the discussion—allow other people to identify their own characteristics and predispositions.

1. **With which villager do you most strongly identify?** Is it the person who is *cautious, kind, courageous, truth/God seeking*, or *enjoying* simple pursuits in the moment? You can choose more than one villager *or* a type of person who is not listed—*creative, organized, controlling, spontaneous, independent, people pleasing, outgoing, to-yourself, dramatic, serious, emotional, logical, disapproving, approving*, etc.

2. **Has your approach to life changed over the years,** or is your character steady?

3. **Did each of the five villagers have a choice about how he or she reacted** to the challenge of tiger, or was each person's actions predetermined by his or her inherent physical, mental, intellectual, and/or temperamental characteristics?

4. **Would the concept of *predispositions* explain why people have different reactions to the same experiences**—disrespect from children, critical comments from relatives, being late or on time for events, neatness and order, and so on?

5. **Is it good to have people with different predispositions** in the same village, family, or marriage?

6. **Why did the person who enjoyed simple pursuits find something that escaped others in their searches?** Does this mean that the way of *being in the present in the moment* has advantages or is better than the way of *caution, kindness, courage*, or *seeking*?

7. **Can a person be present in the moment along with a predisposition to react in a particular way?** Could a cautious, kind, courageous, or prayerful person be present in the moment?

8. **Are you guided more by your *beliefs* or by your *experience* of events** in the present moment?

9. **What was the unity underlying each villager's approach?** A Taoist sage said, *People argue because they have lost touch with the unity underlying apparent distinctions.* When you have arguments with your spouse, can you find the unity in your opposing positions?

10. **What was the role of the tiger and the stone?** Was the tiger chasing the people away from the stone or leading them to it? Why was the stone more radiant when people *wondered* about it together? What do you have in your relationship or family that gives you moments of peace and awe? What simple tasks do you do together? What do you both cherish? Are you still "sleeping in darkness?"

References

The American Heritage dictionary of the English language. (1969). Boston: American Heritage.

All-Seeing Eye. Retrieved October 8, 2009, from www.urbanthreads.com/.

Angel & Crying Baby. Retrieved October 2, 2009, from www.victorianembroidery-and-crafts .com/free.

Assagioli, R. (2000/1965). *Psychosynthesis: A collection of basic writings.* Amherst, MA: Synthesis Center.

Beattie, M. (1987). *Codependent no more: How to stop controlling others and start caring for yourself.* Center City, MN: Hazelden.

Balsekar, R. S. (1992). *Consciousness speaks: Conversations with Ramesh S. Balsekar.* Redondo Beach, CA: Advaita Press.

Barbor, C. (2001, May/June). The science of meditation. *Psychology Today, 34,* 54–59.

Beck, J. S. (2007). *The Beck diet solution.* Birmingham, AL: Oxmoor House.

Beck., J. S. (1995). *Cognitive therapy: Basics and beyond.* New York: Guilford Press.

Bennett, B. (2002). *Emotional yoga: How the body can heal the mind.* New York: Simon & Schuster.

Ben-Shahar, T. (2007). *Happier: Learn the secrets to daily joy and lasting fulfillment.* New York: McGraw-Hill.

Benson, H. (1975). *The relaxation response.* New York: HarperCollins.

Bowen, M. (1978). *Family therapy in clinical practice.* New York: Jason Aronson.

Bowlby, J. (1980). *Attachment and loss: Loss, sadness and depression* (Vol. 3). New York: Basic Books.

Bradberry, T. (2007). *The personality code.* New York: G. P. Putnam's Sons.

Bright Idea & Super Hero. Retrieved October 2, 2009, from www.dreamstime.com.

Browne, M. H., & Browne, M. M. (2007). *You can't have him—he's mine: A woman's guide to affair proofing her relationship.* Avon, MA: Adams Media.

Burns, D. (1980). *Feeling good: The new mood therapy.* New York: Avon Books.

Byron Katie. *The work.* www.thework.com/index.asp.

Campbell, R. S., & Pennebaker, J. W. (2003) The secret life of pronouns. *American Psychological Society, 14*(1), 60–65.

Chapman, G. (1992). *The five love languages.* Chicago: Northfield.

Cohen-Posey, K. (2000). *Brief Therapy Client Handouts,* Hoboken, NJ: John Wiley.

Cohen-Posey, K. (2008). *Empowering dialogues within: A workbook for helping professionals and their clients.* Hoboken, NJ: John Wiley & Sons.

Cohen-Posey, K. (1995). *How to handle bullies, teasers, and other meanies.* Highland City, FL: Rainbow Books.

Cohen-Posey, K. (2008). *Making hostile words harmless: A guide to the power of positive speaking for helping professionals and their clients.* Hoboken, NJ: John Wiley & Sons.

Cope, S. (2007). *The wisdom of yoga: A seeker's guide to extraordinary living.* New York: Bantam Books.

Davidson, R. J., Kabat-Zinn, J., Schumacher, J., Rosenkranz, M., Muller, D., Santorelli, S. F., Urbanowski, F., et al. (2003). Alterations in brain and immune function produced by mindfulness meditation. *Psychosomatic Medicine, 65,* 564–570.

Devil Fish. Retrieved October 9, 2009, from www.urbanthreads.com/designs/clip_art?category_id=86 www.urbanthreads.com/designs/clip_art?category_id=86 www.urbanthreads.com/designs/clip_art?category_id=86 http://www.i-heart-god.com/free_satan clip_art.htm

Eimer, E. (2008). *Hypnotize yourself out of pain now*. Bethel, CT: Crown House.

Ellis, A. (1997). *A guide to rational living*. Chatsworth, CA: Wilshire.

Farmer, S. D. (2006). *Animal spirit guides: An easy-to-use handbook for identifying and understanding your power animals and animal spirit helpers*. Carlsbad, CA: Hay House.

Fincher, S. F. (2000). *Coloring mandalas for insight, healing and self-expression*. Boston: Shambhala.

Forward, S. (1986). *Men who hate women and the women who love them*. New York: Bantam Books.

Galvin, M. (2007). *Clocks and clouds*. New York: Magination Press.

Goleman, E. (1988). *The meditative mind: The varietiies of meditative experience*. New York: Penguin Putnam.

Gottman, J. M., & Silver, N. (1988). *The seven principles for making marriage work*. New York: Crown.

Guigenvich, S. (2007). *The Self-hypnosis diet: Use the power of your mind to reach your perfect weight*. Boulder, CO: Sounds True.

Haley, J. (1967). *Advanced techniques of hypnosis and therapy*. New York: Harcourt Brace Jovanovich.

Hall, L., & Ostrof, M. (1999). *Anorexia nervosa: A guide to recovery*. Carlsbad, CA: Gürze Books.

Hall, L., & Cohn, L. (1998). *Bulimia: A guide to recovery*. Carlsbad, CA: Gürze Books.

Hammond, C. D. (1990). *Handbook of hypnotic suggestions and metaphors*. New York: W. W. Norton.

Kabit-Zinn, J. (1994). *Wherever you go, there you are*. New York: Hyperion.

Kluger, J. (2009, February 12). The biology of belief, *Time*, p. 64.

Kranowitz, C. S. (2005). *The out-of-sync child: Recognizing and coping with sensory processing disorder* (rev. ed.). New York: Berkley Publishing Group.

Leuner, H. (1969, January). Guided affective imagery (GAI): A method of intensive psychotherapy. *American Journal of Psychotherapy, XXIII*(1), 4–22.

Losier, M. (2003). *Law of attraction: The science of attracting more of what you want and less of what you don't*. New York: Hachette Book Group.

Manfred, E. (2009). *He's history; You're not*. Guilford, CT: Globe Pequot Press.

Mavromatis, A. (1987). *Hypnagogia: The unique state of consciousness between wakefulness and sleep*. London: Routledge.

McKay, M., & Fanning, P. (2000). *Self-esteem: A proven program of cognitive techniques for assessing, improving and maintaining your self-esteem*. Oakland, CA: New Harbinger.

Mills, J.C. (2005). *Sammy the elephant*. New York: Magination Press.

Munch, E. (1895). *The scream* (lithograph). Retrieved June 6, 2009, from http://en.wikipedia.org/wiki/The_Scream.

Newberg, A. (2006). *Why we believe what we believe*. New York: Simon & Schuster.

Packer A. J. (1992). *Bringing up parents*. Minneapolis, MN: Free Spirit.

Panksepp, J. (1998). *Affective neuroscience: The foundation of human animal emotions*. Northants, UK: Oxford University Press.

Papolos D., & Papolos, J. (2006). *The bipolar child: The definitive and reassuring guide to childhood's most misunderstood disorder*. NY: Broadway Books.

Papp, P. (1983). *The process of change*. New York: Guilford Press.

The Pointing Finger. Retrieved June 6, 2009, from www.aperfectworld.org/ (metaphors).

Powell, C., & Forde, G. (1995). *The self-hypnosis kit: Discover the power of hypnotherapy to improve your life*. New York: Penguin Books.

Promislow, S. (1997). *Making the brain body connection*. Vancouver, BC: Enhanced Learning & Integration.

Rider Waite Tarot Deck images. Retrieved June 5, 2009, from http://en.wikipedia.org/wiki/Rider-Waite-Smith deck.

Roderick, K. (2005). *Kirtan kriya*: Yoga for age proofing postmodern minds. *Yoga Times*.

Rossman, M. (2000). *Guided imagery for self healing*. Tiburon, CA: New World Library.

Salsberg, S. (1995). *Loving-kindness: The revolutionary art of happiness*. Boston: Shambhala.

Schwartz, R. (1995). *Internal family systems therapy*. New York: Guilford Press.

Shapiro, F. (2001). *Eye movement desensitization and reprocessing: basic principles, protocols, and procedures*. New York: Guilford Press.

Shapiro, F., & Forrest, M. S. (1997). *Eye movement desensitization and reprocessing: The breakthrough therapy for overcoming anxiety, stress, and trauma*. New York: HarperCollins.

Shimoff, M. (2009). *Happy for no reason: 7 steps to being happy from the inside out*. New York: Free Press.

Shinoda Bolen, J. (1984). *Goddesses in everywoman: Powerful archetypes for women*. New York: Harper & Row.

Shinoda Bolen, J. (1989). *Gods in everyman: Archetypes that shape men's lives*. New York: Harper & Row.

Stevens, J. O. (1971). *Awareness: Exploring, experimenting, experiencing*. Boulder, CO: Real People Press.

Stone, H., & Stone, S. (1989). *Embracing our selves: The voice dialogue manual*. Novato, CA: New World Library.

Thirdeyeman. Retrieved June 5, 2009, from www.crysallinks.com.

Tipping, C. (2002). *Radical forgiveness*. Lancaster, UK: Global 13 Publications.

Tolle, E. (2008). *A new earth: Awakening to your life's purpose*. London: Penguin.

Utter, B. (2007). *Pick and plan: 101 brain compatible strategies for lesson design*. Thousand Oaks, CA: Corwin Press.

Van Epp, J. (2007). *How to avoid falling in love with a jerk*. Columbus, OH: McGraw-Hill.

Weiner Davis, M. (2003). *The sex-starved marriage*. New York: Simon & Schuster.

Whitaker, K. (1991). *The reluctant shaman*. San Francisco: HarperCollins.

Williams, M., Teasdale, J., Segal, Z., & Kabat-Zinn J. (2007). *The mindful way through depression*. New York: Guilford Press.

Wisdom, S., & Green, J. (2002). *Stepcoupling: Creating and sustaining a strong marriage in today's blended family*. New York: Three River Press.

Wolf, A. E. (1991). *Get out of my life, but first could you drive me and Cheryl to the mall?* San Francisco: HarperCollins.

Wood Vallely, S. (2008). *Sensational meditation for children*. Asheville, NC: Satya International.

Woodall, M. K. (2001). *How to talk so men will listen*. Lincoln, NE: Writers Club Press.

INDEX

STUDY PACKAGE
CONTINUING EDUCATION
CREDIT INFORMATION

MORE BRIEF THERAPY CLIENT HANDOUTS

Our goal is to provide you with current, accurate and practical information from the most experienced and knowledgeable speakers and authors.

Listed below are the continuing education credit(s) currently available for this self-study package. *Please note: Your state licensing board dictates whether self study is an acceptable form of continuing education. Please refer to your state rules and regulations.*

COUNSELORS: PESI, LLC is recognized by the National Board for Certified Counselors to offer continuing education for National Certified Counselors. Provider #: 5896. We adhere to NBCC Continuing Education Guidelines. This self-study package qualifies for **4.5** contact hours.

SOCIAL WORKERS: PESI, LLC, 1030, is approved as a provider for continuing education by the Association of Social Work Boards, 400 South Ridge Parkway, Suite B, Culpeper, VA 22701. www.aswb. org. Social workers should contact their regulatory board to determine course approval. Course Level: All Levels. Social Workers will receive **4.5** (Clinical) continuing education clock hours for completing this self-study package.

PSYCHOLOGISTS: PESI, LLC is approved by the American Psychological Association to sponsor continuing education for psychologists. PESI, LLC maintains responsibility for these materials and their content. PESI is offering these self- study materials for **4.5** hours of continuing education credit.

ADDICTION COUNSELORS: PESI, LLC is a Provider approved by NAADAC Approved Education Provider Program. Provider #: 366. This self-study package qualifies for **5.0** contact hours.

Procedures:

1. Review the material and read the book.

2. If seeking credit, complete the posttest/evaluation form:

   -Complete posttest/evaluation in entirety; including your email address to receive your certificate much faster versus by mail.

   -Upon completion, mail to the address listed on the form along with the CE fee stated on the test. Tests will not be processed without the CE fee included.

   -Completed posttests must be received 6 months from the date printed on the packing slip.

Your completed posttest/evaluation will be graded. If you receive a passing score (70% and above), you will be emailed/faxed/mailed a certificate of successful completion with earned continuing education credits. (Please write your email address on the posttest/evaluation form for fastest response) If you do not pass the posttest, you will be sent a letter indicating areas of deficiency, and another posttest to complete. The posttest must be resubmitted and receive a passing grade before credit can be awarded. We will allow you to re-take as many times as necessary to receive a certificate.

If you have any questions, please feel free to contact our customer service department at 1.800.844.8260.

PESI LLC
PO BOX 1000
Eau Claire, WI 54702-1000

MORE BRIEF THERAPY CLIENT HANDOUTS

PESI

PO BOX 1000
Eau Claire, WI 54702
800-844-8260

Any persons interested in receiving credit may photocopy this form, complete and return with a payment of $20.00 per person CE fee. A certificate of successful completion will be sent to you. To receive your certificate sooner than two weeks, rush processing is available for a fee of $10. Please attach check or include credit card information below.

Mail to: PESI, PO Box 1000, Eau Claire, WI 54702 or fax to PESI (800) 554-9775 (both sides)

CE Fee: $20: (Rush processing fee: $10)   **Total to be charged** _____

Credit Card #: _____ **Exp Date:** _____ **V-Code*:** _____
(*MC/VISA/Discover: last 3-digit # on signature panel on back of card.) (*American Express: 4-digit # above account # on face of card.)

                        LAST   FIRST   M.I.

Name (please print): _____ _____ _____

Address: _____ Daytime Phone: _____

City: _____ State: _____ Zip Code: _____

Signature: _____ Email: _____

Date Completed: _____ Actual time (# of hours) taken to complete this offering: _____hours

Program Objectives After completing this publication, I have been able to achieve these objectives:

1. Identify specific handouts that would be relevant to various client presenting problems.	1. Yes No
2. List handouts that would facilitate interaction between counselor and client.	2. Yes No
3. Describe how handouts can be used to promote communication between parents, spouses, or family members.	3. Yes No
4. Formulate questions that would help clients apply information in a handout.	4. Yes No
5. State how handouts can be used to increase clients' understanding of and motivation for treatment.	5. Yes No

PESI LLC
PO BOX 1000
Eau Claire, WI 54702-1000

ZNT042820   CE Release Date: 9/14/2010

Participant Profile:
1. Job Title: _____   Employment setting: _____

1. For which issue would the handouts Loving Kindness Mantras (2.10) and Raising Self-Esteem (6.11) be helpful?
a. A person who had retired from a successful career but isn't sure how quickly she wants to start a new venture in life.
b. A man who is fearful of getting back into the dating scene because of bad choices he has made in the past.
c. A person who fears that her husband will find someone more attractive and intelligent than she is.
d. A man states his family complains that he talks and lectures too much.
e. A woman who is puzzled that she can no longer please her partner who now belittles her constantly.

2. A person holds in her frustration until she explodes. Choose the handout that would not be helpful.
a. Mindfulness: Breath by Breath (2.2)
b. Angry Automatic thoughts (4.4)
c. Tempering Anger (6.8)
d. Talking So People will Listen (7.26)
e. Can we Just Talk? (8.12)

3. Which handout could a therapist use to guide a parent and child in an exercise to improve bladder control?
a. Entering Trance (1.2)
b. Entrancing Kids (1.12)
c. Mini Meditations for Minors (2.12)
d. Be the Boss of Your Brain (4.22)
e. A Parent's Power Tools (8.1)

4. Which handout would a therapist want to review with a client to help him be less demanding of with his wife's housekeeping?
a. Entrancing Unwanted Habits (1.7)
b. Personality Awareness (3.22)
c. Discovering the Me that Is Not OCD (6.2)
d. Anger Log (6.14)
e. Relationship Fundamentals (8.10)

5. Which handouts could a family read together to identify the cause of tension in the home?
a. The Community of Self (3.5) and Pictures of Personality (3.12)
b. The Power of Negative Thinking (4.5) and Keep the Good Thoughts Rolling (4.9)
c. Practicing Happiness (6.12) and Surviving a Family Backlash (7.9)
d. Turning Disputes into Discussions (7.10) and The Tale Of The Tiger's Eye Treasure (8.15)
e. Surviving Picky Parents (8.3) and Surviving the Taxing Teens (8.2)

6. A Parent's Power Tools (8.1) and Blending Families (8.14) are designed to for couples to read together to help them be more unified in their parenting practices. Choose the answer that would not help them be more unified.
a. Using the handouts to decide if their expectations of each other are too high.
b. Using the handouts to identify who's parenting approach needs to change.
c. Using the handouts to rate themselves on how often they use suggested strategies.
d. Using information in the handouts to decide with which strategies they both agree.
e. Using information in the handouts to decide which strategy they want to put into immediate action.

7. Which question would help clients apply information they read in a handout? Choose the best question.
a. How will you use the ideas in Erotic Trances (1.11) to make your wife want to have sex more often?
b. Which image in Connecting With Your Self (3.6) best represents the real you?
c. Which thoughts about yourself did you change after reading Your Beliefs—Helpful or Harmful (4.6)?
d. What strategies will be too difficult for you in Not Thinking Yourself Too Thin (6.20)?
e. What responses in Hardcore Bully Busting (7.11) would you like to use with kids who call you names?

8. After leading clients in any of the meditation activities in Mindfulness Matters (Chapter 3) what question would help them with their practice of meditation? Choose the most helpful question.
a. When you practiced meditation, were you able to clear you mind of all thoughts?
b. Which meditation practice will be easiest for you to do this week?
c. Did you meditate every day?
d. When you became aware of thoughts while meditating just now, did you simply notice them or did you return to your breath (or mantra)?
e. What lines do you remember from the dis-identification exercise in the Witness Within (2.5)?

9. Some handouts are designed to increase clients' motivation for treatment. What activity or instruction would not increase a client's involvement in treatment?
a. Have a client read Automatic Thoughts (4.3) and Self talk Case Study (5.5) to decide which approach he or she would like to use in treatment.
b. Lead people with aches and pains in the yoga exercises in An Invitation to Yoga (2.11) and tell them they need to find a therapeutic yoga class.
c. Ask clients to rate how strongly they agree with the assumptions in Therapy For Self Empowerment (3.1)
d. Begin filling out the Thought Record Form (4.13) with a client during a session and ask him or her to continue recording automatic thoughts and formulating new viewpoints at home.
e. Ask clients to read the handouts Three Steps to Self-Talk (5.2) or Examples of Constructive Self Talk (5.3) after using constructive-self-talk in a session.

10. Which of the following questions would increase a client's motivation for treatment? Choose one.
a. Which of your fears about self-hypnosis were relieved after reading Information about Trances (1.1)?
b. After taking the steps in The Journey to Forgiveness (6.6), did you stop feeling angry?
c. What did you learn in Transcending Trauma (6.7) that helped you feel better about your car accident?
d. What ideas can you use from Acts of Love that Renew Romance (8.7) to make your wife spend more time with you?
e. After reading Undoing Dependency (8.10), what did you realize you need to change in yourself to make your husband stop drinking?

PESI LLC
PO BOX 1000
Eau Claire, WI 54702-1000

ABOUT THE CD-ROM

Introduction

This appendix provides you with the information on the contents of the CD that accompanies this book. For the latest and greatest information, please refer to the ReadMe file located at the root of the CD.

- A computer with a processor running at 120 Mhz or faster
- At least 32 MB of total RAM installed on your computer; for best performance, we recommend at least 64MB
- A CD-ROM drive

Note: Many popular word processing programs are capable of reading Microsoft Word files. However, users should be aware that a slight amount of formatting might be lost when using a program other than Microsoft Word.

System Requirements

Using the CD With Windows To install the items from the CD to your hard drive, follow these steps:

Platforms

1. Insert the CD into your computer's CD-ROM drive.
2. The CD-ROM interface will appear. The interface provides a simple point-and-click way to explore the contents of the CD.

If the opening screen of the CD-ROM does not appear automatically, follow these steps to access the CD:

1. Click the Start button on the left of the taskbar and then choose Run from the menu that pops up. (In Windows Vista and Windows 7, skip this step.)
2. In the dialog box that appears, type d:\setup.exe. (If your CD drive is not drive d, use the appropriate letter in place of d.) This brings up the CD interface described in the preceding set of steps. (In Windows Vista or Windows 7, type d:\setup.exe in the Start > Search text box.)

Using the CD with A MAC

1. Insert the CD into your computer's CD-ROM drive.
2. The CD-ROM icon appears on your desktop, double-click the icon.
3. Double-click the Start icon.
4. The CD-ROM interface will appear. The interface provides a simple point-and-click way to explore the contents of the CD.

The following sections provide a summary of the software and other materials you'll find on the CD.

What's on the CD

Content Includes all client handouts from the book in Word format. Handouts can be customized, printed out, and distributed to clients in an effort to extend the therapeutic process outside the office. All documentation is included in the folder named "Content."

Applications   The following applications are on the CD:

OpenOffice.org   OpenOffice.org is a free multi-platform office productivity suite. It is similar to Microsoft Office or Lotus SmartSuite, but OpenOffice.org is absolutely free. It includes word processing, spreadsheet, presentation, and drawing applications that enable you to create professional documents, newsletters, reports, and presentations. It supports most file formats of other office software. You should be able to edit and view any files created with other office solutions. Certain features of Microsoft Word documents may not display as expected from within OpenOffice.org. For system requirements, go to www.openoffice.org.

Software can be of the following types:

- Shareware programs are fully functional, free, trial versions of copyrighted programs. If you like particular programs, register with their authors for a nominal fee and receive licenses, enhanced versions, and technical support.

- Freeware programs are free, copyrighted games, applications, and utilities. You can copy them to as many computers as you like — for free — but they offer no technical support.

- GNU software is governed by its own license, which is included inside the folder of the GNU software. There are no restrictions on distribution of GNU software. See the GNU license at the root of the CD for more details.

- Trial, demo, or evaluation versions of software are usually limited either by time or functionality (such as not letting you save a project after you create it).

Troubleshooting

If you have difficulty installing or using any of the materials on the companion CD, try the following solutions:

- **Turn off any antivirus software that you may have running.** Installers sometimes mimic virus activity and can make your computer incorrectly believe that a virus is infecting it. (Be sure to turn the antivirus software back on later.)

- **Close all running programs.** The more programs that you're running, the less memory is available to other programs. Installers also typically update files and programs; if you keep other programs running, installation may not work properly.

- **Reference the README file.** Please refer to the README file located at the root of the CD for the latest product information at the time of publication.

User Assistance

If you have trouble with the CD-ROM, please call the Wiley Product Technical Support phone number at (800) 762-2974. Outside the United States, call 1 (317) 572-3994. You can also contact Wiley Product Technical Support at http://support.wiley.com. John Wiley & Sons will provide technical support only for installation and other general quality control items. For technical support of the applications themselves, consult the program vendor or author.

To place additional orders or to request information about other Wiley products, please call (800) 225-5945.